ANNALS OF COMMUNISM

Each volume in the series Annals of Communism will publish selected and previously inaccessible documents from former Soviet state and party archives in a narrative that develops a particular topic in the history of Soviet and international communism. Separate English and Russian editions will be prepared. Russian and American scholars work together to prepare the documents for each volume. Documents are chosen not for their support of any single interpretation but for their particular historical importance or their general value in deepening understanding and facilitating discussion. The volumes are designed to be useful to students, scholars, and interested general readers.

Voices of Revolution, 1917

Mark D. Steinberg

Documents translated by Marian Schwartz

Documents compiled by
Mark D. Steinberg, Zinaida Peregudova, and Liubov Tiutiunnik

Yale University Press
New Haven and London

This volume has been prepared with the cooperation of the State Archive of the Russian Federation (GARF).

Designed by James J. Johnson and set in Sabon Roman type by The Composing Room of Michigan, Inc. Printed in the United States of America.

Library of Congress Cataloging-in-Publication Data

Steinberg, Mark D., 1953–
    Voices of revolution, 1917 / Mark D. Steinberg ; documents translated by Marian Schwartz.
        p.   cm. — (Annals of Communism)
    Includes bibliographical references and index.
    ISBN 978-0-300-10169-0

    1. Soviet Union—History—Revolution, 1917–1921—Sources. 2. Soviet Union—History—Revolution, 1917–1921—Public opinion. I. Title. II. Series.
DK265 .A544   2001
947.084′1—dc21

                                                                2001026309

A catalogue record for this book is available from the British Library.

The paper in this book meets the guidelines for permanence and durability
of the Committee on Production Guidelines for Book Longevity of the Council
on Library Resources.

10 9 8 7 6 5 4 3 2

Yale University Press gratefully acknowledges the financial support given for this publication by the John M. Olin Foundation, the Lynde and Harry Bradley Foundation, the Historical Research Foundation, Roger Milliken, Lloyd H. Smith, Keith Young, the William H. Donner Foundation, Joseph W. Donner, Jeremiah Milbank, the David Woods Kemper Memorial Foundation, the Daphne Seybolt Culpeper Foundation, and the Milton V. Brown Foundation.

Contents

Illustrations

peace. Long live Soviet Power. The Kadets are enemies of the people and do not belong in the Const.[ituent] Assembly."

FACSIMILES OF DOCUMENTS

Document 12. Appeal to the Petrograd "People's Committee" from Matvei Frolov, day worker on the Perm Railroad, 25 April 1917.

Document 83. Poem sent to *Izvestiia* by a wounded soldier, Ilya Ladanov, received 22 September 1917.

Document 127. Letter to Lenin from five peasants, Moscow Province, received 7 January 1918.

page xv

MAP

Provinces of European Russia, 1917

Acknowledgments

There may be works of research and writing that are the creation of a lone scholar, but this is not one of them. Indeed, part of the pleasure of making this book lay in the many collaborations and discussions that helped give it life. This book began as part of a larger and somewhat different project in collaboration with Daniel Orlovsky and Genrikh Ioffe, and I benefited from our many useful and pleasurable discussions about 1917 and Russian history. Without the help of the staff and administration of the State Archive of the Russian Federation (formerly the Central State Archive of the October Revolution), especially its director Sergei Mironenko and assistant director Vladimir Kozlov, this book could never have been written. In particular, I am deeply grateful to Zinaida Peregudova and Liubov Tiutiunnik, staff archivist-historians, who, between my own repeated visits to Moscow, searched through hundreds of files of documents looking for texts for possible inclusion. Other colleagues and friends in Moscow helped in many essential ways: Mark, Natasha, and Dmitry Lapitsky, and Valery and Larissa Brun-Tsekhovoy. Research assistants at Illinois also helped greatly in identifying documents in newspapers that might be included and in assisting with annotations: Marjorie Hilton, Susan Smith, Zoria Shapira, Vladka Shikova, Gregory Kveberg, and, in Moscow, Sasha Steinberg. I would also like to thank Patricia Kennedy Grimsted, whose knowledge of Russian archives has been invaluable. The professional reference staff of the Slavic and East European Library at the University of Illinois, especially Helen Sullivan, have been of much help.

The documents chosen for this collection were translated with great skill by Marian Schwartz. Ekaterina Betekhtina, a professional linguist from St. Petersburg University, took time from her own scholarly work and teaching to help me grapple with some of the more difficult linguistic issues and obscure references. Her very astute reflections on the language of these texts constitute the afterword to this volume.

Many people have read and commented on part or all of the text: members of the Midwest Russian History Workshop (one of the best settings I know for collegial and critical scholarly discussion), Diane Koenker (my valued colleague in Russian history at Illinois), Boris Kolonitskii of the St. Petersburg branch of the Russian Academy of Sciences, and students in my graduate seminar on the history of imperial Russia. The anonymous readers at Yale University Press offered both encouragement and many useful suggestions. Finally, I would also like to express my intellectual debt to the scholars and participants who have written on 1917 in the many years since the revolution.

At Yale University Press, Jonathan Brent has been a leader in advancing this important series, Annals of Communism. Vadim Staklo assisted with many important details in the life of this project. Susan Abel edited the text with sensitivity and skill. Mary Pasti handled many final tasks.

I am grateful to the many generous sources of financial support that facilitated work on this project: Yale University Press, the Yale Center for International and Area Studies, and, at the University of Illinois, the College of Liberal Arts and Sciences, Helen Corley Petit for an annual professorship in her name, the Research Board, the Department of History, and the Russian and East European Center.

Finally, but not least, Jane Hedges and Sasha Steinberg not only contributed to the book in concrete ways, but tolerated and even understood and made possible the many hours I took from time with them to give to this project, for which I am deeply thankful.

Note on the Documents

The majority of documents in this collection were translated from originals held in the State Archive of the Russian Federation in Moscow, formerly the Central State Archive of the October Revolution. Assisted by two archivist-historians on the staff of the State Archive, I sought selections for this volume after reading through hundreds of individual letters, collective appeals, and other writings sent by lower-class Russians, primarily from the central regions of the empire, to institutions and individuals of authority in the new revolutionary Russia: notably, to the Office of the Minister-President of the Provisional Government, the Main Land Committee of the Provisional Government, the All-Russian Central Executive Committee of Soviets (including recently declassified collections of "antisoviet" letters and resolutions), the national newspaper of the Soviet, *Izvestiia* (most letters were never published), and the Constituent Assembly. In addition, I searched through popular political newspapers and existing published collections of documents (mainly Soviet collections prepared in the 1950s); I selected texts from these as well, after checking them whenever possible against the originals (the original text is used as the basis of the translation here). The bibliography contains a full list of the archival fonds, newspapers, and published sources used. My aim in selecting documents has been to convey both a balanced picture of the range of concerns and opinion among ordinary Russians in 1917 and the rich vitality of ideas and emotions that made the revolution not only one of the most momentous political events in the twentieth century but a time of exceptionally intense and complex social and personal experience and striving.

The original texts are all in Russian. Given that most of the authors lacked much formal education, these texts are often filled with a rich mixture of popular speech, combinations of official and literary languages, and nonstandard usage. Issues of style are discussed in the afterword by the Russian linguist Ekaterina Betekhtina, who also assisted me in editing the translations. In the translated texts of these documents we have tried to preserve a sense of this rich and complex language. Misspellings and grammatical mistakes in Russian usage have not been preserved in the English translation.

All documents are presented in full (except Document 121, as stated in a note to that document). Ellipses in the text, a common stylistic device in Russian writing, appear in the originals. Formatting, punctuation, and spelling in the documents have been standardized in the translations to make them easier to read. Capitalization of terms, however, which tends to show meaning rather than simply reflect rules of grammar, has been preserved. Signatures to resolutions and other collective appeals are often represented by the notation "[signature]" or by an indication of the number of signatures, rather than by listing names (the signatures are often not legible in any case and were often omitted when the documents were published in the newspapers). Sources of documents are provided in the separate list of document and illustration credits.

Dates in the collection are all given according to the "old-style" Julian calendar, in use in Russia until 1 February 1918. In 1917, the Julian calendar was thirteen days behind the Gregorian calendar in use in most of the Western world.

Provinces of European Russia, 1917

Introduction:
The Language of Popular Revolution

We loved those dissonances, those roars, those ringing sounds, those unexpected transitions when we heard them from an orchestra. But if we really loved them, rather than simply letting them tickle our senses while we sat in a fashionable theater after dinner, then we must hear and love these sounds now, when they are pouring out from the orchestra of the world. . . . With your whole body, your whole heart, your whole mind—hear the Revolution.

ALEKSANDR BLOK, 9 January 1918

Modern revolutions are exceptionally loquacious events. Words fill public spaces—in newspapers, leaflets, proclamations, letters, posters, and an endless stream of talk—as individuals and groups battle over who should hold power (at the national center, but also in more intimate localities of village, town, neighborhood, and workplace), over who has right on his side, and over how power should be used. Physical action, including force and violence, is certainly essential to struggles for power. But words give these actions shape and substance. Words inspire, encouraging large numbers of people to think that it is important and worth the effort (even vital) to take part in meetings, participate in strikes or demonstrations, choose among new claimants to political leadership, draft various appeals, and even write personally to leading public figures. And words beget words, as individuals and groups deploy new and old political languages and endeavor to make use of words and phrases—especially those made more potent by their association with the revolution—to express their own thoughts and needs, which were until then only half articulated.

The collapse of the tsarist autocracy in Russia in late February 1917 opened a verbal Pandora's box. The American journalist John Reed, who observed the revolution firsthand, was amazed by all "the Talk, beside which Carlyle's 'flood of French speech' was a mere trickle"; by the thousands pouring out of factories into courtyards and streets to listen to "anybody, whatever they had to say, as long as they would talk"; by the ubiquitous and endless meetings and lectures; and by "the spurting up of impromptu debate, everywhere."[1] The editors of the daily newspaper *Russkie vedomosti* (Russian news), writing in September 1917, found words to be the only certainty in 1917: "There is no authority, no legality, and no effective political action in Russia, but there is an abundance of political words."[2] These gatherings for talk ranged from elaborate assemblies of delegates from around the country to meetings in factories and villages and among soldiers to spontaneous discussions in public squares, on street corners, in trams and trains, in homes, and at work. And all this talk was echoed—and roused—by printed words. Newspapers, pamphlets, leaflets, posters, and other publications poured off the presses and filled public and private spaces. Meetings produced a growing mountain of resolutions, appeals, petitions, and instructions. Huge numbers of individuals, too, including many barely literate villagers and workers, put pen or pencil to paper or sat down to type (sometimes writing on mere scraps, for this was all that was available or could be spared) to address letters to institutions and individuals with power or, by asking newspapers to print their letters, to speak to various publics or to the whole nation.

The texts in this collection represent only fragments of the whole body of such writing (see Note on the Documents). They have been chosen, however, to convey some sense of the richness and complexity of the Russian revolution of 1917: not just as a struggle between competing political parties and organizations over power and ideology, but as a human story to be understood from the perspectives of individuals—in particular, relatively unprivileged Russians. In other words, this book is intended as a window onto what the revolution *meant* to ordinary Russians—whose experiences and motivations gave living meaning to the abstractions (democracy, freedom, class polarization, radicalization, socialism) with which we normally describe the history of this landmark event—rather than as another account of what *happened*. Of course, even the best sampling of popular voices can only record what was made public. We do not hear the voices of people who felt deeply alienated from the revolution or voices speaking of private and personal meanings of the revolution. We also hear men more than women. Still, the texts say a great deal about many of the ideas, values, and desires that gave meaning to the revolution. And though these texts concern mainly politics and social relationships, they speak of these as concerning everything from the most tangible and immediate needs to the most abstract and even philosophical questions.

These texts represent the public voices of people identifying themselves as workers, peasants, or soldiers—categories with which almost all lower-class[3] Russians identified themselves. We see here various types of texts: collective resolutions and appeals from meetings of workers, soldiers, or peasants (ranging from mass assemblies to meetings of committees of representatives to informal gatherings of individuals deciding to write together), letters from individuals, and poetry written by self-taught lower-class authors. These texts were sent either to institutions and individuals in authority or addressed, through the press, to particular social groups or to the whole country. Some documents were mere lists of demands. Many, though, were more fervent, seeking to convince, cajole, beg, and berate those they addressed. Poetry reached even further in trying to voice argument and emotion. Through verse, relatively untutored writers sought to express, in a richer language than formal or declamatory or epistolary prose allowed, their understanding and feelings about the revolution.

The approach to understanding the revolution that has shaped this collection owes much to the directions other scholars have taken in exploring the Russian revolution and its meaning. In the years since these upheavals dramatically changed the shape of modern world history, historians have debated alternative explanations of the main events: the fall of the autocracy, the social conflicts during the months between February and October, the role of different political parties, the Bolsheviks' rise to power. For many years, most of this work sought answers in the study of political leaders and institutions, and in the competing ideologies and personalities of key figures. By the 1960s, however, attention had begun to shift dramatically toward sustained investigations of the movements and motivations of social classes. Soviet historiography, of course, had always taken seriously this social history of the revolution—but Marxist and Leninist dogmas forced a rigid conformity to a certain interpretive model, though Soviet historiography too began to explore alternative formulations in the 1960s and 1970s. These new social historical studies, which proliferated in the 1970s and 1980s, looked beneath the political surface to explore the actions and aspirations of workers, soldiers, and peasants. The major argument to result from this work was important and influential:

"A deep and deepening social polarization between the top and bottom of Russian society undermined the Provisional Government by preventing the consolidation of a political consensus."[4] This discontent, it was shown, coalesced around the idea of political and social power belonging to lower-class groups alone, an idea that only the Bolsheviks, among the major political parties, were willing to support and put into action.[5]

More recently, influenced in part by wider trends in history and other disciplines, historians of Russia have begun to look more closely and critically at the deeper *cultural* processes in which ideas are formed and articulated: at how words, images, symbols, rituals, myths, and other discursive forms shape the world people see and the actions they take in it. Older social historical writing about the revolution tended to treat language not as itself an object of analysis but as a reflection of largely rational responses to tangible social, economic, and political conditions and possibilities. Thus, questions about whether workers (for example) were skilled or unskilled, young or old, male or female, or employed in small shops or large factories were seen as far more essential to understanding and explaining workers' mental worlds than were questions about how cultural discourses (language, symbols, myths, and so on) shaped the ways the material world was understood, or structured the ways in which individuals and groups envisioned the possible.[6]

By comparison with the various innovative cultural histories of the French Revolution, the story of 1917 in Russia still needs to be told with greater attention to the vital complexities of language, culture, and meaning. To be sure, the language of the Russian revolution has not been ignored. As early as the 1920s, a Soviet linguist examined the language of 1917 and the years following, though his focus was on structures—vocabulary and usage—rather than on the formation of meaning.[7] Most important, social historians of the role of lower-class groups in the revolution (especially workers) often carefully examined resolutions, strike demands, and instructions to deputies, though mainly to document the patterns of political and social radicalization and the nature of popular discontent and demands.[8] Still, recent reviews of writing on 1917 have justifiably noted the failure of existing work to pay adequate attention to "the discursive construction of the world of the workers, as well as that of peasants, soldiers, or the 'bourgeoisie,'"[9] and the "depressingly unadventurous" approaches that have dominated writing on the revolution.[10] It is high time, they argue, to take up the intellectual challenge of the "linguistic turn" in the humanities, which has resulted in "a deepening recognition of the ways in which 'reality' is produced through language."[11] Some of the most recent work on the revolution has begun to answer this challenge. Attention to language (and, increasingly, to ritual and symbol) has become more systematic, and historians have become more sensitive to the complexities of the meanings that discourse shapes and conveys. In particular, in some recent articles, a few authors have focused directly on how various groups in 1917 made use of vocabularies of democracy, class, state power, citizenship, and socialism.[12]

Voices

The texts collected here have been chosen to take readers deeper into this discursive world of the revolution, to encourage readers to ponder the uses and meanings of words and what they reveal about what the revolution signified to the millions of ordinary Russians who experienced it and, in various ways, took part in making it. But we must be honest about the obstacles to such knowledge and recognize the complexity of these voices. Whose voices were these? This is not entirely obvious. We know that these texts were written by people who identified themselves as workers, soldiers, and peasants. But what did this mean? Partly, it can be taken at face value. Many of these authors are identifiable as urban wage laborers, rural villagers, or rank-and-file soldiers who had been drafted from the lower classes. The style and manner of writing in most of these texts provide further evidence of a lack of the education enjoyed by more privileged Russians: awkward use of formal discourse, incorrect word use, corrupted expressions, and odd mixtures of dramatic rhetoric, official language, and popular slang.[13] Some writers clearly had more ability than others. These facts and distinctions only begin to point to the complexity of the answer to the question of whose voices these were.

Self-descriptions could mask a great deal. After all, people's reasons, especially in 1917, for saying that they were workers or soldiers or peasants were as much political as social. For many Russians, these groups defined the *narod*, the common people who were the foundation of the nation, the subalterns who had most suffered from Russia's inequalities and lack of freedom, and thus the people who were the essential reason and the motive force for democracy in Russia. Thus, that a common laborer, a skilled lathe operator, or a salesclerk might call himself simply a "worker," or that a "soldier" might be either a raw peasant recruit or a junior officer who had once been a clerk or a literate proletarian was less an effort to disguise "real" identities than to express an important part of these identities. Still, those more specific identities remained present and important. Even more subtly, broad self-identifications obscured important differences within groups: of gender, age, education, social experience, and ethnicity, not to mention personality.

Collectively written texts were especially likely to blur such particularities. We know very little about the actual authors of such texts. Sometimes their names are mentioned. Sometimes we know that they were, for example, junior officers, relatively experienced socialist workers, or peasants who had once lived in the city. Most often, their identities and experiences are obscured behind the screen of collective representation. No less important, we cannot see the complex process of influence and discussion that produced the final text—the efforts by activists to have their ideas prevail, the arguments and exchanges of ideas, the borrowing from newspapers or other texts that lay at hand.

As this suggests, the question of whose voices these were is not just a matter of who wrote the texts or even of who discussed and approved them. More distant voices were present as well. Even when we know that it was a common worker or peasant writing, we must be wary about imagining that finally we have found direct and pure expressions of "authentic" popular mentalities, ideas, and values that are somehow separate from the wider political and cultural world. It had been a long time since the Russian lower classes could be said to have lived in cultural isolation. Especially after the middle of the nineteenth century, ordinary Russians were increasingly exposed to formal and informal education and to a growing flood of magazines, newspapers, and books, including a large body of publications directed at common readers. In 1917, reading, especially of newspapers, was as much a part of the everyday life of the revolution as meetings, demonstrations, and strikes. Reading the press, one worker told the leaders of the Soviet in Petrograd, was no less essential to the common people in 1917 than bread itself.[14] And the influence of the press and other publications on the way workers wrote and even spoke in 1917 was profound. Many petitions and resolutions repeated standard phrases found in the speeches and newspapers of the day or even, as if adapting a template, based their texts on others that had appeared in the press or were circulating among workers, soldiers, and peasants. Indeed, those attending meetings were often simply asked to endorse a resolution adopted by a party or another organization and to send this on in their name.[15]

Most texts, though they did not conform so closely to models, still reveal the influence of, and deliberate efforts to make use of, various authoritative vocabularies (of the Soviet or the Provisional Government, of political leaders and parties, and especially of the press and books).[16] Like other expressions of lower-class culture—indeed, to an even greater degree in such deliberately public expressions, meant for others to understand—these resolutions, appeals, and letters took form through a complex intellectual interchange across social boundaries. The image of the revolution simply lifting the lid off a stifled society and allowing the authentic voices of the people to be heard may have a certain allure for us in our attempts to understand the past, but this image leads us to ignore a great deal of dialogue and interaction—an exchange of voices that was more intense than ever during the revolution.

This said, the social experience of these authors also mattered: it made a difference in how they viewed and described the world around them, how they understood and used language and ideas. Relative inequality and powerlessness affected the meanings and uses of words and ideas, as did material need, fear of hunger, or the looming threat of death or mutilation at the front. In translating for their own use the bookish language of revolutionary politics—including many literally foreign terms, like "democracy," "republic," "constitution," "revolution," "socialism," and "bourgeoisie"—people sifted new words together with older ideals; social experiences and needs with new possibilities; and a desire to "speak one's heart" with a desire to make oneself heard and understood by others. At the same time, to complicate all this still more, the revolution magnified the normal instabilities and ambiguities of language. In the use of language, as in much else, revolutions are luxuriant, even promiscuous, times. They are times of experimentation and daring in which normal routines, orderly hierarchies and relationships, established boundaries and restraints, and even familiar meanings of things are unhitched and destabilized. The intellectual ferment and disorder of revolutionary Russia made these processes of intellectual influence, borrowing, interpretation, and appropriation all the more intense.

A complex subjectivity was at work when lower-class Russians crafted their letters and resolutions: a process of deciding to write, choosing words, articulating a style, and trying to voice ideas that reflected diverse influences and interpretations and served varied purposes. For all the inherent limitations of these documents—the voices we do not hear, the speakers' deliberate appropriation of discursive styles that were not their own—the results are astonishing in their richness. At this momentous and trying time, huge numbers of common people were determined to give voice to their needs, values, and ideas—and to their feelings. Though elusive and difficult to interpret, emotion was central to the construction of meaning and argument in 1917. The February revolution evoked exceptionally high emotion, even jubilant and euphoric expectations of dramatic transformation. Later, as many grew disappointed, various combinations of frustration, anger, and despair complicated the emotional terrain of revolutionary discourse. Emotion nevertheless remained central to the way people experienced the revolution.[17] When words were spoken aloud, feeling could be expressed through tone of voice, pace of delivery, and gestures. On paper, style conveyed mood and tone. The emotional style of these texts varied partly according to their form and purpose, but the tendency toward moral fervor and strong emotion was pervasive, and no less essential than form and purpose to understanding the revolution as human experience.

Freedom: Space and Light

Following the February events, freedom was the watchword of the revolution. The first act of the new government (and, it would turn out, its main practical achievement) was the promulgation of fundamental civil liberties—freedom of speech, assembly, and the press, the end of legal restrictions based on religion, nationality, and class, the abolition of the old police institutions, and amnesty for political prisoners. For diverse social and political groups, the whole meaning of the February revolution was entwined with the notion and the vocabulary of freedom—of the end of "tyranny" and of the opening up of vast new fields of possibility for all citizens. Ordinary Russians (after initial anxiety, especially among peasants, about how they could survive "without a tsar")[18] were drawn strongly to the language of freedom. More than any other term, "freedom" seemed to capture people's thoughts and feelings about what the end of the old order could mean. The collapse of tsarist autocracy and the promulgation of civil rights and freedoms by the Provisional Government was treated as a mythic, even mystical, time: as emancipation from slavery bought with blood, as redemption for generations of suffering, as the promise of "happiness" and a "great future," as a "sacred" moment of "Resurrection" and the source of "infinite feelings" and "Great Joy" (see, for example, Documents 1, 4, 21, 26, 38, 45, 51).[19] In later months, disappointment tended to replace this early euphoria about freedom. But the emotional tone remained high; then, however, it was expressed more in bitter anger and even hatred against those who had "betrayed," even "crucified," freedom (Documents 26, 74, 108, 113).

What was freedom exactly? How was it defined substantively by lower-class Russians? In part, like the widespread image of broken chains, "freedom" represented a negation of a long history of subjugation, lack of rights, and repression. No more, it was said, would workers or peasants or soldiers be beaten or mistreated, denied the right to freely voice their needs and to struggle for them. As many historians of 1917 have argued, for large numbers of lower-class Russians freedom meant being left alone to conduct their lives according to their own volition. In other words, freedom meant "liberty"—in the sense conveyed especially by the Russian word *volia*, which simultaneously connoted "will," notably popular will, and a lack of restrictions or constraints. Concretely, such a vision of freedom meant, for example, that forest guards should no longer fine and abuse peasants for hunting, collecting berries, or grazing their animals in the wood (Document 38). Taken to the extreme, the implication was that there should be no external authority at all. The peasant-worker and former soldier A. Zemskov, for example, writing in late March, argued that "freedom and state order are incompatible," for "every state authority (even in democratic states) is founded on coercing its own subjects." The influence of anarchist ideology would seem strong here, though Zemskov explicitly rejected the anarchist label. And to be sure, his arguments are more practical and immediate than theoretical. Where is freedom, he asked, when "millions of voiceless slaves are still being led like sheep to the cannons and the machine guns and the officer is still treating the slave as if he were a mere thing," when those who refuse to participate in this senseless and discriminatory slaughter are still punished as before, when force is still used against those who oppose the new order (whether in the name of further political or social progress or in an attempt to return to the past)? Class resentment and distrust as much as anti-authoritarian theory seem to have motivated Zemskov's constant criticisms of the "bourgeois" intellectuals (both liberal and socialist) who had become the new rulers, and of the "modern economic order and modern culture" that shackled ordinary workers. What do the people most want, he asked, what is the people's idea of freedom? It is for all elites—"the noble and the merchant and the scholar and the poet and the journalist and the lawyer and the priest"—to "climb off their back" (Document 6).

By the summer of 1917, many lower-class Russians felt not only that this freedom had not been realized but that the freedoms won in February were being eroded and stolen by the same elites (indeed, Zemskov's mixed list of elites was a fairly accurate portrait of the composition of the Provisional Government) and that repression and tyranny were returning. Resolutions and letters chastised the new rulers for antilibertarian acts of restoration: for the death penalty, for harsh punishments for political crimes, for restrictions on meetings, and for censorship (Documents 62, 63, 64, 66). Similarly, after the October revolution, the Bolsheviks' efforts to secure their new authority with a "proletarian dictatorship" led to often passionate cries of outrage at the "destruction and desecration" of the freedoms "we fought and died for" (Documents 106, 114).

To describe popular ideas about freedom in a purely negative way, however—as the absence of external authority—obscures a great deal of thinking about the positive meanings of freedom. First, it is clear that lower-class Russians could and did view freedom as an abstract principle, as an absolute good (though this ethic, as will be seen, could exist side by side with its contradictions). The tendency to describe civil liberties formulaically—"freedom of speech, the press, assembly, unions, and strikes and the inviolability of the person" (Documents 40, 126) or as "liberty, equality, and fraternity" (Documents 37, 42, 118)—suggests not just mimicry of an established language of rights, but a belief that these liberties had a fixed and external status, that they existed already as matters of principle. Sometimes this was explicit, as in talk about "the rights of man" or the "absolute principle" of a free press (Document 104).[20] Indeed, for many, freedom was a moral achievement, a mark of dignity and honor: freedom meant that Russians could now "unbend [their] shoulders" (Document 5) and "stand proud and tall" (Document 3).

Most often, the principled and moral nature of freedom was asserted when irresponsible and egoistic uses of liberty were criticized. Soon after February, in much of the nonleftist press, one began to hear a steady critique of lower-class Russians for what was said to be their willful and irresponsible intoxication with liberty (as in the article by V. Shulgin that was the subject of protest in Document 29) or their use of freedom to advance only their own narrow material interests. In response, in many public appeals and resolutions lower-class Russians sought to refute these claims or at least (for they often had to admit that others acted in just such a way) to assert their own readiness to "sacrifice personal interests" for the sake of freedom, to endure, for example, harsh working conditions and low wages in the factories, or, at the front, suffering and even death, in order to support the new free order and ensure the victory against the Germans that would preserve freedom (Documents 13, 23, 45). Numerous appeals in 1917 criticized other workers, soldiers, or peasants who, it was said, viewed freedom as a time of wild liberty (*volia*) and arbitrary willfulness (*proizvol* [see Document 72 and note]) when there were "no authorities" and people could do what they liked and take what they could: when, for example, they could engage in unrestricted woodcutting in the forests, ignore officers in the army, beat up anyone they didn't like, refuse to work in a regular manner, and get drunk constantly.[21] This was not real freedom, insisted the more "conscious" peasants, soldiers, and workers. Real freedom, as members of an elected soldiers' committee (clearly frustrated by the behavior of their constituents) insisted in a long and rambling appeal to rank-and-file soldiers, required order, responsibility, a sense of duty, and moral self-discipline (Document 77). Real freedom called for sacrifice of personal material interest and self-restraint to curb the willful exercise of liberty (amoral and self-serving volia), a self-control that was said to be a matter not just of necessity and survival[22] but of "duty," "honor," "morality," and respect for others.

Other principles supported such arguments that freedom must be grounded in responsibility and restraint. Particularly common were ideas about responsibility before the nation and the people. In numerous resolutions, appeals, and letters, lower-class Russians wrote of freedom as the salvation of the nation as a whole—of Russia, or "Rus" (the emotionally resonant ancient name of the country and its people, especially its Orthodox core), or even "Holy Rus." Repeatedly, writers from the lower classes spoke of the principle of devotion to the narod (nation, in the broad sense of the whole Russian people), *rodina* (homeland, land of birth and origin, hence often translated as "motherland"), or *otechestvo* (fatherland). For the sake of this "new free Russia," for the country's "renewal," the selfish pursuit of partisan and particularistic interests must not be allowed to dominate people's behavior or consciousness. In the name of the freedom of the nation, various groups were criticized for forgetting the common good— fellow workers or soldiers, leftist political parties (especially the Bolsheviks), the "bourgeoisie," or "counterrevolutionaries" (Documents 25, 69, 74, 77, 84, 108). It is telling that soldiers offered such public rebukes especially often. In serving their country, soldiers were repeatedly told that they were fighting for Russia's freedom, an idealization of their role that they seemed inclined, at least for a time, to believe.[23]

Competing (and often combining ambiguously) with this embracing ideal of the "nation" as defining responsible limits to freedom was the more restricted principle of "the people"—the *narod*, a Russian word that combined the meanings of nation and common people. In 1917, though, the emphasis was most often on the common people, or even on the common people *as* the nation. Idealism about the unity of "the people" was rife in the aftermath of the February revolution. In appeals and letters, common people wrote with an almost mystical admiration of the "spontaneous" unity of the narod, of how the people were "so closely unified [*druzhno*] and unanimous that no one bothered to sort out who was walking shoulder to shoulder" (Document 26). Abuses of freedom in the pursuit of narrow social or party interests were regularly criticized as violating the high principle of unity of the people. Amid the conflicts and crises of the spring and summer, appeals often spoke of the need for unity among all the "political parties of the proletariat" (Document 54), of devotion to "the interests of the [working] class as a whole," as opposed to the interests of "factions and sects" (Document 57), of the need for disciplined unity around the soldiers' committees and other popular organizations (Document 77), and especially of obedience to the representative will of the common people as expressed in the soviets (Documents 54, 55, 70). Increasingly, organized groups of workers and soldiers reproached their fellows for lacking this spirit of "solidarity" and worried about the spread, dangerous to true freedom, of indiscipline and disorder among the people (Documents 81, 84).

In giving a positive connotation to freedom, lower-class Russians also linked it to a very concrete discourse about social needs and social good. As letters and resolutions stated repeatedly, now that the people were free, they needed food, land, education, and peace (though whether military victory was a precondition for peace was a matter of heated dispute, especially in the early months). More simply, freedom should bring—in the words and phrases used constantly in these texts—"happiness," "joy," "a new life," a "good life." As one group of soldiers (describing themselves as "all peasant farmers, workers, or employees") wrote in early April, freedom must allow "self-betterment" so that "labor" would become not a "shameful and heavy yoke," but something "for the joy and happiness of man" (Document 27). The Petrograd factory worker Maria Kutsko hoped that freedom for women to work outside the home would afford the opportunity to make "this life more beautiful, pure and bright for ourselves, for our children, and for the whole working class" (Document 20). For a group of peasants in Viatka province, "liberty" (*volia*) meant free education for their children and an end to poverty and dependency ("we are sick and tired of living in debt and slavery"). In an even more plain-spoken but still vivid and complex formulation, "liberty" was defined as "space and light" (Document 40). In peasants' writing, the frequent linkage of "land" and "liberty"—an echo of the famous phrase *zemlia i volia*, which had a long history in peasant thought and in Russian populism—was a terse and resonant expression of an assumed inter-dependency: without land there could be no liberty; without liberty there could be no land (Document 48). In other words, more land, peasants were certain, would ensure an end to the poverty that prevented them from exercising their own will (*volia*), that blocked the path to a better life; as long as the rich and the powerful controlled the lives of peasants, their desire for land would remain an impotent dream.

As these arguments may suggest, freedom was often viewed in socially specific (some would say parochial) ways, as a good that not all people merited, as a good that must benefit "the people" rather than the rich or the "bourgeoisie." This assumption is illustrated by attitudes toward freedom of the press. Most lower-class Russians, it would seem, did not view press freedom as an "absolute principle," but rather as one that must take account of the interests of the lower classes and the revolution. Thus, already in March and April, workers were beginning to complain about the "foul slander" and lies directed against them in the "bourgeois press" and to echo the proposals of leftist parties for "boycotts" and even closures of "bourgeois" newspapers (Documents 7, 8, 9, 10). By the fall, calls for class censorship had become much more common, especially among urban workers. Some workers and soldiers, like most moderate socialist intellectuals, insisted that true freedom of the press must recognize the rights of even disagreeable and hostile voices (Documents 69, 70), but many more people evidently believed that true freedom necessitated silencing the voices of those who opposed the struggles and demands of workers, soldiers, and peasants and thus threatened the "freedoms" won through the revolution. After the July Days, when a number of leftist (mainly Bolshevik) papers were closed down, it was not unusual to hear demands that combined, in a single sentence, demands for "restoration" of "freedom of the press" and for the "banning of the counterrevolutionary press" (Documents 66, 71, 87). These complaints against the bourgeois press often struck a moral note, though mixed with political ideas and class hostilities. Freedom of the press, it was often implied, should not include the right to "slander" the people. Even when demands for censorship along class lines were not made, criticisms of censorship by the Provisional Government typically defined press freedom in social terms: as an "inalienable right of the people," as an essential condition of their "struggle for social liberation" and cultural "rebirth" (Document 62). This grounding of freedom in practical and social argument was especially vivid in antiwar letters that began to appear more and more frequently by the summer of 1917. Repeatedly, soldiers and others asked what good freedom was to them if they were dead (Document 67)—an argument quite unlike the declarations, so common in the early spring, that the people were ready to fight to the death for freedom. Deep distrust of social and political elites was a powerful solvent breaking down heroic dedication to freedom in the abstract.

Political Power: Order and Justice

State power, the formal objective of revolutionary change, was viewed in a similar light. The importance of political power in the minds of a large number of lower-class Russians is evident even superficially in the huge numbers of letters, petitions, appeals, and resolutions directed at individuals and institutions in power. Some of these were individual appeals for help—for intervention in local matters such as the firing of a hated foreman or the expulsion of a corrupt official. Most, however, were general appeals—to the Provisional Government and its leaders, and especially to the soviets, as representatives of the people's interests before the government, to hear the voice of the people and adopt a correct course: to preserve freedom; to promote justice; to suppress counterrevolution; to ensure that people had food, land, peace, and education; and, in general, to ensure the people's "happiness" and secure a "new" and "good" life for the people. By midsummer, as disappointment with the results of the revolution and with the actions of the Provisional Government grew, people began to focus more and more attention on state power itself as holding the answer to their needs and desires. Questions about who should control the government, what policies should be adopted, and what sort of political order should be established by the coming Constituent Assembly became regular topics of discussion.

Strong and unified political authority was for most ordinary Russians a necessity (though there were dissenting voices). For some, this meant the unity of the Provisional Government and the soviets (especially as represented by the Petrograd Soviet and then by the All-Russian Central Executive Committee of Soviets), but for many, and increasingly, this meant "all power to the soviets." Again and again, authors of petitions and resolutions and letters spoke of the necessity for "firm authority" (*tverdaia vlast'*—one of the most ubiquitous phrases in these texts—e.g., Documents 17, 92, 95), for "unitary authority" (*edinaia vlast'*—Document 65), for a state possessing the "necessary fullness of power" (Documents 15, 41). Demands for soviet power were very often framed by this desire for a strong and unified political authority in the country. "Enough talk," it was said; the time had come for a "strong democratic government."[24]

The political-cultural context for these complaints should be kept in mind. After so many years of struggling against autocratic monarchy in Russia, which had viewed government as a paternalistic and authoritarian power responsible for the totality of the nation's life, the liberals who led the Provisional Government de-emphasized the state as the key force in transforming the country and placed their confidence instead in the workings of an active citizenry behaving responsibly in a society based on law. Besides, until new national elections established a properly elected government, their leadership of the state was legally only "provisional," and therefore they felt that they must exercise restraint. Meanwhile, the leaders of the Petrograd Soviet hesitated to exceed what they considered their own limited authority as the representatives only of particular social classes, not of the whole nation.

The idealization of strong state power tended very often to be personalized in the desire for strong and good leaders. Just as many lower-class Russians had once looked to the tsar to care for his people "like a father" (Document 3), many now articulated a new revolutionary "cult of leaders."[25] Numerous appeals and letters addressed various "freedom fighters," Soviet leaders, and socialist ministers—especially Aleksandr Kerensky, the most popular leader in the first months after February—as trusted leaders (*vozhdi*) and even as saviors who would bring the people happiness: "You are our friends you are our saviors and we trust you and our hope is in you for the salvation of the working population of Russia and our confidence is in you" (Document 94). "Let all the socialist ministers you lead remain at their posts," a telegram to Kerensky read; "be brave and steadfast, be merciless and stern with enemies of the people—only you can save Russia and lead her out into the light" (Document 99). This inclination to personalize political authority has been explained most often as the persistence of "a monarchic mentality," an echo of the "traditional authoritarian-patriarchal culture."[26] More was involved here, however, than simply the persistence of authoritarian tradition or the belief in strong power for its own sake. Strong power, especially when personalized, was understood, like freedom, as a source of justice, as a means to ensure the coming (in words often heard here) of salvation, truth, freedom, and fraternity.[27]

Ideas about strong power were entwined with beliefs about how this power should be used and, no less important, whom it should serve. In part, the desire was for resolute authority to restore order to the country: to suppress banditry and crime, to unite people in a common purpose, and, especially, to revive the collapsing economy. The impotence of the existing government was a constant cause of complaint. And few hesitated to endorse the need for "merciless" measures, "cruelty to enemies" (*zhestokost' k vragam*), and "dictatorship" to ensure such order (Documents 63, 84, 98).[28] Sometimes, lower-class Russians felt that this dictatorial authority needed to be directed against indiscipline among the people themselves—"who don't recognize discipline that isn't welded together with bare knuckles and an iron fist" (Document 92)—and against enemies of the revolution and of Russia on the Left: "to put down strikes by force and get the defense factories going; . . . to introduce iron discipline into the army by force," to arrest and punish the Bolsheviks (Documents 91, 98).

Most often such strong or even dictatorial authority was classed as a "democratic" power—in other words, one that served the interests of the poor against the rich. The country, it was said, needed a "firm and democratic authority" that "express[ed] the people's will" (Documents 53, 87). Sometimes, appeals for political intervention on behalf of the poor and the subordinate were quite specific and personal. Workers, peasants, and soldiers repeatedly turned to the government, and especially to the Soviet in Petrograd, the "democratic" authority, to act as their advocate in local social conflicts: a railroad worker in the Urals wanted the Petrograd Soviet to "take measures" against a supervisor (Document 12), a peasant in Novgorod Province wanted the Soviet Executive Committee to force the local chief physician out of office (Document 43), and peasants in Poltava Province denounced the local priest and the peasant elder heading the *volost* commune and asked the Soviet authorities to "take measures" against them (Document 44). Most often, appeals for strong democratic power more broadly sought "dictatorship aimed against the counterrevolutionary bourgeoisie" (Document 63). This was far from being a vague abstraction or mere slogan. Most writers were quite specific about what they meant in practice: the government should establish a bread monopoly to prevent hunger, should distribute land to the poor, introduce "control" (democratic supervision) over management in industry, control prices, confiscate clothing and shoes from the rich, expropriate "superprofits," and suppress the bourgeois press, and ultimately should create a strong government "founded on and responsible to the popular masses" (Documents 66, 87, 126).[29] The language of "socialism" in 1917, though less widespread than that of "democracy" or "freedom," encompassed similar meanings. "Socialism" was a term of exclusion: a vision of political authority by and for the common people. Socialism, it was argued, cannot be reached through a bourgeois republic but only through the power of the workers themselves (Document 6); "socialist" papers are those which address themselves to and serve the interests of the poor (Document 50); socialism means "popular sovereignty" (Document 113). At the same time, socialism was an embodiment of the ideal of a just state. "The socialists are trying to win equality and brotherhood on earth," a group of peasants wrote the Petrograd Soviet in April, "and that's why they are our comrades" (Document 40).

Class: Enemies and Friends

Freedom and power both, as should be evident, were often understood in the light of a view of the social and political world as divided between enemies and friends, between others and oneself. Popular distrust and even hatred of the rich and powerful already had a long history by 1917, nurtured by quite tangible social and political inequalities, as well as by decades of radical and socialist agitation and teaching. In 1917, as before, this popular language of class was often much more flexible than the precise notions about social structure that Marxist activists had in mind when speaking of the "class enemy." Although that class designation was sometimes used in a specifically Marxist sense to identify the social group whose material interests as owners of the means of production put them in direct material conflict with the interests of the propertyless proletariat, more often "class enemy" was a less precise and more flexible designation of otherness: a sweeping social pejorative for all who were richer or more powerful, a political label criticizing any who opposed the interests of the common people, a moral label rebuking elites for their self-interestedness and egoism.[30] The boundaries in this vocabulary of class were placed differently and were often vague and changeable, but the language of "us" and "others" was pervasive.

Popular talk of "enemies" resumed quite soon after the initial unifying euphoria of the February revolution. In late March, for example, a group of Petrograd workers protested against the "slander that is coming out of our enemies' camp," which was attempting to "sow enmity" between workers and soldiers (Document 7). Here and elsewhere, we find in these texts a dualistic vocabulary of enemies and traitors on the one side and friends, comrades, and brothers on the other. The boundaries between sides, however, were far from stable. Different groups could be and were branded as enemies or traitors: the "rich, the kulaks, and the bourgeois" who benefited from the war (Document 40), but also socialists who threatened the people's freedom by undermining unity or the effort against the Germans (Documents 17, 26). When used to condemn the "bourgeoisie," this term might include, in those early months, the "upper classes," the rich, the intelligentsia (including the "bourgeois-socialist intelligentsia"), the nonsocialist press, or simply anyone who was not on the side of the people (Documents 6, 8, 50). Quite often, the identification of enemies was concrete and even personal, as when letters were written denouncing specific individuals (officials, priests, village elders, foremen, officers, and so forth) as bloodsuckers, Black Hundreds, or enemies (Documents 12, 43, 44, 47).

By late summer, as political and social relations became more polarized, this language of difference and opposition, of oppression and subordination, grew even more pervasive and insistent. "Where are the results of the blood and of the lives of our brothers who fell in the revolution? Where is the new life, that heavenly, joyous, fiery-red bird that flew so temptingly over our country and then hid—as if to trick us?" (Document 57). Such questions were typical and often heard, though by late summer the assumption that appeals of this sort might inspire a positive response had been largely replaced by disillusioned and angry accusations of lies and betrayal. Repeatedly, letters and appeals from workers, peasants, and soldiers voiced anger at leaders who "made promises to us while they themselves were sitting on the thrones where the executioners and murderers used to sit" (Document 74), who "have not justified the people's hopes" (Document 87), who have displayed only political impotence and the inability to fulfill promises. Before October, this frustration had been directed against the Provisional Government and the "conciliationist" leaders of the Soviet; after October it was often expressed toward the new Bolshevik authorities: "I believed in you because you promised good things for us" (Document 108); "where are the promises you made" (Document 113).

Increasingly, the failure of authorities to deliver on the presumed promises of the revolution was seen as stemming from an irreconcilable conflict of interests and of values. By midsummer, we hear constant talk about the "counterrevolutionary imperialist bourgeoisie" or the "privileged [*tsenzovye*] elements" conspiring against the freedoms won through the revolution and against the "entire working class" and seeking to restore the old order (Documents 58, 63, 66, 90). As disappointment continued to grow over the results of revolution— over the unfulfilled promises of peace, bread, land, freedom—blame was invariably placed not on circumstances (economic difficulties, the war, the problems of transition) but on counterrevolutionary intent and simple "treason." For some, especially peasants, it was the Bolsheviks who were the moral and political enemies of the revolution, the "enemies of the fatherland" who needed to be crushed,[31] the "accursed weeds" that needed to be ripped out (Document 123). Some blamed Jews or other outsiders: it was not unusual to hear bigoted excoriations of "Yids" as the most dangerous traitors to the Russian nation, and as the people most to blame for limiting the benefits of the revolution (Document 112).[32]

The main enemy, though, was the rich and privileged—the "enemies of the people" and "traitors and betrayers" of Russia and the revolution who must be "punished" as "contemptible oppressors of the people" for "infringing on the cause of the Revolution and Freedom" (Documents 71, 76, 81). Here, this language of otherness and opposition becomes a language of class, of economic inequalities and subordination. No longer, many soldiers declared, were they willing to shed blood for the "celebration of the bourgeois pocketbook."[33] The natural solution was to end all "compromise" with the "counterrevolutionary bourgeoisie" and to give all power to the soviets, as representing the will of the people. Sometimes, more vividly and ominously, the answer was said to be cleansing the revolution of the "oozing scab" of the bourgeoisie and of the "leeches" who had clung to the body of the country (Document 81), to be "merciless with the enemies of the people,"[34] to save Russia with purifying fire and blood (Documents 52, 102, 131).

"Friends" were less clearly defined than "enemies." Varying and often ambiguous terms of social identification were used to describe the
side opposed to the bourgeoisie: the "working people" or "laboring
folk" (a category itself designated by a range of terms for people who
labored—*trudovoi narod, trudiashchikhsia, trudovye, truzheniki,
rabochie,* and so on—each with its own history and nuances), the
"working class" (a term that could be used in the Marxist sense of industrial workers or more broadly to include all workers, peasants, and
soldiers), the "lower class of workers and peasants," or simply the
"poor" (*bednye*) or the common people (*narod*). These social designations were not synonymous. They variously included and excluded different combinations of workers, peasants, and soldiers, though often
the particulars were rather vague. And even when groups were speci-
fied, the categories often had uncertain boundaries: migrant workers
or "worker aristocrats" might be excluded from the category of
"workers"; the richer "kulaks" and the *otrubniki* (peasants who left
the commune to farm on their own) might be excluded from "peasants"; men promoted into the lower ranks of officers might be excluded from the category of "soldiers."

The use of "democracy" as a collective identification was especially
characteristic of 1917 and illustrative of the tendency to read politics
though a socially polarized lens.[35] While liberals wished "democracy"
to identify all citizens, they had to admit that the more popular tendency was to exclude the "bourgeoisie." As one political dictionary
published in 1917 observed, "Democracy is the whole people, the
poor and the rich, men and women, and so on. Presently democracy
refers only to the poor, to people without resources, that is, workers
and peasants; but this is incorrect."[36] The Soviet and most socialists
used "democracy" only in this restrictive manner. And so did most
lower-class people who spoke out publicly. In popular usage, "democracy" included those who were not privileged and exploitative and did
not conspire against the revolution. It included the working people
and intellectuals who defended the interests of the common people—
thus the Soviets of Workers', Soldiers', and Peasants' Deputies and
their socialist leaders were identified as embodying the will of the "entire democracy," of the "revolutionary democracy" that would triumph "over all the dark forces of the country" (Document 19). Similarly, when "democracy" was used in the older sense to describe a
political ideal, the tendency was to define it not as equal rights and
power for all, but as politics in the interests of the poor. As one group

of soldiers put this quite bluntly in midsummer: "If you defend the poor class, then there will be a democratic republic, but if you defend the interests of the capitalists, then Russia is lost" (Document 73). The language for conveying ideas of nation was treated in the same way. The Russian word *narod* (the people), as already mentioned, can be used to mean either the whole nation or just the common folk. Although the word carried both meanings in the language of 1917, the class-based reading of "the nation" was increasingly dominant in the language of common people. As one officer wrote home to his family in mid-March, describing the "impassable abyss" that divided the thinking of soldiers from that of officers (and, by extension, the thinking of all subalterns from that of all people in authority): "When we talk about the narod, we mean the nation as a whole [*natsiia*], but when they talk about it they understand it to mean only the democratic lower classes [*demokraticheskie nizy*]." Class, this young officer recognized sadly, was an inescapable part of how ordinary soldiers viewed social relationships, their country, and the revolution. "Whatever their personal attitudes toward individual officers might be, we remain in their eyes only masters [*bary*]. . . . In their view, what has taken place is not a political but a social revolution, in which, according to them, we are the losers and they the winners. . . . Previously, we ruled; now they themselves want to rule. In them speak the unavenged insults of centuries past. A common language between us cannot be found. This is the cursed legacy of the old order."[37]

In the wake of the October revolution, expressions of both support for and hostility toward Bolshevik power tended to deploy the same categories of enemy and friend. The Bolsheviks, one Petrograd factory worker wrote at the end of 1917, had proved themselves to be the true "friend" of the "working people," whereas both the bourgeoisie and the moderate socialists of the Provisional Government had proved themselves to be "traitors and betrayers of the workers, soldiers, and peasants" and "enemies of the people" (Document 109). By contrast, another Petrograd factory worker wrote that it was the Bolsheviks who had made themselves "enemies of the people" by failing to satisfy the needs of the poor (Document 106). One thing was consistent: the language of moral, social, and political demonization. To blame for most misfortune were "enemies" who, whether Bolsheviks or bourgeois, were branded as profoundly other: as impostors (*samozvantsy*), usurpers, tyrants, betrayers, traitors, bandits, plunderers, and bastards (Documents 108, 109, 113, 118, 121, 127, 128).

Morality: Honor and Shame, the Sacred and the Profane

For most lower-class Russians, the revolution was a time of great moral significance. The language of moral transformation was ubiquitous in Russia in 1917. The government, the leaders of the Soviet, and the press constantly spoke of the revolution as a time of resurrection and renewal, of good and truth, of the struggle against evil. Lower-class Russians often shared this moral vision of the revolution. The very act of writing by plebeians was presented in a moral framework—as a matter of necessity and truth. Letters from individuals very often included ritualized (though not necessarily insincere) apologies for the poor grammar or style and for the authors' impertinence in troubling their listeners: "Forgive me, an insignificant worker, for being so bold as to address you, a great political figure" (Document 6); "I am addressing the S.R. and S.D. [parties] in my peasant way, simply, for I know no other" (Document 43). At the same time, they insisted on the special moral power and right they had, precisely as untutored common folk, to address those in power: "to express the truth that only a working man capable of speaking the pure truth can feel" (Document 6); to speak "as a genuine son of our dear Russia" (Document 59); to speak from a "consciousness" learned from "suffering";[38] to voice what "the soul yearns to express" (Document 39).

The emotional pathos and fervor with which so many expressed themselves in 1917 was a further sign of moral feeling. To emphasize the great weight, deep truthfulness, and moral necessity of what they had to say, lower-class Russians employed a resonant and emotionally charged language rich with epithets, superlatives, catchphrases, demands, hyperbole, repetition, irony, metaphors, and phrases drawn from the language of the Church and prayer.[39] Occasionally, for extra emphasis, as a further marker of the moral passion they felt, they wrote their whole text out in capital letters or in red ink (Documents 26, 128) or seasoned their letters with curses, violent threats, and profanity. The use of emotional modifiers made clear the moral significance of these momentous times: good actions were heavenly, joyful, shining, resplendent, fiery, and bright, while the work of enemies was bloody, dark, vile, shameful, and despicable. Even ordinary nouns often conveyed a sense of great moment and moral significance: the writers spoke of liberation, joy, glory, happiness, love, light, truth, salvation, oppression, carnage, chaos, destruction, blood, shame, betrayal, and vengeance. The use of metaphors to elevate meaning and mood, and to indicate moral significance, was especially common. To our ears, these metaphors are mostly clichés; but then they still had, especially for the less educated, fresh emotional force: the sun of freedom, redemptive flight, saviors, heaven, and, standing in moral opposition to these, dark clouds, the abyss, the heavy stone of grief, the bleeding heart, and slavery. Such use of metaphor to express moral intent was especially evident in the branding of adversaries as morally alien, as outcasts beyond the pale of humanity: vermin, jackals, bloodsuckers, and vampires.

Honor (*chest'*) was a key notion in the protests and appeals of lower-class Russians in 1917. The English word inadequately conveys the sense of the Russian. The primary meanings of "honor" in most Western European languages bear the imprint of chivalric notions associated with rank and standing: honor as the "high respect, esteem, or reverence, accorded to exalted worth or rank" and as "personal title to high respect or esteem."[40] The Russian *chest'* shares this emphasis on respect and can entail notions of rank and status, but the primary meaning is grounded in notions of respect necessitated by "the inward moral dignity of the person, high personal qualities, integrity, nobility of spirit, and pure moral conscience."[41] Such concerns with moral respect and dignity, and with the insult and injury that affronted these values, were a prominent feature of popular discourse in 1917. These were not new ideas, of course. The concept that all human beings share a natural dignity and the right to respect had occupied a central place in the thinking and arguments of activist workers in Russia since the late nineteenth century. In confronting employers with demands and strikes, for example, workers very often insisted on "polite address" and, more generally, treatment befitting their worth as "human beings."[42] When workers and other relatively literate lower-class Russians voiced their views of the world in print, they often articulated an ethical vision that insisted on every person's inward nature and personality (*lichnost'*, the person, the self), which made every individual naturally deserving of respect and freedom. This ideal emerged out of an ongoing dialogue in the lives of many ordinary Russians between the everyday experience of social subordination and ill treatment and ideas drawn both from traditional notions of honor and from the widespread public discourse about the natural dignity and rights of the human person, which many Russians encountered in reading. Well before 1917, Russian journals, newspapers, and literature, including those read by literate commoners, were filled with such ideas. Reflecting, perhaps, the weight of lived experience in the thinking of ordinary

Russians about the self and its moral meaning, however, the main focus of the concern with honor and dignity was on *violations* of this ideal.[43]

Lower-class Russians were themselves the targets of such criticism. As before 1917, criticism from educated Russians of immorality and ignorance among the lower classes was echoed (and transformed) in a critique by many lower-class Russians themselves of the everyday culture of the majority of ordinary people. The socialist intellectuals on the Executive Committee of the Soviet in Petrograd regularly warned that boorish and crass behavior (for instance, soldiers' coming to blows with sailors over seats on a train or widespread drunkenness) undermined the revolution.[44] Similarly, many outspoken workers, peasants, and soldiers repeatedly insisted that the revolution, as a historic opening to a new world, necessitated the improvement of the individual, especially the plebeian, more than ever before. "Culture" was the notion around which these arguments were constructed. Culture was understood partly in a utilitarian and political way: greater learning and knowledge were essential to ensure that Russia had the sort of "conscious" population that could understand and defend the revolution; but thinking about culture also had a distinct moral logic: people, especially those demanding rights and respect, needed to learn how to live with the honor and dignity they merited as human beings. "Now that everyone is free," a group of soldiers wrote to their new leaders, "we wanted to make use of this freedom in the sense of self-betterment, which we need so much now for our new creative life. . . . We are all peasant farmers, workers, or employees. Our lack of enlightenment and our economic impotence allowed the ever powerful and rich to exploit our labor. This corrupted our whole life. . . . We do not want this kind of life any more, we are tired of constantly thinking about nothing but a crust of bread for the next day" (Document 27). Peasants, especially soldiers returning to their native villages, expressed aloud their dismay at the "horrible ignorance" and "darkness" among the majority of peasants and appealed for the Soviet or the government to send books, newspapers, and teachers (Documents 43, 44, 46, 50, 97). Groups of soldiers appealed to the Soviet in Petrograd to "bring us your slogans, come see us, we are waiting for you, send us your speakers. Sow the seed in our hearts, set us on a pure path we can follow unimpeded" (Document 89). Women appealed to activists to help "honest" working women avoid falling "into a pool of debauchery" (Document 14). Workers complained, as the activists among them had for years, about the "vulgar," "banal," "crass," "sideshow" (*zhelto-balaganoe*) culture that still prevailed in workers' districts (Document 61) and spoke of the need for "cultural rebirth" (Document 62). Plebeian poets tried to capture this ideal in grander phrases, writing of "blessed learning . . . / minds inquiring and always searching" (Document 2) and of the constant search for "enlightenment" (Document 5).[45] All made it clear that the persistence of "uncultured" behavior was a matter of personal "shame," as well as political harm, at such a time.

Drunkenness was viewed as one of the most persistent and shameful signs of the people's moral degradation. A wartime prohibition did not eradicate the problem of heavy drinking among the Russian populace. In the factories, activists complained, "men are drinking denatured alcohol, varnish, and other such substitutes. They are drunk on the job, speak out of turn at meetings, shout inappropriate phrases, prevent politically conscious comrades from speaking, and paralyze their organizational work. There is total disarray in the shops. Owing to all the alcoholism, politically conscious workers are suffocating in this kind of atmosphere" (Document 16). After October, the problem persisted, as did moral and political condemnation of it. When, in December, some Petrograd soldiers stormed wine cellars and drank themselves into a stupor, activists castigated their comrades for "this disgrace," which threatened to "drown Freedom and the Revolution in wine." In tsarist times, it was argued, drunkenness was used by the government to "keep the people in ignorance." So, "if drunkenness in and of itself is harmful, then right now, when we are only beginning to live a new life, it is doubly dangerous." Are we going to "behave like Judas," they asked, "and betray everything that is precious and holy to us for a bottle of wine?" (Document 119). For a group of activist peasants, commenting on the pervasiveness of home brew in the countryside, alcohol was nothing less than a "diabolical liquid" (Document 124).

Individual behavior in the political arena was of special concern. As we have noted, "conscious" plebeians regularly worried about individuals who abused liberty for selfish ends or engaged in "disorders." They appealed constantly to their fellows for discipline, responsibility, and restraint. And their arguments were almost always colored by moral notions of honor and dignity. A meeting of workers in Novgorod Province in May, for example, expressed "indignation" (*negodovanie*) at the "overt and covert insults aimed at the men the people have chosen to take Power"—the reference is to the socialists who agreed to join the first coalition government as ministers (Document

15). The July Days—when armed soldiers and workers in the streets of Petrograd demanded soviet power, and disorderly riots broke out in the wake of assaults on the crowds by police and Cossacks—were roundly condemned by more moderate soldiers and workers as a disgrace bringing dishonor to the revolution. For workers at a Petrograd printing house, the armed demonstration and the "fratricidal slaughter" of those days was "the most grievous and shameful page in Russian history," for which they "brand[ed] with shame" and put their "curse" on the radical organizers of this "provocational demonstration" (Document 56).

As discontent with the results of the revolution mounted, so did the disorders, and the moral critique of them. We see this especially in the army, where disobedience and disorder were a particular problem but where, also, the ethic of honor was especially strong. Soldiers deplored the constant disobedience to military orders as "a shameful stain" on the revolutionary people and a "slander" against their interests (Document 70). At the front, soldiers voiced their "indignation" and "curse" against the "disgraceful," "unseemly and scandalous behavior" (*bezobrazie*) among the many "idle, full-bellied, carousing" soldiers at the rear (Document 84). Many expressed anguish over the social violence and hatred that was becoming increasingly widespread during these months. One group of soldiers, for instance, "branded with shame" soldiers who had dragged speakers they disagreed with off their platform and beat them to death (Document 70). Similarly, in the eyes of an artillery soldier, the lynching of a group of arrested officers and the violent settling of "personal scores," which had resulted in the deaths of a dozen men, was a "disgrace and a shame" (*pozor i sram*) and stigmatized all soldiers with an "ineradicable stain" (Document 80). Can one achieve a truly "free life," another soldier asked, by leaving the "true path" to follow the way of "malice, envy, and hatred" (Document 74)? Now, it was said, what was needed was a "pure heart" (Document 77).

When common Russians trained their moral vision on the larger social and political order, as they so often did, notions of honor and dishonor remained central and widespread, though people were far from agreeing on who had the best claims on virtue and who most merited righteous condemnation. Resolutions and letters enumerated virtues and sins: the good that the revolution had been expected to inaugurate and evil yet to be eliminated. Some of these virtues, as we have seen, were generalized social goods: the "dignity" and "honor" of freedom (at least, freedom for the people), the virtues of unity and solidarity (at least among the common people and on the political Left), a politics of concern for the unprivileged, and the triumph of social justice. Likewise, social and political conflict was typically viewed less as a clash of interests or of different but equal points of view than as a fundamental moral struggle between light and darkness, truth and lies, or virtuous friends and evil, even demonic, enemies.

As before 1917, peasants, workers, and soldiers continued to voice resentment at everyday insults they suffered at the hands of elites, at the pervasiveness of "humiliation and insult" (*unizhenie i oskorblenie*) for those living at the lower depths of an inegalitarian and unfree society. "Justice," a ubiquitous notion, was often linked to questions of personal dignity, respect, and honor. In the army, widespread anger at the rudeness of officers toward rank-and-file soldiers, including the degrading use of the informal "you" (*ty*), were embodied in the Petrograd Soviet's Order No. 1, which banned that form of address, along with all "rudeness" to soldiers, as insulting to their dignity.[46] Among urban workers, as Diane Koenker and William Rosenberg have documented, the presentation of demands and sometimes the outbreak of strikes "over issues of dignity and personal respect"—especially polite forms of address and humane working conditions—were frequent, especially among clerical and service workers (industrial workers had already fought and often won those battles before the war).[47] Similarly, many lower-class Russians, when they appealed to the government or the Soviet or to the conscience and commitment of the public, spoke of the need to end "humiliation and insult"—as when soldiers publicly rebuked their officers for calling them "bastards" and threatening to shoot them (Document 24), or female workers described poor working-class women treated without "pity," as if they were not also people,[48] or forced by their poverty onto the "shameful path" of "debauchery" (Document 14). Subordination and oppression, quite typically, were narrated as a moral story of "insult" and "mockery" (*izdevatel'stvo*) (Documents 3, 26, 74, 88).

Much more frequently than before 1917, the concerns of ordinary Russians with social honor and insult were generalized and politicized beyond the immediate injuries of class into broader questions of state policy and social power. As such, concern with direct "insult" as the main violation of honor (and thus with actions that might be corrected) gave way to concern with social "shame" (and with deeper and more essential wrongs that had to be reproved, punished, and eradicated). Arguments in support of the war, for example, were often framed as questions of honor and shame: "The free Russian people

must not dishonor themselves with a shameful peace" (Document 23);
it was wrong to make any "degrading" (*unizitel'nye*) deals (Document
25) or sign a "shameful, dishonorable, separate peace" (Document
26). Some writers, like a group of injured and sick soldiers (who noted
that they were all workers and peasants and supporters of the revolution), condemned the Soviet and the leaders of the Social Democratic
party as "traitors" to the Russian people who took "pleasure" in the
people's "torments" and "humiliations" and whose own political actions were "hellish," "filthy, base, and vile," made still worse morally
by their "hiding behind various masks" (Document 26). More often,
of course, it was the political and social powers that be who were
judged to be the most stained by dishonor. For many, like the workers
representing small enterprises in a district of Petrograd, the war was
nothing but "bloody carnage," and the continued political concessions
by the Soviet a "shameful retreat" before "enemies" (Document 58).

Behind bad political policies, it was felt, must stand bad social
groups. Above all, the rich and the "bourgeoisie" were blamed for the
failure of the revolution to fulfill its promise. Notions of "honor" and
"shame" were so central to this language of social criticism that it is
often difficult to untangle the relation between class hostility and
moral outrage. The two helped shape and give meaning to each other.
Unfulfilled promises were often interpreted, as we have seen, through
a moral narrative of deliberate harm by the rich and powerful. These
moral and social judgments were not identical, though. The suggestions of class determinism (what else, the gist of their assertions
seemed to be, could one expect from the "bourgeoisie"?) did not eliminate the quite different logic of moral choice and hence shame. The
government's crackdown on radicalism and disorder in the aftermath
of the July Days—in particular, the many arrests and searches, the
restoration of censorship and old punitive laws, and the threats of violence against the people—were branded as "shameful" (*pozornyi*)
(Documents 58, 62). The restoration of the death penalty especially
was targeted as "barbaric" and "shameful," the "disgrace of mankind" (Documents 58, 62, 71, 100). Adding insult to moral injury, the
bourgeoisie (though its press, especially) was often said to be guilty of
"slander" (*kleveta*) and "defamation" (*travlia*) (Documents 7, 29, 36,
66, 83, 87, 117). More generally, and with a potent and familiar mixture of social and moral antagonism, the bourgeoisie and the rich were
berated for their egoistic materialism, for earning property and wealth
not through their own labor—the only legitimate moral claim to property, it was argued—but through "various amorous escapades" and

"sly and devious behavior" (Document 40). The new rulers were tarred with the same social and moral brush: they were accused of enjoying the same "stuffed, greasy, gluttonous living" as the old rulers, while the people remained "enslaved," "mocked," and "naked" (Document 74).

After October, such moral criticism reached a peak of intensity. For supporters of the Bolshevik-led overturn of the Provisional Government, opponents, especially fellow socialists and plebeians, were dismissed as enemies of the people and chastised with the people's "contempt and curse" (Document 120). But the strongest language of moral condemnation and demonization was directed against the now powerful Bolsheviks. The peace negotiations with the Germans were condemned as a mark of "ineradicable shame" (Document 104). The closing of the Constituent Assembly and the shooting of demonstrators in early January 1918 was said to be the work of impostors, butchers, and tyrants who betrayed their promises, were "killing off everything holy," had "put blinders on the workers' eyes," and deserved to die "on a pillar of shame" (Documents 112, 113, 128). More generally, the Bolsheviks were regularly anathematized and demonized as moral aliens. They were said to be hooligans (a term that in Russia had acquired the sense of insolent assault on civilized values and culture),[49] villains, bandits, butchers, murderers, and "dark forces" whose actions "degraded" and "shamed" the people and the revolution. They were even categorized as class enemies, though in the same moral sense that the bourgeoisie was defined: as "rich and corrupt," "robbers of the poor," "enemies of the people."[50]

For some lower-class Russians, certainly, their anger grew from a particularly deep sense of betrayal: the Bolsheviks, the presumed friends of the people, had been the most consistent enemy of the bourgeoisie and thus, for many, the object of greatest hope. Throughout the revolution, betrayal by friends was a greater sin, a greater cause for moral outrage, than the abuses of overt enemies. In the eyes of many Russians, the failure of the new revolutionary government to bring peace, bread, and land to the people, and especially the failure of the Soviet leadership to challenge the government, was the first major betrayal. "Disappointment" is an accurate but feeble description of the deep anger and outrage often felt. Disappointment with the Bolsheviks, often seen as the last hope, was even more intense. As a "former Bolshevik" wrote to Lenin in December, "At first I believed in you because you promised good things for us—real peace, bread and freedom. . . . But instead of what you promised, you sold Russia out, gave us no bread, and established a Nicholas II kind of freedom. . . . I curse you and all your comrades in the Council of Usurpers and Betrayers of our native land" (Document 108). The deep moral outrage at this betrayal was evident in the emotional and censorious tone of many of these texts—the seething anger, the pronouncing of curses, the verbal spitting into "shameless eyes" (Document 128), and the vigorous profanity (Document 122). It was conspicuous also in the analogies and metaphors deployed: "with your oprichniki [Ivan the Terrible's notorious personal force] you are like King Herod who would not spare fourteen thousand infants just to exterminate the Great Socialist Jesus Christ among them. You are like Judas who sold Christ for thirty pieces of silver." Indeed, the Bolsheviks suffered in the comparison: "Herod took only baby boys from their mothers, whereas you are taking everyone," and "Judas at least felt guilty and hanged himself" (Document 128).

The pervasive use of religious metaphor and language—including phrases from the Bible and from Old Church Slavic, the language of the church and of prayer—was a potent means to intensify the emotional weight of words and to emphasize their universal and ethical significance. Socialists had long used religious metaphor, vocabulary, and narratives in their appeals to lower-class Russians. And as a number of historians have observed, in 1917, as before, the language of revolution and of socialist democracy appealed to large number of ordinary Russians precisely because it resonated so strongly with Christian values and ideals.[51] For many, the sacred meaning of the revolution was literal—the perceived triumph of specifically Christian values. Thus, for example, when appealing for an end to the war, soldiers argued that it was wrong to kill men who "are not our enemies but are our brothers in the cross and in the divine commandments" (Document 30). Peasants continued to insist that all the land must belong to those who work it, for "the land belongs to almighty God, as His creation, and to all the sons of man, as His heirs in equal part," as long as they shall work it (Document 97). For some, the revolution was "blessed" by God (Document 2) and even was God's will, a "Great Joy" for which He should be thanked (Document 38).

In much of this writing, however, religion and the sacred were present less as a literal expression of Christian belief than as a metaphorical and symbolic language—and, entwined with these functions, as an emotional language. The distinction, of course, was not absolute. The emotional and moral power of religious language and imagery was often due, in the minds of most lower-class Russians, precisely to its resonant source in Christian tradition. For whatever reason, it is clear that many Russians, plebeians as well as the more educated and privileged, found in religious language a more satisfactory means of articulating their feelings about the revolution than in any political or other idiom. Religious language, as deeply emotional, universalizing, and ethical, possessed a quality of mystery and destiny that was an important part of the way many lower-class Russians understood the revolution. As a leading Russian historian of the revolution has written, "From the Revolution was often expected not only concrete social and political changes but a Miracle—rapid and universal purification and 'resurrection.'"[52] This hope was often quite explicit. Letters and appeals spoke of the revolution as the "unexpected resurrection of the Russian people" (Document 26), or as the triumph of "the ideas of the International, which has been resurrected in the streams of Blood of the World War" (Document 62), or as a time of new life for every person "who in the chains of slavery saw his death and in the sunlight of freedom saw his resurrection" (Document 77). Above all, the revolution and its purposes were sacred, holy (*sviatoi*). This was a "holy revolution" (Document 59), which championed "the precious and holy slogans of liberty, equality, and fraternity" (Document 81). Freedom, in particular, was a "sacred" thing, a "holy temple," a "sacred site" (Documents 4, 5, 131). And speaking the truth to those in power was a "sacred duty" (Document 98). Of course, different individuals and groups defined the boundaries of sacred and profane, of good and evil, differently. This was especially noticeable after October, when the Bolsheviks were said by some to be trampling on "everything holy" (Document 113) and by others to be engaging in "Holy work" (Document 118).

The revolution, for many, was a struggle for sacred "truth"—for *istina* and especially for *pravda*. In Russian, *istina* is the truth that is real, authentic, and good, as opposed to that which is false, deceitful, and bad. And *istina* is sacred truth: in the Russian Bible, it is the divine truth of which the Old Testament prophets spoke and the truth that Christ said will save those who know it and "set [them] free."[53] *Pravda*, by contrast, means moral truth: the truth that stands for justice, righteousness, honesty, and goodness. And it is no less sacred. In the words of the Russian Psalter, "Pravda comes down from the heavens" (*Pravda s nebes priniche*).[54] Thus the worker Zemskov wrote that he was speaking the "truth [*istina*] that only a working man capable of speaking the pure truth [*pravda*] can feel" (Document 6). Before the revolution, argued a group of peasants, the people were beaten and suffered "for every word of truth [*pravdivoe slovo*], and for reading books in which the truth [*pravda*] was written" (Document 40). Now, it was said, the revolution must oppose "foul lies" with "holy truth" (*sviataia istina*) (Document 6), must champion the cause of "truth and equality on earth" (Document 27), and must fight against those who, as one group of peasant-soldiers put it, were "trying to shove a stick into the wheel of our cart, which is traveling along the road of truth [*pravda*]" (Document 68).

For many, to travel along this "path of truth" (*put' pravdy* or *pravdivyi put'*) was the most essential meaning and purpose of the revolution (Documents 71, 74). Sometimes sacred truths were named differently. The worker-poet Pyotr Oreshin alluded to these as sacred words that the common people knew better than others: "Was it not in our own crowded hovels / That the tablets of Christ safe were kept?" (Document 102). Another worker-poet, Ivan Loginov, dreamed of "a new free temple [*khram*]" (Document 103). Or, for a group of Novgorod peasants, the revolution was about "life, salvation, and the kingdom of heaven on earth for the people" (Document 94). At times, especially when poetry was the form of expression, such idealism about the truth of the revolutionary cause drew upon mythic traditions that were not solely Christian. We see, for example, especially in poetry, human flight symbolizing transcendence and freedom: "Off with my caftan . . . Across fields I'm flying / On the wings of time" (Document 52), "I walk through the gates flung wide . . . On the wings of flight eternal" (Document 130). The widespread allusions to blood as cleansing, purifying, and saving, and to the sun as a symbol of purity and salvation, were similarly powerful images that drew widely from Christian and other mythic beliefs and stories: "The blood they sacrificed has bought / This sacred freedom to our nation" (Document 4); "the time will come . . . when a bloody storm will pass over the world" (Document 25); "the Firebird" has "embraced vast Rus in her bloody wing" (Document 52); in the "sunlight of freedom" is "resurrection" (Document 77); "you bear the Sun of the New Life" (Document 131). Notions and images of "saviors" who would lead people to the realm of truth and justice had similarly ambiguous sources. For some, the living men now ruling Russia, or heading the Soviet, were "saviors" (Document 94). But others looked still to the future: "Now another Savior of the world must be born, to save the people from all the calamities happening here on earth and to put an end to these bloody days" (Document 74).

We clearly see a number of salient themes and patterns in the public statements of lower-class Russians in 1917: the high value placed on the idea of freedom (though this was often viewed more as a collective than as an individual good), a strong love of nation (though construed in multiple ways), a constant and typically concrete discourse of social needs and values that often translated liberty into a "democratic" freedom that must serve the interests of the poor, a view of state power as favoring the common people over (and often against) the privileged, a ubiquitous perception of the world as divided between enemies and friends, and a strongly moral vision of politics and social relations that was shaped by notions of dignity and insult, honor and shame, truth and falsehood. Readers will no doubt find other themes and patterns.

We must not overstate the consistency and cohesion of this alleged popular social vision, however. First and most obviously, great differences existed among people. There were concrete political disagreements: Should the war be supported? Are the demands for greater local power by workers in their factories, by soldiers in their regiments, and by peasants in their struggles over land signs of progress for the revolution or harmful acts of disunity and selfish particularism? Should the Soviet maintain its coalition with the Provisional Government or take all power into its own hands and away from the "bourgeoisie"? Very often disputes over policy were translated into larger and even more consequential questions: Who is the enemy? Who shames the people and the revolution? Who are the real champions of freedom and truth? Answers varied and opinions changed.

We must also notice what we do not hear. Not everyone wrote to the government or the Soviet or the press in 1917. Those who did tended to feel a connection with politics. Most supported the revolution in some way and wished to voice enthusiasm or express disappointment. These views do not exhaust what the revolution meant to ordinary Russians, though. We do not hear the voices of people who might have still longed for the tsar, for example, or—probably even more widespread—those of people who were cynical about politics. We do not hear much about women. This is partly because most Russians writing resolutions or letters to people in authority were men—not only because men were more likely to be literate, but also because the public sphere was still seen by most Russians as a masculine domain. However, even when women wrote to the Soviet or to the government or to the public in 1917, they tended either not to speak specifically about women and their needs or to represent women's place in politics in traditional terms. Very often, women presented themselves in conventional images as sorrowing mothers or as weaker citizens needing protection (Documents 13, 14, 46, 126), though sometimes they openly challenged these traditional ideas about women's nature and place. (Document 20). In many ways, gender is implicit in these writings: in images of women as mourning mothers and wives and of men as public actors whose virtues were heroism and courage (*muzhestvo*, in Russian a word linguistically very close to *muzheskii,* which means "masculine"). We do not hear much about personal life, either. The public discourse of the revolution was mainly about public matters. The revolution certainly meant more than this to many people—it affected relationships with family and friends, feelings about oneself as an individual, anxieties about the meaning or sense of life. Talk about insult and morality pointed to the private implications of public relationships and behaviors, but much else remained unspoken. The revolution also meant less to many Russians than one might imagine from reading these documents: a good deal of everyday life continued to be ordinary or momentous quite regardless of the course of the revolution. Politics was not everything, even in 1917. This too has to be seen as part of the meaning of the revolution, and as part of what we do not hear in these texts.

Finally, we must recognize how uncertain many people were about the revolution and how ambivalent and contradictory people's worldviews often were. The frequent descriptions in writings by lower-class Russians of themselves and especially of other workers, soldiers, or peasants as "horribly ignorant," "illiterate," and "unenlightened" were not merely rhetorical flourishes. The frequent requests for newspapers, books, and teachers—above all, for someone to explain the unfamiliar and confusing vocabularies and rhetoric of the day and the Babel of political ideologies—reflected real uncertainties and confusion. "I beg you to send provocateurs [*sic*] here because . . . I don't know what's going on there in Petrograd because the newspapers do not reach here from Petrograd" (Document 44). "All of us positional [frontline] troops ask you as our comrades to explain to us who these Bolsheviks are and what party they belong to because we don't know them or their opinion" (Document 75). That this request came from a group of soldiers who insisted that they were "little by little going over entirely to the side of the Bolsheviks" is rather telling. No less important, as the documents collected here vividly remind us (though scholars of social attitudes sometimes tend to forget), individuals can view their world, and judge it, in contradictory ways. The universal language of human dignity and rights, for example, can coexist and become mixed with deep hatred for people classed as "others" or as enemies. Optimistic visions of justice and freedom do not preclude doubt and despair. It would be a mistake to reconcile such contradictions too neatly. Ambiguity and ambivalence are no less part of the ways people define their identities and values and compose their opinions than are sharp convictions and strong faith. For the ordinary Russian, fragmentation of opinion and uncertainty of knowledge were no less part of the intellectual world of 1917 than were revolutionary certainties.

When the Bolsheviks came to power in Russia in October 1917, they could draw considerable support from popular opinion—from deeply felt notions about class difference, from wide popular disappointment with the failures of the moderate socialists who had compromised with and even joined the "bourgeois" government, from a belief in the need for strong state authority. However, the new Bolshevik rulers also had to contend with popular ideas that were much less suited to their purposes and values—ideas about liberty, morality, and nationhood that often clashed with the Leninist vision and methods, suspicion of all who held power, an impatient and unforgiving insistence that the state serve the immediate and concrete interests of the laboring classes. No less troubling to the Bolsheviks, they had to contend with silence and uncertainty, with a population whose views remained divided, distracted, and unstable.

PART 1

Liberty, Desire, and Frustration:
The First Months of the Revolution

And is it not the Firebird that has now at last
Embraced vast Rus in her bloody wing?

PYOTR ORESHIN, May 1917

To understand what happened in Russia in 1917, and especially what the revolutionary events of that year meant for the people who experienced and took part in them, we must view the revolution as part of a much longer age of change and crisis in Russian life. The texts that follow these introductory pages, after all, speak of the experiences and concerns of more than a single year. Of course, these documents are most obviously commentaries on the events of the day: the fall of the monarchy, the formation of a new government, the continuing hardships of war and economic crisis, and the struggles of various groups and individuals for influence and power. These appeals and other writings are often filled with the worries and idealism of the moment. But they also express experiences, values, and desires formed over the whole span of people's lives. We must therefore begin this introduction to the events that surrounded the making of these texts with a look at the larger picture of Russian life on the eve of war and revolution.

Fin-de-Siècle Russia

Already before the turmoil of 1917, most Russians had experienced dramatic changes in the social landscape in which they lived. At the end of the nineteenth century and the beginning of the twentieth, cities and industry were growing rapidly, creating expanded social opportunities but also new challenges and hardships and increased instability. Peasant villagers, whose lives had long been circumscribed by the local and the traditional, more and more often migrated between agrarian and industrial work environments, and huge numbers of peasants moved out of the village entirely. A middle class of white-collar employees, businessmen, and professionals (doctors, lawyers, teachers, journalists, engineers, and the like) was also growing. Even nobles had to find new ways to subsist in this evolving economy. Viewing these many changes, and trying to define new patterns and order, contemporaries spoke of the formation of new classes—the proletariat, for example, or the bourgeoisie. Such social generalizations, though helpful, minimize the extent to which individuals were brought together, and divided, along multiple and crisscrossing lines of occupation, status, ethnicity, gender, age, and belief. If anything, it was becoming less and less simple to speak of clearly defined social groups or boundaries in Russian society. And not only were groups fractured in various ways, but the boundaries that defined them were increasingly blurred by crossings of migrating peasants, worker intellectuals, gentry professionals, and the like.[1] These were times of vitality and flux more than of orderly change, and the uncertainty, no less than the formation of new groups and identities, shaped the experience of living in late imperial Russia.

One of the most significant developments in Russia in the late 1800s and early 1900s was the expansion of public life. This growth of "society" (*obshchestvo*), of a sphere of civic activities situated in a social space beyond private life and not completely under the control of the state, made an enormous difference in the lives of many Russians; arguably, it also provided a needed foundation for the possibility of democratic civil society in Russia. The forms of civic activity were many and vital. Voluntary associations proliferated. They included interest groups such as literacy and temperance societies, business and professional associations, workers' mutual assistance funds, private schools, and varied cultural circles and associations. After the 1905 revolution, newly legalized trade unions and political parties, which were allowed to field candidates for elections to the new legislative State Duma, joined this widening and increasingly lively arena of civic life. In addition, some important institutions that stood on the uncertain boundaries of state and civil life—universities, public schools, law courts, and the organizations of local rural and urban self-government—also often gave individuals a place and a stake in the emerging civic life. The great expansion of the press helped stimulate and support all this civic vitality. Newspapers and periodicals multiplied and won wide circulation and influence. Journalists helped give voice and shape to public opinion about a range of social issues (though explicit politics were not tolerated by the censors). And literary works, which often explored important questions concerning society and morality, and often appeared first in journals or magazines, reached more readers than ever before.[2]

This growing civil society in Russia advanced along a difficult political road. The Russian government was deeply ambivalent about the emerging public life. On the one hand, the government wished its subjects to participate actively in building a modern economy and society—required, at the very least, for effective national defense. At the same time, many officials (including the tsar) were suspicious of autonomous participation by individuals in civic life. And so the government kept a close watch and reached out as needed to control or suppress activities that seemed too threatening. Censors supervised and disciplined the press. Police or other official representatives of state authority were present at most public meetings. And the security police, the notorious Okhrana, secretly infiltrated legal as well as illegal organizations. When it was judged necessary, newspapers were fined or closed, organizations banned, and activists arrested. In effect, however, this constant surveillance and scattered repression often acted more to irritate and anger the public than to silence dangerous ideas. Russia was changing in ways that reached beyond the control of its traditionalist state.

In the realm of ideas, a great variety of political ideologies competed for public attention and sympathy. Before 1905, political parties were illegal, though many had formed illegal organizations, often depending in large part on the work of political émigrés living abroad in Western Europe. The establishment of limited civil rights and of an elected national parliament (the Duma), as a result of the 1905 revolution, allowed many organizations to come at least partly out into the open, campaigning for seats in the Duma and expressing their views in legal newspapers, journals, and pamphlets (though with due caution, for the censors forbade and punished many forms of criticism), but also in underground publications. The range of ideologies and organizations was impressive and most would play some part in the conflicts of 1917.

On the conservative and nationalist right stood groups contemptuously branded Black Hundreds by their critics. The largest and most

influential of these was the Union of the Russian People, founded in
1905, but there were other, similar organizations, each with its own
particular blend of right-wing ideology. Most were vehemently opposed to liberalism and socialism, discontented with the flux and disorders of modern life, and often violently hostile to Jews and other minorities, as alien to the allegedly true spirit of the Russian nation. They
tended to support the old romantic ideal of the Russian state governed
according to the traditional principles of orthodoxy (theistic authority
rooted in divine power and will), autocracy (the unrestricted power of
the tsar), and nationality (the spiritual bond of unity between the di-
vinely inspired autocrat and his Orthodox Christian people). Support
for their views came mainly from among the landed nobility, the officer corps, the Orthodox Church, and the imperial court, as well as
from among the lower middle classes.[3]

In many ways, the emperor, Nicholas II, notwithstanding stereo-
types about his disengagement and ignorance, was an exemplary conservative. In his view, politics must be rooted in moral virtue and religious faith and these must be defined by tradition. His criteria of
virtue—order, family, and duty—were viewed as both personal ideals
for a moral individual and rules for society and politics. Individuals,
social groups, and the system itself must show self-restraint, devotion
to community and hierarchy, and a spirit of duty to country and tradition. Religious faith helped bind all this together in Nicholas's thinking: as a source of comfort and reassurance in the face of contradictory
conditions, as a source of insight into the divine will, as a source of
state power and authority. Indeed, perhaps more than any other modern monarch, Nicholas II attached himself and the future of his dy-
nasty to the myth of the ruler as saintly and blessed father to his people. This inspiring faith, it can be argued, was blinding. Unable to
believe that his power was not God-given or that the true Russian people were not as devoted to him as he felt he was to them, he was unable
to see coming the storm that swept him and the monarchy away.[4] This
failure, however, did not prevent these romantic conservative ideals
from appealing to many Russians even after the monarchy vanished.

Democracy was without doubt the dominant political idea in Russia
in 1917. And notwithstanding clichés about Russia's political culture,
the country had a long tradition of democratic thought. Since the end
of the eighteenth century, a whole pantheon of Russian intellectuals
had promoted ideals about the dignity and rights of the individual and
the ethical and practical necessity of civil rights and democratic representation.[5] These ideas were at the heart of Russian liberalism, but

liberals were not alone in espousing democracy. Populists, Marxists, and anarchists all claimed this democratic heritage as their own. And feminist arguments about respect for women as human beings and about women's right to participate as equals in economic and political life, which influenced many political movements, drew on the same sources.

The liberals who came to power after the tsar's abdication in 1917 represented a mix of nonparty independents and representatives of three of Russia's main liberal parliamentary parties: the Union of 17 October (Octobrists), the Constitutional Democratic party (Kadets), and the Progressist party (although the party had ceased to exist organizationally by 1917, former members remained active in politics). The Octobrist party represented the conservative wing of organized liberalism. Established by liberals who accepted as sufficient the limited political concessions Nicholas II had offered in his manifesto of 17 October 1905, Octobrists generally cooperated with the tsarist government. On the eve of the war, however, even the Octobrists were increasingly at odds with Nicholas II's policies, and they could often be heard criticizing the government in the Duma, where the Octobrists, owing in large part to the government's manipulation of the franchise, formed the largest single bloc of deputies.[6] To the left of the Octobrists was the liberal party that would play the largest role in 1917: the Constitutional Democratic party, also known by its formal name, the Party of the People's Freedom. The party's leader was a Moscow history professor, Pavel Miliukov. The Kadets viewed the semiconstitutional order created as a result of the 1905 revolution as unfinished and inadequate. Although not opposed in principle to a monarchical system— indeed, their model was the British political order—the Kadets insisted that a government should be responsible to a democratic parliament elected on the basis of universal, direct, equal, and secret suffrage ("four-tail suffrage"). The Kadet party also sought social reforms to improve the lives of ordinary Russians. Their concern reflected more than simple social conscience or political maneuvering. It was essential to their particular political idealism. Unlike most Octobrists, who were solicitous of the needs of landowners, or the Progressists, who openly spoke for the interests of large-scale industry and finance, the Kadets deliberately avoided being seen as representing the interests of any one class. They insisted that they were "above class" and even "above party." This ideal may have been partly self-delusion in a society increasingly fractured along class and party lines. But it also reflected their particular ideas about the state and the nation. Although devoted to the liberal ideal of individual rights, Kadet liberals tended to view nations as forming social communities held together by free association and patriotic solidarity. The national social community was seen to overshadow both individual and class, and Kadets saw the true democratic state as properly acting in this communitarian spirit. These assumptions would have enormous political consequences for the liberal democratic government established in 1917. They gave rise to noble political dreams and practical political courage; but they also bred an intolerance of—even an inability to understand—the class anger and class struggle that continued to grow in 1917, even as liberals (and many moderate socialists) tried to construct a new democratic polity.[7]

Further to the left stood various groups of socialists, a powerful force in both popular organizing and state politics in 1917. Populist socialism, the oldest tendency, represented in the prewar years by the Socialist Revolutionary Party (known as the S.R.'s) and the Trudovik (Laborist) faction in the Duma, viewed the whole laboring narod, the common people, as their constituency and socialism as a society embodying, above all, the ethical values of community and liberty. Marxists, who were increasingly numerous and influential, were organized mainly around the Russian Social Democratic Workers' Party (RSDRP) and believed they possessed a more "scientific" and rationalistic ideology. For them, socialism was the historically certain successor to capitalism—its more rational and progressive replacement—and the industrial proletariat was the class whose interests and struggles would bring this new order into being. This simple divide between populists and Marxists, however, only begins to suggest the complex variations among socialists. Populists differed among themselves over such issues as whether the use of terror was legitimate or useful, what the importance of peasant communalism was, and whether and on what terms to ally with liberals. Marxists differed among themselves—often with considerable rancor—over questions of organization (for example, how centralized and authoritarian the party should be), tactics (such as whether workers should ally with other classes), strategy (whether Russia was ready for socialism), and philosophy (what was the relative importance of ethics and revolutionary faith, on the one hand, and of scientific reason, on the other). Many of the differences among Marxists were embodied in the 1903 split in the Russian Social Democratic Workers' Party between Mensheviks and Bolsheviks. There were also factions within these two groups, and numerous intermediary groupings.[8]

Further complicating these lines of Left and Right, Russian public life, especially in the years after 1905, was influenced by the organization of political parties and associations on the basis of gender and ethnic or national identity. Women were inspired, as so many other Russians were in these years, by the subversive notion that all individuals, as human beings, possessed a natural right to honor and respect. Ideas of women's equality—and an organized women's movement—grew steadily in the nineteenth and early twentieth centuries. This movement too, however, was divided along ideological lines. While liberal reformers directed their activities toward enhancing women's opportunities through education, petitions to the government (especially for voting rights), and philanthropy, radicals linked women's equality to a complete overthrow of the existing political and social order, to which end many women joined underground revolutionary organizations. After 1905, political reform having become an official goal of the government, opportunities for civic organization greatly increased, and the feminist movement thrived in a highly visible way. Liberals and socialists alike began publishing journals for women, and various organizations were formed—most notably, the Union of Equal Rights for Women.[9]

Russia, of course, was an empire, and many of its subjects were not ethnic Russians. Formally, and by tradition, the empire was idealized as a cosmopolitan collection of separate nations and polities (a political *rossiiskaia imperiia* rather than an ethnic *russkaia imperiia*) under a single monarch who recognized and cared for them all. (Thus, the emperor officially bore the titles of rulers of dozens of former principalities and nations: he was not only Emperor and Autocrat of All the Russias, but also Tsar of Georgia, Grand Duke of Finland, Prince of Estonia, Lord and Sovereign of the Iverian, Kartalinian, and Kabardinian lands, Hereditary Lord and Suzerain of the Circassian Princes, and Lord of Turkestan, along with many other claims to represent the empire's nationalities.) In practice, the governing elites throughout the empire were almost always ethnically Russian (or culturally Russified) representatives of the imperial center, and native ethnicities often suffered from prejudice, subordination, and discrimination as "aliens" (*inorodtsy*) within an empire ruled by Russia. In addition, the many ethnic groups whose histories were not linked to a conquered nation-state or principality, notably Jews, but also many Muslims, formerly nomadic peoples, and others, faced even greater contempt and discrimination. This discrimination was made more oppressive by a sustained policy, in the final years of the empire, of forced cultural Russification and decreased tolerance for cultural difference.[10] In response, nationalist movements grew steadily in the prewar decades, especially after 1905. Often beginning with the efforts of intellectuals seeking to reclaim and revive their cultural heritage—especially in the Baltic states, Poland, Ukraine, and the Caucasus, and among Jews—nationalist groups organized and appealed for greater cultural autonomy, especially language rights. For others, including many Jews, painful personal experiences with bigotry and discrimination led to a more generalized commitment to fight inequality and repression. Thus, many Jews and other non-Russians were to be found in Russia's liberal and radical movements. Even cultural nationalism was increasingly politicized in these years, however, as repression helped push many nationalists into active opposition to the tsarist order. And since the liberals of the Kadet and Octobrist parties opposed all forms of nationalism as contrary to their ideal of a unified nation of citizens enjoying equal rights as individuals, it was to the socialist parties that nationalists often turned.[11]

Ideas about society and politics that gave purpose and meaning to people's actions and statements in 1917 were to be found not only in the main political ideologies or movements of the time. Indeed, even these ideologies and parties must be understood in the context of the complex and dynamic cultural life of the time: literature and the arts, social thought, philosophical and ethical ideas, and even popular culture. And like so much else in these years, Russia's cultural life was filled with both vitality and contradiction, with a spirit of enthusiasm, creativity, and idealism, but also of discontent, anxiety, and pessimism. In literature, the visual arts, and music, for example, new works challenged long-standing traditions of realism, classical balance, and moral utility and proposed ways of seeing and feeling that were both inspiring and troubling. The widespread search for beauty and meaning led down diverse aesthetic and philosophical paths—toward, for example, a spirituality that sought beauty as well as truth by turning away from the material and social world (rejecting the intelligentsia's traditions of social progressivism); fascination with exoticism and transgression, even the demonic; and explorations of sensuality, death, and delusion or of melancholy and despair. Much of this work emanates a sense of impending doom or apocalyptic rebirth. The emphasis, however, was very often on the pessimistic. And the modern city was often at the center of this troubled vision of the world: the city's night life, with its cabarets, streetwalkers, crime, and murder, its oppressive industrial rhythms, its cold surfaces and dark shadows. At the same time, many writers and artists expressed a feeling of liberation as they embraced the vitality and uncertainty of modern urban life: creative individuals felt free of the old restraints of "bourgeois" cultural convention and reveled in the possibilities for exploration, individuality, eccentricity, experimentation, and innovation.[12]

Not only artists and writers worried about the meaning of living in the modern world. Large numbers of Russians, including many with only a rudimentary education, were preoccupied with similar questions. The press, including the mass-circulation commercial press, engaged actively, even obsessively, in such discussions. Journalists and others writing for newspapers and journals portrayed the physical and social landscapes of cities as at once desirable sites of opportunity and vitality and disturbing places marked by cold indifference, greed, exploitation, immorality, and suffering. The press was filled with stories about the wide range of troubling (but also alluring) phenomena of modern life in Russia: nightclubs and cabarets, prostitution and suicide, the defiant antimorality of "hooligans," bizarre murders, vitriol-throwing women, clever swindles, car races, fires, accidents, and scandals of all sorts. Questions of morality, values, and cultural meaning preoccupied many of those who wrote for large public audiences. The press regularly featured stories about, for example, the disintegration of civic moral order, ideals of proper social behavior, social injustices, moral values conveyed in art and literature, national character, sex (the widespread public discussion of which raised important questions about gender roles, the individual, modern life, national virtue, and social order), and death (especially about the moral quandaries posed by suicide and murder).[13]

Inseparable from all these social and cultural phenomena and discussions was the far-reaching religious renaissance that took place in these years—mostly outside the structures and control of the Church and sometimes directly opposed to it. Mysticism, occult spirituality, and other forms of religious searching ("God-seeking," it was called) spread widely among educated Russians. Among the lower classes as well, mass movements developed around charismatic nonconformist preachers (who preached sobriety and self-respect and the nurturing of the inner life and who reminded the poor that they would inherit the earth). Baptists and other Protestant denominations were increasingly successful, Tolstoyan communities arose, and a revival and an intensification of popular Christianity were widely apparent (from claims of miraculous healings by icons to visitations by saints or the Virgin

Mary). For many, it should be emphasized, this intensified spirituality was not a comforting new faith but preparation for a coming apocalypse.[14]

All these changes in Russian life, this ferment of ideas and arguments, and the many uncertainties of the time were part of the lives of ordinary Russians and shaped the ways people responded to the events and rhetoric of 1917, as can be seen in the documents presented here. These documents also express more specific, and often quite tangible, features of the life of the lower classes in Russia. Peasants, for example, had good reason to be attracted to ideas of a more just social and political order, and also to approach such ideas with their own particular reasoning. The abolition of serfdom in 1861 left peasants legally free but still economically dependent on landowners, who retained control over much of their former holdings. As a result, rural common people focused all their discontents on a single goal: land. "Land hunger," as it was often called, can be attributed to the material poverty peasants endured—a poverty shaped by enormous population growth (which, paradoxically, was due partly to improvements in economic conditions and medical care), low agricultural productivity, high taxes, and changing needs and wants as the economy modernized. Ideas of justice, however, were shaped by more than just the material facts of poverty. No less important was an elementary theory of property, common to peasants in many countries, that land should belong to those who worked it. To be sure, had economic conditions for the peasants improved, it is possible that the dream of getting all the land, of a "black repartition," might have faded with time. As it was, economic conditions only reinforced this long-standing ethical idea.

Poverty and land hunger only begin to describe the peasant outlook on the eve of war and revolution. Fuller understanding requires us to look more closely and carefully at the impact of tradition and change in village life. Rural festivities, rituals of passage in the lives of individuals, veneration of icons, spiritual practices that the established Church sometimes condemned as pagan magic, and communal enforcement of moral and economic standards remind us how strong the currents of tradition were in peasant life. Tradition provided peasants with a rich store of meaning with which to make sense of the social and political world around them. Popular notions of what was economically just, for example, nurtured strong convictions about labor as the sole source of value, and hence as the sole source of legitimate income or property. Traditions of popular justice—especially communal rituals shaming individuals who violated communal norms (particularly when those individuals had asserted their own needs and desires above the community's)—remind us of the high value peasants placed on community solidarity and on moral order and reciprocity. Peasant religion reveals a folk Christianity that was not merely ritualistic (as many critics and historians long argued) but that was suffused with a deep feeling for the sacred, a certainty that much lay beyond the grasp of human reason, and a strong sense that truth and morality, however rarely seen in the world or practiced by peasants themselves, were an absolute against which all people could (and eventually would) be judged. Traditional peasant life was not idyllic, however. It was poor and often brutal. While possessing strong ethical principles and spiritual feeling, peasants could often be bigoted, cruel, violent, and hypocritical.

At the same time, peasant life and culture was changing constantly. Complaints by educated elites about the "degeneracy" of peasant popular culture (seen in the ways peasants celebrated festivals, for example) were a sign. However these transformations in peasant life were judged (after all, some observers saw modernization where others saw degeneracy), it is clear that peasants were living and thinking in new ways. Change was facilitated by the movement of growing numbers of peasant villagers to and from industrial and urban environments, but also by the migration of city culture into the village by means of material goods, the press, and word of mouth. Complaints that peasants were becoming "slaves to fashion" pointed to the infusion of commercial culture into the countryside. Increasingly, we find villagers dressed in city clothes, buying timepieces, purchasing manufactured objects to decorate their homes, and acquiring newspapers and books. Perhaps even more important, we see in peasants' behavior a growing sense of individuality and a growing desire to satisfy personal needs and exercise their own will in the world. We see this, for example, most vividly in the lives of women, whose constricted and socially subordinate position in patriarchal village life had long been the norm. More and more often, village women were to be heard, in their songs but also less covertly, voicing discomfort and anger over their customary place and asserting their rights to happiness and respect. Wearing city clothes and cosmetics, for example, might signify a heightened sense of self and pleasure, as might efforts to marry men who had been out of the village, or to answer insults with legal suits. For the many women who found work in the cities or in rural industry, perhaps only as temporary migrants, these were sites not only of hardship and danger but also of personal independence, sexual freedom, and new sources of happiness and knowledge.[15]

Urban workers were caught up even more thoroughly in these tides of change. Workers, of course, would pose a particular danger to both the old tsarist regime and the new democratic one in 1917. They had clear material reasons for discontent: overcrowded housing with often deplorable sanitary conditions, long hours at work (on the eve of the war a ten-hour workday six days a week was the average, and many were working eleven to twelve hours a day by 1916), constant risk of injury and death from very poor safety and sanitary conditions, harsh discipline (workers had to fear not only rules and fines, but also the foreman's fists), and inadequate wages, made worse after 1914 by steep wartime increases in the cost of living. At the same time, urban industrial life offered plenty of benefits, though these could be just as dangerous, from the point of view of social and political stability, as the hardships. The proletarian experience tended to encourage workers to expect more from life. Acquiring new skills often gave workers a sense of self-respect and confidence that heightened their expectations and desires. Living in cities, workers encountered material goods such as they had never seen in the village. Most important, they were exposed to the influences of the larger culture, with the particular intensity that came from living in the city. Reading was an essential part of this, as urban workers were likely to be literate or to become so. Not only was *what* they read a source of dangerous ideas: more subtle but no less subversive, the very act of reading and becoming more "cultured" brought a sense of self-esteem that made the ordinary humiliations and hardships of working-class life harder to endure.[16]

Social and political discontent, of course, was not an inevitable and natural response to material conditions. It did not exist apart from acts of thinking about the world and giving it meaning. Workers and peasants had first to see their conditions not as the inescapable lot of the poor but as correctable wrongs. In other words, discontent required an awareness of notions of justice and right and a belief that alternatives existed. Russians could draw on traditional sources of such ideas: religious ethics and old communitarian values, for example. But fresher sources abounded and offered a more up-to-date language with which to talk of change. Journals, newspapers, pamphlets, and books spread ideas among ordinary Russians about universal rights, the natural equality of all human beings, and the mutability of every political order. Notions of justice, entitlement, and progress were becoming dangerously widespread among Russia's poor. Popular discontent, of course, did not express only ideas about justice, democracy, and rights. It also reflected a great deal of anger and resentment. Once aroused to open protest, as in 1905–1906, many lower-class Russians expressed through their behavior not only a desire to be treated as social and political equals—"as human beings," as they liked to say—but also a desire to punish and humiliate, even to dehumanize, those who stood above them and whom they blamed for their sufferings. In this spirit, workers violently forced foremen and employers out into the streets and sometimes beat them, occasionally to death. Peasants broke into the mansions of the gentry, smashed belongings, and set on fire houses, barns, and other property. The lives of the poor had encouraged dreams of revenge and reversal as well as of justice.[17] The fall of the old order and the proclamation of democracy and freedom in 1917, as the documents following reveal, offered the greatest opportunity yet to speak of, and act upon, all these ideals, desires, and feelings. The war, of course, had made these questions all the more pressing.

War and Revolution

Wars have always been moments of truth in Russian history, times when the empire and its politics were shaped (as during the wars of Peter I and Catherine II) and times (especially in defeat) when the weaknesses of the empire and its politics became clear, and reforms were forced onto the state agenda.[18] World War I, of course, was no ordinary war. It was a protracted modern war requiring unprecedented mobilization of society and the economy as well as of military machinery and personnel. Russia had never been through such a trial. Initially, however, the outbreak of war in August 1914 quieted political and social protests and focused hostility on an external enemy. This patriotic unity did not last long, however. As the war dragged on inconclusively, war-weariness took its toll. More important, though, was a deeper fragility, evident from the start. Even though many ordinary Russians joined anti-German demonstrations in the first weeks of the war, hostility toward the Kaiser and a desire to defend their land and their lives did not necessarily translate into enthusiasm for the tsar or the government. Some voiced hostility toward the war from the outset, as was evidenced by scattered antidraft riots. Most people, however, filled with a mixture of skepticism, anxiety about self and family, and what has been described as "sullen resignation," faced the onset of war with a striking silence. The war often fed into suspicions that the rich and powerful were pursuing their own interests, not those of the poor or even of the whole nation. At least, ordinary Russians were painfully aware, war always meant sacrifice and loss.[19] By contrast, Russia's generals at this moment spoke with pleasure about the brave and righteous enthusiasm of the nation's fighting men and of their own good spirits.[20]

However people felt when the war began, before long many began to speak of the war as nothing less than a catastrophe. Casualty rates were the most telling sign of disaster. By the end of 1914, only five months into the war, nearly four hundred thousand Russian men had lost their lives and nearly a million had been wounded. Far sooner than expected, scarcely trained recruits had to be called to active duty, a process repeated throughout the war as the staggering losses continued to mount. The officer class also suffered dramatic turnover, especially among the lower ranks, which quickly filled with soldiers freshly promoted from below. These men, usually of peasant or working-class backgrounds, would play a large role in the politicization of the troops in 1917. The huge losses on the battlefields were not limited to men. The army quickly ran short of rifles and ammunition, not to mention uniforms and food. By mid-1915, men were being sent to the front without arms; they could be equipped, it was hoped, with arms recovered from fallen soldiers on the battlefields. With good cause, soldiers felt that they were treated not as human beings or even as valuable military personnel but as raw material to be squandered by the rich and powerful. To add to the misery, by the spring of 1915, the army was in steady retreat. It was not always orderly. Desertion, chaotic flight, and plunder were not uncommon. By 1916, however, the situation improved in many respects. Russian troops ceased retreating, and some modestly successful offensives were even staged that year, though at great loss of life. Also, the problem of shortages was largely solved by a major effort to increase domestic production. Still, by the end of 1916, morale among soldiers appears to have been even worse than during the great retreat of 1915. The fortunes of war might have improved, but the war itself, which continued to drain away the strength of the country and the lives of so many families and individuals, remained an oppressive fact. The crisis in morale, argued Allan Wildman, a leading historian of the Russian army in war and revolution, "was rooted fundamentally in the feeling of utter despair that the slaughter would ever end and that anything resembling victory could be achieved."[21]

The war was devastating not only to soldiers, of course. Millions of civilians, fleeing the front line, became refugees, crowding cities in the interior, wandering in search of work, often feeling angry and alienated, and often viewed as yet another sign of disorder and crisis in the country.[22] The lives of those who were not forced to flee their homes were deeply affected by the loss of husbands, fathers, and sons to the army. And most important for all, by the end of the first year of war, were the manifold indications that the economy was breaking down under the increased burden of wartime demand. The main problems were food shortages and rising prices, caused by a combination of factors: the draft had resulted in a dearth of labor at the largest estates; supplies were diminishing and prices for basic consumer goods were rising (owing to production shifts, transportation problems, and high demand); smallholding peasants preferred to produce for their own needs rather than for the market (especially since money was losing value and there was little to buy); and the government was printing quantities of new bills to pay for military production (a difficulty made worse by the huge loss of tax revenues that had resulted from the wartime prohibition on the manufacture and sale of alcoholic beverages). Although the causes were complex, the effects were simple and clear, especially for the urban lower and middle classes. Inflation rapidly forced down real incomes, and inadequate supply of goods made it difficult for people to buy even what they could afford. Shortages were a particular problem in the capital. In Petrograd (as St. Petersburg had been patriotically renamed at the start of the war, so that it would sound more Slavic), distance from supplies and poor transportation networks made matters particularly bad. Shops closed early or entirely for lack of bread, sugar, meat, and other provisions. Meanwhile, the lines grew for what remained. It became increasingly difficult both to afford and to obtain food. Not surprisingly, strikes increased steadily beginning in mid-1915. So did crime. Mostly, though, people suffered and endured—scouring the city for food (working-class women in Petrograd reportedly spent about forty hours a week in food lines),[23] begging, turning to prostitution or crime, tearing down wooden fences to stoke the heating stoves, grumbling about the rich, and wondering when and how this would all end.

With good reason, government officials responsible for public order worried about how long people's patience would last. A report in October 1916 by the Petrograd branch of the security police, the Okhrana, warned bluntly of "the possibility in the near future of riots by the lower classes of the empire enraged by the burdens of daily existence."[24] By early 1917, reports from secret police agents—who lived and worked among people of various classes—pointed to the widespread signs of mounting danger: meetings in and around factories, at which speakers complained about high prices, bread shortages, the war, and the corruption and irresponsibility of the government; work stoppages and demands for higher wages and a direct supply of bread; the closure of factories when workers announced that they were simply too hungry to work and needed to search for bread; the dissemination of subversive leaflets and proclamations by an astonishing variety of parties, unions, and committees; street demonstrations, complete with red flags and revolutionary songs and banners; scattered instances of violence against police and Cossacks; assaults on businesses, especially food shops; and the appearance of guns and other weapons in workers' hands. Agents also reported numerous muggings, robberies, suicides, and fires.[25] Agents employed to keep under surveillance "the progressively inclined and oppositional segment of the capital's society" similarly reported, by January 1917, "a wave of animosity in broad circles of the population against those in authority."[26] Among the working-class women who stood out in the cold in the long and often unmoving bread lines in Petrograd, the mood was especially tense. According to a report in February 1917 by an agent of the Petrograd Okhrana, "These mothers, exhausted from standing endlessly at the ends of lines, and having suffered so much in watching their half-starving and sick children, are perhaps much closer to a revolution than Messrs. Miliukov, Rodichev, and Co. [leaders of the Kadet party], and, of course, they are much more dangerous."[27] Socialists did what they could to give political direction to the discontent. Although socialist parties and organizations, which had largely been suppressed under wartime conditions, could offer little direct guidance to this movement, thousands of party members and others who had been influenced by socialist ideas—and perhaps had experience in the revolutionary upheavals of 1905–1907—were active among workers, soldiers, students, and other groups.

Liberals too were contributing to the pressure building toward a political and social explosion. At the very start of the war, many liberals appealed to the autocratic government to establish a "government of national confidence." The government ignored such pleas, not to mention the even more radical demands for a "responsible" government— meaning, in the language of the day, a cabinet approved by the elected Duma. At the same time, in accordance with the liberal commitment to building an organized civil society, they established public voluntary associations to aid the war effort—in this instance, to help promote and coordinate relief and military production. Many of the leaders of these organizations would help lead the first post-Romanov government. As the war effort faltered and discontent deepened, liberal criticisms of the government, in the Duma and throughout the press, grew increasingly impassioned and hostile, adding to the tense and expectant public mood.

Still, liberals hesitated to defy the tsar's authority openly, much less seek power. They were trapped by their own political logic into maintaining a frustrated stasis: though they foresaw a political upheaval if nothing changed, they were deeply committed to principles of legality and thus opposed in principle revolutionary action; they were also justifiably afraid of provoking popular revolution in the streets. Thus, when the Duma reconvened on 14 February 1917, a day marked also by strikes aimed at reminding the Duma of public discontent, the leader of the dominant Progressive bloc of deputies, the Kadet Pavel Miliukov, vehemently opposed those in the Duma who were demanding revolutionary action. He insisted that "the word and the vote" must remain their only weapons. Indeed, a war of words was launched in the Duma, but it seemed only to underscore the real powerlessness of the body, as it devotedly remained within its legal mandates. In this unstable situation, many liberal Duma deputies felt a tragic foreboding: "The deputies wander around like emaciated flies. Nobody believes in anything. Everyone has lost heart. Everyone feels and knows his powerlessness. The situation is hopeless."[28] Only when revolution broke out in the streets of the capital were liberals forced into serious political action.

During January and February 1917 not only did the number of strikes increase dramatically, especially in cities like Petrograd and Moscow, but their character and purpose changed in important ways. The strike movement had broadened. Now, workers from the biggest and most restive factories were joined by workers who had not previously been involved in strikes, including growing numbers of women. Strikes were also becoming less and less effective. Economically desperate, workers made demands—such as wage increases of 50 to 100 percent—that may have seemed reasonable in the face of the terrible inflation but were extreme from the employers' perspective. Not surprisingly, employers, often unable even to keep operating on a regular basis because of fuel shortages, tended to reject such demands and sometimes responded with lockouts instead. Finally, many strikes were openly political: workers walked off the job on 9 January, the anniversary of "Bloody Sunday" 1905, on 12 January to protest the delay in reconvening the State Duma, and on 14 February when the Duma did reopen. In addition, in many "economic" strikes the workers made political demands. Various leftist political parties encouraged these strikes, but they in no way controlled events. Indeed, though the numbers, breadth, anger, and politicization of the strikes all grew steadily in late February, the strikers appeared to have no clear direction or plan.[29] The movement had, however, acquired a powerful symbolic focal point: bread. The ravages of inflation, widespread shortages of fuel, food, and clothing, anger over the war and government policy, and deep distrust of the rich and powerful all seemed to coalesce around a single outrage: the lack of bread.

On 23 February (8 March) 1917, thousands of women textile workers walked out of their factories—partly in commemoration of International Women's Day but mainly to protest severe bread shortages. Already large numbers of men and women were on strike or idled when their factories closed down owing to lack of fuel or when their employers had shut them out in retaliation for strikes. These women stopped at any factories that were still in operation and called on workers to join them. They marched through the streets, repeatedly shouting, "Bread," and "Give us bread." As the crowds swelled, many protesters headed toward the city center, where demonstrations for women's rights, uniting women from various classes, were already under way. Although it was still winter, the weather was relatively favorable to being outside. After some terribly cold months, Petrograd enjoyed a brief thaw in late February. Still, the mood of these crowds of workers was not especially springlike. According to police reports, the demonstrators were in a nasty mood, as their behavior reflected. Workers armed themselves, mainly with knives, metal tools, and pieces of iron, for what they expected would be bloody fights with the police and Cossacks. And as they marched, demonstrators broke store windows, halted trams, and threw rocks and chunks of ice at the police.

During the next two days the strike, abetted by the efforts of hundreds of rank-and-file socialist activists, spread to factories and shops throughout the capital. By the 25th, virtually every industrial enterprise in Petrograd was shut down, as were many commercial and service enterprises. What with the mild weather and the feeble police response, the streets and squares of the capital filled with crowds. The demands—displayed on banners and repeated in the shouts of demonstrators and in speeches at rallies—escalated, with the encouragement of activists, from demands for bread to appeals for ending the war and abolishing the autocracy. Demonstrators marched and protested all the more boldly as it became evident that the police, under orders not to fire on the crowd, hesitated to stop them. Indeed, many Cossacks and soldiers showed sympathy with the crowds. The use of force tended to anger people all the more. Students, white-collar workers, and teachers joined workers in the streets and at public meetings. Although the crowds were generally peaceful, the potential for mass violence was barely contained: some workers carried sticks, bolts, screws, other pieces of metal, and, sometimes, pistols; crowds smashed shop windows, especially those of food and bread stores; looting became more common; and police officers were attacked and beaten—fatally, on a couple of occasions. Socialist activists condemned the violence and vandalism, but the frequency of such outbreaks increased. Meanwhile, in the Duma, liberal and socialist deputies denounced the current government more vehemently and demanded a responsible cabinet of ministers. Even so, the movement lacked any clear direction. People took to the streets to voice their discontent, not to resolve it. These protests were still, as even many socialists at the time recognized, only "disorders," not "revolution."[30] The next step, which would turn this movement into a revolution, was taken by the government.

On the evening of Saturday, 25 February, Nicholas II sent a fateful telegram to the chief of the Petrograd military district, General Sergei Khabalov. Nicholas refused to believe warnings about the seriousness of these events and instead accepted his wife's reassurances that this was mere "hooliganism," attributable in large part to the warm weather.[31] The tsar made his impatience clear: "I command you tomorrow to stop the disorders in the capital, which are unacceptable in the difficult time of war with Germany and Austria."[32] On Sunday, 26 February, when most workers were off work even if they were not on strike, the streets of Petrograd again filled with demonstrators. Police and soldiers, as ordered, fired systematically into the crowds, wounding and killing hundreds. The show of force convinced many socialist leaders that the regime was still sufficiently strong and determined to restore order.[33] This successful use of force also convinced the Council of Ministers (which had doubted that force could succeed and so had begun discussions of political compromise with the Duma) to reinforce the police effort with a legal blow to democracy. They recommended to Nicholas that he prorogue the Duma. He gladly agreed.

Leaders of the strike movement and of the government, however, both underestimated the psychological and moral effect on the soldiers themselves of the order to shoot at demonstrating civilians. Although some refused, the majority obeyed the orders on the 26th. As the soldiers returned to their barracks, however, they began to think and talk—and to decide whether to follow orders or their consciences on the following day. Most important, for their actions would be critical the next day, junior officers, who were generally literate men from working-class or peasant backgrounds, also met to consider what to do. The answer soon emerged. Mutiny, often led by lower-ranked officers, spread through the barracks of one regiment after another. On the morning of the 27th, workers in the streets, many now armed and ready for combat with troops, were met by insurgent soldiers, many with red ribbons tied to their bayonets. With this disintegration of military authority in the capital, effective civil authority collapsed.

Panic spread quickly through the government. By the night of the 27th, the cabinet submitted its resignation to the tsar and proposed a temporary military dictatorship. By contrast, senior military commanders, fearful that repression would further inflame unrest, and possibly persuaded by appeals made to them by representatives of the Duma that only a new government of ministers approved by the representatives of the nation could bring calm to Russia and sustain the war, joined the chorus of voices advising Nicholas to make political concessions to appease the population. Faced with what amounted to a mutiny of his own military command, Nicholas accepted the inevitable and abdicated on 2 March, hoping by this last act of service to his nation, he stated in his manifesto, to end the disorders and bring unity to Russia.[34] The form of Nicholas' abdication was a fitting symbol for the political situation at the moment. Formally, Nicholas passed the reins of supreme power not to the Duma (which he had dissolved) but to his brother, who refused "this heavy burden" at such a "time of unprecedented war and popular unrest."[35] Power, in other words, was less transferred than dropped. The rest of the story of 1917 (and beyond) was partly about who would (or could) pick up power and hold on to it.

In the Tauride Palace, where the Duma had met and toward which many people in the streets turned, looking for direction on the 27th, two political forces stepped forward to fill the rapidly growing vacuum of state power: the liberal members of the Duma and the socialist organizers of the Petrograd Soviet. The Duma liberals were the obvious candidates for power, but they hesitated. The leaders of the moderate liberal Progressive bloc, which predominated in the Duma, found themselves hindered by the tsar's order that had prorogued the

Duma. They were, after all, liberals—not revolutionaries—who believed in a society based on law and proper democratic procedure. How, then, could they justify taking control of the situation? They tried to convince Nicholas II to cancel the decree closing the Duma, but he refused. By contrast, a minority of Duma liberals, though sharing these anxieties about legality, were willing to take a more pragmatic approach, for they were worried about the spreading chaos and felt a sense of moral responsibility to act even beyond the limits of formal legality. So, on the afternoon of 27 February, a third of the Duma's deputies assembled at the Tauride Palace to discuss the question of power. To be sure, still sensitive to questions of legal propriety, they did not claim to be the Duma: they deliberately met in a room other than the Duma's regular hall and called their gathering a private meeting. They also rejected proposals that they declare this rump Duma a new government or even some sort of constituent assembly that would lay the groundwork for new elections and a legitimate government. Rather, they declared themselves a "Provisional Committee of members of the State Duma for the restoration of order in the capital and for the establishment of relations with public organizations and institutions."[36]

Events, however, forced them to go beyond this hesitant first step. Faced with increasing civil disorder and the appearance of another body claiming a large measure of public authority—the Soviet of Workers' Deputies, led by socialists—the Provisional Duma Committee announced, on the morning of 28 February, that it had found itself "compelled to take into its hands the restoration of state and social order."[37] By 2 March, freed by the tsar's abdication to act, and forced to act in order to stop the spread of anarchy, the members of the committee began to call themselves a Provisional Government, to acknowledge that a "political overturn" (*gosudarstvennyi perevorot*) had occurred, and to recognize, according to the minutes of the first formal meeting of the new cabinet, "the necessity of defining precisely the scope of the powers of the Provisional Government." Although the old laws of the Russian state were now judged to be null and void, it was assumed that a new constitutional legal order would have to await the convening of a constituent assembly.[38] In the months that followed, this spirit of political hesitation would persist. It would undermine, with grave historical consequences, the government's ability to control events and specifically to halt the coming to power, on the back of a plebeian rebellion, of Bolshevik-led radicals.

The effective power of the Provisional Duma Committee, and later of the Provisional Government, was also challenged by the authority of an institution that claimed to represent the will of workers and soldiers and could, in fact, mobilize and control these groups during the early months of the revolution—the Petrograd Soviet of Workers' Deputies. Calls to establish a soviet (or council) of elected workers' deputies were heard from the moment the strike movement began on 23 February. The model for such a soviet was the workers' councils that had been established in many Russian cities during the 1905 revolution, including St. Petersburg and Moscow. In February 1917, striking workers elected deputies to represent them, and socialist activists began organizing a citywide council to unite these deputies with representatives of the socialist parties. On 27 February, socialist Duma deputies, mainly Mensheviks (the larger faction of the divided Social Democratic party) and Trudoviks (who were populists), together with other socialist activists (again, mainly Mensheviks), took the lead in organizing a citywide council. They issued a public call for elections in all factories and, recognizing the key role soldiers were playing in events, invited "troops that have gone to the side of the people" to elect a deputy from each company.[39] That evening, the first meeting of the Petrograd Soviet took place in the Tauride Palace, the same building where the new government was taking shape.

The leaders of the Petrograd Soviet also hesitated to act beyond what they considered their legitimate authority. They believed that they represented particular classes of the population, not the whole nation. Besides, they were convinced that Russia was not ready for socialism. It was still too economically, socially, and culturally underdeveloped. What Russia needed, socialists from almost all of the parties represented in the Soviet agreed, was democratic rights. With Western Europe as their model (and, for many, Marx's writings on capitalism, the bourgeoisie, and history as an ideological guide), they assumed that the liberals of the Duma (the "democratic bourgeoisie") were destined and most qualified for this role. Indeed, the leaders of the Soviet, meeting as the Executive Committee on 1 March to discuss the question of state power, decided that their most urgent task was precisely to compel the hesitant "bourgeoisie" to take power and introduce extensive democratic reforms in Russia, especially the replacement of the monarchy with a republic, guaranteed civil rights, a democratic police and army, abolition of religious and ethnic discrimination, and organization of elections to a constituent assembly.[40] They met in the same building as the emerging Provisional Government, not to compete with the Duma committee for state power but to exert the most effective pressure on the new government. They acted, in other words, as a popular democratic lobby.

The difficult relationship between these two centers of power would shape the politics of 1917 to a considerable degree. The structure of the relationship was established at a meeting between the Executive Committee of the Petrograd Soviet and representatives of the Provisional Duma Committee held late at night on 1 March to discuss the question of power. The Duma leaders understood that the Soviet could control the crowd in Petrograd—and, by extension, the Russian lower classes—whereas they could not, so they sought the Soviet's endorsement of their state authority. In turn, the leaders of the Petrograd Soviet, wishing to influence the policies of the new government without taking responsibility for them, came to this meeting prepared to bargain. The representatives of the Duma committee conceded almost immediately to most of the Soviet's terms and further agreed, in governing, to "take into account the opinions of the Soviet of Workers' Deputies," though the committee members were also determined to prevent "interference in the actions of the government," which would create "an unacceptable situation of dual power."[41] In fact, this was precisely what was being created, though this dual power, as it was often called, was the result less of the actions or attitudes of the leaders of these two institutions than of events outside their control. The complex political history of 1917 was shaped above all by the everyday politics playing out in the streets of the cities, in factories and shops, in barracks and in the trenches, and in the villages.

A Festival of Liberty and Fraternity

The first days and weeks in the life of the new "free Russia" were a time of joyous celebration of freedom and unity, of the rebirth as "citizens" of the tsar's subjects. As seen in many of the letters and resolutions written by workers, soldiers, and peasants in the first month of the revolution, huge numbers of people felt intoxicated with joy, with the liberating sense of a dramatic break with past suffering, with an embracive spirit of mutual love and sacred unity. Observers marveled at the "good nature" of the crowds of soldiers and workers in the streets.[42] Symbols and gestures of goodwill and unity were everywhere in evidence. Strangers talked on the streets as if with friends. Café owners and private citizens offered demonstrating workers and soldiers food or a place to rest. Everywhere, people displayed the color red to signal their support for the revolution: red armbands or red rib-

bons in buttonholes, red strips of material on bayonets, buildings and
vehicles decorated with red banners.[43] A reporter for the London
Times observed a tea shop with a handwritten sign ("crafted ungram-
matically and badly spelt") welcoming all fellow citizens to eat and
drink for free "in honour of the great days of freedom." The owner,
dressed in a red shirt, personally distributed rusks, bread, and unlimited tea to his many guests.[44] During street battles on the 25th, a young
girl offered a symbolic gift of red roses to Cossacks preparing to charge
a crowd; they accepted the offering and turned away from the attack.[45] Many treated the revolution as a sacred holiday. In particular,
many evoked Easter—the sacred festival of resurrection and of the
promise of eternal happiness, the holiest and most joyous day in the
Orthodox calendar, symbolically following the privations of Lent.
Those who experienced these days recalled that friends and even
strangers greeted one another as on Easter, kissing one another three
times, and felt the same sense of "exhilaration."[46] Even officers and
soldiers embraced and kissed one another "just like at Easter."[47] People spoke of feeling a sense of "a miracle close by,"[48] of the revolution
as the "resurrection" of the country, opening a "path to the future per-
fection of the spirit."[49]

Throughout Russia, public festivals were staged to symbolize and
reinforce this new sense of national unity and freedom. Festive time,
scholars have observed, always contributes powerfully to dramatizing
memory and trying to fix the meaning of experiences and the ideals of
communities. In revolutionary times, when things are so uncertain and
full of possibility, public rituals of celebration have special importance.[50] March was the festive month of the revolution. Elements of
various existing festive traditions were combined: military parades,
tsarist jubilee celebrations, religious processions, popular carnivals,
and borrowings from the French revolution. In provincial cities,
church bells rang, military orchestras played and marched, and mass
songs were sung (especially the Russian socialist version of the Marseillaise). In villages, peasants dressed in holiday clothes participated
in religious processions of thanksgiving and kissed each other with joy.
Of course, many celebrated by getting drunk. As visual political symbols, though some carried the old national white-blue-red tricolor, red
flags predominated (often improvised by tearing the upper stripes off
the old flag). Imperial double-headed eagles were removed from public places or covered with red cloth.[51]

Often the most emotionally resonant festivals were funerals,[52] and
the most expressive of these were the ceremonial burials of "freedom

fighters." In many cities, elaborate ceremonies were staged to bury the martyrs who had fallen to state violence in the February days. (Document 4 was probably written for such a ceremony.) The biggest of these, widely reported in the press, was the burial of the individuals who had died in the fighting in Petrograd in late February. On 23 March nearly two hundred men and women were interred in a common grave in the Mars Field as victims of the old regime, martyrs, and heroes fallen for "the people's freedom." The burial was declared by the Petrograd Soviet to be a "national funeral." The mood, by all accounts, was joyous and exultant. It was a "national holiday," a "celebration of resurrection," a holiday of freedom and unity. Banners inscribed in numerous languages and decorated perhaps with a symbol of the nation (often a young woman) or an image of a fraternal handshake uniting classes emphasized the spirit of solidarity that was the central theme of the funeral, as did the participation of citizens from all classes and the tolling church bells. In the months following, the burial site became an important symbolic center for the new order—a place for rallies and speeches proclaiming the solidarity of the whole nation behind the revolution, and the virtue and sacredness of its cause.[53]

Certain prominent individuals also contributed to forging the spirit of revolutionary unity and joy that marked these early weeks of the revolution—and often themselves came to symbolize it. Free Russia's first prime minister (retitled "minister-president"), Prince Georgy Lvov, exemplified the idealism of these early days. By background both an aristocrat and an activist in liberal civic organizations, Lvov exemplified the coming together of old and new elites. Most important, like many other liberal leaders of the Provisional Government, he spoke constantly of his commitment to a government that would always put the "common good" of the nation above class interests or particular ideologies.[54] Even more than Lvov, though, it was Aleksandr Kerensky who most represented the fraternal and national ideal of the revolution. A member both of the Executive Committee of the Petrograd Soviet and of the Provisional Government (minister of justice until May, then minister of war and navy until September, when he became commander-in-chief, and, from July through October, also prime minister), Kerensky was idolized by many as a symbol of the revolution—and with good reason. In the February days, no other member of the Duma so boldly went out into the streets of the city to voice support for the demonstrating workers and soldiers. None was so ready as he to defy the tsar's order disbanding the Duma. And

Kerensky was the most convinced and energetic advocate of the political coalition that united the "bourgeois" liberals and the plebeian soviets—the national unity of the "living forces of the nation," in the popular phrase at the time—that characterized Russian politics between February and October. He literally "personified" national unity, and he was lionized in just this way: as "the genius of Russian freedom," "the noble symbol of the noble February Revolution," a leader guided by moral and spiritual principles, a man whose name, "covered in glory," was "a synonym for the beauty, purity, and clarity of our 'smiling' revolution." Kerensky himself cultivated a political style in tune with this role—evident in his efforts to maintain good relations with both liberals and socialists, his emotional speeches, and his "democratic" dress (he wore a black tunic rather than a suit and tie) and manner (he greeted everyone in the same "familiar and friendly way," even shaking hands with the doormen to government buildings).[55] Kerensky's role and image, as the historians Orlando Figes and Boris Kolonitskii have observed, and as some of the documents following reveal, "corresponded to the conciliatory spirit of fraternity and national unity—the spirit of *sobornost'*—that marked out that first euphoric spring."[56]

The Provisional Government began its work by endeavoring to realize these high ideals of freedom, unity, and citizenship. In a matter of weeks, the new government freed thousands of political prisoners and exiles; proclaimed freedom of speech, press, assembly, and association, and the right to strike; abolished flogging, exile to Siberia, and the death penalty; removed legal restrictions of rights based on nationality or religion; granted women the right to vote and run for office; began preparing for elections to a constituent assembly on the basis of universal, secret, direct, and equal suffrage; and started work on land reform.[57] In their own self-image, as well, the liberal leaders of the new government articulated a broad and inclusive notion of the revolution that placed the individual citizen at the heart of the new order. This was an ideal of citizenship that disregarded class interests or particularistic needs in favor of ideals of national unity and concord. In accordance with their long years of struggle against autocracy, the liberals de-emphasized the state as the key force in transforming the country in favor of faith in an active civil society. The public discourse of the government and its leaders was filled with the language of citizenship, nation, morality, justice, law, duty, and rights. Or, in the words of the new head of state, Prince Georgy Lvov, speaking with the press in early March, the revolution reflected the deep commitment of all classes to the "common good of the nation."[58] Indeed, inspired by populist ideals and the spirit of February, he often affirmed publicly his admiration for the people's wisdom and generosity, for the "great heart of the Russian people, filled with the spirit of love for one's neighbor."[59]

Struggles for Everyday Power

As so many of the documents that follow make clear, this celebration of freedom and citizenship masked (and only barely, at that) conflicts over power and meaning that lay just beneath the surface. The signs were visible from the first. The February days were not simply a euphoric celebration of liberty and solidarity. These were also days of popular rebellion and assertion, of anger and hatred, of sometimes violent attempts to put forward the separate power of the poor. Alongside stories of café owners feeding demonstrators and girls giving roses to Cossacks, and of talk about the fraternity of citizens and the spirit of Easter, words and actions of quite another sort were often to be seen. Crowds broke into weapons factories and arsenals to arm themselves. They attacked prisons, freeing arrested revolutionaries and criminals alike, invaded police stations, and often set ablaze these two agencies of state control. Policemen—long-despised "pharaohs" who were now further guilty of violence against demonstrators in February—were beaten and killed. Witnesses recalled with horror the sight of crowds beating fallen policemen with the butts of rifles, kicking them in the head until they died, and stomping on their already lifeless bodies.[60] The display of guns and automobiles—symbols of power—in the hands of commoners was a leitmotiv of this theatricalized rebellion. Trucks and cars were "requisitioned" by soldiers and workers who crowded into them and sped through the streets, waving red flags and often shooting into the air. Everywhere, soldiers, workers, students, and others were walking or driving about armed—draped in cartridge belts and often carrying several weapons, which they would fire into the sky in belligerent exultation. Even "girls," observers noted, were "driving around the city, God knows where, in God knows whose cars."[61] Looting and pillaging were common: wine stores were broken into, store windows were smashed, goods were stolen from various businesses, and the homes of the rich were robbed. Public drunkenness was rampant.[62]

What did this disorder and violence mean? Even many socialists were appalled by it. The Petrograd Soviet condemned it as mere "hooliganism"—the familiar cultural code word for senseless defiance of civilized rules and norms.[63] For the socialist writer Maxim Gorky, this was not a real "revolution" at all, but "chaos," and proof of Russians' "Asiatic savagery" and "political ignorance."[64] Others, though they might share his dismay, recognized a certain necessity in all the disorder and destructiveness. "The excesses, the man-in-the-street's stupidity, vulgarity, and cowardice, the muddles, the motor-cars, the girls," argued Nikolai Sukhanov in his memoir, was "what the revolution could not in any circumstances avoid, without which nothing similar had ever happened anywhere."[65] The meaning often ran deeper, though. The cars and guns and violence were in part symbolic gestures: variously signs of anger and frustration over conditions; of oppression avenged and hierarchies overturned; of liberation from old authority; of a new public power for the poor; and of new ideas of order and justice. Everyday power—immediate and direct power exercised by people in the places where they lived and worked—was particularly crucial. When crowds of workers, soldiers, and other townspeople took control of city streets in massive meetings, demonstrations, and processions or beat up figures of public authority (especially police), they were demonstrating their authority in the public sphere. Most important, they carried these efforts into the everyday settings where hierarchy and authority were most immediate and tangible in their lives: factories, workshops, army units, trenches, and villages. In the weeks and months following the February revolution, efforts by lower-class Russians to assert power in the places where they lived and worked became increasingly common and widespread. These actions were not necessarily attractive or admirable; but they were not without meaning, either.

Following the fall of the autocracy, workers of all sorts acted to dismantle the authoritarian managerial order and to assert their presumed rights to greater control over labor conditions and to more respectful treatment. New demands were made, and strikes declared, to increase wages and benefits, improve working conditions, and end degrading management practices such as informal forms of address, physical compulsion, and other marks of "factory despotism." Very often, especially in the first days after February, workers acted directly (even theatrically) to redress their complaints about managerial power. Workers sometimes simply ignored the orders of supervisors and employers or were rude in their presence. Against the foremen and managers who had most offended, some workers took more decisive action: running them out of the shop, beating them up, or even murdering them. In an act that had strong symbolic as well as practical meaning, workers sometimes seized the most hated foremen and managers, forced them into wheelbarrows, dumped waste on them, shouted abuses at them, and wheeled them into the streets (in Petrograd, if a canal was handy, the ritual expulsion might end with the victim's being dumped into the granite-banked waters). Further, workers in huge numbers joined organizations that could advance their control over management and public life: trade unions, factory committees, local worker militias, and soviets. Most famously, talk of "workers' control" was increasing, though in these months it still meant not complete worker management but worker oversight and supervision of production, work discipline, hiring, and firing. Still, as with all such actions, the goal for workers was greater power over their everyday lives.

Views differed with regard to how threatening these demands were. Many officials in the new government (especially the new economic ministers, Aleksandr Konovalov and Mikhail Tereshchenko), progressive industrialists, liberal party activists, and the moderate socialist leaders of the Petrograd Soviet spoke of Russia as coming to enjoy a Western European model of labor relations in which mobilized and organized labor would ensure the orderly resolution of conflicting class interests. The legalization of strikes, trade unions, and factory committees was a step toward this goal. The government also promoted the establishment of factory-level and citywide conciliation boards (*primiritel'nye kamery*), on which workers and management were represented in equal numbers, to resolve differences without strikes. Not a few industrialists, sharing this hopeful vision of reformed labor relations, conceded to workers' demands for higher wages and even for an eight-hour day (often enough, they had little choice) and recognized factory committees and unions. The Petrograd Society of Industrialists, expressing the still optimistic views of many employers, declared, "We believe that the free citizen-industrialist and the free citizen-worker will find a common language in which to communicate [and] will find normal forms of mutual relations."[66] Soviet and trade union leaders, especially those from the Menshevik party, spoke similarly of creating a "constitutional" order in the factory and other workplaces and appealed to workers to advance their class interests in an "orderly" and civically responsible manner, avoiding "spontaneity" and "force."[67]

The spirit of conciliation was fragile, however, as many of the documents presented here vividly attest. Workers and employers tended to approach conciliation differently. Whereas employers believed that their concessions to workers would lay the foundation for worker moderation in the future, workers were inclined to see their successes as the basis for further struggles and as reason to expect further victories. Persistent inflation and faltering production (especially as fuel and supply shortages forced temporary closings) made the fulfillment of further demands less and less likely after early spring. In general, employers grew frustrated with workers' continued demands. Echoed and emboldened by much of the press, which increasingly criticized workers for irresponsible and selfish demands (a subject of much comment and contention, as we shall see in the documents), employers complained publicly about workers' "outrageous" requests and disorderly work habits, irresponsible during a time of national and economic crisis. Workers answered these accusations by declaring them to be the foul "lies" of the bourgeoisie, who had no real sympathy for workers' needs and sufferings.[68] Discontent with the policies of conciliation grew rapidly on both sides during March and early April. New waves of strikes in April and May, and the lockouts with which many employers responded, made it increasingly fanciful to continue to speak of a "common language" uniting workers and employers as "citizens." These widening social rifts were made still greater by workers' disappointment with state policies on such key political issues as the continuation of the war.[69]

Soldiers too were engaged in struggles over everyday questions of power and authority. Most rank-and-file soldiers were peasants. And in 1917, huge numbers were very recent recruits called up to fill the places of the thousands who had fallen in battle. As soldiers, though, they were no longer simply peasants. A young man who became a soldier or a sailor escaped the conventional strictures of the village community, gained some basic skills, and might feel a special sense of pride as a man defending his country. At the same time, he faced the particular and often brutal hardships of military life (even when not at the front): meager and low-quality food, harsh discipline and punishment, concerns about his family having to survive without his labor, and the looming threat of crippling injuries or death as long as the war persisted. Perhaps the most oppressive feature—for it was this that would draw the most protest in the early months of 1917—was the constant reminders of the degrading social inequalities and subordination that all lower-class Russians suffered: the need to address officers as "Your Honor," "Your Excellency," even "Most High Radiance," depending on rank; the condescending way soldiers were addressed in the second person singular (*ty*); and rules that forbade soldiers from walking in parks, riding inside trams, visiting theaters, or smoking in public.[70]

In the wake of the great mutiny that helped bring down the old government, a struggle for everyday power erupted. In trenches, urban garrisons, and barracks throughout the country, soldiers challenged established authority. Huge numbers simply deserted, to help their families survive, to participate in the rumored division of estate lands among peasants, or to escape the hardships and dangers of war.[71] Hordes of unattached soldiers crowded railway stations and trains, fled to cities away from the front, or returned to their villages. Newspapers were filled with stories portraying deserters not only as a symbol of civic breakdown but as a tangible cause of disruption: bullying civilians, stealing food, violently resisting arrest, stirring up peasants. "The streets are full of soldiers," an official in the Urals town of Perm complained in the middle of March. "They harass respectable ladies, ride around with prostitutes, and behave in public like hooligans."[72] Much worse (from this same point of view) were the actions of the soldiers who remained at their posts. Officers who refused to recognize the new government or the authority of elected soldiers' committees were arrested and new officers elected in their place. No less important was soldiers' rejection of the everyday signs of traditional authority. Many soldiers refused to salute their officers or address them in the required forms, were openly rude to them (knowing that they no longer had the power to retaliate), dressed with defiant sloppiness (hats askew, belts abandoned, tunics unbuttoned, cigarettes dangling from their lips), demanded that officers' epaulettes (or at least monarchical insignia) be removed, and flouted the few remaining military regulations, by smoking on duty, for example, or neglecting to stand at attention while on guard duty.[73]

The Petrograd Soviet's Order No. 1, issued on the first day of March, and the Declaration of the Rights of Soldiers, drawn up by the soldiers' section of the Petrograd Soviet and published in *Izvestiia* on 15 March 1917, stimulated this social upheaval in the military. There were plenty of other stimuli, to be sure: news of the fall of the autocracy and of social rebellion throughout the country; the passing of new laws ensuring civil liberties for all; the abolition on 12 March of the death penalty, including at the front, and the replacement of military field courts and the direct disciplinary authority of officers with new courts at which soldiers and officers had equal representation. Moreover, on 11 May the government approved a revised version of the Declaration of the Rights of Soldiers; and the army officially approved the establishment, from company to division levels, of soldier-officer committees (most of whose representatives were to be drawn from the lower ranks). Still, Order No. 1 was the first text, and remained the most important one, to represent and encourage the soldiers' revolution. Although the order was formally only a ruling of the Petrograd Soviet and was intended only for troops stationed in Petrograd, it was quickly disseminated throughout the country (in leftist newspapers and pamphlets, by telegraph, and by Petrograd troops rotated to the front) and treated as a fully authoritative order for all.

Order No. 1 amounted to a charter of soldiers' power and rights. The authors were a group of soldier-deputies to the Petrograd Soviet assisted by Nikolai Sokolov, a radical lawyer and member of the Executive Committee of the Petrograd Soviet, who put their ideas into words and helped give them clearer shape. The order, approved by the Soviet on 1 March, endorsed the revolution in the army that was already under way, while also trying to channel the soldiers' rebellion into a more orderly course. Its mandate was simple and powerful. Military units were to establish soldiers' committees of elected representatives from the lower ranks and send deputies to the Petrograd Soviet, which was to be the final authority controlling the actions of the military. Weapons, vehicles, and other matériel were to be taken from the officers' control and put under the authority of soldiers' committees. Although soldiers were required to maintain discipline in the performance of their military duties, they were to function as free citizens in their private, civic, and political life. Thus, it was no longer necessary, when not on duty, to salute officers, and the old forms for addressing them, such as "Your Excellency" or "Your Honor," were replaced with such new civil forms of address such as "Mr. General" or "Mr. Colonel." Finally, officers were expressly forbidden to be "rude" to soldiers of any rank or to address them with the familiar *ty*.[74] In large measure, the Provisional Government endorsed Order No. 1. Although the government opposed exclusive soldiers' committees (not to mention the expulsion or election of officers, which even Order No. 1 did not advocate), on 7 March the new war minister, Aleksandr Guchkov, issued an order abolishing all military regulations that infringed the rights and dignity of soldiers as citizens, such as required use of honorific titles in addressing officers, officers' use of *ty* in addressing soldiers, and limits on the off-duty activities of soldiers.[75] On 11 May, Kerensky, the newly appointed war minister, approved a modified version of the Soviet's Declaration of the Rights of Soldiers, which similarly insisted on full civil rights for soldiers.

Efforts by soldiers to gain greater freedom and authority consistently overflowed the boundaries set up by both the government and the Soviet. Arrests of senior officers continued (for refusal to accept the new democratic relationship between soldiers and men or on suspicion of "betrayal" of the revolution), soldiers often refused routine orders, antiwar texts were widely read, and unauthorized leaves (as well as plain desertion) were epidemic. "Fraternization" with German soldiers at the front—especially during the Easter ceasefire in early April, when the German command endorsed friendly contacts across the front line as an intelligence operation—was one of the most telling signs not only of Russian frustration with the war but also of soldiers' determination to act as they wished. Repeatedly, soldiers left the trenches to meet German and Austrian troops, with whom they conversed in improvised sign language, exchanged cigarettes, alcohol, and other gifts, visited in the others' trenches, played music, and drank.[76] The Russian men spoke of German soldiers as "innocent brothers."[77] Still, violent lynching of officers was extremely rare after early March—though this was not necessarily a sign of moderation. As the leading historian of the military during the revolution commented, "the helplessness of the officers was demonstrated daily, so that there was little reason to resort to excesses."[78] By May, as preparations for an offensive got under way, unrest again began to increase rapidly. At the same time, in a reminder of how contradictory popular involvement in the revolution remained, many soldiers continued to insist on their devotion to their military duties and to uphold proper discipline and loyalty. The language and arguments of soldiers heard in the documents that follow give expression to both this rising discontent and the persistent uncertainties and disagreements.

In the countryside, too, struggles for everyday, local power were as important in the early months as questions of national or international politics. While the village commune and its periodic assemblies remained at the center of everyday authority in the village, the traditional dominance of the village patriarchs was challenged and undermined by younger men, by women, by literate peasants, and by peasants who had worked in the city or served in the army (including deserters and men on leave). Ad hoc peasant "committees" and "assemblies," usually formed at the levels of volost (township or parish) and district and often influenced by Socialist Revolutionaries, were new and increasingly authoritative forms of peasant power. Whatever forms of organization they favored, though, peasants began to meet and debate regularly, passing resolutions and appealing to those in authority to pay more attention to peasants' needs. As the texts following make clear, the most important issue in their eyes was power over the land. "Land is freedom," peasants repeatedly declared. For most of them, the meaning of the revolution, the meaning of the declaration of freedom, was that the long desired "black repartition"—the redistribution of all agricultural land into the hands of those who worked it directly—was finally about to take place. Until the summer, most peasants voiced confidence that the Provisional Government (or a constituent assembly, which the government would quickly convene) would pass a land-reform law transferring estate lands to individual proprietors; however, especially in heavily populated areas where large tracts of land were not in peasant hands and population pressures intensified the peasants' need for additional land (above all, in the central agricultural and middle Volga regions), peasants were increasingly willing to satisfy their needs and their sense of justice directly through their own actions. During March, direct seizure of land was relatively rare—partly because most peasants still believed it was better (and safer) to wait for the government to authorize land redistribution, but also because sowing of the fall crops would not begin until April at the earliest. Instead, peasants marched on local manor houses or government offices to demand lower rent for land use and the obligatory sale of seed grain, livestock, and agricultural tools at "fair" prices. Timber for firewood and repairs they cut in the forests illegally.

Most often, especially in the first weeks after February, peasants took actions that demonstrated their view of the revolution as a social upheaval in which the balance of local power would be reversed and the oppressions and insults of the past avenged. More than half of all recorded peasant actions in March involved the destruction of estate property or, less commonly, personal violence.[79] Frequently (though far less often than in September and October), large crowds of peasants, armed with pitchforks, axes, shovels, scythes, and sometimes guns, marched against local manor houses. Very often, these crowds simply intimidated landlords or their agents into meeting a list of demands, but violence often accompanied these demands. Agricultural machinery (which reduced the need for peasant labor) was smashed, stored grain was stolen, and grand estate houses were burned to the ground.

By April and May, as the planting and mowing season started and as the government made it clear that no land redistributions would be authorized until a constituent assembly could be convened in the fall, peasants began to seize private lands. Almost always, in these seizures, peasants acted as an organized community, planning and carrying out these efforts through village communes or through newly established peasant committees. These seizures, though they tended to be less destructive than actions taken earlier in the spring, were also a more deliberate effort to increase peasant power. Peasants formally declared woods, meadows, and other common lands to be under their control, and they redistributed private or state lands and began cultivating them, often ripping up the boundary markers separating peasant fields from estate lands. Peasants also used less direct methods to gain control of estate lands: they would force a drastic reduction in rent on estate lands they were leasing (or simply refuse to pay the rent at all); or they might disrupt work on lands farmed with hired workers (by running laborers off the estates, damaging machinery, and confiscating tools, seed, and livestock) to pressure owners to rent out the fields to local peasants.[80]

These constant, disruptive, and emancipating seizures of everyday, local power involved not only peasants, soldiers, and workers but also women, students, youth, and national, ethnic, and religious minorities (categories, of course, that overlapped). Women, whose activism often cut across class and political lines, demanded full voting rights (attained in midsummer) and continued to protest against prostitution and sexual harassment. Many women made their presence felt by participating actively in labor organizations and protests, in village assemblies and peasant rebellions, in civic organizations, in political movements ranging in ideology from anarchist to conservative, and even in the army, where they served not only as nurses but also as volunteer soldiers in special women's battalions (most famously, the Women's Battalion of Death, formed in May). Of course, not all women acted publicly out of feminist convictions. Many continued to hold quite patriarchal views of gender roles, even as they took an active part in civic struggles to advance their own interests and ideas.[81] National, ethnic, and religious minorities also participated in larger class and political movements, while many actively nurtured the new cultural and communal autonomy granted by the government and, in some cases, campaigned for national independence.[82]

Again and again, we see groups and individuals challenging established hierarchies of power and honor. In assessing these struggles, we might recall the already quoted comment in mid-March of a young and liberal-minded army officer: "In their view, what has taken place is not a political but a social revolution, in which, according to them, we are the losers and they the winners. . . . Previously we ruled; now they themselves want to rule. In them speak the unavenged insults of centuries past. A common language between us cannot be found."[83] At the same time, as many of the following documents make clear, this sharp division between us and them, however painful it may have been to individuals who wished for a broader spirit of revolutionary community, was still far from fixed, and the boundary was nowhere near as clear-cut as it would become after the political disappointments and crises of late spring and early summer.

Political Crises: April to June

Popular attitudes toward the government that replaced the autocracy, as so many of the letters and resolutions here show clearly, were divided and fractured. Enthusiasm for the new freedoms and for the country's new leaders combined with suspicion of individuals and groups labeled variously as the rich, the upper classes, and the bourgeoisie.[84] Distrust and discontent intensified as frustrations grew over the continuing economic disorder (especially inflation and shortages), the failure of the government to control "enemies" of the revolution, and the hardships caused by the seemingly endless and clearly unsuccessful war. The intensification of local struggles for everyday power reflected the distrust and disappointment with the politics of the state, with the perceived failure of the government to intervene effectively to protect and advance the interests of the people. Letters and resolutions, sent by the thousands to those in authority, also warned of growing discontent. A study of resolutions passed by Moscow workers in 1917, for example, found, for the months from March through June, growing disenchantment with the war (visible, for example, in resistance to appeals from the government and the Soviet, starting 6 April, to buy Liberty Bonds to support the war effort), growing support for expanded soviet power, criticism of socialist participation in the government, and increasing numbers of appeals for government or Soviet intervention in the collapsing economy.[85] This pattern of deepening discontent was repeated throughout the country and can be seen as well in the texts presented below, most of them letters or resolutions sent to the press or directly to the government or the Soviet. On occasion, the government was directly and dramatically confronted with popular frustrations in the form of mass demonstrations, especially on the streets of the capital.

The first of these upheavals occurred in late April 1917, in connection with the government's war policy. On 27 March, under considerable pressure from the Petrograd Soviet to renounce annexationist war aims, the Provisional Government issued a Declaration on War Aims that insisted on the purely defensive goals of the war and declared that "the aim of free Russia is not domination over other nations, or seizure of their national possessions, or forcible occupation of foreign territories."[86] A political compromise rather than the preferred policy of the government, the declaration was further weakened as a policy statement by being addressed only to Russian citizens and not to other nations. Pressure on the government continued, to issue a formal diplomatic note to the allies stating that the terms of the declaration were official government policy. When a note on war aims was finally produced, however, it gave rise to the government's first major political crisis.

On 20 April, the newspapers published the text of a diplomatic note concerning the Provisional Government's war policy that Foreign Minister Pavel Miliukov had sent to the allies two days before.[87] The note assured the allies that the declaration to Russian citizens on 27 March did not mean that Russia was no longer committed to fighting until "decisive victory" or that Russia would not "fully observe" the treaty obligations worked out by the tsarist government with the allies. The note also spoke of readiness to impose "guarantees and sanctions" after the war. These statements were widely, and probably justifiably, understood as implying, among other things, that Russia fully supported the war aims of Britain and France and intended to continue to demand control of Constantinople and the Dardanelle straits for itself, according to the agreement with the allies in 1915; after all, Miliukov had already spoken out publicly in support of this policy. The contents of the note clearly contradicted the foreign policy on which the Petrograd Soviet had been insisting: in the short term, acceptance of the war only in the interests of defending the revolution against German militarism; in the long term, "peace without annexations or indemnities" and the principle of "self-determination of peoples." The note also seemed to contradict the government's own Declaration on War Aims of 27 March. Many thought that the note proved the declaration to have been an act of political deceit and hypocrisy.

Left-wing newspapers said as much in blistering articles attacking the note on 20–21 April. By 21 April, large crowds of protesters (including soldiers with arms) took to the streets of Petrograd and Moscow to denounce "Miliukov-Dardanelsky," the "capitalist ministers," and the "imperialist war." Numerous counterdemonstrations voiced support for the government and the war, and a few violent clashes took place between the two groups. Also occasionally heard were calls for soviet power as the only way to ensure a speedy and democratic end to the war. The Soviet leaders, however, were not prepared to take control. Most of the Menshevik and Socialist Revolutionary leaders of the Soviet continued to believe that the time had not yet arrived for a worker-based socialist government in Russia. So they did what they could to calm tensions and heal the bloody rift. They called on demonstrators to return to their homes—and the crowds obeyed, revealing the Soviet's considerable authority. And when, on the 22nd, the government, showing good political sense, assured citizens that Miliukov's note had been misunderstood and that "guarantees and sanctions" meant only limitations on arms and international tribunals, the Soviet leaders hastened to accept the explanation.[88]

Most important, and most dangerous for the future popularity of the Soviet's moderate leadership, the Executive Committee of the Petrograd Soviet agreed to participate in a coalition government. The "April Days" had brought on the "April Crisis," a highly public debate over the proper composition of the government in view of the clear unpopularity of a purely "bourgeois" cabinet. After much argument, dire warnings and threats, and two major resignations (of the war minister, Aleksandr Guchkov, and the foreign minister, Pavel Miliukov), on 2 May the socialist leaders of the Soviet agreed in principle to enter into coalition with the liberals, in order to bolster the government's flagging public support and to influence policy more directly by accepting ministerial positions, although a minority of them. After heated negotiations between the Soviet Executive Committee and the Provisional Government, on 5 May six socialists entered the cabinet.[89] The coalition policy was sanctioned during the next couple of months not only by the Petrograd Soviet but by national gatherings of deputies from soviets throughout Russia: the First All-Russian Congress of Peasants' Soviets, which convened on 4 May, and the First All-Russian Congress of Soviets of Workers' and Soldiers' Deputies, which began meeting on 3 June. From that moment on, popular discontent had to come to terms with a government in which the soviets had a voice but in which they were also complicit. As many of the documents collected here indicate, many Russians began to view this arrangement as a capitulation to the enemies of the people.

The one major national party that refused to join the "bourgeois" government, the Bolsheviks, began to benefit from its stance of radical opposition, though its radicalism also earned it a good deal of popular anger and contempt. The Bolshevik policy was in large part the work of Vladimir Lenin, the party's charismatic leader. On 3 April 1917, Lenin returned to Russia to enjoy the amnesty the revolution granted him and to convince his party comrades that the moderate course they had taken in relation to the Provisional Government was mistaken. He arrived, controversially for some, after being allowed by the German government to pass though Germany in a sealed train (sealed because the German government was happy to have him subvert Russian politics but feared the effects of Bolshevism on their own). On the day following his return, he issued a call to his party to turn the bourgeois revolution into a socialist revolution. These "April Theses," as they would be titled a few days later when published in the party newspaper, *Pravda*, shocked even many Bolsheviks with their dramatic call for revolution against the "bourgeois" Provisional Government, political power to the soviets, an end to the war, nationalization of land and distribution of it to peasants, and control of industry by workers' councils. Many listeners thought that Lenin, having been away for so long, had simply fallen out of touch with political realities. But he did not relent in the following days and weeks. Many were soon won over to his point of view—and not only those in his own party.

Within the Bolshevik party, Lenin found growing rank-and-file support for a more critical stance vis-à-vis the Provisional Government. Intransigence also helped the party grow rapidly in these months. Already in April, the Bolshevik party in Petrograd numbered sixteen thousand members, compared with only two thousand in February. By late June, the Petrograd party had thirty-two thousand members. It experienced similar growth in other large cities and among soldiers. Clearly, many of these new members were frustrated and impatient. Resolutions at party conferences in April showed strong support for preparing the next stage of the revolution, though without insisting on immediate action.[90]

Even more important than the growing membership or the shift in opinions within the party was evidence that rapidly increasing numbers of lower-class Russians found the Bolshevik arguments appealing, especially the demand to replace the "bourgeois" Provisional Government with some sort of "democratic" (that is, lower-class and leftist) soviet power and to end the war. We see this support in the election of Bolsheviks to various civic bodies. Many factory committees returned Bolshevik majorities in elections of officers, and Bolsheviks had a majority at the conference of Petrograd factory committee representatives at the end of May. In municipal Duma elections held throughout Russia during June, while Socialist Revolutionaries and Mensheviks (usually running as a bloc) consistently won a majority (itself an impressive sign of the democratic victory of socialist ideas in Russia), Bolsheviks were a growing force, especially among working-class voters. Increasingly, in resolutions and other appeals, individuals and groups voiced sympathy for the Bolshevik position (though many others voiced increasing concern and contempt). Finally, the Bolshevik press was gaining in popularity, especially the main Bolshevik paper, *Pravda,* and the soldiers' papers *Soldatskaia Pravda* (Soldiers' Pravda) and *Okopnaia Pravda* (Trench Pravda).[91]

This growing radical sentiment will be evident in many of the documents in this collection (though contrary sentiments also find expression). The radicalization of lower-class Russians became most starkly and dramatically evident in the crisis surrounding the June demonstration in Petrograd. On 3 June, the First All-Russian Congress of Soviets of Workers' and Soldiers' Deputies opened in Petrograd, with more than a thousand delegates in attendance. Most were supporters of the S.R.-Menshevik majority in the existing Petrograd Soviet Executive Committee. The primary questions discussed at the congress concerned the war and the relationship to the government. The majority backed the current Soviet policy of support for the government and for the war. The congress also established a new national executive body, the All-Russian Central Executive Committee of Soviets (VTsIK). Inside the congress, the Bolshevik minority made it quite clear that it opposed the conciliationist policies of the majority and any continuation of the "imperialist" war. For now, it seemed to many, the Bolsheviks were "preaching in the wilderness."[92] Outside the congress too, however, there were troubling signs of discontent.

On 8 June, twenty-eight Petrograd factories shut down in protest against the government's effort to expel the Petrograd Federation of Anarchist-Communists from their headquarters, a secluded villa on the edge of the working-class Vyborg district of the capital that had belonged to the former tsarist minister General P. P. Durnovo. Rumor had it that the villa, which the federation had seized soon after February, had become a sinister site of orgies, witches' Sabbaths, and violent plots, and that huge stashes of guns and bombs were stored there (none of the reports proved true). Not only did workers from the district strike, but crowds and armed workers' detachments gathered to defend the villa, appealing to the Soviet (which was quite unsympathetic) to support them. In part, this action was a reminder that many local workers' groups, in addition to the anarchists, used the villa. No less, it reflected a growing social and political polarization that made even anarchists seem to be more on the side of "the democracy" than bourgeois liberals and conciliationist socialists.[93]

A still more serious sign of disenchantment with the policies of the majority in the Soviet was the demonstration of 18 June. At the very beginning of June, as the meeting of the congress of soviets approached, the Bolshevik leaders began planning an armed mass demonstration of workers and soldiers in Petrograd as a show of strength (or even, according to some accounts, as an incitement to insurrection against the government).[94] On 9 June, the day after the Vyborg strike in defense of the Durnovo villa, proclamations pasted up in working-class districts, signed by the Bolshevik Central Committee as well as the Bolshevik-led Central Bureau of Factory Committees and the Central Bureau of Trade Unions, called for a peaceful demonstration on the following day against "the ten capitalist ministers," against the "revelry and bacchanalia" of rising counterrevolution, against growing restrictions on freedom, and for "bread, peace, and freedom," and "all power" to the soviets.[95] The leaders of the Soviet, angry at the challenge the demonstration represented to their authority and policy, and alarmed by rumors that the real purpose of the demonstration was to start an armed uprising, bluntly warned soldiers and workers that this appeal for soviet power was against the will of the Soviet itself and against a government the Soviet had resolved to support. Such a demand threatened to lead to "civil strife in the ranks of the revolutionary democracy," which would play into the hands of "counterrevolutionaries." In a resolution accusing the Bolsheviks of acting as "provocateurs," the All-Russian Congress, the Executive Committee of the Petrograd Soviet, the Executive Committee of the All-Russian Soviet of Peasants' Deputies (established at the recent congress of peasant soviets), and the Central Committees of the Menshevik and Socialist Revolutionary parties put Soviet authority on the line and forbade the announced demonstration and all other street demonstrations for the next three days. The Bolshevik leadership felt it had no choice but to call the demonstration off.[96] The Soviet leadership, determined to ensure that no demonstration was held, dispatched to factories and barracks throughout the city delegates to the congress charged with persuading workers and soldiers of the dangers of such a demonstration. The delegates' reception was often far from friendly. Still, everyone agreed to stay home. At the same time, the delegates reported back to the Soviet leaders on the mounting discontent with the results of the revolution and with the "conciliationist policy toward the bourgeoisie."[97]

Hoping to reverse this dissatisfaction and bolster "the unity of the revolutionary forces"—a phrase meant to embody the Soviet's policy of coalition as well as the authority of the Soviet against threats from the Left—the Soviet leadership decided to hold its own peaceful demonstration in Petrograd on Sunday, 18 June, and to encourage parallel demonstrations throughout the country. To underscore the message of unity, the demonstration in Petrograd was to consist of a march to Mars Field, the burial ground of the martyrs of February and the chief symbol of the generous and confident spirit of unity and enthusiasm that had marked the early days of the revolution. Still nervous, the Soviet and other organizations barraged the city's population with warnings against carrying arms at the march or engaging in any disorders, and with constant reminders that "unity" was to be the leitmotiv of the demonstration. What occurred, in the words of Nikolai Sukhanov, a Soviet leader, "was a stinging flick of the whip in the face of the Soviet majority and the bourgeoisie."[98] Many supporters of the Soviet line did not even show up. And though marchers, grouped by factory, regiment, and organization, carried a scattering of official slogans—"Unity of Revolutionary Forces," "All Rally Around the Soviet of Workers' and Soldiers' Deputies," "Down with Counterrevolution," "Down with Civil War," "Support the Soviet and the Provisional Government," "Trust in Kerensky," "Armistice"—most of the banners bore the slogans planned for display at the banned Bolshevik demonstration of a week before: "All Power to the Soviets," "Down with the Ten Capitalist Ministers," "Constituent Assembly," "They've Deceived Us with Promises—Prepare to Fight," "Workers to the Factories, Bourgeoisie to the Trenches," "Peace to the Hovels, War Against the Palaces."[99]

On the same day, 18 June, the long-planned offensive in the war began. The Soviet endorsed the offensive as essential to bringing the war to an end. Kerensky, as war minister, went to the front personally and proclaimed the offensive to be a heroic fight for "rights, honor, and freedom" and for "an enduring and honorable peace." He assured the army that "all Russia gives you its blessing." Prime Minister Lvov similarly insisted that the "whole people of Russia" are united behind the revolutionary army of Russia as it "defends the revolution" and prepares "to die for the eternal ideals of freedom."[100] Many Russians, indeed, were enthusiastic about the offensive and hoped it would restore the unity of the nation and bring peace to Russia and a chance to build a stable and free country. Others were already beyond such faith. They were, in the words of some of the documents collected here, "perishing" under the continued oppressions of the "bourgeois and the despots," sick of "sacrificing our sons to the capitalists' inflamed greed," "exhausted, mutilated, and sick," and tired of waiting for "land and liberty."[101]

The deepening popular alienation from the government and even from the Soviet in these months suggested to some observers a complex and troubling crisis in Russian life. The writer Maxim Gorky, for example, like many on the Left, viewed the rising popular fury as a troubling sign not of an impending advance toward greater freedom and democracy but as the next step toward an abyss of cynicism and destruction. How else, he asked, are we to understand the swelling language of hatred, the pointless vandalism, the beatings and cruelty, the barbaric destruction of books and art when peasants stormed the homes of the gentry, and the antisemitic bigotry of many lower-class Russians (directed variously against Bolsheviks, the Soviet, and the liberal bourgeoisie).[102] Educated Russians tended to view the popular upheavals in a similar light. Russia is "turning into a Texas," a liberal newspaper commentator wrote in late May, into a land of lawless disorder, lynchings, excess, and the brutish struggle to survive.[103] Ordinary Russians sometimes shared these anxieties, as can be seen in the documents following, while others continued to look to the revolution, and even to a new upheaval, with hope that it might bring peace and democratic order to Russia and to the world, a "new and free happy life." The situation, and the ways people understood and felt about the revolution, remained deeply divided, unstable, and uncertain.

· 1 ·

"Long Live Free Russia," by Mikhail Serafimovich,
a private in the reserve cavalry, March 1917.

I most humbly ask the gentlemen editors if you might not find a way to put the verse copied out below in your newspaper.

> "Long live free Russia."
> The joyous cry floods my soul—
> "Long live our freedom,"
> The red flag stills my heart.
> A leaden weight has fallen,
> The world dreams a shining dream . . .
> I'm young again, my body drunk,
> My soul replete with feelings.

With feelings as vast and endless
As drops in the cup of the sea.

Priv.[ate] in the G.[uards] Res.[erve] Cavalry Regiment
Mikhail Serafimovich

· 2 ·

"The Russian National Hymn," by the factory worker
"Muzhik [Peasant] Mikula," Novgorod Province, March 1917.

———————

The Russian National Hymn
(to the tune of "How glorious . . .")[1]
Blessed is the Father of all—
The God of Gods inscrutable!
Who creates from nothing, from mortal life,
Joyous souls immutable.

Blessed too are all the nations
And every living creature,
Wondrous nature's emanations,
And matter inanimate of feature.

Blessed too are work and learning,
Dreams, ideas, experience,
Minds inquiring and endless searching,
And the anguished heart's disturbance.

Blessed is every work and offering,
that teaches and perfects the mind:
'Tis this that brings both joy and suffering,
Yet henceforth this shall be our guide.

Blessed is our Holy Rus—
Our family of nations, tribes,
Our homeland with its bounds unloosed,
Its freedom and its law prescribed.

Blessed is the new republic
Of our cherished nation's power,
With a leader now elected
By this huge dear land of ours.

Blessed is our sacred promise:
Behind our president to stand
Behind our country, firm and tireless,
Be there peace or war at hand.

Blessed is our Russian language
That brings together all our brethren,
A union free of town and village
Under our own elected sovereigns!

Muzhik Mikula
March 1917

1. *"Kol' slaven nash Gospod' v Sione"* (How glorious is our Lord in Zion)—well-known Russian spiritual, nonchurch hymn, written toward the end of the eighteenth century. The melody was based on folk and religious tunes. In the nineteenth century, the hymn was performed at many official religious ceremonies. In 1917, during the rule of the Provisional Government, there were unsuccessful attempts to use the melody as a national anthem.

· 3 ·

"On the Old Tsarist Regime," by Fyodor Korsun, a private
in the infantry reserves, Orenburg Province, March 1917.

On the Old Tsarist Regime

For Russia, for freedom,
For the people, Hurrah!
No longer shall our blood be drained by tsar above.
Freedom is ours now, we must give it our love!
The whole royal house into treason did turn,
Freedom is ours now, at the harness they'll learn . . .
Our tsar, the traitor, drank the blood from our veins,
And kept Russian freedom locked up in chains . . .
The court of the tsar with whoring was loose,
The Russian tsaritsa made the tsar all confused . . .
The Russian tsaritsa our freedom would seize . . .
To the Germans accursed our freedom would cede . . .
For Russian freedom and this, the tsar's treason,
Russia's crown from the tsar was taken with reason . . .
That traitor, our tsar, evil-doer and more
Did not have the sense to drive out all the whores . . .
In the court of the tsar, the beloved of all,
Was Grishka Rasputin,[1] a filthy soul . . .

Grishka Rasputin disturbed the tsar's house,
While feasting her eyes on him was the tsar's spouse . . .
To Russia they would prove their power and mettle,
And to the Germans surrender Petrograd the capital . . .
At last to this matter we are putting an end,
The tsar and Rasputin took counsel as friends . . .
There was treason afoot throughout the tsar's court,
while blood spilled in streams, for Russia's tsar we had fought . . .
The tsar like a father his nation should keep,
but his nation he treated instead like sheep . . .
We have no tsar, brothers, and do not forget,
There is no one now to drink what blood we have left . . .
Our blood ever growing, we will stand proud and tall,
Breathing free in this new life, giving our all . . .
No more will our flesh be torn or blood drained from our veins,
Destroy now we must the old power, the old reign . . .
The sun now in Russia burns so brightly, it shines,
And Russia blooms vivid, a flower so fine . . .
Rejoicing, the sun sits in our sky in the clouds,
at our feet the old government lies covered in shrouds . . .
the power of old goes to rack and to ruin,
while Russia sings loudly its dear freedom tune . . .
The power of yore, so proud and so old,
collapsed in a moment and died, stone cold . . .
The world raised its prayers for the tsar, but now,
not even a single person would bow . . .

For the trap opened, gaping, all of a sudden,
and into it the tsar's power has tumbled . . .
Citizens free, for our rights new today,
Let us shout out the people's thunderous
                                        Hurray . . .

Composed by Fyodor Afanasievich Korsun, private, 241st Infantry Reserve Regiment (Orenburg Province, Orsk Uezd [County], village of Sev-
astopol)
My address: 241st I[nfantry] R[eserve] Regiment, 1st Company, 4th Pla-
toon
        Fyodor Afanasievich Korsun

Mr. Editor of *Russkoe slovo* [Russian word].[2] I have the honor to ask you
most humbly to find a place for this little piece in *Russkoe slovo*.
    And so with respect,
        Free citizen
        Fyodor Af. Korsun
Please heed my plea.

1. Grigory Yefimovich Rasputin (1864–1916) was the famous peasant "seer" and "healer" who gained considerable influence in the court of Nicholas II. Stories of his debauchery tarnished the reputation of the imperial family. He was assassinated in December 1916.

2. *Russkoe slovo* (Russian word), with a circulation of over one million in 1917, was the most important daily newspaper in Moscow. Broadly liberal in its political orientation, *Russkoe slovo* supported the Provisional Government. See the glossary for descriptions of the main Russian newspapers and periodicals mentioned in the documents.

· 4 ·

"To the Fallen Freedom Fighters," by metalworker Demian Semyonov, Viazma railroad depot, Smolensk Province, 17 March 1917.

———————

To the Fallen Freedom Fighters
Memory eternal to all who have fought.
For freedom through great tribulation!
The blood they sacrificed has bought
This sacred freedom for our nation.
   Much they suffered, their needs subdued,
   Awaiting the dawn with freedom's hope . . .
   For naught their pleas and howls flew
   To the ear of the tyrant, to the tsar's own throne.
Despise he did our patient people,
Though drowned they be in blood and tears!
In royal grandeur, basely—feeble,
He tried to drown in wine his fears.
   The people's terrible forces ignited,
   Recalling the tears long since shed . . .
   "Peace and freedom!" they recited
   Commingled with their cries of "Bread!"
Our pleas for bread they would not abide,
and instead of bread sent bayonets, lead!
In sacrifice too many comrades died[1] . . .
But they tore the crown from the despot's head.
   In our hour of trial, you did not despair,
   You sallied forth with naked chest . . .
   May the earth be a bed as soft as air!
   And know—your sacrifice is bless'd!
You unlocked the prisons, the shackles' teeth
To the ground you threw the tyrant's yoke,
Immortal glory is your wreath
Through you the dawn of freedom broke!

Metalworker, Viazma depot
Demian Semyonov
Viazma, Smol.[ensk] Prov.[ince]
Kaluzhskaia St., Sedov Lane
Balakin h.[ouse], Grigoriev apt.
Please put the attached poem in the newspaper.

D. Semyonov
At your service

1. The Russian phrase used here, "zhertvoiu pali" (fell victim), echoes the famous song "You fell victim in the fateful battle."

· 5 ·

"Dawn Has Broken," by the sailor Stepan Stepanov,
Baltic Fleet, 28 March 1917.

———————

Dawn has broken. Arise, tribe oppressed,
Arise, oh nation, from your chains and knout
From seed sown under the yoke detested
A cornucopia of fruit did sprout.

Unbend your shoulders powerful
Should any disturb the blood-soaked path,
Henchmen of a tsar so wrongful,
Never can they take your gains, your freedom flag!

Who would trespass on your temple holy,
Or dare defile that sacred site,
No, they cannot: you are a hero, a titan mighty,
All men fall silent in your sight.

S. Stepanov
28 March 1917

Esteemed Editor,
I am completely unfamiliar with the rules of versification and far from literate. The accursed despot has not let me study since my childhood days. My out-of-the-way school with its primer and book of hours did not bring any enlightenment to the area of my mind.

But now is a great and terrible time and all of us must work tirelessly, never letting up. I want very much to be useful and to help the great cause, the people's cause, in some way.

Here. 9th Baltic Fleet Crew
9th Barracks, 5th Company sailor
Stepan Nikolaevich Stepanov

Workers

· 6 ·

Letter to Minister of Justice Aleksandr Kerensky, with a cover letter
to Chairman of the Petrograd Soviet Nikolai Chkheidze,[1] from worker
and deserter A. Zemskov, Kuban region, 26 March 1917.

———————

To Comrade N. S. Chkheidze

I hope that you will graciously forgive me for the audacity that I, a worker
you do not know, have allowed myself to address my request, which may
seem strange, to you. I have been so bold as to ask you to give my letter,
which is attached to this, to A. F. Kerensky. I have not addressed it to him
directly because I well know that A. F. Kerensky is inundated with correspondence, both ministerial and personal. Therefore, I think my letter either would never reach him at all or would take a very long time to reach
him, so I decided to send the letter through you, as someone close to him,
and his associate in current political affairs.

Worker A. Zemskov

Kind sir, Mr. Minister,

Allow me, a poor worker living in Russia's hinterlands, to express myself, if only in a letter, on the subject of past and present events in the current historical moment. In addressing you, an individual who professes
proletarian worldviews and is a defender of the interests of the working
classes, I must nonetheless ask you to forgive me, an insignificant worker,
for being so bold as to address to you, a great political figure whose name
is covered in glory, a letter in which I set forth only my own personal opinions and worldviews and, regrettably, for taking up a minute of your very
valuable time, the minute you take to read my letter. I beg you to read my
letter closely, to the end, since in it I wanted to say something that I consider very important: I wanted to express the truth [*istina*] that only a
working man capable of speaking the *pure* truth [*pravda*] can feel.[2] I who
am writing these lines am a natural-born worker, but at the present time I
am a farmhand. I turn to you as a member of the Provisional Government

in the hope that my voice will be heard among those to whom the revolutionary elements of the people have entrusted the *authority* of our renewed state and the administration that is setting up a new democratic state order on the wreckage of the old. I, who live far from Russia's major centers, where different forms of political movement arise and develop with amazing speed, see how violently the political surface of the Russian national sea is bubbling and heaving, and I hear the distinct voices of individuals glorifying freedom and calling on us to safeguard this precious and long-awaited guest. Amid the general uproar, which has even flown as far as my wild steppes, I can distinctly make out the solid voices of the bourgeoisie, the inspiring and stern voices of the scholars, the shrill ones of the university and grammar school students, and the weak ones of the workers and soldiers, and all these voices are spinning out a very, very old song that mankind has already heard a great many times: in ancient Greece from the lips of the Athenian orators, in Great Rome from the lips of the plebeian leaders, here in Russia in glorious Novgorod,[3] in aesthetic France, England, Italy, Austria, and Germany, and in all the states of Europe, Asia, and America. And here first of all I have to say that this song is too old and the politically conscious worker figured out a long time ago that it is the hymn of a foul lie and not the song of holy truth. Here, in Russia, this hymn is now sung very harmoniously, in unison with the *new* government, the proclaimer of the *new* lie, which seems new only to our blind Russian people. You, who are administering the destruction of the old temple of the lie and trying to create a new temple of the new lie, have heard from the Tauride Palace[4] the opinions of all the political parties and organizations; but wouldn't you like to listen to the opinion of a man without party or power? I, a poor worker wracked by hard work and slavery, want to sing to you, the new tyrants, one of the new songs that only a fully conscious laborer could sing. If I had an opportunity to be in Petrograd, I would sing this song from the tribune of the Tauride Palace, but not having that opportunity, I ask that you listen to me through this piece of paper.

Ever since the last Russian autocrat fell from his high throne, you have been hearing on all sides laudatory hymns to the new state order and freedom. The new order is drawn in golden colors. Freedom has its praises sung to the ringing of bells—these are the sounds of the revolutionary days we have known. I, who expose this noise for what it is, am an enemy of state order no matter what it is, but I would sing the praises of freedom more loudly and triumphantly than you would, you slaves of the sinful earth, if freedom were ever to appear to us from somewhere. The whole question, though, is whether it's freedom's praises you are singing. Aren't you singing the praises of new chains that are only going by the name of freedom? Indeed, the facts of the political reality we now know speak so clearly that there is not even any need to refer to history or the opinions of the great many bourgeois scholars who have been reckless enough to hint at a certain portion of the truth, to say without error that freedom and state order are incompatible. Up until the present moment in Russian history, arguments in political debates had to be based on historical facts from the political history of Western Europe. Now that the political ideas of the Russian Revolution have almost been carried out, though, there is no more need to venture abroad for facts: they are right in front of the Russian man. That the tsar is gone the Russian worker has heard—and believes deeply and naively that the hour of his liberation has come, and the honorable Miliukov[5] and the ignoble press declared back on 2 March that "the chains have been lifted from the people." In fact, though, we never had freedom for a single second, even at the very height of the revolution. Rodzianko[6] was so thoroughly frightened by freedom that he called the situation that had come about (on 27 and 28 Feb.) in Petrograd, which was heading toward the realization of this momentary freedom, anarchy, and before the old autocratic yoke could be lifted, a horse collar was made up in rough-and-ready fashion at the Tauride Palace and put on the people's neck to songs and hymns, while the cry went out all around the world: "Freedom!!" In actual fact, however, it's a horse collar. . . . This is how badly the people's vision has been spoiled, that they can't tell the difference between those two things, the collar and freedom! . . . But I am amazed at how boldly and brazenly the people in whose interests the new political order is being built can lie, calling the new state regime freedom. The lie is so blatant that it is utterly superfluous to set forth individual facts to repudiate this lie.

You (I am addressing the Provisional Government) have the audacity to say that freedom has come. But isn't your current power over the people a power that the bourgeoisie delivered to you, based on coercion? Actually, I hardly think you would object if I were to say that every state authority (even in democratic states) is founded on coercing its own subjects. That political authority in democratic states is founded on coercion as well is acknowledged by all the intellectual defenders of these new state forms because the entire activity of the state is expressed in facts of coercion, so at this point it is too late to say no. You have to say yes. Even you, gentlemen, the new rulers of Russia, cannot say you have other means of administering the state apart from coercion. If you admit that authority cannot exist without coercion, then I will ask you a question: What is the opposite of freedom? You will probably say, "Coercion." It follows, then, that where there is freedom, there cannot be coercion, and where there is coercion, there cannot be freedom. Now let us apply this formula to our fatherland. Everyone already knows full well that freedom exists here. However, there exists as well a very popular political authority, i.e., by universal admission, an organ of coercion. This means that according to your false teaching, both coercion and freedom reside here side by side. If this is so, then we can say that even fire can learn to live with water.

The slogan of our era is "Freedom!" "Down with coercion!" Nonetheless, all the leaders of our revolutionary movement who have proclaimed these slogans are professing and energetically supporting harsh military discipline among the troops—that crudest form of coercion. Rodzianko and Miliukov presented this same freedom to the soldiers at the entrance to the Tauride Palace at the very height of the battle for freedom, proposing for the soldiers who had risen up for their freedom the same discipline imposed upon them as far back as the great-grandfathers of Nicholas II, probably. They shout at the top of their lungs that "the chains have been broken and freedom has come!" Devil take it, though, what kind of freedom is this when millions of voiceless slaves are still being led like sheep to the cannons and machine guns and the officer is still treating the slave as if he were a mere thing, when still only crude coercion restrains the multimillionfold army of gray slaves, when the new government (exactly like the old) has the authority to send the entire male population of the country into this bloody abyss (war)? You say that *political* freedom has come. Is that truly so? In fact, we are seeing just the opposite. Any state crime, for example, is punished just as strictly as it was before. Won't you deal just as harshly with those who in the name of their convictions have decided they do not want to take up arms, or that they do not want to take the bloody business any further and have thrown down their rifles? Wouldn't you apply crude coercion (as indeed you already have) to anyone who decides to protest the war in word and deed? Wouldn't you put in prison anyone who took it into his head to agitate against the new political order for the purpose of further political or social progress or for the purpose of returning to the past? So you see, I would like to know just what your political freedom comes down to. I'll tell you: to the protection of the new ~~democratic~~ [crossed out in original] state order that is now being constructed, to permission to praise the new projected form of state governance openly. Consequently, freedom has been granted only to defend and support the existing state order—i.e., rather, the order slated for existence. The people have already had that freedom. After all, Nicholas II never prohibited defending monarchism—i.e., the order that existed at the time.

In professing a lie to the whole world, you, gentlemen, the new rulers, think that the working masses are so intoxicated by your lie that everyone is accepting it as truth without exception. No, gentlemen, in this you are mistaken. Any politically conscious worker who became developed not through any political party, where the bourgeois-socialist intelligentsia shackles his mind, sees perfectly well that this is a lie. Now all the upper

classes want a republic. A handful of naive workers guided by the bourgeois intelligentsia naively assume, like children, that workers will lay the
path to socialism through a democratic republic, but the clever bourgeoisie—in erecting on the ruins of the autocratic regime a new state order
that is called democratic—has been carried away by satisfaction and joy,
seeing what glorious nets it has woven for the working class out of the
democratic republic. So you see, gentlemen bourgeois servants, no matter
how you sing the praises of the order you are creating, which you are calling democratic for the sound of it, the politically conscious worker will
boldly tell you that all these republics and constitutions are new chains
created to fit the modern economic order and modern culture, chains
placed on me, the laborer, with much triumph and rejoicing. This is so
clear that only the worker who has been hypnotized by the bourgeois intelligentsia can fail to see it. . . . Who was the soul of our last revolution?
Miliukov, Rodzianko, Maklakov,[7] the officers, the generals—in short, the
representatives of all the upper classes and, for the most part, representatives of the bourgeoisie. We also see that the bourgeoisie is creating the republic; consequently, if, according to the assumption of the socialists, the
path to socialism runs through the republic, then by creating a republic for
us, the bourgeoisie is leading us toward socialism. That is the absurdity
you have arrived at, my socialist friends! You have probably forgotten the
great words of your great prophet Marx, who said that "the emancipation
of the workers is the task of the workers themselves." The bourgeoisie is
striving for democratic forms of governance because in them it sees the
most convenient method of oppression and exploitation. Isn't this really
why Messrs. Miliukov, Rodzianko, and Maklakov want to establish a
new form of governance—not for themselves but for me, the tormented
laborer on whose back they are riding? This applies to the entire intelligentsia (especially the socialist intelligentsia), which is constantly asserting that in organizing political storms (revolutions) it is guided by a single
goal—the desire for freedom, happiness, and every good for the people,
that it places the good of the working people highest of all, that it cares
about it whole-heartedly and is looking out for it, that it is permeated with
the desire to serve it (i.e., its liberation). How stupid to believe these
words. Do the people really want you to look after them, take care of
them, etc.? No, the people want you to climb off their back. If you want
good, happiness, and all the rest for the people, then climb down off their
mighty back, which you've been riding on and squeezing all the juice
from. Don't live by its labor, don't stuff yourselves on what belongs to others. If you want happiness and freedom for the working people, then climb
down off their back and stand next to me and do my peasant work; take
up the plow with me. Only then will I believe that you might not wish me
ill. . . . After all, you're oppressing the people, and they have long known

that you are riding on their back: the noble and the merchant and the scholar and the poet and the journalist and the lawyer and the priest. You're all nothing but greedy predators making off with the products of our labor. That is what the people are suffering from, and this is where the root of social evil lies. All the people need is for you parasites not to be riding on their back, and once that happens, freed from your yoke, they will govern themselves, and worrying about them will be none of your business. Though probably they will have no call to create a state. We can draw vivid examples and incontrovertible proofs from history and current reality to demonstrate that *any state* is an organ of oppression of the working classes, an organization created to protect bourgeois property, as Bebel[8] said. In particular, his last designation of a state as an organization for protecting bourgeois property is clearly seen during changes in state forms. Here in Russia, under the autocratic order, everyone rebelled against the police, and the old regime was usually called a police regime. But now, under the new order, isn't the people's militia nothing but that same police under a new name? Also organized now are those units of the ~~police~~ militia [crossed out in the original] that are replacing the criminal investigation department—the old spies—an object of popular hatred. Consequently, in the name of protecting bourgeois property, the new government has been forced to resort to the old system of investigation. No sooner did the overthrown police leave their posts than the "people's" militias were set the same goals: protecting property. But what kind of property was this new police called upon to protect? Certainly not the property of the proletariat: the proletariat as it is has been robbed by legal robbers, robbed within the framework of the law, and so has nothing to protect. Consequently, the new state too is directing all its care toward protecting the property of the upper classes, which was stolen from the working class, and to taking every measure to support in this regard the law regulating theft. So no matter how you try to draw us workers into political activity, the politically conscious worker clearly understands that the state is the weapon of his oppression and that this bourgeois organ cannot be used for the purpose of his liberation. Now I have said what I wanted to say, but I would like these words to be heard by those I'm addressing most of all—the members of the Provisional Gov. and their colleagues. I ask you not to christen me with the name of anarchist. I am not an anarchist. I am a proletarian free of prejudice. I ask you to excuse me for my rudeness and form of exposition, for I have been writing not in a study with unlimited free time but in the field on a cart, when I could take myself away from my fieldwork.

The details of my person are these: I am a former Moscow worker of peasant origin from Vladimir Province, Suzdal Uezd, surname Zemskov. As a deserter I've been hiding in the Kuban steppes for more than two years. My address: Armavir, Kuban Obl.[ast], Armavir municipal office,

Refugee Aid Bureau, Aleksandr Antoniuk, for K. Pikovets (I have been residing under the name of refugee K. Pikovets).

With deep apologies,

Worker A. Zemskov
26 March 1917

1. Biographical information on these and other influential individuals can be found in the glossary.

2. Although these two Russian words for truth are sometimes used synonymously, *istina* is properly defined as the opposite of "lies," as all that is real, authentic, and true. *Pravda* entails more applied meanings: justice, rights, righteousness, honesty, and goodness (see the discussion in the introduction).

3. Novgorod had long been a symbol in the Russian historical imagination of preautocratic Russian democracy. Ruled from the twelfth to the fifteenth centuries by its *veche*, a popular assembly uniting the municipal population and free rural dwellers, Novgorod was brought under the autocratic centralizing control of the ascendant Moscow state in the mid-1400s.

4. The Tauride Palace was built under Catherine the Great for one of her favorites. The State Duma met there 1906–1917. In March, both the Petrograd Soviet and the Provisional Government met in the opposite wings of the palace.

5. Pavel Nikolaevich Miliukov (1859–1943) was one of the organizers of the left-liberal Constitutional Democratic (Kadet) party. He was named minister of foreign affairs in the first cabinet of the Provisional Government.

6. Mikhail Vladimirovich Rodzianko (1859–1924) was one of the leaders of the moderate liberal Octobrist party and a leader of the Provisional Committee of the State Duma during the February revolution.

7. Vasily Alekseevich Maklakov (1869–1957) was a political activist and lawyer and one of the founders of the Kadet party in 1905.

8. August Bebel (1840–1913) was a Marxist political activist of working-class origin. One of the founders and leaders of the German social-democratic movement and of the Second International, he wrote many popular books on Marxism.

· 7 ·

Appeal to soldiers from the workers of the A. M. Ouf machine, metal,
and engineering factories, Petrograd, 28–29 March 1917.

The Ouf Factory

On 28 and 29 March, at meetings of workers from the A. M. Ouf factories, the issue was raised about the unrelenting accusations made by factory owners and some of the press against the workers, and also about the agitation being conducted among the soldiers in order to set them against the workers. To put an end to the reprimands that allege the workers are regularly late for work, it has been resolved that the entrance be locked at exactly eight o'clock in the morning, and that late workers, if there are any, not be allowed in to work. At the suggestion of one of the workers, it was resolved to publish the following appeal to soldiers:

> At a time when the entire people, and the working class even more so, were in despair, left without a crust of bread, and our comrade soldiers were without their ration, the old authorities of our autocratic government greedily hoarded their savings, which they had stolen from the Russian people, leading a carefree life and paying no attention to the situation our state was in. The working people and the soldiers went out into the streets demanding bread, and there they were fired upon by supporters of the old government. Now that the struggle is coming to an end, at a time when we, the workers and soldiers, should be walking hand in hand, there is powerful agitation under way and a hostile attitude toward us workers. We, the workers of the Ouf factory, in a gathering of eight hundred people, loudly protest the disgraceful and insolent agitation aimed at us, the workers, by dark and ignorant persons. We declare that we and the soldiers have common interests; there are no enemies among us, for we are all the working class. This lie is coming not from our camp, for it is bubbling up in an underhanded way, from underground, fearful of just retribution.
>
> Comrade soldiers! The slander that is coming out of our enemies' camp must be stopped immediately. We must declare that workers and soldiers are one and that we will not allow our enemies to sow enmity between us. We workers declare that we will not allow our enemies this lie, since we are working, and we are not making excessive demands, for we have always lived on just our own earnings. We and our comrade soldiers have together also freed ourselves. We declare that our comrade soldiers and we workers shall henceforth fight for our interests—the interests of the working people. And to our enemies, who are attempting to divide us, we loudly declare, "No! Stand back! For you are our enslavers, for you are living off our labor, you are breathing through us, and it's you who depend on us, not we on you."

During the meeting of 29 March, representatives of the Volynsky, Litovsky, and the 6th field-engineer regiments appeared and were greeted ecstatically by the workers. In a series of speeches, the workers asked them to tell all the soldiers that not only are the workers not allowing defense work to be disrupted, but that until the peoples of Europe respond to the call for peace, out of necessity, as long as the bloody slaughter continues, the workers will labor with heightened energy to supply the army with all it needs to defend the homeland and our hard-won freedom from outside threat. The workers pointed out to the representatives of the troops that the work stoppages were due to a lack of materials and fuel. In particular, one of the Ouf factories operated only ten days in February, and now the workers of an entire department (340 men) have been dismissed, even though they had not presented any economic demands whatsoever and had not even managed to introduce the eight-hour workday.

In their speeches in response, the soldiers' representatives assured the workers that the army does not believe the foul slander of the bourgeois press and that the soldiers know the secret purpose of this slander—to make the workers and soldiers quarrel, and that the soldiers have taken up the slogan "Ever with the People." In conclusion, the soldiers' representatives promised to tell their comrades about the workers' fraternal readiness to give their all for their work, for the needs of the army, and expressed their assurance that if the workers and soldiers unite, no threat to Russian freedom can frighten them.

· 8 ·

Resolution of workers of the Putilov metal and machine factory,[1]
Petrograd, 31 March 1917.

Considering the fact that the rumors being spread by the bourgeois press to the effect that workers are striking and leaving the army without shells are a foul lie and are being spread to weaken the revolution and sow strife between the working class and the army, the workers of the Putilov factory resolve:

1. To address a request through their representatives to the Soviet of Workers' and Soldiers' Deputies demanding that the Provisional Government make statements in the press saying that these kinds of rumors are a foul lie and take measures to put a stop to these rumors.

2. Because the bourgeois newspapers *Russkaia volia* [Russian will], *Novoe vremia* [New time], *Vechernee vremia* [Evening time], *Birzhevye vedomosti* [Stock exchange gazette], *Rech'* [Speech], *Malen'kaia gazeta* [Little newspaper], and *Gazeta-kopeika* [Kopek gazette][2] are a mighty weapon in the hands of the bourgeoisie, to boycott these bourgeois newspapers, while trying in every possible way to support and disseminate our workers' press.

3. To have our comrade workers from all the other plants, factories, and workshops of Petrograd join us in our resolution and support our boycott.

4. To print the names of the newspapers being boycotted, as well as the resolution, in *Izvestiia Soveta rabochikh i soldatskikh deputatov* [News of the Soviet of Workers' and Soldiers' Deputies], *Pravda, Rabochaia gazeta* [Workers' newspaper], *Zemlia i volia* [Land and liberty], and *Delo naroda* [Cause of the people].[3]

This resolution will be passed later at a meeting of the military organization of the PK RSDRP [Petrograd Committee of the Russian Social Democratic Workers' Party] (thirty unit representatives).

  1. The Putilov works was one of the largest and most technically advanced metal and machine factories in Russia. It employed about thirty thousand workers in 1917 in a wide variety of shops engaged in metal forging, steel making, and machine construction.
  2. See the glossary for details on these newspapers, which represented a variety of political points of view.
  3. Socialist newspapers affiliated with major leftist political parties or with the Soviet (see the glossary).

· 9 ·

Resolution of workers of the Petrograd Pipe Factory,[1] printed
in the Soviet newspaper *Izvestiia* (Petrograd), 4 April 1917.

We, the workers of shop no. 3 at the Petrograd Pipe Factory, having assembled in a meeting of 2,600, are deeply indignant at the persecution on the part of the bourgeois press and various dark and ignorant persons who, while trying to sow hostility between workers and soldiers, say that the workers are not working but only demanding an increase in their wages and an eight-hour workday. This, comrade soldiers, is not true. We appreciate the gravity of the present moment and, aware that our brothers and fathers are sitting there in the damp trenches, defending our Free and Great Russia, we are prepared to work not eight but twelve hours, and more if necessary and if we have the metal, material, and fuel. We ask you, comrade soldiers, not to believe the various provocative rumors but to select a delegation and send them to see us in the factories. We will bring you up to date on our work. Only in this way can you be convinced that all the persecution that has been stirred up represents nothing but a desire to break the close bond between the soldiers and workers.

With comradely greetings, the workers of shop no. 3.

Chairman of the meeting, F. Golakhov
Secretary, I. Gavrilov

  1. The Petrograd Pipe Factory (Trubochnyi zavod) employed nearly nineteen thousand workers at the beginning of 1917.

· 10 ·

Resolution of the workers of the "Old Parviainen" metal and machine factory, Petrograd, 13 April 1917.

We, the workers of the "Old Parviainen" factory, having assembled at a factorywide meeting of 2,500 men beginning on 13 April, and having discussed the issue of the current moment, have resolved:

1. To demand the removal of the Provisional Government, which has served only as a brake on the revolutionary cause, and to put power into the hands of the Soviet of Workers' and Soldiers' Deputies.

2. The Soviet of Workers' and Soldiers' Deputies, resting as it does on the revolutionary proletariat, must put an end to this war, which has benefited only the capitalists and landowners and has sapped the strength of the revolutionary people.

3. To demand from the Provisional Government the immediate publication of the secret military accords concluded between the old government and its allies.

4. To organize a Red Guard and arm the entire people.

5. To express a protest against the issue of the "Liberty Loan,"[1] which in fact serves as an enslavement of this freedom.

6. To requisition the printing presses of all the bourgeois newspapers conducting persecution against the Soviet of Workers' and Soldiers' Deputies and the workers' press and to put them at the disposal of the workers' newspapers.

7. From now on, until the printing presses are confiscated, to boycott the following newspapers: *Russkaia volia, Novoe vremia, Vechernee vremia, Rech', Den'* [Day], *Malen'kaia gazeta, Kopeika [Gazeta-kopeika], Zhivoe slovo* [Living word], *Sovremennoe slovo* [Modern word], *Petrogradskie vedomosti* [Petrograd gazette], *Petrogradskii listok* [Petrograd sheet], *Petrogradskaia gazeta* [Petrograd newspaper], *Yedinstvo* [Unity].[2]

8. To protest against England's interference in our domestic affairs and against delays for emigrants.

9. To requisition all food products for the needs of the broad masses and to set fixed prices on all consumer items.

10. To bring about the immediate seizure of landowners', appanage, cabinet, and monastery lands by a peasants' committee and to put the means of production into the hands of the workers.

11. To protest the withdrawal of revolutionary troops from Petrograd.

12. To recognize that in no instance may the Provisional Government use money to issue pensions to former ministers and their families—those fundamental enemies of the people.

Chairman, S. Ustinov

1. The "liberty loan" or "freedom loan" (*zaem svobody*) was the effort by the Provisional Government to raise revenue after the revolution. Cautiously approved by the moderate socialist leaders of the Soviet, a major campaign in the press began on 6 April, calling on Russians of all classes to purchase liberty bonds. The Bolsheviks opposed the campaign.

2. Mostly centrist, liberal, and moderate socialist papers (see the glossary).

· 11 ·

"From the Council of Elders of the Tula Brass Cartridge Factories,"
printed in *Izvestiia*, 15 April 1917.

From the Council of Elders[1] of the Tula Brass Cartridge Factories.
Comrade workers and soldiers of Petrograd!

Incredible rumors have been spread among you about our fabulous economic demands (a six-hour workday, dismissal of the directors of technical personnel, and so forth), about internal disorganization, which has led to a total cessation of production, to the detriment of the cause of defense, about how we, the workers of the Tula Brass Cartridge Factories, are exclusively devoted to our own personal demands, while totally failing to take into account the current political situation, the cause of revolution, or the cause of our freedom.

Comrade workers and soldiers of Petrograd, know that these rumors have been unleashed among you by ill-intentioned people desirous of bringing trouble, dissension, and mistrust into our workers' milieu. Comrades, know that we are fully mature politically, we carry the red banner of Revolution high, we dearly value the cause of our Freedom, we are capable of sacrificing our personal interests for the good of our common cause, and we know what to demand and when. Comrades, know that we still have the same old ugly working conditions, the same more-than-eight-hour, overtime work, the same old wage rates. If the output of our Tula Cartridge Factories is not at capacity, then this is not our fault but the fault of the old criminal government, which permitted a general collapse of the entire country, a general industrial crisis, a shortage of materials, fuel, etc., a fate that did not bypass our Tula factories either. So, comrades, do not believe the ill-intentioned rumors any more—do not permit the thought, either, that such a major workers' center has not understood its class interests, has not placed a high value on the cause of freedom.

Presidium: I. Kapteltsev, A. Kolykhalov, A. Kotlyer

1. The Council of Elders (*Sovet starost*) was an elected body of workers' representatives existing in some large factories, established by prerevolutionary law (see glossary).

· 12 ·

Appeal to the Petrograd "People's Committee" from Matvei Frolov,
day worker on the Perm Railroad, 25 April 1917.

To the Petrograd People's Committee[1] of Soldiers' and Workers' Deputies
From a day laborer on the 13th section, precinct 34
of the Perm R.R. service line
Matvei Gerasimov Frolov

Appeal

Matvei Gerasimov Frolov hereby makes his most humble request to the
soldiers' committee and the workers' deputies. Comrade Citizens! Come
and cast off the stone that was placed on our hearts by the despots of the
old government, for we only have a few moments left, and these are the
very hardest breaths of all. Comrades, come and take the iron chains off
us. They chafe so painfully that we cannot move. Citizen Comrades! Send
us the man with the keys, and open the doors that have been sealed shut all
these ages, where the freedom of the century we've waited for so long is
locked up, the freedom for which untold numbers of our very bravest
fighters have fallen. Comrades! Lend us a helping hand. We are perishing
without your mighty hand and indeed will surely perish. They are taking
away our freedom, the bourgeois and the despots. There are popular traditions, and here people say this: the bourgeois would rather die than give
us our freedom. People also say that they have laid up stores of firearms,
cannons, and bullets. This notion gives us ideas of the following content:
that we should make a search through all the buildings. A committee was
organized here, a soviet of soldiers' and workers' deputies, and even
though we can't accuse it of being idle, we aren't seeing anything useful
coming out of it either. Why? Because it's full of the same bourgeois who
used to embezzle public funds. A food committee was organized here, too,
and they have employees on it from the city council, social despots, and
even the old city chief. People say something's finally come of it: they set
an example for the capitalists and even the small merchants in how to
trade. They ratcheted the prices up sky high in every category and secured
them there with a bolt so strong you probably couldn't blow it off with dy-
namite. What else can you expect? It's perfectly possible. Imagine whoever
let employees from the city council move onto the Food Committee. They
were despots and now they're bourgeois. How much difference is there
between them, tell me that, comrades?

We most humbly request that the Petrograd People's Committee of the
Soviet of Soldiers' and Workers' Deputies turn its favorable attention to
this. Join us in our fight for freedom for the benefit of the new Provisional
Government. This appeal was written by day laborer Frolov. True copy.

25 April 1917
Confirmed by the workers of the 34th precinct of the Perm R.R. service line
[In a different hand]: We asked the workers to sign, but the senior worker wouldn't let them. Please take measures against senior worker Viktor Vasilievich Nesterov.

1. Here and below the author seems to be referring to the Executive Committee of the Petrograd Soviet (see the glossary) as the People's Committee (*Narodnyi komitet*, which also could be translated as "national committee").

· 13 ·

"To All Russian Women and Mothers" from the Smolensk Initiative Group of Women and Mothers, printed in the independent socialist newspaper *Novaia zhizn'*, 5 May 1917.

To All Russian Women and Mothers
We, a group of Russian women and mothers, are joining the protest of the working people against the war. We are also extending our hand to women and mothers the world over.

We are deeply convinced that our extended hand will meet the extended hands of mothers the world over. No annexations or indemnities can compensate a mother for a murdered son.

Enough blood. Enough of this horrible bloodshed, which is utterly pointless for the working people. Enough of sacrificing our sons to the capitalists' inflamed greed. We don't need any annexations or indemnities. Instead, let us safeguard our sons for the good of all the working people the world over. Let them apply all their efforts not to a fratricidal war but to the cause of peace and the brotherhood of all peoples. And let us, Russian women and mothers, be proud knowing that we were the first to extend our brotherly hand to all the mothers the world over.

Smolensk Initiative Group of Women and Mothers

· 14 ·

A letter to the Bolshevik newspaper *Rabotnitsa* (Working woman) from a restaurant worker in Petrograd, printed 20 May 1917.

A Letter to the Editor
Is it not time finally to pay attention to the growing debauchery [*razvrat*] both in Petrograd and in the provinces? Who should fight

against this evil if not you? Why is it that in the restaurants "girls" are serving without any pay but live on tips (on charity) from customers? Who if not you can help organize them, the honest ones, who have not already, because of poverty, fallen into a pool of debauchery? I, an honest girl, having neither relatives nor good friends, feel that I too will sooner or later end up on this shameful path, for there is no good pay. The owner of the restaurant told me that if I do not buy myself a dress and patent leather shoes and generally make myself up, then he will dismiss me. If he dismisses me, then that will be the beginning of debauchery, for where can I go without a penny in my pocket? And I am one of many.

With respect,
L.

· 15 ·

From the protocol of a general meeting of workers of the Okulovsky
Paper Factory and local peasants of Krestetsk Uezd,
Novgorod Province, 21 May 1917.

Excerpt from the Protocol of the General Meeting of 21 May 1917

The workers of the Okulovsky Paper Factory Company and the local peasants of Krestetsk Uezd, Novgorod Province, near the Okulovka-Nikol. R.R. station, having listened to the reports of their delegates from the Petrograd Soviet of Workers' and Soldiers' Deputies on the issues of the moment, have issued the following resolution:

Recognizing the tremendous tasks lying before the ministers who are fighting for our freedom, Kerensky, Skobelev, Tsereteli, Chernov, and Peshekhonov, and comparing them with the difficulties advanced by anarchist elements at the present difficult time, they fervently welcome the Coalition Ministry that has been formed.[1] Let our socialist comrades in the Ministry as well as in the Petrograd Soviet of Workers' and Soldiers' Deputies know that even in the remote provinces we hear their summons to save free Russia and know their work and devotion to the people and with them burn with the desire to work for the common goal—the Salvation of Free Democratic Russia. We are indignant that Revolutionary Petrograd is permitting overt and covert insults aimed at the men the people have chosen to take Power. We are indignant that a handful of loudmouths who have not been authorized by reliable organizations or sent by the people with instructions are making speeches of a blatantly anarchist nature, in front of thousands of the people, in the presence of the representatives of Revolutionary Authority. We believe, however, that the Petrograd Soviet of Workers' and Soldiers' Deputies will immediately extend one hand into the provinces toward the soviets of Workers', Soldiers', and Peasants' Deputies and the other to the Provisional Government, thereby reinforcing the necessary fullness of power.

The Peasant, the Worker, and the Soldier understand their civic responsibility. The people hold the revolutionary conquests dear, and the people trust the men they have chosen to occupy the front line in the revolutionary struggle. Comrades in the provinces are developing the revolutionary struggle, and the rear of the Russian Revolution is healthy both physically and spiritually.

Forward, work, for we are with you.

We do not await destruction but believe in the victory of the Russian Revolution.

Long live the Coalition Ministry.

Long live the All-Russian Soviet of Workers', Peasants', and Soldiers' Deputies.

Long live the Democratic Russian Republic.

> Secretary, [signature]
> [Seal of the factory committee of the Okulovsky factory]

 1. The first coalition government (May–July 1917) was formed on 5 May, when six socialists, representatives of the Soviet leadership, agreed to enter the cabinet of the Provisional Government. Five of them are named here (see the glossary for biographical information). P. N. Pereverzev, a Trudovik, was not usually viewed as one of the socialist deputies.

· 16 ·

Appeal to workers from the Committee of Elders of the Atlas Metal and Machine Factory, Petrograd, printed in the Menshevik newspaper *Rabochaia gazeta,* 11 June 1917.

———

Comrade workers! We must report to you that a sad phenomenon has continued and intensified at the Atlas Factory: heavy drinking is flourishing. Men are drinking denatured alcohol, varnish, and other such substitutes. They are drunk on the job, speak out of turn at meetings, shout inappropriate phrases, prevent politically conscious comrades from speaking, and paralyze their organizational work. There is total disarray in the shops. Owing to all the alcoholism, politically conscious workers are suffocating in this kind of atmosphere. You have no strength left to work when barriers go up at every step you take, but what is even more offensive is that politically conscious, advanced workers are participating in this vile business. Comrade workers, if you are alcoholics, isn't it about time you changed your thinking? You're ruining yourselves, you're wrecking production, you're destroying what has been purchased at such a high price: at the price of many lives. Comrade workers! Change your thinking and admit your guilt. You're putting a barrier in front of us, but know that we will not stop for anything or any kind of barrier. Conscious that we are right, we will fight to our last breath. Comrade workers! We ask you to come to our aid, to root out the vile drunkenness—we appeal to you with good intentions; otherwise, you will ruin the freedom bought at such a high price, specifically, many lives. Comrade workers! Remember that you will have to answer to the politically conscious proletariat. We are asking our politically conscious comrade workers from other factories to come to our aid in the fight against alcoholism. Write protests. Work out effective measures in the fight.

> Committee of Workers' Elders
> Atlas Factory

· 17 ·

Protocol of a general meeting of workers and employees of the Vysokovskaia Manufacturing Company Cotton Mill, Moscow Province, 14 June 1917.

Protocol

of a General Meeting of the Workers and Employees of the Vysokovskaia Manufacturing Company, 14 June 1917.
Chairman Vladimir Dmitrievich Bogdanov, Vice Chairman Nikolai Mikhailovich Novikov, and Secretary F. I. Blinov,
Recordkeeper Ivan Matveevich Bogomolov.
A motion was made for the General Meeting to discuss its stance toward the New Coalition Provisional Government and its stance toward the All-Russian Congress of Workers' and Soldiers' Deputies,[1] as well as toward the Petrograd Soviet. The General Meeting resolved: to express its full support and confidence in the New Coalition Provisional Government up until the Constituent Assembly,[2] which they would hasten to bring about as quickly as possible, and we stand solidly behind firm authority, which is now so essential, moreover while joining in on all the resolutions of the All-Russian Congress of Workers' and Soldiers' Deputies and of the Petrograd Soviet. Furiously protesting against the Bolsheviks and their leader Lenin, who do not trust the Provisional Government and want to take power into their own hands, as is obvious from their words spoken at the All-Russian Congress of Workers' and Soldiers' Deputies, which suf-

fered total defeat on all the points of our respected War Minister Keren-sky. We protest the Anarchists' and Bolsheviks' armed protest against the Provisional Government and the resolutions of the All-Russian Congress of Workers' and Soldiers' Deputies, not being willing to submit to the ma-jority. And all this, as we see, is to play consciously into the hands of our enemies and to the downfall of our freedom. Comrades, it is impermissi-ble for self-professed socialists to make these kinds of protests when our enemy the German is standing at the doors of our dear Mother Russia and trying to break them down. After all, it is a disgrace to exploit the igno-rance of the people and lead them into the open arms of our enemies. By means of this separate peace they are demanding. This is betrayal and treason against us, comrades, against our homeland and our allies. We stand for peace without annexations or indemnities and for the self-deter-mination of peoples. There is no place for those kinds of socialists to live among us, the free citizens of Free Russia. Let Lenin and his followers go to Germany and tell them that there it's not as easy as it might seem to make fools of the Russians.

> Chairman of the General Meeting, V. Bogdanov
> Vice Chairman, N. Novikov
> Secretary, F. Blinov
> Recordkeeper, I. Bogomolov

1. The All-Russian Congress of Workers' and Soldiers' Deputies, held in Petrograd 3–24 June 1917, brought together representatives of Soviets and of the leading leftist political parties from throughout the country. It was headed by Mensheviks and So-cialist Revolutionaries (see the glossary).

2. The Constituent Assembly was to be a national gathering of democratically elected representatives of all citizens to determine the course of Russian political life.

· 18 ·

Resolution of the workers of the "Old Parviainen" metal and machine factory, Petrograd, printed in the Bolshevik newspaper *Pravda*, 18 June 1917.

We, the workers of the "Old Parviainen" factory, having discussed Comrade Yevdokimov's report at the general meeting of both shifts on 15 June, consider the policy of appeasement with our country's capitalists, and through them with capitalists worldwide as well, to be ruinous for the cause of Russian and international revolution and for the cause of the world unification of the proletariat.

We call on all our comrade proletarians and semiproletarians of the city, countryside, and army to make a decisive break with the policy of imperialism and appeasement with imperialism, a policy that is aimed at reducing the Russian revolution to the role of humble servant and executor of the instructions of international capital. The Russian revolution, which calls on workers the world over to fight the capitalists, must provide a worthy example for this fight in its consistent and final form. Down with the power of the capitalists.

Long live the power of the revolutionary proletariat and the peasantry! Down with the policy of impotence, the policy of appeasement with the global plunderers! Long live the policy of force, the policy of decisive struggle for the freedom of workers the world over! For the peace of the whole world!

Peace to the hovels! War against the palaces!

In the name of this great struggle, we consider it essential to carry out immediately several measures that are expressed in the following slogans:

Down with counterrevolution!

Down with the ten capitalist ministers!

Down with the "ally imperialists," who stand for the counterrevolution under way!

Down with the capitalists organizing the Italian strikes[1] and secret lockouts!

All power to the Soviet of Workers', Soldiers', and Peasants' Deputies!

Long live workers' control over production and over the distribution of food!

Down with the undemocratic points in the Declaration of the Rights of the Soldier![2]

Against the disbanding of the revolutionary regiments!

Against the disarming of the workers!

Long live the arming of the entire people and especially the workers!

No separate peace with Wilhelm, no secret agreements with the English and French capitalists!

Immediate publication by the Soviet of truly just conditions of peace!

Against the policy of an offensive!

Bread! Peace! Freedom!

1) In the name of the victory of the proletarian-peasant revolution, in the name of the victory of the worker over the capitalists, the peasant over the landowner, we will come out under these slogans for a demonstration on 18 June.

2) We demand the release of Comrade Khaustov.[3]

3) We protest in the most categorical way possible against the persecution and silencing of the Bolsheviks and internationalists by the Social Democrats at the All-Russian Congress of Soviets, against the abusive conduct at the congress aimed at the Bolsheviks by Comrade Gegechkori[4] and the threats of Comrade Tsereteli.

Passed unanimously.

1. "Italian strikes" were "strikes" by employers—that is, mass firings in order to replace the current labor force with more tractable workers (the term also applied to sit-down strikes by workers in retaliation).

2. A first draft of the Declaration of the Rights of Soldiers had been drawn up by the soldiers' section of the Petrograd Soviet and published in *Izvestiia* on 15 March 1917. Referred for discussion to a Provisional Government commission, it was opposed by senior officers as undermining discipline and authority. Kerensky, the new war minister, approved it on 11 May, though only after alterations designed to increase command authority slightly.

3. Flavian Khaustov, a lieutenant in the army, was one of the founders and editor of the Bolshevik *Okopnaia pravda* ("Trench Pravda") and the chairman of the soldiers' committee of the 436th Regiment of the 12th Army. He was arrested 9 June and charged with treason for his articles against the forthcoming offensive. Imprisoned in the notorious Crosses prison in Petrograd, he was freed on 18 June, along with seven other political prisoners, by a crowd of self-described anarchist-communists.

4. Evgeny Petrovich Gegechkori (1879–1954) was a lawyer, political activist, and Menshevik. He was elected deputy from Kutaisi Province to the third State Duma (1907–1912) and was one of the leaders of the Social Democratic fraction in the Duma. After the February revolution of 1917 he was named commissar for the Provisional Government in Kutaisi Province and was elected chairman of the Transcaucasian Soviet of Soldiers' Deputies. In June 1917 he was elected to the All-Russian Central Executive Committee.

· 19 ·

Telegram to the Provisional Government and Congress of Soviets
from a meeting of twelve thousand workers, soldiers, peasants,
and Cossacks in the Kuban region, 18 June 1917.

———————

Received on 22 [June] 1917, 7:10 [a.m.]
Zhlobin
To the Petrograd Provisional Government

Strong in the spirit of our organization and our faith in the victory of revolutionary democracy over all the dark forces of the country twelve thousand workers, soldiers, and peasants and the Cossack regiment of Kuban Oblast and the citizens of Zhlobin at a meeting on 18 June send greetings to the Provisional Government and the All-Russian Congress of the Soviet of Workers' Soldiers' and Peasants' Deputies and express our full confidence that soon the country will hear the voice of firm authority which will put an end to all the counterrevolutionary actions and statements on both the right and the extreme left and bring us closer to peace without annexations or indemnities on the basis of the self-determination of peoples and will lead the country up to the Constituent Assembly.

Presidium of the Meeting

· 20 ·

Letter to working women from Maria Kutsko, a worker
at the Petrograd Munitions Works (*Orudiinyi zavod*), printed
in the Bolshevik newspaper *Rabotnitsa*, 25 June 1917.

Comrade women workers! Not long ago we won higher wages for women at the Munitions Works, and this ought to show us how great is the strength and significance of organization. What would we have achieved if we acted alone, by ourselves? Absolutely nothing! Until 7 June we women workers got only four rubles [a day], which, given the existing inflation, was hard for many to live on, especially for working women with families whose husbands were in the war. So we talked among ourselves about raising wages. We heard that at other state factories women workers had already, with the help of their factory committees, won higher rates. So we got together a general meeting of all the women workers at the plant and, after considering our situation, decided to turn to our factory committee and ask these comrade workingmen to raise our rates like those at other factories.

It is understandable that the factory committee agreed, for, after all, this is a comradely organization, not an owners' one, and they understand our situation. The factory committee requested that we bring them information about the wages of women at other state plants, and when we compiled information about wage rates at Pipe Works, New Arsenal, and Cartridge Works, our factory committee established for us a rate of six rubles and eighty kopeks a day. This was all done calmly, in a friendly way, without any complaints on the side of these men comrades.[1] And why was that? Because we now have our own workers' organization, a factory committee, through which one must always act. Because we have our own general meeting, which one must always attend so that together we can discuss our essential needs. The general meeting went very well. Only one comrade expressed an idea that it is completely impossible to agree with. He said that women will work in the factories only until the end of the war, but after the war is over, they will in all likelihood quit the factories. But we are sure, comrades, that this will not be the case. Where can those women workers go whose husbands, fathers, and brothers return home as cripples, unfit for labor? Who will support their helpless families and children if not we working women? Further, this comrade said that we women workers should not do dirty work in the factories, that we ought to "beautify the lives of men," to "sit at home and occupy ourselves with the domestic economy and not with dirty factory work." But, comrade workers, one can beautify your life not only at home by the stove but also at the factory. We women workers can beautify your life at the workbench, working hand in hand with you to improve our common working lives, to make this life more beautiful, pure, and bright for ourselves, for our children, and for the whole working class. This, it seems to me, is the real beauty and meaning of life.

Woman worker Maria Kutsko

1. As author and readers understood, such solidarity was noteworthy precisely because it was not the norm.

Soldiers

· 21 ·

Telegram to the Executive Committee of Workers' and Soldiers' Deputies from soldiers of the administration of the 17th Mortar Artillery Division, 9 March 1917.

Comrade soldiers and workers! The great events that have taken place in Russia could not have passed us by, we who are far from everything— here, at the front. But if, because of the duty the Homeland demands of us—to defeat the enemy no matter what—we cannot participate in the triumphs of Russia's renewal, then allow us to join with you, if only in spirit, and send our heartfelt greetings to the new free Russia. We are all her sons, and all as one wish her to be free, independent, and happy. Only for such a homeland can one die in peace, conscious of a duty fulfilled. With the help of God and the people, and under the guidance of our superiors, we all hope that the hour is at hand when these triumphs will be joined by a new one—the triumph of ultimate victory over the enemy.

Soldiers of the administration of the 17th Mortar Artillery Division, 9 March 1917, active army.

· 22 ·

"Letter from the active army," 10 March 1917.

10 March 1917

Greetings, dear comrades and citizens of our free country!
I congratulate you on your victory over our internal enemy. I am

touched to the bottom of my heart by your concern and your efforts to bring down the monarchist yoke. I beg you, dear comrades, not to abandon your cause, and to work hard to keep our frontline active army supplied with ammunition. Now not a single enemy airplane can slip by us—without being shot up—we fire our shells at them. . . .

Dear comrades, today we are giving our oath to the Provisional Government to be loyal defenders of free Russia; if you support us with ammunition, we will endeavor to hasten the victory over the enemy, but before we can inflict the first blow on him, the German people will probably demand from their Kaiser the same kind of freedom as we, the citizens of free Russia, have won. . . . I hope that through our joint efforts we will achieve an honorable peace.

Dear comrades, do not stint with your help, everyone do what he can, for our provisional committee[1] and for the good of our freedom.

Your devoted colleague,

N. Mikhailov [supported by seven signatures]

1. On 27 February 1917, a private meeting of a number of leaders from the prorogued State Duma established a Provisional Committee "to restore order and to deal with institutions and individuals." On 1 March, the Provisional Committee reached an agreement with the Petrograd Soviet about an appointment of a provisional government.

· 23 ·

Appeal to soldiers, workers, and other citizens of Russia
from the 8th Siberian Rifle Division, 16 March 1917.

Delegates from units of the 8th Siberian Rifle Division stationed at the battlefront gathered on 16 March and unanimously resolved to direct the following appeal to all the soldiers of the Russian army, all the workers, and all other citizens of Russia:

The liberation of the Russian people has now been accomplished. The sun of freedom has started to shine over our homeland. We believe that our homeland has honorably endured the difficult trials of the dark past and, now that it is free, can look forward to a great future. We believe that the free Russian people must not dishonor themselves with a shameful peace. Their freedom, their entire future, will be decided by this war. War to the end, to total victory. Freedom cannot be reconciled with disgrace. Comrade soldiers of all Russia: We must give our homeland victory, which means perfect order and close, honest collaboration with the officers. The discipline of the troops and the talent of our military leaders are what make our army fearsome [*groznyi*]. Let us invest all our fervor, all our strength, in this—and we will be victorious. Comrade workers, our fervent greetings to you. You and the soldiers have given your blood and your lives to open the way to freedom for the people. We will not disgrace ourselves by ceding our freedom, our happiness, to the enemy. Now we are expecting you to make an all-out effort for the defense. We know now that there is not a single party among you that desires peace, peace no matter what. We know that the German ruling class is waging a war for mastery over us, and we are waging a war with them for our independence and freedom. But freedom and defeat are mutually exclusive. There will be victory, there will be peace, and then will come the time for a final resolution of economic issues. Remember that discord and disagreement will lead us to defeat and the restoration of the overthrown order. Citizens of the Russian land, the history of our people has been forged from the work of each one of us. We have endured a difficult period, we have won our freedom. We must strengthen it. Victory will guarantee our freedom. The army has not and will not regret lives; but victory, and with it freedom, can come only from an organized and unanimous effort.

Long live free and great Russia and its first people's government!

· 24 ·

Letter to the Petrograd Soviet from soldiers of the 61st Siberian
Rifle Regiment, 18 March 1917.

Gentlemen deputies of the Committee of Workers' and Soldiers' [Deputies]! We simply cannot endure the old authority and regime. The gentlemen officers are issuing punishments just as they always have and are not giving us any of the freedom that our brothers have won. We keep hearing about "freedom of speech" but we don't have [it]. The officers don't let us speak and are fully prepared to shoot us. On 15 March, two soldiers deserted because of officers' harassment. Our detachment was lined up when the head of our detachment approached, and we were given the command "Attention," and he walked up and said, "I don't want to greet such bastards, and if anyone dares address me, I'll open fire." And so for no reason at all they put us under armed guard for twenty hours at a stretch and we couldn't talk at all. Which is why we ask you, Gentlemen deputies, to free us from the old rule and arrest them. And throughout the regiment they treat us in the old way, won't let us organize, and threaten to restore the old rule, which we cannot allow, naturally. Not only are the gentlemen officers not trying to get closer to us but, on the contrary, they've started harassing and punishing us. And so, Gentlemen deputies, either you arrest them yourselves or give us orders on how to deal with them. There is no way for us to assemble, because the entire regiment has been dispersed, one each to a company. Or recall them, because we don't want this kind of commander for our regiment and leader of our detachment, because we have already spilled our blood three times, and he calls us bastards. All of us are willing to lay down our lives for our freedom and for our existence and our dear homeland and to defeat the cursed enemies. And we feel that the day of freedom has started shining on us, too, but our people are still afraid to take [it] because there is no one to inspire us, and they won't allow us any meetings.

Once more we ask you, Gentlemen deputies, to take immediate [measures] to resolve this request or give us orders. And in order to confirm the truthfulness of the lines set forth above, we sign,

Soldiers [eighteen signatures]

· 25 ·

Appeal to Petrograd workers from the Tsarskoe Selo[1] Garrison
Soldiers' Committee,[2] 24 March 1917.

The Tsarskoe Selo Garrison Committee, which brings together all the units of the garrison, and which was formed on 7 March of this year, at its session on 24 March, passed the following appeal to the workers of the Petrograd region [*raion*].

Comrade workers! According to information in our possession, work has still not resumed at several of Petrograd's plants and factories. Among the many reasons for this (the shortage of fuel, the simultaneous dismissal of a large number of experienced supervisors and others the workers disliked), your demands for very high payments for your work have been far from insignificant here. We know that you are right, comrades: the entire people groaned under the lash of the autocratic-capitalist regime, but in this year of great national calamity, of war, when the salvation of the Homeland depends on the productivity of the factories, their work cannot slacken or halt. It pains us, it pains us terribly, to think that you, whose blood has mixed with our soldier blood on the pavement of Petrograd, to the firing of the tsar's machine guns, have forgotten this so quickly.

It is not about ourselves we speak. We are in the rear, far from the front, far from the battle effort. Remember those who are in the trenches, comrades, under the threat of death, injury, or harsh captivity, who are sacrificing themselves for the homeland, and not for two or three hundred rubles but for seventy-five kopeks a month! The gray Russian muzhik [peasant] is sitting in the trenches and, without trying to make any kind of deals, which would be degrading at such a time, doing his great deed without a murmur. The time will come, though, when a bloody storm will pass over the world, the gray hero will return to his native villages, settlements, and towns, and he will present a bill, a long bill, written in the blood of millions of his brothers, and the workers in the rear will have to pay that bill.

No matter what happens in this country, no matter how much the people's attention has been captured by the abrupt turn from the dead grip of autocracy to freedom and to a bright new life, at the front life goes on as before. The enemy is just as close and just as dangerous, assembling his regiments for a crushing blow against Russia. Our defenders need bread to gain the strength to repulse the enemy, they need clothing to keep from freezing in the cold damp earth of the trench, they need weapons and ammunition to defend the homeland.

Think about this, comrades.

Executive Commission of the Tsarskoe Selo Garrison Committee

1. Located fifteen miles from Petrograd, the town of Tsarskoe Selo (tsar's village) grew up around a complex of royal palaces built in the eighteenth and early nineteenth centuries. The Alexander Palace was the primary residence of Nicholas II and his family and the site of their house arrest from 8 March to 1 August 1917.

2. The proliferation of soldiers' committees in the army, especially at the front, during 1917 was one of the most salient expressions of popular efforts to exercise power from below. Analogous to urban and rural soviets, elected soldiers' committees tried to assert control over a wide range of functions in the army. Their role as representatives of rank-and-file interests was officially recognized by the army high command at the end of March. Increasingly, especially above the regimental level, these committees were in the hands of the better-educated, more urbanized, and most politicized soldiers, often workers and white-collar employees by background, and frequently junior officers in rank.

· 26 ·

Letter to Chkheidze from "Sick and injured Russian warriors," 31 March 1917.

Citizen Chkheidze! We are peasants and workers who have been at the front, who fervently love our homeland, which has been stained through the ages with our blood, who were born and died throughout vast Russia with the single dying thought of how one day our long-awaited and much-desired freedom would come. We, the lucky descendants of our grandfathers and fathers, have become witnesses to this unexpected resurrection of the Russian people, which occurred so spontaneously and suddenly, so closely unified and unanimous that no one bothered to sort out who was walking shoulder to shoulder. Rather, everyone burned with the single thought of overthrowing as quickly as possible the detested order that for ages has been leading the Russian people to shame and ruin. With what tenderness and hushed reverence did each of us admire the beautiful sun of freedom that has risen. How much indescribable joy we felt for this unified, brotherly work. But our joy was premature. The newly risen sun of Russian freedom began first to be obscured by fluffy clouds, then by storm clouds, and now by sinister thunderclouds that could block it out and hide it completely. But who is to blame? Who has been driving these sinister clouds? After long consideration we have reached the conclusion that the guilty party for all these clouds is none other than the Soviet of Workers' Deputies—that is, the leaders of the S.D. party, whose numbers include both you and Kerensky. It has become clear to us now how far-sighted the autocratic German order was that reigned in Russia. Together with Berlin they prepared in advance for the event of revolution by creating entire bands of well-organized people who worked fearlessly both in the State Duma and in various institutions and departments, in unions, in factories and plants, and wherever necessary to send you out under the loud sign of members of the S.D. Workers' Party—that is, as defenders of the people against oppressors. Your headquarters were located in the police department, and you had offices in all the security offices,[1] and it was these bands, under your leadership, that took the Russian revolution into their own traitorous hands in one fell swoop, exploiting the Russian people's lack of preparation and organization against your perfidious bands. The entire work of your party (and I mean not the party whose majority consists of the countless ignorant masses but its leaders, including you) is conducting an underground, traitorous, hypocritical tactic using the same German money, and of course for the benefit of the Germans alone. You are now not clandestine but overt German spies and provocateurs, and just as the overthrown German court and its agents did everything they could toward Russia's enslavement by Germany, intentionally, with this goal in mind, leading the Russian people into slavery and degradation, so you too have donned a mask, shouting at every crossroads, Down with the war, with the Provisional Government, with work, no matter where, and demanding the complete insubordination of everyone, not excluding the army and the navy, to anyone but your band. Capitalizing on a moment of confusion that resulted from the unexpected Divine joy of the Russian people, you, like predatory beasts in ambush, sank your claws into the youthful body of the Russian revolution in order ultimately to tear it to shreds, introducing all kinds of terrible disorder [*smuta*][2] among the Russian people, becoming autocratic dictators, publishing all kinds of orders among the citizenry, the army and navy, that have led only to the disintegration that is so ruinously reflected in everything, especially the army, that buttress and defender of our newborn freedom, trying to crowd out the administration of the country, the Provisional Government, to which the troops swore an oath and in which the entire Russian people believe, knowing each of its members, and not only the details of their biographies, and seeing their crystal-pure, selfless work for the good of their people and for strengthening their freedom. The Provisional Government is not acting by force and threats, as you do, but is following a straight and open path, not silencing anyone at meetings or in the press, and if it agrees to your forced bid, then it is only because it regrets the precious blood of the Russian people and does not want to spill it inside the country and at such a time over you mercenary German servants. Your posters shout blasphemously about the brotherhood of peoples, whereas for you brotherhood works in only one direction, toward your one master and guide, the German people, and it is only with them and for their benefit that you try to do everything, preparing in various ways the same shameful, dishonorable, separate peace that was so dear to the overthrown German court. You are intentionally acting separately from the socialists of other countries, our allies, being reluctant not only to bring up with them all the issues of war and peace but actually avoiding them, knowing ahead of time that you will not find among them traitors to their homeland—in other words, provocateurs overseen by Berlin. In Russia you have woven yourselves a sturdy nest under the protection of the old German regime for the support of which, as a sign of gratitude, you have with such unity expressed your hellish intent to ruin the Russian revolution, which indeed you have already attempted to fulfill, and now you can triumph, for your goal is partially achieved and your labors have not been in vain. Thanks to you and others of like mind, a treacherously evil act has been committed against the Russian people and its freedom, the disintegration that you intentionally sowed so assiduously in the army—not to obey their superiors, and to throw down their weapons and go home—has accomplished its purpose, and thanks to your preparation, your German masters shot tens of thousands of free Russian men at Stokhod.[3] You are clearing the road for the German hordes, just as it was cleared before by the German autocrats, so that they would be given everything they wanted. At the same time, you purposely shut your eyes to where, under your supervision, not only the defense factories began abandoning operations but also those in all the branches of the country's economic life, in such a way as to make the rear take a fateful step and thereby create a counterrevolution and keep the Russian people from defending their freedom, you safeguard just as jealously as the old autocrats did every living German, allowing them the perfect opportunity to put the brakes on and throw a monkey wrench into the wheels of free Russia, you let all of them stay on as leaders in the factories and plants, not excluding even those working in defense at the head of production, and your sole common goal is to dig a grave for the Russian people as quickly as possible. Soon we may learn that Riman and Rennenkamf and Sukhomlinov[4] and all the butchers and torturers of the Russian people, along with the entire former tsarist family, which once protected you, is going to be freed by you on bail, to be under your protection. Amid your hellish plans, you have not stopped to consider what is happening to our brothers there, who have fallen into the hands of the Russian people's ferocious sworn enemies, thanks to the treacherous snares you created in collaboration with the accursed overthrown German autocrats. It is obvious that they, like the old autocrats, are total strangers to you, and those atrocities, those mockeries, those humiliations, which they endure there and as a result of which people are perishing, not only do not alarm you but in fact afford you pleasure. Oh, if you were true brothers of the Russian people and not traitors, you would be able to defend our brothers and fathers, as our allies are doing—in fact, under your protection there are several times more Germans not just living but reigning in Russia than there are our brothers among them—but these of course are the kinds of actions that are inversely proportionate to your tasks, as they were for the former autocratic rulers. Your task is to inflict only harm on the Russian people, using all the measures so richly bequeathed to you by the old regime. You don't allow the newspapers to print any reports about your base actions—not only not from individual citizens, but not even from entire associations and resolutions from various meetings. You get rid of them by force, going so far as to murder citizens you have no use for. You make illegal arrests and do much more that is filthy, base, and vile, something you inherited from your collaborative work in the old security police. Remember, though, that no matter how you traitor snakes hide behind various masks, afraid to take them off, so that no one recognizes you, no matter how anonymously you act, like various pretenders and provocateurs, the Russian people will find you out, they will record your shameful names and will demand that you answer for deliberately shooting at them in war and for the troubles within the country; they will demand an answer perhaps sooner than you suppose, but they will never let you, as enemies of their freedom, go unpunished. Well, I have no more strength to write, my wounds ache, and I am in tears over the sufferings each of us has had to bear from you barbarians in the war. It is getting dark, although we burn with the desire to rejoin the ranks as quickly as possible in order to pay you barbarians back for the torments of our brothers and to make a peace that is worthy of the Great Russian People and their glorious allies, not that shameful one you want. May the curse of the Russian people be upon you.

Sick and injured Russian warriors
Moscow, 31 March 1917

1. The reference is to the Okhrana, the prerevolutionary political security police. In their fight against political opposition, they recruited a broad network of agents who worked under cover.

2. *Smuta* is a term evoking disorder, upheaval, and deep social conflict. The most famous and defining smuta in Russian history was the Time of Troubles (*Smutnoe vremia*) in the late sixteenth and early seventeenth centuries, when Russia was wracked by decades of dynastic crisis, civil war, social rebellion, and foreign intervention.

3. Stokhod is a river in Ukraine. In the summer of 1916, the Russian army took the offensive against the German and Austrian military forces in the region of the Stokhod River. After a month of tense and bloody battles, the Stokhod operation ended without success.

4. Tsarist generals. As a colonel of the Semyonovsky Life Guards Regiment in December 1905, at a time of armed uprisings throughout the country, Nikolai Karlovich Riman had led a notorious punitive force to suppress rebellion. Pavel Karlovich Rennenkamf (1854–1918) was a cavalry general, also notorious for his leadership of a punitive force to suppress revolutionary disturbances by soldiers in 1905–1907. He commanded the 1st Army during World War I until his discharge and retirement in 1915. Vladimir Aleksandrovich Sukhomlinov (1848–1926) had been a cavalry general since 1906 and had served as minister of war from 1909 to 1915. He was arrested and imprisoned for treason in March 1916 and sentenced to life imprisonment in 1917 but was then released in 1918 because of old age.

· 27 ·

Letter to Chkheidze from Soldiers of the 2nd Battery Assembly,
Caucasus army, 3 April 1917.

To the Commander of the 2nd Battery of the 2nd Caucasus Artillery Division
At a general meeting on 3 April of this year, we resolved to ask you, Colonel, sir, to permit us to address the following letter to State Duma Deputy CHKHEIDZE:
[Handwritten note in margin:] Approved, very happy to have this sent immediately, [signature]

Deeply respected State Duma Deputy Mr. Chkheidze,
Now that everyone is free, we wanted to make use of this freedom in the sense of self-betterment, which we need so much now for our new creative life. We were in chains, ignorant and helpless. Now the chains have been broken and we are free, yet we remain as ignorant and helpless as ever.
Before long there will be a Constituent Assembly. We do not want to be mute and passive voters and deputies. We want to know what this or that form of rule holds in store for us.
We are all peasant farmers, workers, or employees. Our lack of enlightenment and our economic impotence allowed the ever powerful and rich

to exploit our labor. This corrupted our whole life. Labor by its very nature is intended for the joy and happiness of man, but it has been transformed into a shameful and heavy yoke. We do not want this kind of life any more, we are tired of constantly thinking about nothing but a crust of bread for the next day, but we do not know how to do this, although we do believe that it is possible.

Therefore we have decided, with the permission of our battery commander, to ask you, deeply respected deputy, Mr. Chkheidze, for help. We have heard of you many times as a fervent supporter of truth and equality on earth, which is why we decided to turn specifically to you. Do not deny our request, if it does not put you to too much trouble: please send us by mail books with popular accounts dealing with all the questions enumerated above.

We ourselves do not know books or where to get them. We will send the money for the books immediately upon receipt of a bill. We will be endlessly grateful. We ask you to send the books addressed to our battery commander, Caucasus Army

> Chairman of the battery meeting, senior scribe, [signature]
> Delegates of the assembly, [three signatures]
> Officer representative, [signature]

· 28 ·

Letter to Chkheidze from soldier workers of Transport Repair Workshop No. 2, Uman, Kiev Province, 3 April 1917.

Uman, 3 April 1917

We, the soldiers of Transport Repair Workshop No. 2, sincerely sympathize with the Great Cause and are walking hand in hand with the proletariat toward the attainment of a better future life. After years of struggle with the Romanov tyrants, the foul throne of Nicholas II was overthrown by a powerful hand; the tyrants' nest came crashing down and all the slaves of Nicholas II are sitting under lock and key, and these will all get the appropriate punishment for their crime before all Russia—plunging peaceful peoples into a bloody slaughterhouse, winning their fortune off the bones and blood of their less fortunate brothers, bringing the country to the point of total devastation, allowing infants to be lost from hunger and cold. Seeing the starving shadows of their little children, mothers could not endure it and did away with themselves. At this difficult moment for our Homeland, on top of all this horror, Tsar Nikolasha and Sasha the libertine[1] started mocking Russia, filled the whole palace with various and sundry sorcerers and horse thieves, made a funeral feast of lies and debauchery on the warm blood of the workers and soldiers. The pathetic coward Nikolasha, seeing there was no escape from the deadly noose, unleashed a torrent of blood, abandoned the throne, which was bursting at the seams, and fled to the front and the soldiers in order to save the foul throne. Pathetic coward, who could ever believe in you? To save your foul throne. Who needs it, when you have robbed the people of everything—their fathers, sons, and brothers. Your entire reign has passed in blood.

There were no machine guns or other weapons at the front, but in your tyrant's nest there was a machine gun in every window, and they armed all the guards with the latest weapons. Haven't you and your henchmen spilled enough blood? Haven't you carried out enough sentences and executions? Haven't enough freedom fighters suffocated in forgotten cells? Haven't you tried to sell your foul throne as dearly as possible? Did you really need a bloody sacrifice at the very last minute? May you fall off the face of the earth of free Russia, bloody phantom.

Lately the revolution has chewed up thousands of the lives of our best freedom fighters. Eternal memory to you, dear comrades. We vow before your still-warm graves that we will defend the freedom you have won to our last drop of blood and no one will dare infringe on our freedom. They can take it only over our dead bodies.

In light of all this, we are enclosing the money we have collected for victims of the revolution and ask Comrade Chkheidze in the name of the entire detachment, numbering four hundred men, to accept this money, FORTY-TWO rubles, and to print the letter in full in the workers' newspaper, since that is what we subscribe to, and it would be good if other soldiers followed this example. Receiving two and a half kopeks, we share it for this sacred cause.

> Soldiers of Transport Repair Workshop No. 2
> Uman, Kiev Province

1. Derogatory names for Nicholas II and Alexandra that were often used when Russians alluded to rumors of illicit relations between Alexandra and Rasputin and to Nicholas II's powerlessness before this presumed affair. Such rumors and innuendos did much to undermine and desacralize the authority of the monarchy.

· 29 ·

Letter to the Soviet from Sergeant Ia. Z. Mazur on behalf of soldiers
of the Mortar Artillery Division, 11 April 1917.

Mr. Chairman,

On behalf of soldiers of the Mortar Artillery Division, I beg to express
to the Soviet of Soldiers' and Workers' Deputies, in your person, our deep
gratitude for the freedom you have won for us.

We deeply believe you that you will always be on guard for our dear
freedom.

We ask you to do everything possible to get rid of the Black Hundreds[1]
and the underlings of the old mercenary rule. We would be deeply grateful
if you could remove from authority V. Shulgin,[2] who, in the *Kievlianin*
[Kievan] newspaper, issue no. 89, calls you, our dear liberators, prisoners
and convicts.[3]

> Sergeant Ia. Z. Mazur
> 11 April of this year

1. "Black Hundreds," or *chernosotensy*, was a loose term used by leftists and liberals to describe right-wing organizations and individuals. The implication was that they were pogromists at heart if not in practice.

2. Vasily Vitalievich Shulgin (1878–1976) was one of the leaders of the Nationalists in the State Duma. During the February revolution, as a member of the Provisional Committee of the State Duma, he and Aleksandr Guchkov negotiated Nicholas II's abdication on 2 March 1917. He remained active as a conservative publisher, writer, and political activist in 1917.

3. As publisher of the *Kievlianin* newspaper, a conservative literary and political paper published in Kiev, Vasily Shulgin sent a lead essay from Petrograd on 5 April in which he argued that "yesterday's prisoners [*kolodniki*] today feel themselves to be autocrats," a transformation he viewed as perilous: "Liberty, won by one's own strength, intoxicates, and is dangerous, like a strong liquor." Under such conditions, he argued, there cannot be "real freedom," which will exist only when "the human spirit is filled with respect for the rights and beliefs of others." *Kievlianin*, no. 89 (6 April 1917): 1.

· 30 ·

Letter to Minister of War Aleksandr Guchkov from soldiers
of the 64th Infantry Division of the active army, 13 April 1917.

This is our soldierly request to you, Mr. Minister of the new government. We, the soldiers of the 64th Division of the active army, who have
faithfully sworn allegiance to the new Provisional Government, following
the edict issued by you, the war minister. We soldiers have the honor of

humbly asking you for your order to conclude peace as quickly as possible
with our so-called enemies—that is, they are not our enemies but are our
brothers in the cross and in the divine commandments. As we here have
been suffering for two years and nine months, so too have our so-called
enemies. They turn out not to be our enemies but our innocent brothers,
and they owe us nothing, nor we them. And we should not strike at each
other, just as they, Austrians, daily broadcast from their trench to ours:
"Russia, don't fire, let's have peace!" And it's true, we do need peace. It's
time, Mr. Minister, it's time. We sit here in the trenches in torment, in these
filthy wet dugouts, hungry, cold, unshod, tattered. The parasites have bit-
ten us to death, and disease among us that we caught earlier on other
fronts is starting to act; it entered our bones and body in the very first
years and now gives us no rest whatsoever, and the disease demands its
own every time when it is damp or the weather is bad. Here in the trenches
there is no salvation for us from this martyr's life, from this compulsory
task. Here in the trenches we have many men who have been wounded
two or three times and some who have been gassed that we could show
you, Mr. Minister, very many men like that. Mr. Minister! We soldier-sufferers ask you to consider our position as soldiers and join with us in addressing these soldierly sufferings, this torment. We soldiers here at the
front are suffering in the trenches. Back home in Russia we have our wives
and children and fathers, our mothers in their old age are suffering without bread or clothing, since everything has become hard and impossible,
and they write us plaintive, tearful letters here at the front. Why is it
they're crying? Because they, our fathers, are old men, they cannot get a
crust of bread for themselves; they are old, but the children are small, and
our wives cannot cultivate the land we left behind, which at the present
time is overgrown and full of weeds, desolate, and they are suffering without bread. Yes, Mr. Minister, I dare say you are familiar with all this that is
tearing people's lives to pieces. What did we need this for? What is this war
for? Why do we need what belongs to someone else if we have so much of
our own anyway? Our Savior Himself said: "Take not from your brother.
If he is in need, give to him." Why then should we go against the words of
Our Lord Jesus Christ and kill each other? Why should we soak the
ground with human blood, which is dear to every man, so each spurt of
blood is to be regretted. But our elected deputies, whom we sent to speak
for us soldier-sufferers and to stand up for our common interests, have
told your Petrograd deputy, who was here at our 64th Division on 12
April 1917, that our 64th Division wishes to wage war to a victorious conclusion. But no, that's wrong, they, our deputies, are mistaken. We soldiers
do not want the 64th Division to continue the war. Rather, give us peace as
quickly as possible because the people are done for and sick and time is
running out, we are short of everything, and we think that soldiers all
along the front have the same opinion: peace as quickly as possible and

nothing else. Why should we defend the interests of other powers, like this England and France, for instance? Let them do what they like, but we need peace because we are on the brink of complete exhaustion, and we don't need any victory, and for now our enemies are asking us to make peace, but the time will come when we have to ask them. It's time, Mr. Minister, it's time to put an end to this bloody business. We have had enough of the tears shed by our wives, our fathers, and our mothers.

Be so kind, Mr. Minister, as to consider our plight.

We, soldiers of the Russian army

· 31 ·

Letter to the chairman of the Soviet of Workers' and Soldiers' Deputies
from soldier Yegorov in the 753rd Reserve Regiment, no date
(content suggests late April).

To the chairman of the Soviet of Workers' and Soldiers' Deputies

We have heard that you want war and to support our dear allies [*sic*] England. Well, you can support them yourselves. Go into the trenches and fight. You are using our money to take out loans, but we will pay. You are bad defenders for us. Down with war, give us peace. Down with Miliukov. Our 753rd Regiment is standing now in reserve but we won't go back down into the trenches any more. However, it is necessary to replace our comrades, regiments 754 [and] 755, so send Miliukov Guchkov Brusilov Kornilov Gurko Rodzianko[1] and the factory owners, but regiments 753 and 756 aren't going to take their dear comrades' places in the trenches because the blood is ours and the money is ours but the words are yours. Give us peace. A soldier's word is true. Whoever wants war should go into the trenches and fight for the good of England, but we don't need anyone else's good, we've got enough of our own.

Regiment 753 Yegorov

We have heard the gentlemen officers from the armies are saying that the soldiers want war, but did they ever ask the soldiers who are sitting in the trenches? Doubtless not.

1. Conservative politicians and military leaders (see individual names in the glossary for biographical details).

· 32 ·

Appeal to all the soldiers of the 12th Army from the 186th
Artillery Division, 4 May 1917.

All the soldiers of the 186th Artillery Division, shaken by current events, gathered at a general divisional meeting on this 4 May, in a body of all three batteries and their officers, and after discussing the issue of the life and death of the homeland dear to us all, decided as soon as possible to declare the following openly and loudly:

Fighting comrades, glorious heroes of the 12th Army: What are we waiting for? Who are we obeying? The entire Russian nation rejects this war.

The Soviet of Workers' and Soldiers' Deputies has sent a fervent appeal to all the peoples to put an end to the carnage.

Russia is awaiting an answer to this appeal; but comrades, the German people are still silent, Wilhelm's regiments, having taken advantage of our summons, have left insignificant units against us and come crashing down in a great mass on our allies, the French and the English, and have halted their onslaught.

The time is not far off when the German hordes, having beaten our allies, will be thrown back to our front. The enemy will make incredible efforts, and for us this convulsive death spasm of the enemy will be fateful.

We will end the war then. We will end it, comrades.

We will end it not as free citizens, masters of the Russian land, though, but as slaves of the bloody Emperor Wilhelm.

Right now we are standing idle, we are dawdling, but every day of inaction in the trenches and the reserves inflicts tremendous costs on our people.

The country is experiencing a severe economic crisis. The moment is coming when the homeland will be in no condition to give us food and ammunition. It will be 1915 all over again,[1] and the enemy will drive us out, hungry, unclothed, and unarmed.

Brothers, while we still have the strength, we must tear peace from the enemy and not wait for him to dictate to us after he has broken through to the bleeding heart of the young Free Russia.

Thirty-four months of suffering and the millions of lives of our fathers and brothers demands two to three months of concerted effort so we can be free—otherwise it will be inaction and slavery.

Heroes of the 12th Army: Have we really forgotten the deeds of the December battles, when we snapped the German barbed wire with our chests and showed the enemy and the whole world what a real Russian hero is?

The blood of our brothers has still not dried on those fields where we fought, and it calls out to us.

It begs us to defend freedom.

But we are silent.

We were strong when we were slaves. We fought like lions when we were surrounded by betrayal, but now that we are free, we have become weak, like rebellious slaves.

No, comrades.

Let the whole world know that this is wrong.

The revolutionary army with its red banners of freedom shall defend revolutionary Free Russia and hoist on its former borders the Free red banner before which Wilhelm's regiment will bow.

WE BEG OUR VALOROUS ARMY COMMANDER GENERAL RADKO-DMI-TRIEV[2] to gather us around himself, we who are thirsting to save Free Russia or die and will not hesitate a moment to strike at the enemy before it is too late.

Free warriors, glorious soldiers of the 12th Army: Answer our appeal. Let each regiment, each company, squadron, battery, and detachment, each individual warrior who thinks the way we do, without a moment's hesitation, address a plea through the Executive Committee of Soldiers [Iskosol][3] to General Radko-Dmitriev to find the means to unite us, free men who have sworn to achieve the death and destruction of the hydra of German militarism or to die.

We beg those comrades who do not feel strong enough for bloody battle to carry out their duty as citizens and openly and honestly declare that they are too weak for bloody battle and, going back to their peaceful activities, help us to perform our difficult duty to Free Russia and the whole world.

> Chairman of the General Assembly, Captain, [signature]
> 1st Vice Chairman, Senior Bombardier, [signature]
> 2nd Vice Chairman, Ensign, [signature]
> 1st Secretary, [signature]
> 2nd Secretary, [signature]

1. A disastrous year for the Russian armies in World War I. Austrian and German offensives pushed the Russian army back into its own territory. Shells, rifles, and clothing were in short supply. Thousands of refugees clogged paths and roads. Approximately a million men were taken prisoner and over a million were killed and wounded.

2. General R. D. Radko-Dmitriev (1859–1918) was born in Bulgaria, where he began his military service, and he became Bulgarian ambassador to St. Petersburg in 1913. In March 1916 he was appointed a commander of 12th Russian Army, positioned in Riga. Because of his willingness to tolerate soldiers' committees, he was replaced by Kornilov at the end of July.

3. Iskosol, an abbreviation for *Ispolnitel'nyi komitet soldatov*, was the Executive Committee of the Soviet of Soldiers' Deputies of the 12th Army of the northern front. The committee was created in Riga in March 1917 and included mostly Mensheviks and Socialist Revolutionaries.

· 33 ·

A Voice from the Trenches
Brothers and Citizens

Comrade editors, we ask you to find room for our small request and put it out through all the newspapers and send them to us in the trenches. We will be waiting impatiently.

Comrade soldiers and workers,

We ask you to stop your meetings in the streets and your quarreling between the workers and capitalists and soldiers and sowing strife among the nations. Comrade soldiers and workers, don't make trouble for us and don't talk about an offensive. We can't listen to or look at those people who are discussing war until we have freedom and who are saying that we have to attack. Comrade soldiers and workers, we are your brothers and we are your comrades. We are sitting in the trenches without light or happiness, and we hear all the rumors let loose from the rear. Stones have been placed on our shoulders. Comrades and brothers, we are already lost, even without an offensive. We are all sick, we have no strength left. Comrade soldiers and workers, help us. We are alone, we have no strength, and we cannot attack. We don't have the men, and everything is in short supply. We are standing in the trenches, our brothers are going into the trenches on crutches, they have no legs or strength, and everyone is saying we have to attack. Comrades, we don't have to attack and we're not going to. Enough of our brothers have fallen over these three years. We have had enough bloodshed for now. We must end the war no matter what, and if they want an offensive, then we'll mount an offensive against the capitalists and bourgeoisie that are drowning us and killing us and our freedom. We will mount an offensive against them, and then we will end the war that is leading us to our ruin. We are all perishing, and we ask you not to wait for the army to turn its bayonets around and go on the attack. There will be no mercy—the army will not let anyone speak against it. Try hard, comrades, to put an end to the war. Don't wait for us to turn our bayonets around. And that's enough talk about an offensive. We will attack and we will drive everyone out. But comrade workers and soldiers in the rear, act now and end the war.

We will end it soon, only help us, since we don't have to attack and aren't going to.

Division Chairman, Volkov
Secretary, I. Chirkov

Please correct the mistakes in our words and print them in all the newspapers and send them to the trenches for the units.

Composed by Sh.

30 May 1917

· 34 ·

Appeal to reservists from a soldiers' committee at the northern front, June 1917.

Appeal to Comrade Reservists

Comrades, worker-citizens, to you who treasure the freedom we have won this word is directed. Our homeland is going through a difficult time, a time when our fate is being decided, along with our life and our entire future well-being. For more than thirty-five months our fathers and brothers have been shedding their precious blood defending the homeland, which is threatened by danger from a bloodthirsty external enemy.

You well know, comrades, Wilhelm's threats to fulfill the bequest of his grandfather—to devastate all of Slavdom.

We know that in union there is strength and by strength alone we can save ourselves and our descendants. But you, comrade workers, do not wish to unite, you do not all wish to stand as a wall in defense of the homeland, you prize your own skin, forgetting that your fate is in your hands.

By not joining the ranks of the army and not sending support to the comrades in the trenches, you are sentencing them to death, those men who are performing a hard and difficult duty for their homeland and conscience.

Their powers are depleted, they are truly weary, their ranks are thinning. They are awaiting help from the rear, where, as everyone knows, there is much fresh strength, and where all the participation in the common struggle for the homeland is expressed merely in work in the rear for good reward. Wouldn't it be better for you to quit your cozy corners and yield them to the wounded comrades who are no longer capable of battling the terrible enemy?

Comrade workers, consider the position of the fighters at the front and appreciate their deed.

You who have not seen tears or grief, who have not seen men dying in war or experienced the nightmares of battle, shout: "Down with war, we're tired, we're sick of it. Peace, no matter what." And those to whom freedom and the homeland are dear and who look at the future, remembering that our fate and the homeland's depends on us, say something different: "We will not allow a shameful peace but will fight and strive for the speediest yet honest peace that will bring liberation to all enslaved and ravaged peoples." So let us all together, unanimously, stand like a granite wall, let us not allow our cunning enemy to exploit our weakness and strife for his own ends—waiting for the right moment and falling upon us with all his forces. For examples we have only to recall our failure at Stokhod.

Comrades—quit riding on other people's shoulders and go to your brothers in the trenches. Help them defend and reinforce the freedom we have so long awaited.

Do not forget that if we ourselves do not put our future on firm foundations, then our conscience will reproach us and the coming generation will have no good word to say about us.

Committee of the 8th Construction Brigade of the northern front
P.S. We ask other newspapers not to refuse to reprint this.

· 35 ·

"Letter from the Front" to the Bolshevik newspaper *Pravda*, 7 June 1917.

_____

Letter from the Front
Comrades! We have been very sad to read bourgeois newspapers such as *Rech'*, *Birzhevka*,[1] and so on, which assure us that we need war to a victorious conclusion, that we need an offensive to win back the land seized by the enemy. Haven't the bourgeoisie and the capitalists already filled their pockets with bloody coins? We workers and peasants, dressed in our gray overcoats, do not need this bloody slaughter. Enough of decimating peoples, we don't need conquests! We need peace, peace for all mankind. We are exhausted, mutilated, and sick, and after long months of trench life we have no relief. We demand this relief! Let those loudmouths who are demanding war to a victorious conclusion relieve us here. And let us be in the rear defending the interests of free Russia. That is the goal we are striving for.
We send greetings to the workers' newspaper *Pravda*. We believe in it alone and not the bourgeois newspapers. We desire a speedy peace for all peoples. We regret that few newspapers like *Pravda* reach us in the trenches.

Soldiers of the 727th Novo-Silidginsky Regiment
[twenty-five signatures follow]

1. Popular nickname for *Birzhevye vedomosti*.

· 36 ·

Resolution of the soldiers of the 1st Infantry Reserve Regiment, 18 June 1917.

_____

Resolution of the Soldiers of the 1st Infantry Reserve Regiment
We, the soldiers of the 1st Infantry Reserve Regiment, gathered for a meeting on 16 June of this year and issued the following resolution:

The crisis of the revolution has come to a head. The bourgeoisie is closing ranks by the day, gathering around itself dark forces and also attracting politically naive proletarians and peasants. The All-Russian Congress [of Soviets] itself has assured us that the counterrevolution is advancing.

Our most crucial issues have not been resolved at all yet, the slaughter continues, and there is an industrial collapse in the making. We see the rich lining their pockets from this criminal war, and we sense and know that a sinister and terrible famine is approaching. We also see the jackals from the State Duma and State Council reaching out with their filthy paws to strangle freedom. The rights of the soldier are falling by the wayside, so is the reinforcement of the rights of freedom, and in their place Articles 129 and 131 are being advanced once again.[1] Comrade Khaustov was arrested for this, Kharitonov[2] did time for this, the slander that is pouring out with impunity from the direction of the bourgeoisie is for this. . . . How could all this fail to affect us? And finally, the soldier's lack of rights and Mr. Kerensky's decrees on hard labor—isn't all of this a disgrace to our revolution?

But we ask whether anything good has been done for our revolution by our rulers and with regret have replied—no, nothing. We consider the fault for all this to be our rulers' line of conduct. And in particular those ten bourgeois who now sit in the ministry.[3]

Above all, we hotly protest any kind of bourgeois ministry, and we demand that the ten bourgeois make way.

We demand that the All-Russian Soviet of Soldiers', Workers', and Peasants' Deputies seize all power.

And after these first steps are taken, finally, we will set about administering all the freedoms won by the blood of the revolution and implementing the greatest of issues, the end of the criminal slaughter.

In anticipation of all this, we will be alert and on guard for our revolution and will never allow anyone to destroy it.

We will die, but we will vanquish the most accursed, the most evil of our enemies—the bourgeoisie.

Assembly chairman, Sakharov
Secretary, M. Osipov

1. On 4 June 1917, the Ministry of Justice announced that it had introduced, for urgent consideration by the commission revising the criminal code, two articles, 129 and 131, stipulating strict penalties for public incitement to various serious crimes.

2. Probably G. Kharitonov, a soldier from the Caucasus army and a member of the Executive Committee of the All-Russian Soviet of Peasant Deputies.

3. References to the "ten bourgeois ministers" became common in demonstrations against the government after the formation of the first coalition to identify the nonsocialists in the cabinet: G. Lvov (the prime minister), A. Godnev, A. Konovalov, V. Lvov, A. Manuilov, N. Nekrasov, P. Pereverzev, D. Shakhovskoi, A. Shingarev, and M. Tereshchenko. The designation was not entirely accurate however. Pereverzev was a Trudovik—a member of a moderate socialist party represented in the Duma.

· 37 ·

Letter to "Comrade Patriots" from soldiers in the trenches, 27 June 1917.

Comrade Patriots!

When you're sitting at your position in the dirty gray trenches on the front line, chest to chest with your foe, and once in a while you peek out of your little trench at your opponent, your heart involuntarily surges with blood, because you can't wait for the order to attack or else about peace from the Socialist Ministers, or, in short, an order from our leaders leading to a speedy Peace—an honorable Peace based on self-determination for the peoples of all countries, warring and neutral both. Here at last we have seen the first sign of life on the south.[ern] fr[ont]. Our brothers, the first to come to their senses, and at the first call of the Socialist Minister Kerensky, themselves voluntarily went to reinforce Free Russia, sparing neither strength nor life, because they realized the danger that threatens our young Freedom and the entire Revolution and knew that the Prov.[isional] Coalition Government would never forget their families or leave them unprovided for. And here, comrades! We have all heard that our brothers— the wonder-bogatyrs![1]—of the 7th Revolutionary Armies, our valorous "18th of June" regiments, were the first to wake and rise up from their long sleep and move forward, and, with their patriotic chests, to break through all the German redoubts. And they are calling to us for help!

Comrade Brothers! How can we fail to support our Comrade Patriots, the first revolutionary defenders, who showed the German that the Russian Revolutionary Army is strong, that it has a might of iron and civic discipline of steel, and that the Russian troops have all united everywhere, closed ranks, and are very, very tightly coordinated. But they want to disrupt this organization and unification we have and provoke disorganization in the Army. And just who are these people? Well we say that these are certain Bolshevik Anarchists from the Petro.[grad] garr.[ison] who are now traveling up and down the front with the following slogans: "Down with the war," "Down with the offensive." And they are running to the ignorant mass of soldiers with these false words: "You should trust and believe only us and, generally, all the Bolsheviks and their parties—we alone will save you, we will lead you out onto the true path without bloodshed or carnage!" And instead of leading us out onto the path of salvation, they send us into Anarchy; they want us to become Anarchists, like those who were at the Durnovo dacha.[2] But no, Comrades! We are not Anarchists or monarchists, not Nicholas II or Grishka Rasputin, and not Alisy-Kulisy.[3] We are position soldiers, trench rats! We do not recognize Bolshevik Anarchists or their henchmen, but we have always and only trusted the socialist minister Kerensky and the Soviet of W.[orkers'], Sold.[iers'], and Peas.[ants'] Deputies, and also the Central organ and Coalition Provisional Government. Comrades! I'll cite a few examples, since I myself have heard personally from German deserters, who we sometimes have a lot of, nearly every day they desert straight to us in the trenches. When we ask, Why do you go voluntarily? they answer, "To save our skin." When we ask, Might there be peace tomorrow? they state categorically that there will not be peace until Russian soldiers take Berlin or Wilhelm ascends to the throne in Petrograd. Comrades! Did we overthrow our tsarism and Nicholas II just to be German farmhands or to bow at the feet of bloody Wilhelm? No, Comrades! What he wants must not happen. We won't let him be lord and master over Free Citizens. We, your Comrades, will make the utmost effort and will inflict a blow, such a blow that the entire German land will shudder, we will go forth, and with our mighty chests clear ourselves a road through all the barricaded places. And the enemy, seeing such a terrible, all-out defeat looming over him, will extend his hand to us and say, "Peace without annexations or indemnities," and "An honorable Peace based on the self-determination of nations," and will tell our allies, especially France, that he is surrendering Alsace and Lorraine to France.

We fervently ask the socialist Ministers and the Soviet of W., Sold, and Peas. Deputies to keep provocational agitators, such as the Anarchist Bolsheviks of the Petrograd garr., away from the front. Just a few days ago we had a meeting here at the N. Infantry Regiment where representatives of the Petrograd garrison were present. When they were asked, Who are you? they replied, "We are Bolsheviks from the Petrograd garrison," but in fact we don't know who they are. Bolsheviks or Mensheviks, Social Democrats or Socialist Revolutionaries, or Kadets. But from what they said it became clear that instead of inspiring the position soldiers, they were sending them in the opposite direction. Here is their slogan: "Down with the Provisional Government!" "Down with the war." From all that was said by the Petrograd garr. representatives it became clear that they were agitating in favor of the Anarchists. But no, Comrade Brothers! We are neither Anarchists nor Monarchists. At the first call of our Socialist Minister A. F. Kerensky we will go wherever he orders us. Yes, and at the present time, Minister A. F. Kerensky himself is our second for the fighting on the southern front.

Long live the first, inspired, Revolutionary Armies of the South. Front!
Long live Liberty, Equality, and Fraternity!
Long live our Leader A. F. Kerensky!

> Trench soldiers
> Detachment of infantry scouts
> Inf.[antry] Regiment Number [not given]
> Act[ive] Army
> 27 June

1. Bogatyrs were heroes of the *bylini*, traditional heroic epic poems. The bogatyrs were known, above all, for their great might and heroic achievements (*podvigi*) as warriors.

2. Durnovo dacha—a secluded villa of a former government minister in St. Petersburg. Anarchists had seized the villa and turned it into their headquarters until they were arrested in early summer.

3. A contemptuous popular nickname for the tsaritsa, Alexandra, who was known as Alice by her English grandmother, Queen Victoria. *Kulisy* is a word referring literally to the wings or backstage of a theater, and thus, by analogy, to things theatrical and going on in secret.

Peasants

· 38 ·

Letter to *Izvestiia* from the peasant Nikolai Burakov, Perm Province, 30 March 1917.

Please let this be in your newspaper. The peasant in the village waits impatiently.
30 March

Glory be to you, Lord. We have lived to see the Great Joy. We have lived to see complete Freedom and the word of freedom, for which in the old days the land captain in the volost [township] and village assemblies[1] would truly fine us five rubles apiece and even put us under arrest. Now we are free citizens, and we speak freely and we can express all our thoughts freely, and we can defend our interests for the good of the homeland and the entire people. We express our deep and great gratitude and sincere greetings to our new Government and the freedom fighters. But I, a free peasant of the village, cannot hold in my heart one other torment and heavy oppression of the village: the gloatingly unjust and idiotic reprisals of the forest guard, who has been drinking the peasant's blood for many long years. Now we see and hear that there is freedom everywhere and the new government writes to us that now there is nothing owned by the state in Russia, that everything is publicly owned by the entire people.[2] But we also have the heavy oppression of the village by the old regime from the old government. Nothing has changed at all. Brutal force is still used, just as always. The forest guard continues to fleece and claw us. They would sell the forest, impose a fine on the innocent peasant, and make the buyer the witness. They are trusted, not we; we can never find justification for ourselves. And then we peasants are renting land from the state. Everyone already knows what the price for plots is nowadays. So once again we don't have the right to let a horse or a cow take a step onto a plot without a ticket, but these snakes of the night have stopped giving tickets at all, even if it's for all the livestock. And even if you've come to the fields to cultivate a plot of land, don't you dare unharness your horse from the cart to graze even for a few minutes. If the forest guard caught you, he'd give you a fine as big as he liked. And that blood-sucker is believed. And when you leave the field, don't you dare cut any grass to take home for the horse. If you come across a forest guard and have even a pood [thirty-six pounds] of grass he'll punish you then and there any way he pleases. He'll pull out a revolver and take the horse by the rein and start either hacking at the wheel or at the spokes, if he doesn't break your scythe on the wheel, tipping the cart over to dump the grass out in the middle of the road, and slap you with a fine as big as he wants. And he is believed. You don't even have the right to stop at a plot for berries or for white mushrooms or to pass through for hunting—there's a fine for everything. To this very day, all these forest guards remain in their jobs, and not only have they not been disarmed, but no change of any kind has been made. Everything is still done the same old way, going from gar-den to garden, making general searches, but not wanting to stand sentry in the field. He has a pretty nice life for himself in the village. But the peasant is an ignorant person and keeps his opinions to himself, and even though he opposes all this, he puts up with this cruelty to the end. But he still longs for freedom, if only for his horse and cow. The old government called on us to do our best to hold on to our young livestock and to raise as much livestock as we could. Meanwhile, though, you are not allowed to take one step into an open area with a cow or a horse. I think that this has been completely forgotten in these hard times. Or they haven't gotten around to it yet. But I think that our liberators who gave us freedom in everything ought to do something about this. They should liberate us from this, too, and take whatever measures they have to against the old regime. We wait impatiently for this other freedom.

Kamyshlovsk Uezd, [Perm Province,] Tamykulsk Volost.
Nagibina village
Citizen Nikolai Burakov

1. The village assembly (*skhod*) was the gathering of the heads of households that governed the village community or commune. The volost (usually translated as "town-ship" or "parish") was an administrative and judicial combination uniting several vil-lages. Land captains (*zemskie nachalniki*), also translated as "land commandants," were appointed state officials who, from 1889 to 1917, exercised broad discretionary power in managing peasant administration and justice, including confirming peasant officials and decisions of village and volost assemblies and courts. This office was abol-ished after the February revolution of 1917.
2. The Provisional Government expropriated crown lands after the fall of Nicholas II and began work on land reform, but did not declare that "everything is publicly owned by the entire people," a principle much closer to the agrarian program of social-ists.

· 39 ·

Appeal to the Orel Uezd Land Commission,[1] Orel Province,
from peasant farmer Nikolai Savinykh, 6 April 1917.

To the Orel Uezd Land Commission
From a peasant from Orel Uezd,
Posadskaia Volost and village
Nikolai Aleksandrov[ich] Savinykh

Petition

I most humbly request the Orel Uezd Land Commission to inform me at
its first opportunity as to what I'm supposed to do with my piece of land
[otruba]. The time has come for me to clear and dig up stumps, but I don't
know what to do. There are people here who are spreading rumors that
with the restoration of people's rights the whole procedure for land regulation is going to collapse and our notorious Commune,[2] which is good
only for idlers and parasites who see nothing beyond their nose, will again
be in full force. Does Russia, which has thrown off the yoke of autocracy,
really have to go backward when the slogan of cultured European nations
is "Forward"? Who would call the blind man mincing backward free?
No, better the deadman's noose, better death, than a single step back. The
commune—what is that? Here I have a strip of land for one soul, which at
best is three arshins wide,[3] but two of them, thanks to my efforts at plow-
ing deep and all around, yield nothing but loss, which means that two-
thirds of my land goes for naught, so even with the most favorable harvest
I myself receive two, at most two and a half. So, here is the whole solution
to the mystery of our Orel Uezd, which is perishing from hunger and is fed
only by imported grain. The whole point is not too little land but the commune. The commune's supporters are unwittingly putting around Russia's
neck the most terrifying noose of Autocracy. Almost all the peasants are
aware of this, only not all are free of their centuries-old stagnation, which
grips the ignorant peasantry like iron pincers, but it's pointless to go on
about this subject because you, gentlemen, members of the Land Regulation Commission, know this much better than I. Only I most humbly request that you support the truly free Russia and not the blind man mincing backward. May the slogan of free Russia be "Forward!" Down with
the centuries of ignorance! What other than the commune is slowing the
progress of our peasant farmer? Under communal practice, were he even a
genius and worked twenty hours a day, he still could never work his way
out of poverty such as ours! Take the noose called the commune off our
neck, and in five years you positively won't recognize our peasant, so far
will he have progressed. True, we do have some who are dissatisfied with
the new order; except these aren't peasants but people who feed them-

selves off side earnings, for example, trade and so on, and also some utter ignoramuses who are not worth paying any attention to. I most humbly beg the Orel Uezd Land Regulation Commission to forgive me for writing too much and not sticking to the point, but what can you do? The soul yearns to express itself. We put so much work in last year, and suddenly it all comes crashing down. No, God forbid. It's a bad joke.

In the name of almost our entire village, we most humbly request that you inform us what is valid: our plots of land or, again, the despised commune, and inform us immediately, because the land requires cultivation from us that does not allow for delay.

> Peasant from the village of Posadskaia,
> Nikolai Aleksandrov Savinykh

6 April 1917

1. In promoting land reform, the Provisional Government established a Central Land Committee to collect relevant data and help plan the coming land reform. A network of local committees was formed at the level of the province (*guberniia*), county (*uezd*), and canton or township (*volost*).

2. The peasant commune, *obshchina* or *mir*, was a long-standing institution of peasant self-administration.

3. One arshin equals twenty-eight inches.

· 40 ·

Letter to the Petrograd Soviet from the peasants of Rakalovsk Volost, Viatka Province, 26 April 1917.

We, the undersigned peasants, citizens of Viatka Prov., Slobodsk Uezd, Rakalovsk Volost, having gathered on 26 April 1917 in a volost assembly, have deliberated, and have decided to send the following to the Soviet of Soldiers' and Workers' Deputies, with a copy to the Provisional Government:

Our 1st thought and decision is the following: for us to not have a tsar, because we have now found out that they were always enemies of the people, and the last tsar also carried on a friendship with the Germans, was surrounded by them, and so we request that the Soviet of Soldiers' and Workers' Deputies write in its newspapers and conduct propaganda in favor of a democratic republic with a president at its head.

Our 2nd thought is the land; the land must be transferred to those who labor on it. Cabinet, appanage, monastery, church, and major estate owners' lands must be surrendered to the people without compensation, for they were earned not by labor but by various amorous escapades, not to mention through sly and devious behavior around the tsar. As for land from small estate owners, this should be recognized by our Constituent Assembly, elected on the basis of universal, direct, equal, and secret vote, [the land taken] with compensation, redeemed out of state income collected from a progressive income tax. All the laws must be written by persons who were chosen by the people, since they are promulgated for the people.

Our 3rd thought is about liberty [*volia*]. We are sick and tired of living in debt and slavery. We want space and light. We need for our young people to be taught in higher schools—this is necessary, but it must be at the state's expense, because we don't have money of our own: the tsars have collected so much from us, and they hired guards using our money, and they lashed us with whips for every word of truth, and for reading books in which the truth was written, they put us in prison. And thus we demand freedom of speech, the press, assembly, unions, and strikes, and the inviolability of the person; under this kind of freedom we ourselves will write how hard it is for the muzhik plowman to live and how to improve our bitter lot.

Our 4th thought is a terrible one—about the war. We are sick and tired of it, we pity our brothers, fathers, and sons, and we regret their blood, but we need to beat the German because he wants to encroach on our freedom. We will die rather than give him our freedom, for it is so very precious to us, and if the German repudiates his conquests and indemnities, and if the allies agree to it, too, then we should begin peace negotiations with him, and we ought to make the peace be so that there are no more wars in the world, since the only profit from them goes to the rich, the kulaks,[1] and the bourgeois; working people know only indescribable harm from war. The socialists are trying to win equality and brotherhood on earth, and that's why they are our comrades. We stand for replacing the standing army with a people's militia.

Next, we have read in the newspapers that they want to deport Nicholas II to England and set pensions for the high dignitaries, the old enemies of the people, and therefore we ask that the Soviet of Soldiers' and Workers' Deputies under no circumstances allow the former tsar to be deported to England. Our people are still ignorant, but the capital the tsar has is great, and they could put out big money for bribes, which could begin to shake our young freedom, maybe even provoke a counterrevolution. Do not allocate any pensions to former high dignitaries at all.

We have also decided that we will give our vote for the Constituent Assembly to whoever defends the needs laid out above, and we will publish this in the newspapers for other, fellow peasants to read, think about, and to stand up for these same interests, because they are the same for us all. Although we are now citizens of equal standing, we consider the title "peasant" a mark of honor; peasant means grain producer and breadwinner—with his grain he feeds all of Mother Rus, and in a free state we remain a "free citizen-peasant."

The dual power that the bourgeoisie and their newspapers keep talking about is not what we see in you, dear comrades. On the contrary, we see true defenders of the working people. Be bold and courageous, defend the interests of the working people to the end; may we labor together successfully; do not fracture apart, but merge into a single whole.

Sincerely yours,

> Citizen-peasants
> 130 illiterate men
> Chairman of the Rakalovsk Committee, Ognev
> Secretary, Ponomaryov

1. Literally, "fist"—a wealthy peasant who was seen as exploiting others.

· 41 ·

Letter to the Petrograd Soviet from "a peasant," 27 April 1917.

Protest

Kind Sirs,

Citizens, Soviet of Workers' and Soldiers' Deputies, I apologize for troubling you to listen to a few words from me, a peasant. We have been following the newspapers about the misunderstandings you have had in Petrograd, and we are shaken to the depth of our souls by your actions and your poorly thought-out outburst and action against the Provisional Government.[1] How did you ever find the nerve to take up arms against unarmed citizens and soldiers, and how did you have the conscience to fire at soldiers? You killed three [*sic*] or five men, soldiers without whom you could not have gotten your freedom. You workers have covered yourselves in shame by spilling the blood of the soldier-citizen, and the black mark of innocent blood will remain on you, indeed you are like that ungrateful pig that, foraging under a venerable oak, stuffed its belly full to bursting and is now with its snout digging up the very oak that made it full and happy.[2] I also ask you, What right do you have to speak and demand anything from the government elected from the people and with the trust of the people and invested with all the fullness of Power? From our ministers to whom we have entrusted our destinies, life, and property, who took an oath and pledge of allegiance to the Republic and promised to lead it to the Constituent Assembly? And when the people express their will, they alone will have the honor and glory we have invested in them. What right do you have to speak and demand anything from them without asking the entire people, especially all the peasant millions? You are only a handful of members of the Soviet of Workers' and Soldiers' Deputies, you are only eighty men there altogether,[3] but there are 3,000,000 (three million) workers in all of Russia together. Isn't this the voice of the Whole people? You have no right to demand peace without annexations and indemnities, but you should wait to listen to what the whole people will say when the Constituent Assembly starts. First of all, we have to vanquish the enemy, to kill the lion, to skin him, and then to beat the unbeatable lion. But you offer peace terms, which just shows you're weak and cowardly. You're all cowards. For how many millions did you betray your fatherland? Your duty is only to make sure that the Government properly fulfills its duties, that it fulfills its promises of freedom. There's no doubt that if they fail, if the old Government wins, then it won't be those ministers who will be the first to swing from the Gallows with their legs kicking. You haven't appreciated these labors either, that people sacrificed their lives, risked life and property for the good and salvation of the Homeland. You ought to be ashamed of yourselves. Didn't your conscience and Mind and the Will of Your soul and good sense suggest anything to you, traitors to your Homeland? I'll tell you another thing—I was in church on 23 April 1917 and I saw two daughters, twins, born from one mother, who had died simultaneously, and I stared closely at them, at the miracle of nature and at the prophecy for our fatherland, which has two powers at the helm.[4] The thought flashed through my mind: These are the sign of the Time, and though one little girl was a little bigger and fuller than the other and more sturdily built, their little faces looked alike. And I thought that it's also happened here in our fatherland, we have our two powers, and it falls to them to lead the country to a Constituent Assembly and it also falls to them to die, like these two little girls, this marvel, this miracle of nature, a portent and a prophecy. Verily, I say to you, I am indeed a witness. So I call God's blessing down upon you, and may the Lord God come to your aid. In unity lies our pledge of happiness and prosperity; unity is the power and will of the entire Russian people, the happiness and prosperity and ripening of all earthly fruits. You should follow the example of Minin and Prince Pozharsky:[5] when our fatherland was in danger, they sent a call to the people and thus saved their Fatherland Moscow and all Holy Rus, so if you dare express a protest against the Government, we will not give you our confidence or any money. And what will you do then without money? Your Red Oranges[6] won't get you anywhere without money. That idler Napoleon was a Genius, and he said that for war you need money and more money. You can't have victory without it. The two little girls again: one fuller and sturdier—this is the ministers elected by the people and invested with their trust—the second a little weaker—this is your power—less than the first's; so don't you go getting all high and mighty. God opposes the proud and gives the meek grace. Amen. May the Lord's blessing, peace, and unity be upon you. In unity is strength and the pledge of our future happiness and prosperity.

I remain sincerely yours,

A peasant
27 April 1917

[Note added by hand in the margin] Please read this and pass it on to Rodzianko.

1. A reference to the April Days, the mass demonstrations in the streets of Petrograd triggered by reports that the Foreign Minister Miliukov had sent a note to the Western Allies assuring them that Russia was committed to the war policies of the old government.
2. A reference to Ivan Krylov's fable, "The Pig Under the Oak."
3. The number is approximately that of the members of the Executive Committee of the Petrograd Soviet. The Soviet itself had more than a thousand deputies.
4. The complex political relationship between the Provisional Government, which held state power, and the Petrograd Soviet, which commanded enormous influence and authority as the representative organ of the lower classes, was a situation often called "dual power" (*dvoevlastie*).
5. Kuzma Minin, a butcher by trade, and Dmitry Pozharsky, a prince, united to lead a national army of resistance to Polish and Swedish invaders during the Time of Troubles in the early seventeenth century. They were symbols of national and spiritual revival and solidarity across social barriers.
6. *Apel'sinye Krasnye.* The meaning of this expression is obscure. It may be a reference to the Red Gift campaign, in which many workers donated all of their earnings from 16 April (the Sunday preceding International Workers' Day, 18 April, or 1 May in Western Europe and elsewhere), which was designated as a special workday to purchase gifts for soldiers—cigarettes, candy, shaving supplies, and reading materials. Another possible reference is to the recently announced "Liberty Loan." Finally, it might be an allusion to the anarchist slang for bombs—"oranges." Red Oranges would thus be socialist bombs, though in the context of 1917 and in reference to the Petrograd Soviet the allusion is unclear.

· 42 ·

Resolution of an assembly of heads of households from seventy-five villages, Istra Volost, Liutsinsk Uezd, Vitebsk Province, early May 1917 (received by Soviet Central Executive Committee, 6 May).

———————

Citizens of Russia, village heads of households [*sel'skie khoziaeva*], residents of seventy-five villages, gathered at an assembly [*skhod*] and resolved: 1) To express gratitude to our freedom fighters, to the revolutionary people, and to the provisional executive committee of the State Duma, who saved Russia from traitors and plunderers of the national wealth, who overthrew the autocratic order, the old authority. 2) To immediately remove from the ranks of the Istra Volost administration all lackeys of the old regime. 3) To dismiss for good the old volost administration: the volost head [*starshina*], the scribe, the elders, the judges, and the peasant police, who have hung on up until now, picking us clean—one should remember that no matter how well you feed an old wolf, he'll still be drawn to the forest. 4) To rename the old Istra Volost administration the Istra public [*obshchestvennoe*] administration. 5) To elect immediately a provisional executive committee from the heads of households of the seventy-five villages, no matter what their confession, literate, honest, and sensible people, at least sixteen men. 6) To elect one commissar[1] and two policemen in every village to carry out security and to maintain order in the region of the seventy-five villages. 7) To elect from the number of members of the provisional executive committee a commission on the manufacture of lumber materials made up of at least four men chosen on the basis of universal, equal, direct, and secret voting, in order to provide rural citizen-proprietors with firewood and building materials. This commission must gather information from all seventy-five villages about how much firewood and building material are needed in the course of the year, according to the tariff worked out by the general meeting; in accordance with the resolution of the general assembly, to demand that local landowners release the required amount of firewood and building material from the forest tracts close to each village. The duties of this commission shall include making sure that the landowners cannot sell any forest land to private persons without first informing the provisional executive committee. 8) To elect an agricultural commission of at least four men from among the members of the provisional executive committee, in order to stockpile and order agricultural equipment: plows, harrows, threshers, harvesters, mowers, grain cleaners, ready-made horseshoes, nails, iron, scythes, and so forth; as well as seed, grain, and feed directly from wholesale warehouses. 9) To elect a commission for the honest distribution and issuance of money from the treasury ration set aside for families of those drafted into the army. 10) To elect an inspection committee. 11) To elect a chairman of the Provisional Executive Committee of the Istra public administration—a citizen with a strong and revolutionary personality who is not sympathetic to landowners' interests; he should be a fervent fighter and defender of the rights of liberty, equality, and fraternity. 12) To send this resolution of ours for their information to the commissars for Liutsinsk Uezd and Vitebsk Province.

---

1. Commissar, from the French commissaire, was a term already in use before 1917 to describe an individual invested with governmental powers for a particular purpose. Used increasingly in 1917.

· 43 ·

Letter to *Izvestiia* from a peasant and former soldier, Andrei Sunin,
Novgorod Province, early May 1917 (received 16 May).

Private of the Volynsky Life Guards Regiment[1] Andrei Kuzmich Sunin
who participated in the revolution, on 27 and 28 February, in Petrograd.
Three times wounded, and after 16 March given three months' sick leave
from the regiment to recuperate. Getting home, I see around me in the village a sleep from which there is no waking and horrible ignorance. They
are still living in the past and moaning about how we can go on living without a tsar. No matter how many words you try to convince them with, they
keep singing the same old tune. There is no kind of organization, and they
are not going to do anything about it. They can't decide even to send their
representatives to so much as the volost governing committee. They keep
putting their hopes on one thing: that because we're illiterate, that's why
we don't know what to do or how to act. Likewise in the village, there is no
order. It's a very sad way of life in the countryside. No help, no one wants
to do anything for anyone else. But they keep hoping for something. Are
they praying, waiting for a miracle from heaven? In the uezd center here in
Belozersk there is something incredible going on. In the town office, and
the zemstvo office, the same people are still governing who once sucked
our bloody sweat. I'd like to replace one skinflint, that bloodskinner
[*krovoder*], so he won't be in an official position. He serves in the town office. He's also the chief physician in Belozersk. He lost all his honor on
bribes and such, and now you can't hold a single commission for evacuated
soldiers without him. Several volosts have already written resolutions to
bar him, but nothing helps and they don't know how to proceed. This man
is Petrov. There was also one good man. A member of the S.R. party twelve
years ago, L. Sergeevich Kholopov. He immediately took upon himself the
post of Belozersk Commissar. I'm sorry that for some reason he's going
away now. But the thing is, we never seem to get anywhere. The village
doesn't get any instructions and we don't know where or how to begin.

So I am addressing the S.R. and S.D. [parties] in my peasant way, simply, for I know no other. I most humbly request you give this your attention.

Send some newspapers and appeals to our cooperative, the Solmas
Union of Consumer Societies, which includes several villages. So we'll
have something, even a little bit, to use for convincing the ignorant
masses.

Or else my heart will break and it doesn't know what to do or how.

My address: Novgorod Province, Belozersk, Solmas Station,

A. Kuz. Sunin

I left my regiment in Petrograd on 29 March. I served in the Volynsky Life Guards Regiment in the Fourth Company. Evacuated wounded three times over the whole campaign during 2 and 1/2 years. I will send you my last per diems, but for God's sake send us explanations for everything—that is, how to organize volost and rural committees, etc.

I am very eager.

1. The life guards regiments were elite, privileged military units in the Russian army, created to reward high achievement and to inspire regular detachments. During the February revolution many guards' regiments joined the opposition to the tsarist government.

· 44 ·

Letter to *Izvestiia* from a peasant and former soldier, Nikifor Tatianenko, Poltava Province, 12 May 1917.

———————

Letter to the editor!

Comrade soldiers and workers,

I categorically declare that in our the village of Belogorenka in Poltava Prov., Lofitsk Uezd, Luksk Volost, we do not have any provocateurs.¹ The people here are ignorant and not united. Half the population of the village sticks to the old order—things with them are still done strictly according to the old way. There is a committee, but they elected its members from those people who do not care about the people but only about their own pocket: the priest and the volost elder who even before used to say that we would live better when the German conquered us. Measures need to be taken with them now.

Comrade soldiers, I beg you to send provocateurs here because I can't deal with this alone and I don't know what's going on there in Petrograd because the newspapers do not reach here from Petrograd.

Send a newspaper here from your offices free of charge, unite the ignorant people. If you don't have an account for sending it out for free, then we will take up a collection for *Zemlia i volia*.

The peasants gather for meetings, but they don't decide anything or resolve any problems, because they don't know and no one has explained to them what a democratic republic or a nation means, what annexations and indemnities are, and so forth, and even if someone started to explain it, they still wouldn't understand. Comrade soldiers and workers, send a newspaper here so that we could at least take issues from the newspapers and tell people what's going on in Petrograd.

Comrade soldiers and workers, do not forsake my request, send newspapers. From here I will inform you in writing what is going on in the provinces.

Address: Lofitsk Uezd, Poltava Prov., Luksk Volost, to the village Belogorenka

Nikifor Danilovich Tatianenko

1. The author has evidently confused the meaning of this term with other relatively new and unfamiliar words in the public political discourse of the day—all difficult to decipher, given that their origins were not Slavic. Properly used, "provocateur" was a strongly negative term for secret agents of the police who worked to undermine and destroy revolutionary organizations by encouraging actions that would result in failure and arrests. The author may have had in mind the term *propagandisty* (propagandists).

· 45 ·

Appeal to the peasants from a Committee of Soldiers' Deputies,
printed in the Menshevik newspaper *Rabochaia gazeta*, 12 May 1917.

Comrade peasants, our fathers and brothers!

Our freedom, our liberty, is in danger. Rumors have reached us that say certain wild, dangerous people are going from one remote village in our vast and long-suffering Homeland to another and burning the landowners' hay, burning the grain, killing the livestock, demolishing structures. And seeing them, our ignorant, uninformed peasants are joining the robbers to menace and plunder landowners' estates.

We, your sons and brothers who wear the soldier's gray overcoat, call upon you from our trenches: Stop! What are you doing? Do you want to leave our army without bread, meat, or fodder? Do you want the Germans to capture us with their bare hands right here as we starve? Do you want to wreck our Homeland and your own freedom? Do you want us to have Tsar Nicholas back with the old ways, the birch rods, the gallows, the penal detachments, the guards, the Ingush?[1] Instead of land and liberty, do you want poverty and misery worse even than before? If not, then don't lay a hand on anyone else's property, and maintain order. Wait calmly and patiently for the New Government to establish new laws in the state. Even this summer the Constituent Assembly, the new Duma, is going to be gathering in Petrograd. Select your most reliable people to go there, people who will stand up for you, and then this Constituent Assembly will look into all your complaints and satisfy all your needs.

And so sell your grain to the New Government, help it establish order in the rear. Then we will quickly drive our stubborn enemy out of our native land and return to you more quickly for a new and free happy life.

Committee of Soldiers' Deputies
540th Sukhinichsky Infantry Regiment

1. People from Ingushetia in the Caucasus. Soldiers from the Caucasus were sometimes formed into special regiments, especially the famous "Wild Divisions." Many Russians feared and despised such soldiers because of their reputation, in combination with ethnic prejudice against them.

· 46 ·

Resolution to the Soviet and the Provisional Government from peasant citizens in the villages of Osnichkovo and Andreevo, Petrograd Province, 11 May 1917.

Resolution [*Prigovor*][1]
11 May 1917

To the Soviet of Peasants', Workers', and Soldiers' Deputies and the Provisional Government.

We, the undersigned citizens of the villages of Osnichkovo and Andreevo, having attended a general meeting on this date, discussed the question of State Order and the Land, and also all the needs of society, and unanimously resolved:

1. The state must be based on a Democratic Republic under federatively autonomous governance.

2. The entire administration must be elected by direct and universal, equal and secret vote.

3. Freedom must be without any and all restrictions.

4. Election of judges.

5. Schooling must be at the expense of the State. Parents will subsidize the first three years of study, but the rest of the time spent in study must be at the expense of the State—that is, full room and board, since we teach our children not only for ourselves but for the good of our entire state.

6. The land in its entirety must belong to whoever cultivates it, since the land was taken away from us by forcible authority and so the land should transfer into the hands of the working people. We the citizens of the villages of Osnichkovo and Andreevo, not having a sufficient amount of land, have, between 1861[2] and 1917, been buying haymakings, that is, grass for mowing, from landowners and kulaks annually, and considering the kulaks or landowners to be benefactors because they leave us the discards from their properties, which for their own use wouldn't pay for itself—that is, does not justify hired labor, and we pay for such throwaways whatever prices our benefactors feel like setting. [We pay] for tiny amounts of cuttings in scattered locations, such that in these fifty-six years we have already paid many times over whatever the land is worth, but the land still remains someone else's, and if we live on the single strip of a five-desiatina- [thirteen-acre][3] per-capita allotment and you reap from twenty-five to forty-five poods [nine hundred to sixteen hundred pounds][4] of hay

per allotment, then you can't feed a couple of sheep, to say nothing of a horse or a cow. But since our location is northern, arability, that is arable land, requires in addition to cultivation also fertilizer for the soil, so you can't live without livestock; moreover, of this small amount of allotment land, a third is unusable—that is, not just for haymaking but even for grazing livestock. The earth was Created by God for everyone in equal measure, and people should be its equal owners, except for the bowels of the earth, where there are deposits of ore and mineral wealth—this should belong to the State and not to usurpers and kulaks, so that all mineral wealth goes to the State and not to rich private speculators.

7. The war against Germany must be fought to a victorious conclusion. There can be no talk of peace until there is not even one armed German soldier standing on the land of free Russia. We citizens will devote all our efforts and will go as one man to defend free Russia and will sacrifice everything in return for protection against the enemy of our fatherland, which is why we are asking the Provisional Government and the Soviet of Workers' and Soldiers' Peasants' Deputies to consider us a reliable buttress and support both in manpower and in material assistance.

Hereby sign Citizens, men and women both, who have reached the age of twenty years, of Petrograd Prov., Novo Ladozhsk Uezd, village of Osnichkovo,

> [forty-nine signatures—seventeen men and thirty-two women—
> most signed by a common hand]

Owing to illiteracy and on their personal request, we sign both for them and for ourselves,

> [seven signatures: three women and four men]
> Village of Andreevo

1. The assemblies of peasant communes used *prigovor* to designate a formal resolution. The word implies a legal decision and was also used by the courts.
2. The year that serfdom was abolished in Russia.
3. A desiatina equals 2.7 acres.
4. One pood is about thirty-six pounds.

· 47 ·

Letter to *Izvestiia* from a village in Ukraine, 21 May 1917.

———————

21 May 1917

Greetings

Dear Comrade Il. Konstantinovich—I am sending you my comradely respects, and then I am informing you of the fact that I received your letter, for which I thank you. You inform me in writing concerning the Romashkovskin peasants. When you were in our village, you suggested to the peasants that they subscribe to the newspapers for the enlightenment of life and they promised to collect money for a newspaper. When you went home, they forgot. You instructed the peasants that they need culture, but the peasants go on living like cranks, the way they always have. Over and over I have suggested to the muzhiks[1] that they subscribe to the newspaper. But I myself subscribed to a little newspaper *Izvestiia Soveta Rabochikh i Soldatskikh Deputatov* [News of the Soviet of Workers' and Soldiers' Deputies], I get it three times a week, but I don't have enough money to subscribe any more. Our news is bad: they have set up Committees in the village. The richest men joined the committees, so there are lots of misunderstandings. We don't have any grain, so the poor muzhiks ask the committee to organize redistribution of grain from the rich muzhiks. There's nowhere to buy it for money here. Everyone who had extra grain hid it, and they do not sell it to the poor and upset matters worse. Dear comrade I. K., I beg you to submit a petition in my name if you can. I submitted one but haven't received an answer yet. Or you could look into the fact that our priest belongs to the Black Hundreds and isn't obeying the New Government. Everywhere in our Ukraine they are saying prayers for the new Government and requiems for the old, but he refuses to pray for freedom and says that we ourselves should hold services for our New Government. He supports the old regime in his liturgies prays for the old bloodsucker Nicholas II when people are present. A priest was arrested for this in Pigoravka. Be so kind—you must know better who to inform about this. For we are an ignorant people, as you well know.

1. The author of this letter alternates between two words for peasant—*krest'ianin* and *muzhik*. The latter term is more colloquial and more complexly textured in meaning. Among peasants themselves it was a slightly intimate term, but it also could hint at personal and cultural ignorance and crudeness, and thus be a term of contempt.

· 48 ·

Protocol of a meeting of the Sadki village committee, 8 June 1917.

Protocol

On 8 June 1917, we, the undersigned citizens of the Sadki Village Public Executive Committee,[1] in the presence of the chairman Ivan Guzenkov and members of the Committee Ivan Goncharov, Onisim Riabov, and Stepan Kotov, at a general meeting, decided to pass the present Protocol as follows. Through the Sadki Committee we will express the needs of the entire people—that is, what we need, what kind of need we have, that the people demand for themselves a better share so that along with freedom they can also get all the land transferred to the working people without any compensation, in order that the slogan "Land and Liberty" may become truly the people's. For the very first time it fell to the lot of the Russian peasantry to have the honor to proclaim a great slogan: "Land and Liberty," i.e., all the land and all the liberty to the working people, the land belongs to the entire working people, which cultivates it with its own labor and sweat. But the land belongs to the peasant commune [*mir*], to the working community. This land cannot be sold, cannot be an object of buying and selling. The peasant knows that the land is the main foundation of his life, that he cannot exist without the land, for the land feeds every peasant and there is no tender word the peasant would not apply to the land: dear mother, beloved benefactor, our native land gives us food and drink, shoes and clothing. It is because our peasantry is accustomed to regarding the Land as the commune's Land that the call for "Land and Liberty" arose among us, proclaiming that the land should belong to all the working people. This came from the very source: the basis of peasant life is land and labor. Without labor the peasant cannot exist, or without land either. From these two principles of land and labor come the foundation of his life, without this he cannot be. This is why in the Russian native consciousness the only reason land has any value is because labor has been invested in it. Because if land is considered a possession, then it is only because he labors on it and so comes to consider it his property. As an object created not by the hands of man, land in the people's view is like air, like the sun, it cannot belong to anyone. It is an object for all mankind—and so we have unanimously passed the present protocol at the general meeting of the Sadki Executive Committee [expressing] our essential needs of the whole people. Hereby sign

> Literate: Ivan Goncharov, Ivan Skibin, Ivan
> Grebenikov, Stepan Kotov, Anisim [*sic*] Riabov
> For the committee: Ivan Kovtunov, Ivan Tkachev
> Chairman, Ivan Guzenkov

1. No province is indicated. Sadki is a name shared by many villages in Russia.

· 49 ·

Resolution from "citizen-tillers of the soil," Kursk Province, 29 June 1917.

We citizen-tillers of the soil of Kursk Province, Korochansk Uezd, Podoleshansk Volost, vill.[age of] Provorot, gathered in a general assembly of seventy-eight households on 29 June 1917 and discussed issues concerning future arrangements in our dear homeland and about the land.

1) We recognize that the best form of rule in a state is a Democratic republic since only under that kind of order can the people develop.

2) Education must be universal and compulsory up to sixteen years and at state expense; for poor children dormitories should be set up where full board for the children is at state expense; in higher educational institutions everyone without exception must study who so wishes, but not according to the kind of rules that were published recently by Mr. Manuilov,[1] where the doors of higher educational institutions remain closed as before to certain people wishing to get in. That is unacceptable.

3) All the appanage, cabinet, monastery, landowner, and privately owned land must be transferred to the working peasantry without compensation, for we have been paying it for hundreds of years already and it has been more than paid for and washed in our sweat and blood, which means there can be no question of compensation. Prohibit the buying and selling and leasing of land forever; there must not be ownership over land, the land must be transferred for use only to whoever works it.

4) We express our complete trust in the Soviet of Soldiers', Workers', and Peasants' Deputies and the Provisional Government.

5) Here we resolved to take up a collection to benefit the families whose breadwinners fell in battle against Wilhelm's troops on 18 June of this year: for Freedom, Land, and Liberty. The money collected, forty-one rubles fourteen kopeks, we are dispatching, and we request that it be conveyed immediately as intended.

> Chairman, Yegor Zenin
> For the secretary, N. Boitsov
> [Stamp beside signatures:] Village elder, Provorot Commune,
> Podoleshansk Vol.[ost], Korochansk U.[ezd]

---

1. Aleksandr Appolonovich Manuilov (1861–1929) was an economist, educator, and liberal political leader. He was one of the founders of the Kadet party in 1905 and member of its Central Committee (1905–1917). Rector (President) of Moscow University (1908–1911), he became minister of education in the Provisional Government (March–July 1917).

· 50 ·

Letter to the Soviet from peasants of Lodeina village,
Vologda Province, 3 July 1917.

To the Soviet of Workers' and Soldiers' Deputies
3 July 1917
Peasants of Vologda Prov., Nikolsk Uezd,
Shetkinsk Volost, vill.[age of] Lodeina

Comrades, we appeal to you—help us. It has been four months since the rusty chains of vile tsarism were smashed and our tyrants and oppressors swept away. Construction is under way on Democratic principles. All around us people are organizing meetings, associations and assemblies, organizations, political unions, lectures—all this is essential at the present historical moment. This is what has bypassed our locale, our volost and village.

Comrades, we ask you to come help us and have pity on our village, bring enlightenment to our ignorant, downtrodden laborers. Although there is a tiny group of politically conscious people, still they are not strong enough to fight two hundred to one. We have no material either to use to convince the ignorant muzhiks and superstitious women and to give them explanations. We don't have newspapers or literature, or any chance at getting them. We subscribed to *Zemlia i volia* two months ago—but it hasn't come and they didn't send a reply. Instead of socialist newspapers, they are sending us *Russkoe slovo, Birzhevye vedomosti,* and *Pravitel'-stvennyi vestnik* [Government herald].[1] We are very unhappy about this. The population in almost the whole volost is under the influence of capitalism and the bourgeois.

Comrades, consider our request and send our population down the path of democracy and the path of equality and brotherhood and unity. Send us newspapers and literature.

Hereby sign the committee of the village of Lodeina (of said volost)

Chairman, P. Konev
Members, K. Konev, Vasily Rykov, F. Pankov
Secretary, T. Konev

1. See the glossary.

· 51 ·

"A Flame of Gold Ablaze," by the worker and soldier Pyotr Oreshin,[1]
printed in the Socialist Revolutionary newspaper *Delo naroda*, 14 May 1917.

A flame of gold ablaze
The nighttime sky lit bright.
Did we not for ages toil like slaves
Bent before the tsar's brute might?

No freedom to us was given
And land they would not yield
Like clockwork we were driven
To a shameful blackened field.[2]

Will no one in the village
Read this letter from my son?
It's from the war and simple
We are dark and so undone.

A flickering golden flame
Its wing of crimson bowing
Brothers, when will liberty reign,
Brothers, where now are we going?

My hut by light encircled,
Joy like wine intoxicating,
In the field, 'neath sun descended,
A spring afoot, pristine.

On my knees so thankful falling,
"Lord, glory be to Thee!"
Shimmering angels softly walking,
Round my darkened hut and me.

1. Pyotr Vasilievich Oreshin (1887–1938) was born in Saratov to a family of workers. He completed three years of primary school and then wandered around Russia for
years, engaging in various kinds of wage labor. He began publishing poems in newspapers in 1911. He served at the front during World War I. Politically, he described himself vaguely as a "neo-populist." After February 1917, his work appeared mainly in
publications associated with the Socialist Revolutionary Party. After October 1917, he
would be often categorized as a "peasant poet," because of his pastoral themes and
his "unproletarian" ideological point of view.

2. Literally, a "black pit of shame" (*chernaia iama pozora*), an allusion, in popular
language and folklore, to prison (especially debtors' prison) and hell, and hence a symbol of poverty, lack of rights, and moral degradation.

· 52 ·

"In the Fields," by Pyotr Oreshin, printed in *Delo naroda,* 28 May 1917.

In the Fields

Past ravines, the fields and steppes
Have filled the air with rosy haze . . .
The peasants marching close in step
Through villages free, their flags ablaze.

Land and liberty—words more fine
Than gold—our motto: Liberty, land . . .
The distant steppe now ripped by knife,
Blue raiment snatched by fire's hand.

Past forest dark a glow is blazing,
Like laughter come alarms of joy . . .
Ah, isn't that our sovereigns' palaces
On fire 'neath the northern sky?

Off with my caftan! . . . 'Cross fields I'm flying
On the wings of time, engulfed by flame . . .
Suddenly down roads they're running,
From every side they ran, they came.

—Down with the ruin of centuries,
The palaces of the tsar, who held the serf! . . .
The river of blood is racing nearer
In the ring of thawed but unplowed earth.

From up above hang fiery streaks,
The birds cast shadows on level fields . . .
Whose screams are in the bush, whose shrieks?
In the smoking bushes, whose voiceless shade?

I run behind a darkened hut,
A pink glow towering round. . . .
Shrill and pained, alarm bells sob,
In fields, tocsins weap and mourn.

Their anger hurled in chasms black
Is that not their bell, its brassy ring?
And is it not the Firebird that has now at last
Embraced vast Rus in her bloody wing?

1. Soldiers posing by tank after joining the revolution. Written on their vehicle: "FREEDOM! / 28 February / Armored Division / 1917."

2. Soldiers at the ceremonial funeral for the fallen in the revolution, Mars Field, Petrograd, 23 March 1917. Banners read: "Eternal Glorious Memory to the Fallen Comrade Fighters for Liberty," "Long Live the Democratic Republic," and "In Organization Is Strength."

3. Women demonstrating, Petrograd, March 1917. Their banner reads: "If the woman is a Slave, there will be no Freedom. Long live the Equality of Women."

4. May Day demonstrators, Palace Square, Petrograd, 18 April 1917 (post-card). Banners read: "Long Live the Democratic Republic," and "Long Live Socialism."

5. Demonstrating restaurant and café workers, Petrograd, spring 1917. Banners read: "Down with Tips," and "We stand for respect for waiters as human beings."

6. Soldiers, possibly deserters, spring 1917.

7. Soldiers participating in political demonstration, Petrograd, 18 June 1917 (postcard). Banner reads: "Long Live the World International."

8. A worker, a soldier, and a peasant—studio photograph taken in the first days after the October overthrow of the Provisional Government. The banner reads: "Workers, Soldiers of all Countries, demand immediate peace. Long live Soviet Power. The Kadets are enemies of the people and do not belong in the Const.[ituent] Assembly."

DOCUMENT 12. Appeal to the Petrograd "People's Committee" from Matvei Frolov, day worker on the Perm Railroad, 25 April 1917.

Солдатская Жизнь

Лежу на койки раненый
Какъ мнѣ вѣкъ прожить,
въ, О Какъ жизнь утратилъ,
И кровь свою пролилъ.
...ратилъ я всю силушку,
...а родину свою.
А, раны какъ зажмутъ,
апять въ окопъ пойду.
здесь жить нетъ моей моч..
Здесь вездѣ и всюду люди
Насолдата здесь клевещутъ!
Вотъ И живи какъ хочи.
Эхъ несчасныя солдаты,
Что про насъ говорятъ?
Посмотрѣлъ на генераловъ
Что они творятъ.
Филодрес Илья Ладановъ

DOCUMENT 83. Poem sent to *Izvestiia* by a wounded soldier, Ilya Ladanov, received 22 September 1917.

DOCUMENT 127. Letter to Lenin from five peasants, Moscow Province, received 7 January 1918.

PART 2

Crisis and Upheaval:
From the July Days to Bolshevik Power

For we received a stone instead of bread, and instead of the promised golden
rain we got a hail of steel bullets that knocked down a tenth part of the
country and infected the rest with malice, envy, and hatred. Now another
Savior of the world must be born, to save the people from all the calamities
in the making here on earth and to put an end to these bloody days.

SOLDIER A. KUCHLAVOK, August 1917

The military offensive that began in late June of 1917 highlighted—and deepened—the frustrations and enmities that were beginning to tear apart the new Russian political order. Announced as a heroic fight for "rights, honor, peace, and freedom," and endorsed as such by the All-Russian Soviet of Workers' and Soldiers' Deputies, the offensive inspired both enthusiasm and disgust. For many, especially at the front, the first quickly disintegrated into the other. Following on the initial notices of success in the campaign, ominous reports by division commanders described the rapid collapse of fighting spirit among the troops, collective refusals to move into fighting positions, threats of violence and assaults against officers, and mass desertions.[1] Particularly troubling was the brutal beating on 21 July of several members of the Soviet Executive Committee who were trying to persuade soldiers to obey orders and move into position. Ironically, the leader of this delegation of Soviet activists was Nikolai Sokolov, who had helped draft Order No. 1, the charter of soldiers' rights.[2] Aleksandr Kerensky, the war minister, had to admit in a confidential telegram from the front to the rest of the cabinet on 24 June, barely a week into the offensive, that "the mood of breakthrough and enthusiasm created in the first days . . . turned out to be unstable, so that after the first days, sometimes even after the first hours, of battle, this changed and spirits fell."[3] By early July, newspapers were reporting publicly what government officials and military commanders already knew: not only had the offensive failed, with Russian forces everywhere under attack and the losses heavy and mounting (even before the German counteroffensive began on 6 July), but it had stimulated still greater discontent with the war and with the policies of the government and the Soviet, and greater disorder at the front. Everywhere, as the following documents reveal, Bolsheviks were fostering these troubles, and benefiting from them.

The July Days and Their Aftermath

By early July, Bolsheviks had been talking for some weeks already about armed action to achieve soviet power. Certain groups were especially attracted to such a plan, particularly Bolshevized soldiers in the Petrograd garrison and sailors at the Kronstadt naval garrison, radicals in the Vyborg district committee of the party in Petrograd (Vyborg was a neighborhood with a heavy concentration of industrial workers and garrison soldiers), and members of the party's Military Organization. Such radical talk was encouraged not only by general discontent with the policies of the coalition government but by a particular irritant: the news that the government planned to start sending garrison units to the front to assist in the offensive—contrary to the agreement in late February between the Petrograd Soviet and the government that all garrison troops would remain in their places in order to "defend the revolution." Lenin and other Bolshevik leaders also talked openly about the soviets' taking power, but they counseled patience, insisting that the seizure of power must be carried out in a disciplined manner and only when there was a high probability of lasting success. The Bolshevik leadership was divided over when that time would come. Many lower-class Russians, however, especially rank-and-file Bolsheviks in Petrograd, felt that the time for waiting had passed. At the very least, many were convinced, the offensive and the preparations to send garrison soldiers to the front called for a forceful demonstration of opposition.[4]

Complicating the coming clash, a government crisis broke out on the day before the July demonstrations began. On 2 July, four ministers, all members of the liberal Kadet party, resigned in protest from the Provisional Government. Ostensibly, the cause of the resignation was an agreement, negotiated by a small delegation of ministers (Kerensky, the Menshevik minister of post and telegraph Irakly

Tsereteli, and the independent foreign minister Mikhail Tereshchenko), to grant a large measure of autonomous political authority to Ukraine, in particular to the nationalist and leftist assembly known as the Rada. This issue, however, was merely a catalyst. As the Kadet leaders explained in the party's formal declaration of withdrawal from the coalition cabinet, the incident was only a painful example of a deeper problem: the failure of their socialist partners to concern themselves with national interests, as opposed to party or class interests.[5] The Kadets too had grown impatient with the policies of the coalition government. Prime Minister Georgy Lvov, an independent, shared this sense that the coalition had failed, though he doubted that the Kadets cared any more about the common good than did the socialists. He too, it seems, had decided to resign, though he would wait until 7 July to announce his decision. He had decided to leave the government, he explained privately, because he felt that he had "reached the end of the road," as, he believed, had his "sort of liberalism." Shortly after, in a private letter written on the night of 3 July, amid the first upheavals of the July Days, he viewed the future with even deeper pessimism. He saw ahead only upheaval and destruction: "slaughter, famine, collapse at the front," and the utter destruction of "the cultural inheritance of the nation, its people and civilization."[6]

On the morning of 3 July, with the active involvement of Bolshevik and anarchist activists, soldiers of the 1st Machine Gun Regiment, located in the Vyborg district, met to plan an armed demonstration (or perhaps—for the historical record is ambiguous—an armed insurrection). They elected a Provisional Revolutionary Committee to coordinate action and send representatives to urge other military units and major factories to join in. Some regiments and factory groups rejected the call for an armed demonstration as dangerous and disloyal. But large numbers of soldiers and workers agreed to join the demonstration. Many, it seems, were prepared for it to become a revolutionary insurrection. As planned, in the early evening of 3 July, the center of Petrograd began to fill with tens of thousands of armed soldiers and workers.

Nothing like this had been seen in the streets of the capital since the February revolution. Soldiers and workers took control of the city center, confiscated automobiles and drove about aimlessly, fought with police and Cossacks, and frequently shot their rifles off into the air. By 2:00 a.m., on this first night of the rebellion, sixty to seventy thousand soldiers and workers (including many women and children) had taken to the streets, of whom most were massed outside the Soviet headquarters in the Tauride Palace. The crowds grew even larger and more threatening over the course of the following day, when heavily armed sailors and workers from the nearby Kronstadt naval base sailed into the city and marched to the Tauride as well. More striking than these similarities, however, were the differences from the February days. Most noticeably, the crowds lacked the embracive, multiclass character of February. As one participant wrote, "The cockades of officials, the shiny buttons of students, the hats of 'lady sympathizers' were not to be seen. All that belonged to four months ago, to February."[7] Also, by all accounts, the mood was darker and angrier. Especially on the fourth, shootings were reported all over the city, and the toll of injured and dead began to rise. On at least one occasion, when Cossack and military cadet snipers fired at a crowd from the rooftops, a riot broke out: apartments were broken into, well-dressed passersby beaten up, shops looted, and windows shot out. In many places, violence broke out wherever civilians encountered Cossacks or other forces of authority. Sometimes vague fears that someone was shooting at demonstrators (even though only the demonstrators themselves might be shooting into the air) inspired people to fire into the windows of apartments where the "bourgeois" lived.

The press regularly reported such "excesses" and "outrages," and many workers and soldiers, as some of the documents collected here show, experienced the same disgust at this chaotic and often senseless rebellion. Maxim Gorky, like many socialists, argued that these were the actions not of a revolutionary crowd but of a blind and cowardly mob with "absolutely no idea of what they were doing."[8] Nevertheless, as the documents here also show, these protests gave expression to a good deal of clearly directed anger and hatred: against the military offensive, against the war, against the bourgeoisie. The protesters also had a concrete goal: to put all state power into the hands of the soviets of workers', soldiers', and peasants' deputies. What was not clear was how to achieve this end, especially when the national center of the soviet movement, the All-Russian Central Executive Committee of Soviets, refused to take power. There were some shouts that the Soviet Executive Committee ought to be arrested for "surrendering to the landlords and the bourgeoisie."[9] Mainly, however, the crowds were trying to convince the Soviet to hear their pleas, to take control of the movement and of the government. Workers from the huge Putilov plant, present in the thousands, declared that they would not leave until the Soviet Executive Committee agreed to arrest the "capitalist ministers"—the workers were unaware, as was most of the public, that several of the ministers had already quit—and take power. This goal of persuading the Soviet leaders to take control of the government—but also the underlying currents of frustration with and distrust of the very Soviet leaders they were asking to take power—finds its best illustration in one of the famous (though possibly apocryphal) scenes of the July Days. When an increasingly volatile crowd of soldiers, workers, and Kronstadt sailors, who had gathered outside the Tauride Palace on 4 July, insisted on talking with one of the socialist ministers, the Soviet leaders sent out Viktor Chernov, the leader of the Socialist Revolutionary (S.R.) party and minister of agriculture. He tried to mollify the crowd by explaining the logic of the Soviet position on the question of power and describing the useful work of the socialist ministers, but without success. In the midst of the confrontation, an angry demonstrator, shaking his fist, expressed the frustration and contradictory feelings of the crowd when he shouted at Chernov, "Take power, you son of a bitch, when it is handed to you!"[10]

The Soviet Executive Committee, now faced with the defection of the main block of liberals from the government and with armed demonstrations in the streets, began an extended debate on the evening of 3 July. Pressure on the Soviet leadership to confront the question of power increased still further when the workers' section of the Petrograd soviet,[11] influenced by a Bolshevik majority and by reports of the Kadet resignations, voted earlier that evening to call on the All-Russian Soviet to take state power into its hands.[12] Just before midnight on the night of 3–4 July, as the crowds outside kept growing, a special closed meeting of the Soviet leaders (a joint session of the executive committees of the All-Russian Soviet of Workers' and Soldiers' Deputies and of the All-Russian Soviet of Peasants' Deputies) debated what to do. The moderate majority indignantly branded the demonstrations a "counterrevolutionary" attempt to "dictate with bayonets" decisions of the Soviet and placed the blame on the Bolsheviks.[13] In the end, the Soviet leaders made it clear that they would not tolerate being forced to take power, a course which, in any case, they considered premature and dangerous.

After much uncertainty, temptation, and ambivalence, the Bolsheviks also refused to lead this movement to power. Historians still argue about the role of the Bolshevik party in the July Days. Were the demonstrations a carefully orchestrated, though ultimately unsuccessful, attempt by the Bolshevik party to seize power? Were they part of a complex strategy for testing the waters of popular support in preparation for a later Bolshevik coup, or an attempt by Bolshevik radicals to

compel a reluctant leadership to act? Or were the protests a largely un-
coordinated action by radicalized soldiers and workers, one that the
party at first reluctantly agreed to support and then, as events un-
folded, considered using to take power, only to back away as it became
clear that success was unlikely? On one point, there is no disagreement: rank-and-file Bolshevik activists played a big role in these
events. It is also clear that many looked to the party for leadership.
Crowds often included in their route a stop at the headquarters of the
Bolshevik party, located across the Neva River from the center of town
in the former mansion of the ballerina Mathilde Kseshinskaia (reputed
to have been the mistress of Nicholas II before his marriage). Here,
party speakers offered the crowds encouraging words, and the party's
Military Organization worked out plans to coordinate the demonstrations. There is also little doubt that the goal of overthrowing the Provisional Government was on the Bolshevik agenda. "In the mind of
each of us," an activist later wrote, "was the thought of seizing
power."[14] The question was when. Whatever the initial plan, the quite
reasonable fear of failure stayed the Bolsheviks' hand. Lenin and the
Central Committee, though certainly tempted, evidently recognized
that they still did not have enough support among the population outside the capital or among soldiers at the front—a justifiable concern,
as evidenced in many of the documents presented here. Besides, the
Bolsheviks would be put in the untenable position of seizing power in
the name of the Soviet but against the clearly voiced will of the Soviet
leadership itself.[15] In the absence of such leadership from either the Soviet or the Bolsheviks, the movement disintegrated. A heavy rainfall on
the evening of the fourth conveniently drove most of the crowds from
the streets. Gradually, those who remained, or who returned after the
rain ended, recognized the pointlessness of further demonstrations and
returned to their homes and barracks. Petrograd's white night still
rang with the occasional shot or the crash of broken glass, but these
sounds now signified only retreat and frustration.

   At this point, a reaction began, fueled by allegations that the Bolsheviks were acting at the behest of the German government. The Trudovik (Laborist) minister of justice, Pavel Pereverzev, had decided to
release to the press information, collected by a government investigatory commission, that purportedly demonstrated—though the evidence was not sufficiently irrefutable for the government to take legal
action—that Lenin and the Bolshevik party had received both money
and instructions from the German government. The right-wing press
made full use of this rather slender evidence to excoriate the Bolsheviks

as vile traitors to the nation and as enemies of the Russian people. In Petrograd and elsewhere, violence was directed against presumed Bolsheviks (or, by extension, other socialists, Jews, or anyone else who was blamed for the disorders). Many socialists—whether they believed the charges about German money or not—also condemned the Bolsheviks as guilty of fomenting disorder, bloodshed, and dangerous divisions among revolutionaries. For its part, the government launched a vigorous crackdown on the party. The editorial offices and printing plant of *Pravda* and the party headquarters were raided, sacked, and shut down, and hundreds of Bolshevik leaders were arrested. Lenin, along with a few other key leaders, went into hiding.

The effort to reestablish order and unity in the country was not limited to measures of repression against the Bolsheviks. The breakdown was, after all, widely viewed as far exceeding what the Bolsheviks had done in Petrograd in early July. Indeed, as many of the letters and appeals in these documents indicate, even Russians living far from the centers of power and from the streets of Petrograd often had the troubled sense that disorder and disintegration were widespread. As Maxim Gorky had commented already at the end of June, in an editorial in his newspaper, *Novaia zhizn'* (New life), "Everybody agrees that the Russian state is splitting all along its seams and falling apart like an old barge in a flood."[16] Many would have added that Russian society was splitting apart no less inexorably. The resignations of the Kadet ministers from the Provisional Government were a response to this breakdown, an attempt to prod the government into taking bolder measures to restore order. At the other end of the political spectrum, the armed demonstrations of the July Days were also an attempt to force authorities to create a viable order. Prime Minister Lvov conveyed the same message, again from the right, when, on 7 July, he announced that he too would resign. He could not serve in a government, he stated, echoing the earlier Kadet complaint, in which socialists were "sacrificing national and moral values to the masses in the name of demagogy and as a play to the galleries."[17] In particular, he was appalled by the encouragement socialists seemed to be giving peasants to seize private lands. Arguing that "strong authority" was the most essential thing at this dangerous time for the revolution, Lvov asked Kerensky to succeed him as prime minister. As Lvov told a reporter, Kerensky perfectly combined the requisite elements of authority: he was head of the military, "symbol of the revolution," and "possibly the only practical man among the socialists."[18] Privately, Lvov explained his reasoning more bluntly: "In order to save the country, it is now necessary to shut down the Soviet and shoot at the people. I cannot do that. Kerensky can."[19]

Indeed, immediately after Kerensky's return from the front on 6 July, the largely socialist interim government, the government for the salvation of the revolution, as it was unofficially dubbed, embarked on a sustained effort to restore political and civic order. At the same time, as Lvov recognized, the government was shifting leftward. On 8 July, the government issued a new program that voiced its strong commitment to the soviet and socialist agenda: an international peace conference, elections to the Constituent Assembly (the date was set as 17 September, though this would later be revised to 12 November), increased local self-government, state regulation of the economy and of labor relations, land reform, and the abolition of all civil ranks, orders, and estates.[20] Not surprisingly, many liberals found this program unacceptable and for that matter illegal in that it preempted decisions that only the Constituent Assembly should make. At the same time, the program was set in the framework of an increasingly conservative policy on restoring order through disciplinary action.

At an emergency overnight session on 6–7 July, the government approved a series of wide-ranging decrees stipulating arrest and punishment for anyone engaging in "arbitrary actions, arrests, and searches," publicly inciting people to disobey lawful orders, or perpetrating violence against any part of the population.[21] Over the next few days, loyal troops were employed to restore order and to arrest people known to have participated in violent acts during the July Days, to oust anarchists forcibly from the Durnovo mansion, and to retake the Peter and Paul Fortress, which had been occupied on 4 July by rebellious Kronstadt sailors. Military units that had taken an active part in the events of 3–4 July were disarmed and disbanded. Then, partly in response to demands the Kadets had set as their condition for returning to the government, several decrees were promulgated with the aim of ensuring greater social order and discipline throughout society. On 12 July, the death penalty was restored for military personnel at the front who had been convicted by field courts (officially "military-revolutionary courts") of "heinous" crimes such as treason, desertion to the enemy, flight from battle, refusal to fight, incitement to surrender, violence against persons in authority, disobeying orders, and mutiny. At the same time, the government banned all street processions in Petrograd until further notice and authorized the closure of any publications that advocated disobedience to military orders (this authorization was formalized, on 20 July, with the restoration of military censorship over the press).[22] Finally, on 18 July, Kerensky appointed as the new commander in chief Lavr Kornilov, a tough-minded Cossack general already greatly admired in conservative circles for his strong advocacy of military and civic discipline. His standing in the eyes of those on the political Right was further enhanced when, in response to Kerensky's offer, he set his conditions for accepting the post of commander in chief: complete autonomy with regard to operations and command appointments, the extension of the death penalty to soldiers in the rear, and recognition that he had formal responsibility before only his own conscience and the nation.[23]

Symbolic gestures reinforced the message, confidently voiced by many newspapers of the day, that a Rubicon in the political culture of the revolution had been crossed after the July Days. A funeral, as on so many earlier occasions, captured the political tenor of the moment. The government designated 15 July as the date for the public burial in Petrograd of Cossacks slain by insurgents during the July Days. In a solemn religious ceremony, ministers, foreign diplomats, invited dignitaries, Cossacks, and well-dressed crowds accompanied these "loyal sons of free Russia" who had fallen while "performing their revolutionary duty" to their graves in the cemetery at the Alexander Nevsky Monastery. Before those assembled, Kerensky swore that "all attempts to foment anarchy and disorder, regardless of their source, will be dealt with mercilessly, in the name of the blood of these innocent victims."[24] A few days later, on 18 July, Kerensky seemed further to signal his government's return to certain political traditions by moving the offices of the cabinet into the Winter Palace (and taking Alexander III's suite for his personal use). Concomitantly, he moved the Soviet out of the Tauride Palace, the traditional seat of representative government in Russia, and into the Smolny Institute, a former school for daughters of the nobility that was located much further from the center of the city.

In this new atmosphere, various right-wing and conservative groups became bolder and more active. The press reported on the growing visibility of extremist right-wing groups and of street-corner rallies where speakers called on listeners to "smash" the Jews, who were blamed both for leftist radicalism and for "bourgeois" oppressions.[25] On the more moderate right, a "private conference" of members of the last State Duma, organized by the revived Provisional Committee of the Duma, met on 18 July in the Tauride Palace (from which the Soviet had just been expelled). Faced with what the organizers called the "horror, dishonor, and shame" that reigned at the front and with the de facto seizure of state power by "irresponsible organizations," backed by the "elemental movement of the dark popular masses," the Duma Committee presented a proclamation for discussion at this special conference. The proclamation called for the formation of "a firm and strong government" to restore order until the Constituent Assembly convened to decide on the form of the new state. Some speakers at the meeting went even further in condemning the "fanatics," "madmen," and "traitors" who were destroying Russia. Especially controversial were speeches (which, widely reported in the press, evoked storms of protest)[26] by the former Duma deputies A. M. Maslennikov and Vladimir Purishkevich. They vehemently chastised the soviets for the breakdown of authority in the country and proposed calling the State Duma back into session as "the only organ capable of saving Russia."[27] Inspired by much the same spirit, in industry, many employers decided that it was time to take a much firmer stand against workers' "unreasonable" demands and efforts to interfere in the decisions and prerogatives of management.[28]

Kerensky's willingness to push the government toward the right helped him finally to win the agreement of the Kadets to join a new coalition with socialists—though only after he threatened resignation on 21 July and then agreed that ministers would serve as individuals, not as representatives of parties or other social organizations. This second coalition government, headed by Kerensky and comprising ten socialists (Socialist Revolutionaries, Mensheviks, and Trudoviks) and seven liberals (mostly Kadets), began work on 25 July. It continued the effort to restore strong authority and order in the country. Between 26 July and 4 August, the government expanded military censorship to cover mail and telegrams as well as the press, granted the War Ministry and the Ministry of the Interior the right, for the duration of the war, to close or administratively prohibit any meetings that might "constitute a danger to the war effort or to the security of the state," authorized administrative arrest and deportation of any individuals viewed as a threat to freedom or "internal security," and restored hard labor as punishment for acts of violence against the state or for possession of arms intended for such use.[29] As the documents presented here show, even many lower-class Russians welcomed these measures as necessary to restore firm authority and to preserve the gains of the revolution. Many, however, condemned the laws as a betrayal of the revolution and as the sign of a deepening counterrevolution that would benefit only the rich and powerful. Like the July Days themselves, the growing reaction evoked mixed and divided feelings. While many suffered from the social disorder all around and demanded strong government and order, others were no less discontented with the policies of the government coalition, with the endless and painful war, and with the continuing economic hardships.

The Moscow State Conference

A key step in the government's effort to unite diverse constituencies around its authority and program was the national State Conference held from 12 to 14 August. In the announcement of the meeting, made a month earlier on 13 July, the whole of organized civil society was invited to send representatives: "all political, public, democratic, nationalities, commercial, industrial, and cooperative organizations," including city dumas, zemstvo boards, academic institutions, trade unions, soviets, and political parties, as well as members of past State Dumas, high military officers, and, in the capacity of observers, foreign dignitaries. Tellingly, the meeting was to be held in Moscow, the traditional national and spiritual center of the country and, no less important, a more conservative and peaceful place than Petrograd.[30]

In the weeks beforehand, it became increasingly clear that, as the Kadet party newspaper observed on the eve of the meetings, the conference would serve not to unite the country or strengthen the government, "but only to underscore the intrinsic contradiction of two irreconcilable tendencies."[31] As the conference approached, the public discussed how to respond. On the one side, a rising tide of conservatism was evident at preliminary meetings of industrialists, landowners, professionals, liberal and right-wing parties, and other "bourgeois groups" (as they were called by the Left). For example, at the Conference of Public Figures (*obshchestvennye deiateli*), held in Moscow on 8–10 August, which brought together representatives of officers' organizations, Cossacks, the old Duma leadership, industrialists, merchants, academics, professionals, liberal parties, and others, speakers called for a "strong unified national government" that would break with the "utopianism" of the socialists, which they blamed for the disruptions and agony that the revolution had brought Russia. It was necessary to create a government that could "save Russia" by introducing order and discipline and setting the country on a "healthy" course.[32] By contrast, socialists blamed Russia's sufferings on the greed of the bourgeoisie and warned of growing counterrevolutionary sentiments and of portentous preparations on the Right. The strongest statements came from the Bolsheviks, who called for a boycott and one-day protest strike against the conference, which they condemned as nothing less than a "parliament for counterrevolution," a gathering of "saviors of the profits of the landowners and capitalists."[33]

Although the Soviet leadership ordered the Moscow proletariat not to strike, when the conference opened the trams were not running, most of the city's large factories were silent, and many cafés and restaurants were closed (including those in the Bolshoi Theater, where the conference was held, so the delegates had to serve themselves at the buffet).[34] Demonstrations remained peaceful, yet the crowds that had gathered outside the theater were clearly hostile to the assembled representatives of the "bourgeoisie"—the men in "morning coats, frock coats, and starched shirts," who were in the majority, according to a reporter.[35] Once again, it appeared that the radical distrust of the bourgeoisie voiced by the Bolsheviks resonated strongly among lower-class Russians. A great many of the documents presented here echo that distrust.

Inside the conference, the mutual recriminations continued. The Cossack general Aleksei Kaledin, for example, argued that for "the salvation of the native land" political meetings and assemblies should be prohibited, officers given full disciplinary rights, and all soviets and committees abolished (these proposals aroused commotion and cries of "counterrevolution" on the Left but applause and shouts of "That's right!" from the conservative majority). By contrast, socialists like Nikolai Chkheidze blamed the "enemies of the revolution" for taking advantage of the failures at the front, the economic collapse, and the growing discontents of the lower classes to benefit their own selfish interests and to turn back the achievements of the revolution. Both sides repeatedly made appeal to the principles of unity and the common good, as against the rule of particular social or party interests. The two sides stood far apart, however, in their interpretation of who was selfish and who was sacrificing for the good of all. As the meeting went on, Kerensky had to intervene repeatedly to ask the audience to refrain from constantly cheering or deriding speakers, and to advise the speakers not to provoke such outbursts deliberately. "We must preserve order," he argued, "in the general interests of the state."[36]

The dominant opinion and mood at this conference were conservative. Kerensky himself seemed to endorse the arguments of the Right in his opening address. In ringing words, he insisted on the absolute need for national unity, the government's readiness to meet all challenges to its authority "with iron and blood" (a phrase that met with thunderous applause), the need to ensure that the Russian empire would stand as a great power in the world of nations (hence the impossibility of a separate peace), the need to defend the unity of the Russian state even as autonomy was granted to different nationalities, and the need to uphold the honor and discipline of the Russian army.[37] The real sensation at this meeting—and the most ominous sign of impending counterrevolution, in the eyes of many observers on the Left—was the speech on the second day of the conference by General Lavr Kornilov, the new commander in chief. His speech was inelegant and blunt, especially by comparison with Kerensky's passionate and florid rhetorical style; but the message was clear: it was essential to halt continuing losses of land and men in battle and the indiscipline and disorder in the army. Many found his words moving, though the actual speech may have been less important than the reputation of the man who gave it: an individual many Russians had begun to view (sometimes in almost mythic terms) as a strongman ready to save Russia. When he arrived by train in Moscow, he was met by a military honor guard and an orchestra, crowds of officers and dignitaries, and throngs of "ladies in gaily colored dresses," who pelted him with flowers. In a brief welcoming speech, the Kadet Fyodor Rodichev echoed the many statements in recent days that spoke of Kornilov as a savior and leader, urging him, "Save Russia and a grateful people will crown you." After he returned to his railway carriage, where he waited before addressing the conference, streams of civil and military leaders visited Kornilov to express their support. When he arrived at the conference, he received a standing ovation from the majority, while representatives of the soviets and other leftist groups remained sitting, provoking shouts of contempt ("serfs," some shouted) and demands that they stand and honor Kornilov.[38]

The Kornilov Mutiny

The Kornilov affair grew naturally out of this rising summer flood of talk about disorder, betrayal, and danger, and about the need for discipline, unity, and strong authority. The affair itself, which oscillated between the ominous and the absurd, was the result as much of confusion and misunderstanding as of conspiracy.[39] The consequences were nonetheless enormous. For some weeks in late July and early August, Commander in Chief Kornilov had been pressuring Kerensky to enact a series of military reforms: in particular, to curtail the power of soldiers' committees, restore capital punishment for soldiers in the rear as well as at the front, and place workers in defense industries under military discipline. He viewed Kerensky's vacillating answers as further evidence that the government was a prisoner of the Soviet, and even that the government itself was staffed by disloyal and perhaps treasonous men. Adding to the sense of danger were widespread rumors, which Kornilov and his supporters strongly believed, that the Bolsheviks were planning an uprising. Even a date was mentioned: 27 August, the half-year anniversary of the revolution. Increasingly, Kornilov saw himself as the man who could rescue the government, and Russia, from the control of the Left and save the state from its own weakness. He was encouraged in this self-ideal not only by public figures on the Right and the conservative press but also by increasingly well-organized associations of military officers (especially the recently formed Union of Russian Officers), businessmen, and landowners. Although the evidence is sketchy, some of these groups appear to have been raising funds and laying plans for a military coup. Other signs also suggested that a coup was in the making. In particular, in the first weeks of August, Kornilov, as commander in chief, began to move loyal troops from the front to positions closer to the capital, though his purpose may have been, as he claimed, merely to prepare in case of a Bolshevik attempt to seize power.

Although we cannot know for certain what Kornilov was planning during those weeks, we do know that he believed it essential to end the political power of the Left and to establish a strong government, even a temporary dictatorship that would impose civil order and create a robust political center. Most important, Kornilov appears to have believed that Prime Minister Kerensky shared this belief. Certainly, Kerensky had been talking tough in recent weeks. He had promoted Kornilov, whose views were no secret. On 23 August, Kerensky's deputy war minister, the Socialist Revolutionary Boris Savinkov, arrived at staff headquarters with Kerensky's approval of tough new measures to restore discipline to the army and the nation. Then came the rather bizarre exchange of views between Kerensky and Kornilov through the intermediary of Vladimir Lvov, a former Duma deputy, the Provisional Government's chief procurator of the Holy Synod (the state's lay administrator of the Church) until July, and an active participant in the work of conservative groups seeking to "save" Russia from imminent collapse.

The story of these fateful communications is muddled by a profusion of contradictory memoir accounts, though it appears that what happened was something like this. On 24 August, Lvov arrived at staff headquarters in Mogilev, where he presented himself as an official emissary of the prime minister. This was probably a misrepresentation (or, at least, a self-deception on Lvov's part). Lvov had indeed met with Kerensky on 22 August to present the views of conservative groups on the need for a new government coalition. It is not certain, however, that he was (as he later affirmed, but Kerensky denied) formally authorized to represent the prime minister in negotiations with Kornilov and others about forming a new government. In any case, it appears clear that when Lvov arrived at staff headquarters, he and Kornilov discussed not only the formation of a new government but also the possibility of a military dictatorship to be headed by Kornilov. Whether the discussion took place in accordance with a proposal actually sent by Kerensky or with Kornilov's belief that Kerensky had made such a proposal because Lvov falsely claimed that it was so or with both men's understanding that they were defying Kerensky's authority (but deciding to dissemble) depends on whose account of these meetings one believes. In any case, when Lvov returned to Petrograd on the 26th, he informed Kerensky that Kornilov was demanding a new government with dictatorial powers for himself—specifically, martial law in Petrograd, the resignation of the current government, and the transfer of all civil and military authority into the hands of the commander in chief. Kerensky treated this proposal as a hostile ultimatum, backed by the implied threat of a military coup. To obtain the necessary written proof of this conspiracy to convince the other ministers to authorize resolute measures against the popular Kornilov, Kerensky arranged to communicate directly with the commander in chief later that evening by direct telegraph. The effort to prove Kornilov's mutinous intent, however, did no more than secure the ambiguous confirmation that the content of "the communication made to him [Kerensky] by V. N. [Lvov]" was true. Nor did it clarify matters when Kornilov confirmed his request that Kerensky come to staff headquarters at Mogilev: the latter interpreted this as a plan to place him under arrest; Kornilov and his supporters claimed that they were trying to protect Kerensky in the likely event of a Bolshevik coup.

Whether this was a tragicomedy of misunderstanding or a darker tale of deliberate deception, the results were dramatic. Kerensky called an emergency meeting of the cabinet to describe the "conspiracy" and ask for full authority to suppress the coup. In support of his request, the ministers agreed to resign, giving Kerensky dictatorial power. At 4:00 a.m. on Sunday morning, 27 August, Kerensky sent a telegram to Kornilov dismissing him and ordering him to return to Petrograd at once. Kornilov, who evidently interpreted this dismissal as proof that Petrograd and the government were now in Bolshevik hands, hastened the movement of troops toward the capital. Next, refusing all proposals for mediation, Kerensky issued a sensational statement to the nation (which appeared in special Monday morning editions of most newspapers on the 28th) informing the country of Kornilov's plan to seize power and declaring that he, Kerensky, was preparing to take all measures necessary "for the salvation of the motherland, liberty, and the republican order" against those wishing to "take advantage of the grave condition of the country to establish a regime opposed to the conquests of the revolution."[40] In response, Kornilov issued his own statement, declaring these accusations to be lies and provocations, and accusing the government and the soviets alike of acting, under the pressure of the Bolsheviks, in "complete harmony with the plans of the German general staff," to destroy the army and "tear apart the country from within." He called on all those "in whose breasts a Russian heart is beating" and who "believe in God and in the Church" to pray to the Lord God to "save our native land." He also declared himself ready "to die on the battlefield of honor rather than to see the disgrace and infamy of the Russian land."[41] Expressing support for Kornilov were most of his army commanders as well as a number of chiefs of staff and other senior officers. In particular, the Union of Russian Officers encouraged the mutiny by sending telegrams to all army and navy headquarters urging "tough and unflinching support" for Kornilov and for removal of the Provisional Government.[42]

Over the next few days, as Kornilov's troops headed toward the capital, and as the Provisional Government issued fevered appeals but hesitated over what concrete measures to take against the threat, the Soviet leadership took charge of organizing resistance. On 28 August, the Soviet established the Committee for Struggle Against Counterrevolution, to organize the defense of the capital. The committee included representatives from the two national soviet executive committees (of workers and soldiers and of peasants), the Petrograd soviet, the Central Council of Trade Unions, and the S.R. and Menshevik parties, but also the Bolsheviks, whose renewed popularity among lower-class Russians could not be ignored. The Soviet also arranged to have Trotsky and other popular Bolshevik leaders freed from prison, to help mobilize popular support. The Committee for Struggle—along with local soviets, trade unions, factory committees, and party organizations— kept citizens informed of events and of pronouncements from the government and various social organizations, helped distribute arms to garrison units, took steps to protect supplies of food to Petrograd, sent representatives to appeal to the rank-and-file soldiers marching under

Kornilov's command toward the city, worked with the union of railway workers to disrupt the rebels' advance, and encouraged workers to arm and organize to protect factories and workers' districts. In emulation of the Committee for Struggle, ad hoc defense committees were established in various Petrograd neighborhoods as well as in other cities and even some rural areas. Often organized by local soviets, these committees were known variously as revolutionary committees, military-revolutionary committees, and often committees for the salvation of the revolution. Although the soviet forces were well prepared for battle, no actual fighting was necessary. Agitators easily persuaded the advancing troops, including Cossacks and the notorious "Savage Division" from the Caucasus, to stop their advance (especially when they learned that Kerensky did not support Kornilov's action). By 30 August, the mutiny was over.

The Dissolution of Coalition Politics

Paradoxically, the main outcome of the Kornilov affair was to compound the problems that Kornilov (and Kerensky, for that matter) was trying to rectify. The government became less than ever a "strong power": the Soviet's authority and influence over the government were enhanced; the increasing authority wielded by the panoply of committees, unions, local soviets, and other institutions hastened the fragmentation of national administrative authority; the popularity and influence of the Bolsheviks grew dramatically; and military indiscipline, industrial disorder, and agrarian conflict reached crisis proportions. "The fragile foundations of the only recently built edifice of democratic Russia," observed an editorial writer in the Menshevik newspaper *Rabochaia gazeta* (Workers' gazette), were crumbling.[43]

Kerensky, resisting the political polarization and fragmentation around him, was still determined to create a strong government committed to law and order and based on a coalition of liberals and moderate socialists. The leaders of the Soviet, however, on whose agreement coalition depended, were less sanguine. They had become increasingly mistrustful of the Kadets, who had so often blamed socialist reform plans and the power of the soviets for all the disorder and who had been suspiciously supportive of Kornilov. Also, the Kadets had become for many ordinary Russians a symbol of pro-war, anti-democratic politics. Beyond this, the Soviet leaders faced increasing and often fervent popular pressure to abandon coalition with the "bourgeoisie." Huge numbers of resolutions and appeals—especially by workers and soldiers—voiced the widespread popular desire, intensified by the tangible threat of counterrevolution and the rightward shift of the nonsocialist parties, for a "democratic" government. This meant a government that excluded, and even openly opposed, the "counterrevolutionary bourgeoisie." In other words—words increasingly used at the time—this meant "soviet power," even "revolutionary dictatorship." To add to the pressure on the Soviet leadership, a number of influential popular organizations passed resolutions to this effect in the aftermath of the Kornilov affair, including regional soldiers' committees, local soviets, trade unions, and others. On top of this, at a meeting of the Petrograd soviet on 31 August, a strong majority voted for a Bolshevik resolution to create an all-socialist government that would exclude propertied elements.[44]

The question of what kind of government should replace the collapsed second coalition was the subject of a joint meeting of the national executive committees of the workers', soldiers', and peasants' soviets held from 31 August until the morning of 2 September. More than at any time previously, a large number of Mensheviks and Socialist Revolutionaries seemed ready to break with the liberals and attempt to protect the revolution both from the Right and from the Bolshevik Left by establishing a national government made up only of "the democracy." As Matvei Skobelev, a Menshevik and former labor minister, acknowledged, "in recent days many of us have undergone a mental revolution" and could now support the view that only a purely "democratic" government without the bourgeoisie could save Russia and the revolution. Many, however, resisted these arguments, including Skobelev himself, who feared that only a broad coalition could save the country from chaos and defeat. Yet others remained too skeptical of the bourgeoisie and the liberals to approve a coalition. The resulting decision was an unstable compromise. On the one hand, the soviet executive committees rejected resolutions by Bolsheviks and by Menshevik-Internationalists (led by Yuly Martov, the original leader of the Menshevik movement) to form an all-socialist cabinet responsible to the Soviet. At the same time, reluctant to agree to a new coalition, they resolved to convoke at the earliest opportunity a congress of all democratic organizations and organs of local self-government, to decide what sort of government could lead the country until the Constituent Assembly convened. In the meantime, they would support Kerensky's government, but they insisted that the government work closely with the soviets and especially with the Committee for the Struggle Against Counterrevolution.[45]

While awaiting the results of the Democratic Conference scheduled for the middle of September, Kerensky continued to try to establish as strong a government as possible. On 1 September, the government announced that full power had been transferred to a temporary directory of five ministers (also called the Council of Five). It would be headed by Kerensky, in his capacities both as prime minister and as commander in chief, joined by four men said not to be affiliated with any particular political parties.[46] At the same time, in a symbolic gesture aimed at the Left, the government formally proclaimed Russia a "republic." Both these actions were undertaken with the goal of establishing "order." A republic was proclaimed "to put an end to the outward vagueness of the state order." The Directory was established to adopt "immediate and decisive measures for restoring the shattered state order."[47] (The name "Directory" was evidently intended to evoke the five-member Directory that tried from 1795 to 1799 to restore order to revolutionary France by opposing both the radicalism of the Left and the counterrevolution of the Right.) In practice, it accomplished little apart from the negotiation of a new coalition, established finally on 27 September.

The Democratic Conference, convened by the Central Executive Committee of the Soviets of Workers' and Soldiers' Deputies and the Executive Committee of the All-Russian Soviet of Peasants' Deputies, was, according to the invitation, meant to be a "congress of the whole of the organized democracy of Russia." Its purpose was to unite these forces and enable them to "pronounce the final word" that would ensure the formation of a "strong, revolutionary authority" that could unite the country, preserve the "freedom that has been won," and thus bring "salvation" to Russia. Invited to participate were representatives of central and regional soviet executive committees (with the largest number of places allocated to the soviets), cooperatives, soldiers' organizations, trade unions, employees' organizations, professional unions (teachers, lawyers, pharmacists, engineers, and so on), zemstvos, and the Peasant Union.[48] The meeting opened on 14 September in the Aleksandrinsky Theater in Petrograd and lasted an entire week.

On the key question of what sort of government should be formed, no clear answer emerged from the conference. The debates, and especially the final votes, revealed at best much confusion and uncertainty and at worst deep and irreconcilable divisions within the democracy. On the socialist and liberal right, many participants—notably, the majority of Mensheviks and Socialist Revolutionaries and most representatives of nonsoviet organizations—insisted that only a broad coalition which included both socialists and liberals, both "the democracy" and the "bourgeoisie," could save the country from further polarization and breakdown. Many others, however, argued, as the S.R. leader Chernov did, that even though coalition was necessary, association with the Kadets was no longer possible. (Some people, though, wondered justifiably how a coalition could include the bourgeoisie but exclude the Kadets, who were practically the only organized nonsocialist party remaining in Russia.) Still further to the left stood many who opposed any coalition—the Bolsheviks, the Menshevik-Internationalists (led by Martov), and the growing faction of so-called Left S.R.'s (who criticized the conciliationist position of the S.R. leadership). In the face of deepening popular hostility to coalition with the distrusted and often passionately hated bourgeoisie (feelings amply evident in the documents here) and profound frustration with the war and the economic crisis, these left-wing socialists argued that the only way to avoid violent upheaval was for the democracy to take power and respond to popular demands for an end to the war, a restoration of eroded freedoms, distribution of land, and revival of the economy. Although Bolshevik moderates (notably Lev Kamenev and Grigory Zinoviev) endorsed these arguments, other more influential party leaders (notably Lenin and Trotsky) found the goal of "peaceful development of the revolution" undesirable, especially if that meant a broad "democratic" coalition. Indeed, in the very midst of the conference, Lenin, still in hiding in Finland, sent two letters to the party leadership in Petrograd rejecting all compromises and calling on the party to begin preparing an armed insurrection.

The vote on these questions, which took place on 19 September, produced typically contradictory results. First, by a margin of only 78 votes (766 to 688, with 38 abstaining) the principle of "coalition with propertied [*tsenzovye*] elements" was approved. The lines along which this vote split were significant, though: representatives of workers' and soldiers' soviets and trade unions were overwhelmingly against coalition, whereas other groups were more supportive. To complicate matters further, in voting on amendments to stipulate what sort of coalition was acceptable, a majority favored excluding the Kadet party as a whole from the coalition, along with members of other parties who had been involved in the Kornilov plot. Finally, to make the meaning of all these votes even more contradictory, when the entire resolution and its amendments were brought to a vote—for coalition with the bourgeoisie but without the Kadets—it was soundly defeated (813 to 183, with 80 abstaining). What this indicated, of course, was not that the majority now favored a socialist government (though clearly, even most of those who favored coalition did not much trust the liberal bourgeoisie). Rather, since many supporters of coalition could not imagine how they could organize a real coalition without the Kadets, they decided to join those who opposed coalition altogether and to reject the whole package. In other words, all the discussions of the conference resulted, typically and dangerously, in indecision and contradiction. As Tsereteli observed, on behalf of the presidium of the conference, the main message of the vote was that there was "no agreement, no unity of will within organized democracy."

The leaders did not give up, though. Determined to arrive at some agreement, the presidium, enlarged by the participation of various invited representatives of different groups, met to find a solution to the impasse created by the contradictory vote of 19 September. The result was a proposal to the conference that a permanent representative body—a preparliament, it would soon be called—should be established that would help form a government and to which the government would be held "accountable and responsible." If "propertied elements" were successfully attracted into the government, then this permanent body would also have to include "delegates from bourgeois groups," though "democratic elements" would remain predominant. On 20 September, this proposal was presented to the conference. Although in many ways it contradicted earlier votes at the conference—especially in that it did not exclude Kadets—it was approved by a strong majority. Some declared these results an encouraging compromise, but most observers judged the conference and its contradictory resolutions to be a complete failure, even a farce.[49] One thing was clear. The still predominantly Menshevik and S.R. leaders of the soviets were adamant in their rejection of demands that "the democracy" take full power. Determined to persist on this increasingly unpopular course, they joined Kerensky in his negotiations with the Kadets to form a new government.

The third coalition government, which formally began its work on 27 September, contained a minority of Kadets, though they held some of the key posts, including that of deputy prime minister. This last coalition government, which lasted only a month, accomplished little, perhaps partly because it saw its main goals as simply maintaining domestic order until the Constituent Assembly could make a "final determination of all important questions on which the welfare of the Russian people depends" and sustaining the war effort while working for a peace agreement. From the first, many viewed this new government with grave doubts. At best, some argued, it represented a necessary compromise. At worst, others felt, it was an impotent collection of nonentities, representing nobody and hence powerless to accomplish anything.[50] In any case, too much now lay beyond the authority of the government to affect or control. Lenin's comment on the situation in late September was not without prescience: "The people are exhausted by the hesitations and delays. Discontent grows openly. A new revolution approaches."[51]

The Bolsheviks Advance

Lenin had good reason to believe that the Bolsheviks' moment on the historical stage had arrived. Indeed, one of the reasons Lenin urged his comrades at the Democratic Conference to abandon efforts to work together with moderate socialists to create a broad socialist government was that the configuration of party forces had changed rapidly in the weeks following the Kornilov mutiny. Recent Bolshevik electoral victories, especially in the Moscow and Petrograd soviets, made it possible and necessary, Lenin now argued openly, for the Bolsheviks "to take power into their own hands." The patience of workers, soldiers, and peasants had run out, he argued. They were ready to support an armed rising against the government. Given the Bolshevik program—immediate peace, land to the peasants without further delay, and the return of the democratic liberties restricted by Kerensky—this would be a government "that nobody could overthrow." His normally cautious view of what was possible gave way to rare excitement and impatience. We "can and must take power," he declared. "History will not forgive us if we do not assume power now." There was no doubt about success: "We shall win absolutely and unquestionably."[52] In spite of considerable skepticism in his own party—including some opposition that lasted right up to the day of the insurrection—a decision to organize the immediate armed overthrow of the government was approved at a meeting of the Bolshevik Central Committee on 10 October.[53]

That the popularity of the Bolsheviks was growing is unquestionable. As many of the documents below suggest, Bolsheviks benefited from deepening political polarization (a rather bloodless phrase with which to describe attitudes often shaped by strong emotions) as liberals and conservatives gravitated toward policies such as those advocated by Kornilov and as growing numbers of socialists and lower-class Russians viewed the government less and less as a force that would respond to their needs and their vision of the revolution. The Bolsheviks, as the only major organized opposition party still standing outside the government, were in a unique position to profit from popular discontent with the government. They also benefited from the growing frustration and even disgust at the compromises of the Mensheviks and Socialist Revolutionaries, who stubbornly refused to abandon the ideal of national unity of all classes.

Evidence of Bolshevik gains, especially in Petrograd and Moscow, was visible already before the Kornilov affair, especially in local balloting for individual factory committees and trade union officers, in the recalls and elections of new deputies to district and city soviets, in receptivity to Bolshevik speakers at soviet meetings, in voting by the soviets on particular issues, and in the growing readership for the Bolshevik press.[54] Elections to the Petrograd city duma on 20 August offered an especially impressive illustration of this rising support for the Bolsheviks. The party launched a huge election campaign in which it offered an unambiguously revolutionary platform: redistribution of the tax burden to the rich to support a policy of improving the everyday lives of the poor; support in the struggles of peasants against landowners, of workers against employers, and of soldiers against officers; and the promise to undo such "counterrevolutionary" measures as the death penalty.[55] When the ballots were counted, the Bolsheviks showed a gain in every district of the city (partly owing to high absenteeism in normally liberal neighborhoods, where political passivity was growing), but especially in working-class neighborhoods. Over all, the Bolsheviks won 33 percent of the total vote in the city, second only to the Socialist Revolutionaries.[56]

After the Kornilov affair, which intensified fear of counterrevolution and exacerbated frustration with the vacillations and conciliations of the moderate socialists, Bolshevik influence grew even more rapidly, paralleled by the growth of the Left S.R.'s among Socialist Revolutionaries. On 31 August, as we have seen, a majority of deputies in the Petrograd soviet voted in support of a Bolshevik resolution for the first time—and this on the most important of issues: one in favor of a socialist government excluding propertied elements.[57] Given that a large number of deputies were absent, the vote could have been an aberration. But it was only the beginning. By 25 September, the Bolsheviks had a sufficiently reliable majority in the Petrograd soviet to reject a coalition government again, to elect a new presidium with a Bolshevik majority, to replace the members of the Executive Committee representing the workers' section of the soviet with a Bolshevik majority, and to elect Lev Trotsky, who had recently joined the Bolshevik party, to replace the Menshevik Nikolai Chkheidze as soviet chairman.[58] In Moscow, Bolsheviks won their first majority in the city soviet on 5 September, in voting on a resolution they proposed on the government question. There, too, they would continue to dominate the voting. Indeed, two weeks after this first Bolshevik success, on 19 September, the Moscow soviet elected a new Executive Committee and a new presidium, both with Bolshevik majorities, and elected the Bolshevik Viktor Nogin chairman, to replace the Menshevik Lev Khinchuk. On 24 September, district duma elections in Moscow actually returned a slight Bolshevik majority (partly due, as in Petrograd, to the apathy of many liberal voters) and showed significant Bolshevik gains in working-class districts, largely at the expense of the Socialist Revolutionaries and Mensheviks.[59] Elections in various organizations and different parts of the country showed similar results. As the lead editorial in the S.R. paper *Delo naroda* (The people's cause) noted with alarm in late September, "Yes, Bolshevism is growing stronger in factories and in the Soviets of Workers' Deputies. Bolsheviks are elected to volost [rural township] committees and to city dumas. They and the 'Left S.R.'s' succeed, and sometimes with no special effort, in passing their 'left' resolutions: 'All power to the soviets,' 'Peace on all fronts.'" This was a disaster in the eyes of the more moderate S.R.'s. It was not a "deepening" of the revolution, but its disintegration.[60]

The weeks that followed brought only more of the same, culminating in the opening in Petrograd of the Second Congress of Soviets of Workers' and Soldiers' Deputies late in the evening of 25 October 1917. The Bolsheviks constituted the largest group—partly because the Executive Committee of Peasants' Deputies, preferring to prepare instead for the Constituent Assembly, had decided not to call on peasant representatives to take part and because, for the same reason, the leadership of most higher-level soldiers' committees had agreed only a week before the meeting to let committees send delegates (though some boycotted anyway). In the democratic flux of 1917, however, these formalities did not detract much from the symbolic importance of the congress as the political focal point of "democratic" Russia. With approximately 300 out of 670 delegates, the Bolsheviks did not actually have a majority; however, half of the 193 Socialist Revolutionaries were from the party's left wing and would give the Bolsheviks a practical majority. As the congress opened, a new presidium was elected with 14 Bolsheviks and 7 Left S.R.'s (the Mensheviks were allotted 4 seats but, as a gesture of protest against the Bolshevik insurrection already under way in the streets of the city, declined to accept them). The political preferences of most delegates were clear from the start. Before the meeting began, deputies filled out questionnaires indicating the position taken by the soviets they represented on the formation of a national government. An overwhelming majority stated that they were committed to the transfer of "all power to the soviets" (505 of the 670 delegates, or considerably more than the 300 who were Bolsheviks). Eight-six delegates were committed to voting for "all power to the democracy"—the principle, voiced at the Democratic Conference in September, of a government including representatives of soviets, trade unions, cooperatives, and other organizations of the democracy, but excluding propertied elements. Seventy-six deputies favored a government of coalition with the propertied elements—though nearly a third of these said that the Kadets must not take part.[61] The congress clearly seemed prepared to endorse the goal of a united democratic socialist government based on all the parties represented in the soviets. Indeed, when Martov, the Menshevik-Internationalist leader, proposed this, both Bolsheviks and Left S.R.'s agreed with his suggestion that discussion of a peaceful agreement among socialist groups was desirable. When the suggestion was brought to a vote, it was approved unanimously.[62] This first move toward creating an all-socialist government was stillborn, however, for events outside the meeting quickly overwhelmed it.

In accordance with a plan worked out by Lenin—who worried, with good reason, that the congress might tie the Bolsheviks' hands by insisting on a Soviet government that would include all socialist parties, or even on a broader "democratic government" excluding only the propertied elements—the overthrow of the Provisional Government was to be presented to the congress as an accomplished fact. Formally, as a mark of legitimacy, the insurrection was to take place in the name of the soviets rather than of the Bolshevik party (though Lenin did not consider this gesture as important as Trotsky and other Bolsheviks did). To ensure this legitimizing connection to the soviets, the uprising was to be coordinated by a Bolshevik-led organization under the authority of the Petrograd soviet—the Military Revolutionary Committee. Also, the Second Congress was to be asked (now that approval seemed certain) to endorse it. On 24–25 October, Bolshevik workers' militias known as Red Guards together with Bolshevik soldiers seized control of major streets and bridges, government buildings, railway stations, post and telegraph offices, the telephone exchange, the electric power station, the state bank, and police stations.

The "preparliament" (known formally as the Provisional Council of the Russian Republic), the assembly of representatives of democratic groups favoring coalition that had been created in the wake of the Democratic Conference, was forcibly dispersed. By the time the congress finally opened, all that remained to do was to arrest the ministers of the Provisional Government, who were barricaded, though not heavily defended, inside the Winter Palace (with the exception of Kerensky, who had fled in disguise on the morning of the 25th). Though the job was not quite complete, Lenin drafted and issued, in the name of the Petrograd soviet, a declaration announcing that power had passed into the hands of the Military Revolutionary Committee. In a speech before the Petrograd soviet in the afternoon, he described the aim of this action: "a soviet government, our own organ of power, without the participation of any bourgeois." With this would come, he declared, an immediate end to the war, distribution of land to the peasants, and workers' control in industry.[63]

By the time the soviet congress opened, the assault on the Winter Palace had begun; the sound of shells being fired across the river from the Peter and Paul Fortress could occasionally be heard in the distance. After the new presidium was installed and the agenda approved, a series of Menshevik and S.R. speakers took the podium to denounce the Bolshevik action as a "criminal political adventure," a coup that subverted the role of the congress, an opportunistic power grab by a single party behind the back of the soviets in whose name it claimed to act, a plot that would surely plunge Russia into civil war, thwart the Constituent Assembly, and destroy the revolution. Not wanting to "bear the responsibility" for those actions, but also certain that "an outburst of popular indignation" would inevitably topple the Bolsheviks once the people discovered that the party could not deliver on its promises, the Mensheviks and right-wing S.R.'s walked out of the congress. Martov, in the name of the Menshevik-Internationalists, made a last, vain attempt to convince the congress to establish a democratic government representing all socialist parties and democratic organizations. Only such a government would be "recognized by the entire revolutionary democracy." Having failed in this effort, Martov and his faction also walked out, though only after Trotsky had gone to the podium and added insult to injury by mocking the proposals for compromise as the pleas of "pitiful, isolated individuals," "bankrupts" whose "role is played out" and who should now go where they belonged, "onto the trash heap of history."[64] Shortly thereafter, in the predawn hours of 26 October, having received news that the palace had been seized and the ministers placed under arrest, the soviet congress approved Lenin's declaration of the transfer of state authority into its own hands and of all local power into the hands of local soviets of workers', soldiers', and peasants' deputies. The congress also promised to propose immediate peace to all nations, to safeguard the transfer of land into the control of peasants' committees, to defend soldiers' rights, to establish workers' control in industry, and to ensure the convocation of the Constituent Assembly as scheduled.[65] Within days, soviets of many other cities seconded this approval. At the same time, large numbers of Russians, including socialists and many from the lower classes, declared their outrage and opposition to this seizure of power.

The Social Revolution

The Bolshevik seizure of state power would have been impossible apart from the ongoing process of social conflict and breakdown that was steadily undermining "the fragile foundations of the only recently built edifice of democratic Russia."[66] In part, these conditions were rooted in an economic collapse that rapidly intensified in the summer and fall of 1917, notwithstanding various regulatory measures enacted by the government. Many factories and other workplaces (including in industries that had been spared such disruptions in the early months of 1917) were forced to close their doors for days or even weeks, owing to shortages of raw materials or fuel. Even when factories managed to keeping running, their efficiency was reduced by falling productivity. Supplies of food to the cities and to the front had dwindled dramatically, causing even "fixed" food prices to rise steeply during the summer and fall. After poor harvests in the fall of 1917, even the countryside was threatened with food shortages. As a major national newspaper reported in late August, the whole country faced "the grim specter of hunger."[67] Contributing to the shortages was a catastrophic breakdown of the railway system, overtaxed by the war, sapped by labor conflicts, and crippled by shortages of both fuel and locomotives, a growing number of which had fallen into disrepair.[68] Material conditions were particularly abysmal for soldiers at the front. Food supplies were low, and as malnutrition rose, so did illness. The short supply of warm clothing, along with food shortages, was a growing concern as cold weather approached. A recent historian has summed up the conditions at the front bluntly: "The plight of the troops went from the unbearable to the unimaginable."[69] In addition to the shortages, they endured death, maimings, and suffering, the disastrous results of the failed June offensive and the German counteroffensive that followed.

People responded to the situation in different ways: some organized to improve conditions; some, as the documents following reflect, raised their voices in public protest and appeal; some participated in the wave of crime, looting, and violence; others succumbed to despair. Throughout 1917, however, a constant theme in the struggles of lower-class Russians was the determination to achieve direct power over their own lives. That power might be deployed as a direct means to meet particular needs—to obtain food, for example, or to protect one's job. It might be put forward as a gesture of distrust and defiance—a way of expressing deep mistrust of elites, of undermining unjust authority, of getting revenge. Power could serve all these purposes. And it was sometimes brutal. It is a mistake to oversimplify or sanitize popular rebellion. Rational social and political purpose was enmeshed with more emotional and expressive intent—with what many contemporaries on both Left and Right saw as "dark, animal instincts."

For workers, especially on the Left, midsummer brought increasingly hard times. Not only did they have to confront continued economic suffering and growing political reaction, but employers and managers were turning decisively away from the policy of concession to workers' demands and beginning to act vigorously to stem the tide of "anarchy" in labor relations. Agreements were broken, new demands rejected, and lockouts declared when necessary. A widely publicized comment by the Moscow industrialist Pavel Riabushinsky (long considered a progressive among business elites) exemplified the hostile new environment for the labor and socialist movements. In his speech opening the national Trade and Industrial Congress in Moscow on 3 August, he warned that the solution to the present crisis would come only when "the bony hand of hunger" grasped soviets, committees, and other "false friends of the people" responsible for the national disorder "by the throat."[70] Most tangibly, workers throughout the country found it increasingly difficult to achieve their demands through negotiations or strikes. Partly reflecting these obstacles to success, the number of strikes fell in July to its lowest point in 1917. By late July, though, the strikes were on the rise again, and frequently larger and more intransigent. Workers made use of all possible forms of labor organization to extend their collective power—cooperatives, trade unions, factory committees, workers' militias (Red Guards), and strike committees.

They also increasingly turned to more direct and often desperate forms of action: food riots, mob attacks on people suspected of hoarding food, and searches for hidden storehouses.[71]

The Kornilov affair helped further exacerbate workers' distrust and hostility toward the rich and powerful, and hence their restiveness. From mid-September to late October, a wave of strikes, greater in scope and intensity than any the country had seen since before the war, swept across Russia. Frustrated and angry, strikers, many of them in industries that had not been actively involved in earlier strikes, tended to demand far more than most employers or government officials (or even many trade union leaders and socialists) considered reasonable. Though repeatedly told that the economy could not sustain their demands, workers insisted on higher wages to compensate for the huge losses to inflation. And strikers, though warned about their violation of fundamental managerial prerogatives, asserted the right to make decisions about hiring and firing. The more that employers resisted and denounced these demands and the more the state, the liberal press, and the Soviet leadership counseled moderation and consideration for "the common good," the more workers in large numbers insisted.[72]

For many workers, especially in large factories, the direct assertion of workers' control over production and distribution through factory committees was the best way to respond to the economic crisis and to oppression. At first, workers' control was primarily defensive and supervisory, though born of a fundamental mistrust of employers and managers. Factory committees insisted on being allowed to supervise production, oversee supplies and fuel, monitor fines and other disciplinary measures, and direct hiring and firing, all in order to make sure that jobs were protected and the factory run fairly. As the economic and social crisis deepened in the early fall, workers' control became increasingly aggressive and interventionist. The principal aim was still to protect workers' livelihoods by keeping the factory running. Factory committees began to take a more assertive stance, however, in the face of employer resistance to further concessions, attempts to restrict the roles of factory committees, and the constant threat of production cutbacks and factory closures due to an economic crisis that many workers suspected was the result of willful "sabotage" by employers and the bourgeoisie as a whole. Forms of action varied. When managers threatened layoffs because of fuel shortages, for example, factory committees might seek out new fuel supplies, arrange for more economical usage of available fuel, arrange for hours to be cut for all, and for some workers to be transferred to different shops, or intervene to decide

who should be laid off. Efforts, mostly unsuccessful, were made to review company finances and control expenditures. In a small but growing number of cases, usually when employers planned to close their
factories entirely, workers acted to remove the existing management
and run the factories themselves.[73]

Deepening polarization and conflict were also strongly in evidence
in the army and the navy. On the part of the authorities, a harsh new
attitude toward lack of military discipline and soldiers' power arose in
the wake of the July Days and the disastrous collapse of the military offensive. Before July, most officers had viewed the soldiers' committees
as a necessary evil and many had cultivated working relationships with
the committees, which, after all, were often the only means by which
they could get things done. By mid-July, however, the situation had
changed. Growing disorder had resulted from the failed offensive, and
officers, encouraged by the new tough language about discipline from
both government officials and senior commanders like Kornilov,
showed less restraint in their dealings with the soldiers' committees.
(Kornilov's appointment as commander in chief on 18 July was seen by
many as an endorsement of his views on the necessity of stringent discipline.) More and more often officers voiced resentment against the
committees, tried to interfere with their activities, and openly proposed that committees and deputies be reined in or even abolished,
that soldiers' meetings be banned, that the Declaration of the Rights of
Soldiers be revoked, and that the old rituals of officer authority
(salutes, formal address, and so on) be restored.[74]

The government and the high command were clearly sympathetic to
the officers' concerns. In July and August, the military command approved a host of new restrictive orders limiting the activities of committees. The act of greatest significance, though—not so much in its
practical implementation, which was rare, as for its symbolic force—
was the reintroduction on 12 July of the death penalty at the front (to
be imposed by field courts), a decision that most officers embraced as
an act of salvation for the army as a whole and for their own right to
enforce military discipline and order. Talk about extending the application to soldiers at the rear soon followed. The effects of this new
spirit of military discipline, however, were often the opposite of those
intended. It was true, according to a secret army report from the beginning of August, that these new rules, and the restitution of officers'
authority in general, had a "sobering effect" on relatively loyal men;
yet in already disaffected units, the result was just the reverse: "unreliable" soldiers became even more infuriated, "regarding the orders on

discipline and the death penalty as a return to the old regime and blaming officers for their publication." As a consequence, "the situation [of the officers] in many units" had become "very bad, even critical."[75]

The Kornilov mutiny, though involving a relatively small number of senior officers, appeared to a great many soldiers as confirmation of their worst suspicions, and they responded accordingly, often brutally. The first news of the mutiny called forth a reaction far out of proportion to the real danger, for the men were responding as much to underlying frustration, distrust, and anger—sentiments strongly reflected in many of the documents presented here—as to the event itself. Soldiers' committees, ready to defend the Soviet and the government, swung into action to ensure that their units would not be used against the revolution. Committees delegated to themselves the necessary authority to combat counterrevolution, including the right to arrest and replace unreliable officers, to control communications, and to countersign all orders and telegrams. At the same time, they counseled organization, tact, and self-discipline—but their appeals on this score often fell on deaf ears. Once the immediate threat of counterrevolution had passed, the gates were open to what has been described as "a momentous groundswell of soldier determination to master their own fate which overflooded all institutional bounds, new and old, and recognized no counsels of restraint or accommodation."[76] A torrent of anger and hatred was unleashed, first and foremost against officers. Meetings approved resolutions calling for punishment and retribution, for replacing "the revolution of flowers and poets . . . by the revolution of fire and sword."[77] Hundreds of officers were removed from authority, arrested, beaten, and sometimes brutally killed.[78] Very soon, soldiers' committees and the soviets were openly criticizing the new wave of anarchy among the soldiers. Soviet leaders and moderate socialists appealed to them for calm and self-restraint. They claimed to understand what drove soldiers to such excesses: "Wrath and fury, grief and fear have filled your hearts" at the threat of counterrevolution; yet they begged soldiers to "control [their] wrath" for the sake of the revolution.[79] Such violence, they warned, was the "poisoned fruit of the Kornilov affair," stimulating in soldiers and sailors "an unreasoning, dark, stupefying hatred and hostility toward commanding personnel," which, in turn, was the "undying echo of immemorial distrust toward the master, now renamed 'bourgeois.'"[80] This was not, they insisted, the true meaning or the spirit of the revolution and could only do it harm.

This outburst of wrath and violence did not last long. Nonetheless, huge numbers of soldiers and sailors made it abundantly clear that their patience with the government had run out. With the cold weather approaching and food and warm clothing in terribly short supply, soldiers were determined that the war must end before winter. They held meetings, passed peace resolutions, harassed their officers, demanded leaves (or simply deserted), and refused to build winter bunkers, repair trenches, stock winter supplies, or participate in training exercises. In September, according to commanders, soldiers everywhere were talking about "peace, warm clothing, and food" and about the need to "put the whole high command to the bayonet."[81] Army intelligence bulletins from the front at that time reported a "complete lack of confidence in the officers and the higher commanding personnel," hostility to every order, and a "defeatist" attitude toward the war.[82] Not surprisingly, Bolshevism reaped the benefit. To be sure, the party as an organization had been severely damaged in the wake of the July Days, and both activists and the party press had a rather weak presence at the front even as late as September, apart from individual Bolshevized soldiers from the garrisons who arrived at the front as replacements. Still, "Bolshevik" themes—especially calls for ending the war immediately and for taking power out of the hands of the bourgeoisie—were ubiquitous. This "revival of 'Bolshevism,'" as Alan Wildman called it, gave those who were actually Bolsheviks the opportunity to increase their influence.[83] They did not miss their chance. By mid-October, staff reports described astonishing Bolshevik gains, resulting in "provocative" resolutions for peace and soviet power, disputes over every order, and new elections of soldiers' committees replacing Menshevik and S.R. leaders with Bolsheviks.[84]

In the countryside, too, patience and trust were running out. Throughout the summer and fall, the government continued its efforts to develop a land reform program in preparation for the Constituent Assembly. In late March, the government had authorized the minister of agriculture (a post held, starting in May, by the Socialist Revolutionary leader Viktor Chernov) to establish a national network of land committees—directed by a Central Land Committee and extending to provincial, county (*uezd*), and township (*volost*) committees—in order to collect data on local conditions and needs with an eye to planning reform.[85] Already in the spring, as we have seen, peasants had begun to act, without waiting for legal government sanction. They marched on local manor houses or government offices to demand lower rents for land use or other changes, illegally cut timber for fuel from the forests, occasionally burned an estate house to the ground, and, by April and May, began to seize private lands. By midsummer, and especially in September and October, after the harvest was in and as food shortages made the coming winter look especially ominous, unrest grew to crisis proportions. Government reports and stories in the press were replete with horrified accounts of "anarchy," "arbitrary action," "destruction," and "pogroms," especially in the densely populated central black-earth and Volga regions (where the long-term pressures of land hunger and social resentment combined with widespread crop failures in 1917 to create even higher levels of unrest). Some peasants continued to appeal to the government to hand over private and monastic lands to them, but most seem to have decided that they would have to enact their own revolution in land tenure and in the rural social order. Peasants seized and divided up livestock and tools, harvested grain, broke into and looted government grain stores (a state monopoly in the grain market had been established in March), and felled trees in great numbers. Crowds of villagers attacked the enclosed private holdings of peasant farmers (*otrubniki* and kulaks)— who had in earlier years separated their lands as private, rather than communal, property—and forced these independent farmers to return to the communal rules of the village. Guards, managers, and servants were beaten up, and some were killed. Finally, peasants told large landowners to hand over their lands to village committees or communes and threatened destruction if they refused. Relatively few estate lands were directly seized in the fall (partly because until the spring sowing peasants would have little immediate need for the land). Instead, peasants focused on eradicating rich landowners from the countryside altogether. Hundreds of manor houses were destroyed in "pogroms," in which crowds of peasants, numbering sometimes in the thousands and armed with pitchforks, rifles, and other weapons, invaded the homes of the gentry, smashed their belongings, and burned the rest to the ground. It often seemed that the aim of these actions was not simply to destroy the homes of rich landowners so that they could not return but also to ritually smash the symbols of their wealth, privilege, and cultural otherness. Peasants took home any tools and materials that could be useful, but they tended to destroy objects having, in their eyes, mainly emblematic significance: fancy furniture, pianos, libraries, statues, paintings, formal gardens, and fish ponds. If reports can be believed, these iconoclastic riots sometimes took on a playful even festive character, a carnival spirit marked by laughing, music, dancing, and drinking.[86]

For radicals on the Left, these social upheavals represented the welcome advent of the "new revolution" that Lenin had seen on the horizon in late September. For conservatives, liberals, and even many socialists—including, as the documents remind us, many lower-class Russians—the deepening crisis in the fall of 1917 revealed a much darker vision of the near future: "anarchy," "destruction," "catastrophe." Like many who commented on these upheavals, the editors of the Socialist Revolutionary newspaper *Volia naroda* (People's will), writing in late September, spoke of Russia's having fallen into a nightmarish abyss: "Against the background of merciless foreign war and defeats of the armies of the Republic, internally the country has entered upon a period of anarchy and, virtually, a period of civil war. . . . Class animosity has flared up everywhere . . . and the singular devastation of Russian life is further complicated by strikes, revolts, upheavals, and outright robberies. In a few more weeks, perhaps a few days, all of Russia will be swept by the fire of dissension, mutual discord, and the complete paralysis of all life."[87] The prospect of an armed seizure of power by the Bolsheviks was viewed by many as certain to push the country over the edge. Many others, however, as documents following also reflect, viewed this new upheaval, which the Soviet newspaper branded an "insane adventure,"[88] as the only remaining path to order, peace, and freedom.

Workers

· 53 ·

Resolution on the July Days by workers of the Shlisselburg Powder Works, Petrograd, 4 July 1917.

Resolution
Passed at the general meeting of workers
of the Shlisselburg Powder Works

We, the men and women workers and the soldiers of the Shlisselburg Powder Works, a total of five thousand people, having discussed the events of 3 July in Petersburg [*sic*], welcome and support our comrade Petersburg soldiers and workers who have come out to fight the counterrevolution, and we declare:

"Enough hesitations! In the name of freedom, in the name of peace, in the name of the worldwide proletarian revolution, the All-Russian Executive Committee of the Soviet of Workers', Soldiers', and Peasants' Deputies must seize power! Executive power must rest in its hands, for it truly expresses the people's will. There is no other way out of the impasse that has come about. The policy of compromise with the bourgeoisie has clearly revealed how utterly bankrupt and ruinous for the cause of freedom it is."

Meeting chairman, N. Chekalov
Accurate: Secretary of the Committee of the RSDRP (Bolshevik), Pushkevich

· 54 ·

Resolution on the July Days by representatives of Petrograd printing workers, 8 July 1917.

The general meeting of the elected workers' representatives of the printing establishments of Petrograd, having discussed the events that took place on 3 and 4 July, hereby declare:

The events of recent days were prepared for by the agitation of the left wing of Russian democracy, which consists of a significant irresponsible minority and which attempted with the help of bayonets and machine guns that happened to fall into their hands to impose their will on all of the revolutionary democracy. For this reason, responsibility for the crisis we are experiencing[1] must fall on their heads. The appeals to workers and units of the garrison bearing arms to come out on the street were made apart from and in defiance of the will of the most authoritative organ of revolutionary Russia, the executive bureau of the CC [Central Committee] of the All-Russian Congress of SWSD [Soviets of Workers' and Soldiers' Deputies].[2]

We, printing workers—part of the Petrograd proletariat[3]—having organized in our own trade union, feel it is essential to stress that henceforth only the slogans and appeals shared by the revolutionary democracy of all Russia will be binding and authoritative for us and we will never respond to the appeals of irresponsible groups or separate socialist parties.

Uniting in our ranks comrades belonging to various political parties, and even some without a party, we consider the sole correct point of view to be that of the Third All-Russ.[ian] Conf.[erence of] T.[rade] Unions on this issue: in close unity with all the political parties of the proletariat, we will do our utmost to support absolutely the authoritative organs of revolutionary democracy—the Soviets of Work.[ers'], Sold.[iers'], and Peasants' Deputies.

1. The reference is to the conservative reaction that was directed against much of the Left in the wake of the July Days.

2. As here, authors of resolutions and letters often mistook or forgot the still unfamiliar name of the Central Executive Committee of the All-Russian Congress of Soviets.

3. This insistent self-identification of printers as part of the "proletariat" is directed against common accusations of craft pride and exclusiveness.

· 55 ·

Resolutions on the July Days by workers and employees
of the Petrograd Metal Works and by the Executive Committee
of Bolsheviks at the factory, 11 July 1917.

A general factory meeting held on 11 July at the Petrograd Metal Works passed the following resolution:

Recognizing that the bloody events of recent days (3–5 July) were a consequence of the disorganizing activity of certain individuals and groups, and the intrigues of agents of imperialist governments and agents of the old order who are trying to introduce strife, enmity, and disintegration into the workers' laboring mass and into the army on the basis of the general [economic] collapse and the fact that the essential needs of the working masses remain unsatisfied, the meeting (of workers and employees) of the Metal Works acknowledges:

1) That for the salvation of the country and the revolution, the entire working people must unite around its elected soviets of workers', soldiers', and peasants' [deputies] to undertake coordinated common action and to struggle against the dark forces of the past.

2) We pledge to serve the country and the revolution, sparing neither strength nor sacrifice, under the guidance of our soviets (of workers', soldiers', and peasants' [deputies]) for the total triumph of the revolution.

3) We demand from our elected representatives strict and precise execution of the will of organized workers in defense of the interests of workers, peasants, and soldiers, and independence and careful deliberation in decisions and oversight over individuals and the activities of any executive power.

4) We demand that everyone to whom power has been entrusted at this critical moment retain his presence of mind, in order not to disarm the revolutionary powers of the people or introduce disorganization through violent actions against the soviets elected by the working masses but, on the contrary, do everything possible to facilitate the organization of the revolutionary army, the workers, and the people on democratic principles.

The meeting believes that the fulfillment of the promise given by the government for the Salvation of the Revolution,[1] to imperiously demand sacrifices, especially from the propertied classes, can introduce enthusiasm, unanimity, and readiness for sacrifice among the revolutionary people.

This resolution was drawn up by representatives from all the parties at the factory (with the exception of the anarchists) and was approved unanimously by eight thousand workers and employees with only twenty abstentions.

By a majority of sixteen votes, one against, with four abstentions, the executive committee of the organization of the RSDRP (Bolshevik) at the Petrograd Metal Works approved the following resolution, which was announced to the representative of the Petrograd committee present at the meeting and will be proposed to the meeting of the entire collective at the factory:

1) We express our full confidence in the All-Russian Soviets of Workers', Soldiers', and Peasants' Deputies, as well as in the Petrograd Soviet of Workers' and Soldiers' Deputies and their executive organs and, consequently, in everything that is resolved by these authorized organizations of the revolution.

2) We put ourselves wholly at the disposal of the Petrograd Soviet of Workers' and Soldiers' Deputies.

3) We demand that the central committee and the Petrograd committee of our party immediately lay aside their positions of authority and put themselves wholly at the disposal of the judicial authority for a strict and thorough investigation into the accusation against them by the bourgeois newspapers of spying for the Germans, so as thereby to prove that a hundred thousand worker Bolsheviks cannot be German agents.

4) We demand that Comrades Lenin and Trotsky immediately surrender to the judicial authority as well.

5) Until the authorized all-Russian and Petrograd conferences [of the Bolshevik party] assemble for new elections for the central committee and the Petrograd committee, the local factory S.D. [Social Democratic] (Bolshev.) organization will no longer consider itself a part of the general [party] organization, and until the conference it will not obey any orders of the central and Petrograd committees.

6) The local factory organization shall consider itself temporarily disbanded until the elected committee of three, authorized at this session, verifies the lists of all the members of our factory organization.

7) In practical work at the factory, our organization will advance arm in arm with the local councils of elders[2] and with local socialist organizations, though still adhering to its own theoretical point of view and convictions.

1. The "government for the salvation of the revolution" was an unofficial designation for the Provisional Government sometimes used following the July Days, especially after Kerensky became prime minister on 7 July.

2. Elected bodies of workers' representatives that existed at some large factories, as established by prerevolutionary law (see glossary).

· 56 ·

Resolution by the printing workers of the former Markus press,
Petrograd, 13 July 1917.

The chromolithography department of the "Russian Printing and Publishing Company, formerly of E. I. Markus"
Extract from the minutes of the Gen.[eral] Meet.[ing] on 13 July 1917

Resolution

We workers of the "Russian Printing and Publishing Company, formerly of E. I. Markus," having gathered to discuss the current political situation, have issued the following resolution (passed unanimously by all those participating in the Gen.[eral] Meet.[ing]). Finding the armed demonstration that took place in Petrograd on 3–5 July of this year to be the most grievous and shameful page in Russian history, when politically naive soldiers and workers went out on the street with weapons, as a consequence of which there was fratricidal slaughter, which took many innocent victims to the grave. Branding with shame and putting our curse on all the organizers of this provocational demonstration, which could lead to counterrevolution, and considering them guilty of all the murders committed at that time, we at the same time express our full sympathy with all those who helped restore order in Petrograd. While giving them the proper and just gratitude and deeply regretting those others who fell in the performance of their duty, we request that these small funds we have collected be accepted for their burial or to benefit their families, at the discretion of the Sov. S. and W. Deputies.

> Chairman of the factory committee, A. Likhtenshtein
> Secretary, S. Dmitriev
> Factory elders, P. Bogomolov, R. Chernov

· 57 ·

Letter to citizens from workers at the Putilov factory, Petrograd, 11 July 1917.

Letter to All Citizens from Putilov Workers
(in explanation of 3, 4, and 5 July)

Citizens! Like a venerable oak standing in the middle of the forest, the giant Putilov factory stands in the middle of state industry, making the earth quake with the heavy blows of its hammers.[1] From all ends of Russia, workers have come to work in it, and while they are working they think thoughts: to the whistle of the saw, the screech of the drive belts, the dispiriting sight of the gun carriages and cannons, gloomy thoughts creep into your mind. In work as hard as prison labor, the mothers and fathers who gave us birth die, and we too are dying right here: in despairing alienation from the joys we envy, from the wealth and culture that is enjoyed not far from us—separated only by a fat monument, the old Narva Gates[2]—by the rich, "educated" minority.

Where is justice?

Where are the results of the blood and of the lives of our brothers who fell in the revolution?

Where is the new life, that heavenly, joyous, fiery-red bird that flew so temptingly over our country and then hid—as if to trick us?[3]

Citizens, this is not the first time the Putilov workers have shed blood for the common interests of the working class. Remember 9 January[4] and refrain from those unfounded accusations that are being heard now on the streets of Petrograd. On these days, 3 and 4 July, we were marching with the pure heart of loyal sons of the revolution and marching not against the Soviet of Workers' and Soldiers' Deputies but in support of it. This is why "All Power to the Soviet" was written on our banners.

When we come out—they fire upon us. This is why some of us, for purposes of self-defense, took weapons along. On 9 January they, the loyal servants of the House of the Romanovs, fired upon us. Now it has been established with certainty that the first shots, as well as some of the answering shots, were organized by provocateurs—enemies of Russian freedom, enemies of the workers.

Citizens: Our renewed life is impatient. By the logic of events, it pushes the revolutionary people inexorably onto the streets and onward. And often the street resolves a dispute. But sadly, we are alone. We do not have sufficient organizational strength. The politically conscious workers are too scattered and often care not for the interests of the class as a whole but for the interests of numerous, and, for us, harmful factions and sects. It is left to us. The "Soviet of Workers' Deputies" seems to have started getting along without workers, and in isolating itself more and more from us, keeping to its own members, it has gone off into minutiae of an administrative nature. And the Provisional Government is already frozen, with everything in bureaucratically dead forms.

It is in this light that the economic and political situation on the eve of the events of 3–4 July appeared before us, workers.

Citizens: Take an honest look at the black, smoking chimneys rising up from the earth. There, at their foot, creating new assets for you that you need, are people just like you, suffering and tormented in bondage by the most complete and fierce exploitation. Class consciousness is maturing slowly there. Hatred is building up in their hearts, and the sweet conditions of another life for all mankind are being written lovingly on their bloody banner.

Down with fratricidal strife.

All citizens to the active support of the Committee for the Salvation of the Revolution—this final push for freedom, repeating the words of its appeal "To Men and Women Workers": "Under neither the boot of Wilhelm II nor the foul yoke of Nicholas the Bloody."[5]

Passed unanimously on 11 July at a full general meeting of the cannon works and passed on to the fac.[tory] comm.[ittee] for publication.

> Chairman, I. Mudrov
> Secretary, I. Smirnov

1. The Putilov factory, with thirty thousand workers in 1917, was the largest metalworking enterprise in Russia before 1917. Putilov workers had a reputation for being militants in the class and political struggles, and many took part in the July Days.

2. Narva Gates—a monument built to commemorate the war of 1812, situated at the northern end of the working-class Narva district, where the Putilov factory was located.

3. An allusion to the Firebird, the mythological symbol of another, better world, and of salvation.

4. On 9 January 1905, "Bloody Sunday," a mass procession of workers, including many Putilov employees, and their families marched to the Winter Palace to present a petition of social grievances to the tsar. Police fired on the unarmed crowds, and hundreds were wounded or killed. The event convinced many workers to reject the autocracy. Bloody Sunday marked the start of the 1905 revolution.

5. This joint resolution of the Executive Committee of the Soviets of Workers' and Soldiers' Deputies and of the Executive Committee of the Soviets of Peasants' Deputies appeared in *Izvestiia*, no. 114 (11 July 1917): 2.

· 58 ·

Resolution of a meeting of workers in twenty-seven small enterprises
from the Peterhof district of Petrograd, 27 July 1917.

On the Crisis of Authority and the Current Moment

Recognizing the extremely critical condition of the Russian revolution
when an adventuristic offensive[1] has led inevitably to serious defeat at the
front and to the disintegration of the revolutionary army, and when the
war, artificially and criminally prolonged by the ruling circles, is leading
the exhausted army into new and dangerous adventures, when under the
influence of bloody carnage, bankers' speculation and factory and plant
owners' sabotage, the agricultural and industrial collapse mounts, pushing the country toward total exhaustion and ruin, when under pressure
from the counterrevolutionary bourgeoisie, the Black Hundreds and the
command staff of the army, the leading majority of the Soviets is shame-
fully retreating and surrendering its positions one after another to its enemies, when through the shameful resurrection of the death penalty and by
field courts-martial,[2] arrests and violence threaten to shed the blood of the
people's conquests, when with the criminal connivance of the ruling parties the tested leaders of the revolutionary democracy have been betrayed,
when before our very eyes, instead of the chains of autocracy, a new slavery has been forged and there has been a wild outburst of tyranny—the
working class cannot remain silent, and we, workers from the small enterprises of the Peterhof district, having listened to a report by members of
the Soviet of Workers' and Soldiers' Deputies, Griaznov and Travnikov,
about the current situation, consider it our duty to state:

1) The new coalition "combination" of the Provisional Government is
frankly doomed to failure and to a new downfall in the near future, as four
months of a chronic crisis of authority have shown fully the entire sense-
lessness of democracy's policy of appeasement with the counterrevolutionary imperialist bourgeoisie. The new so-called government for the salvation of the revolution is incapable not only of saving the revolution but
even of saving itself from bankruptcy, for a good half of this government,
which consists of frankly counterrevolutionary elements, is seeking support among those "vital forces" of the country that make the tsarist regime stink like carrion.

2) A government of unlimited irresponsibility toward the Soviet of
Workers', Soldiers', and Peasants' Deputies cannot enjoy the confidence
of the people, for in this situation the presence of the Soviets, which alone
are capable of saving the country, is reduced to nil. The refusal of responsible factions in the Soviets to participate in the organization of [state]
power is an act of political suicide that we wholeheartedly protest.

3) We demand the immediate repeal of the shameful introduction of the

death penalty. If the penalty has been repealed for Nicholas the Bloody and his gang, then shame on those who would reinstate it for the revolutionary soldier.

4) We protest the insolent attacks made by the high command against the revolutionary organization of the army that exists in the form of regimental, company, and other collectives of the revolutionary army.

5) We protest the arrest of the meritorious leaders of democracy's left wing and the routs and repressions of workers' and soldiers' organizations, for in this we see an open campaign by the counterrevolutionary bourgeoisie against the entire working class.

6) We indignantly protest the closing of the left-wing organs of the workers' and soldiers' press, for this step is frankly counterrevolutionary, depriving the people of the opportunity to prepare for the Constituent Assembly, while at the same time the conservative press of all stripes is openly going about its own corrupting work.

Considering the fact that, given the silent connivance of the ruling parties of the S.R.'s and the Mensheviks, everything set forth above is undoubtedly moving the country toward an abyss of dark reaction and not giving the land to the peasants, control over production to the workers, rights to the soldiers, and so forth, we insist that the leading circles of the Soviet of Workers', Soldiers', and Peasants' Deputies correct its aimless and tottering policy at its very roots, rip out all the various deals with the counterrevolutionary tsarist Duma,[3] reject the errors of the policy of compromise with the bourgeoisie, and stand on the firm ground of the revolutionary class struggle.

With respect to the crisis of authority, we declare that only a revolutionary authority that rests on the proletariat and the poorest strata of the peasantry[4] can facilitate the country's move toward saving the revolution; therefore our immediate task is the irreconcilable struggle for the interests of the very poorest people and for concentrating all authority in the hands of the revolutionary proletarians', soldiers', and peasants' Soviets, which alone can reinforce and extend the gains of the revolutionary people.

Chairman, [signature]

1. The Russian offensive on the southwest front began 18 June. Within days, after fleeting success, the offensive collapsed, as soldiers refused to continue fighting. On 6 July, Austrian and German forces delivered a counteroffensive and broke through the front of the Russian army, which began to withdraw, not always in good order.

2. On 12 March, the Provisional Government had abolished the death penalty in all civil, military, and naval penal laws. Similarly, extrajudicial courts, flogging, deportation to Siberia, and other brutal practices of the old regime were abolished. On 12 July, the government restored field courts (officially, "military-revolutionary courts") and the death penalty in the war zone in order to enforce military discipline.

3. In early July, the Soviet leadership proposed to the Provisional Government that there be a formal decision to dissolve the old tsarist State Duma and State Council as

part of a legal declaration of a republic. The Duma had been prorogued by Nicholas II but not dissolved. And moves were under way to revive its role. On 18 July, in the Tauride Palace, a meeting of members of the fourth State Duma was organized by the Provisional Committee of the State Duma to discuss how the Duma might "save Russia."
    4. This was a familiar phrase, often used by Lenin and the Bolsheviks.

· 59 ·

Letter to Kerensky from Pyotr Arshinov, railroad workshop storeman,
Orel Province, late July or early August 1917.[1]

To Mr. Minister Chairman Aleksandr Fyodorovich Kerensky
From a citizen of Briansk, Orel Prov.[ince],
Pyotr Kuzmich Arshinov, a storeman in the Belogovsky workshops of the Nikol.[aevskaia] R.R.

Even though the holy revolution dictates equal rights and freedom of action and speech, doesn't there nest in some innermost corner of the revolution some statute according to which might be said something like this? Slap an iron harness on those who are obviously leading the Fatherland to its ruin. Rip the accursed weeds out of our native field, dear Russia.
    Aleksandr Fyodorovich! To my great sorrow, I possess no eloquence, but as a genuine son of our dear Russia I beg you to accept my assurances that there are many, a great many, [politically] conscious citizens of the Russian land who look with disgust upon the appeal of the Bolsheviks attached to this letter.[2]

P. Arshinov
P.S. In 1905–1906, the word "bastard" was used only in the newspaper *Veche*.[3] In the attached appeal it is symptomatic.[4]

    1. Based on the dates of publication of the Bolshevik proclamation referred to.
    2. "Ko vsem trudiashchimsia, ko vsem rabochim i soldatam Petrograda [To all working people, to all workers and soldiers of Petrograd]" (24 July 1917), *Rabochii i soldat*, no. 2 (24 July 1917), 1–2, and reprinted in no. 8 (1 August 1917): 1–2. Text also in *Listovki petrogradskikh bol'shevikov, 1917–1920*, vol. 3 (Leningrad, 1957), 56–60. The appeal justified the demonstrations of 3–4 July, called for transferring power to the workers and poor peasants, and accused, the moderate socialist leaders, in sometimes venomous rhetoric, of weakness, cowardice, and betrayal and of leading the country toward counterrevolution.
    3. *Veche* was an extreme right-wing newspaper published in Moscow from 1905 to 1910.
    4. The proclamation, authorized by the second Petrograd conference of Bolsheviks, was evidently written by Joseph Stalin. See I. V. Stalin, *Sochineniia*, vol. 3 (Moscow, 1946), 137–143, 401–402. The offending phrase, similar to the style of discourse that became familiar from Stalin's "Short Course" in the 1930s, was a reference to the post-

July Days, when, in the words of the proclamation, the "insolent bourgeois bastard slings mud at" the "dear and beloved" Bolshevik leaders of the working class.

· 60 ·

Anonymous note to the All-Russian Central Executive Committee of Soviets, late July 1917 (received 4 August).

———————————

Comrades. Please drive out that fucking son of a bitch[1] General Kornilov,[2] or else he's going to take his machine guns and drive you out, that is, your soviet of W.[orkers'] and S.[oldiers'] D[eputies].

Your true friend and comrade.

Also drive out Savinkov[3] because he supports Kornilov. Comrades, take power into your own hands. Ministers and various other bastards are taking a great sin upon their souls, for they're acting like one who would take a man and get him drunk and force him to commit some crime.

Comrades, take every measure to repeal the death penalty because lots and lots of innocent people are going to die.

1. Translating Russian obscene speech into English is difficult, as Russian *mat* (as such swearing was called, a word with the same root as the word for "mother") tends to be far more varied, complex, and lavish than English swearing, and often quite different in form. For example, the original here, *gonite pozhalusta ginirala karnilova k khuiam sobachim* (the many misspellings are in the original), literally means "please drive General Kornilov to the dog pricks."

2. On 18 July, Kornilov had been promoted to commander in chief (see glossary).

3. Boris Viktorovich Savinkov (1879–1925), also known by the literary pseudonym V. Rupshin, was one of the leaders of the Socialist Revolutionary Party. He was involved in the assassination of Interior Minister Viacheslav Plehve in 1904 and Governor-General of Moscow Grand Duke Sergei Aleksandrovich in 1905, after which, to avoid a death sentence, he emigrated to France. He returned to Russia with amnesty after the February revolution. In July 1917, he became assistant war minister to Kerensky. In late August, before the Kornilov "mutiny," he represented the Provisional Government in negotiations with Kornilov about a more cooperative relationship.

· 61 ·

Letter to the editor of *Izvestiia* about a Literary-Musical Evening in Petrograd, 31 July 1917.

———————————

31 July 1917

Dear Comrade Editor,

Allow me through your newspaper to lodge my strong protest. On Sunday, 30 July of this year, at the Putilov Theater, the Peterhof District Committee of the S.R. party organized a literary-musical evening devoted to the memory of people's fighter E. Sazonov.[1] There aren't enough theaters in the workers' districts, and practically no good ones where one can find rest for the soul from one's daily work, and so, believing that the S.R. party, in trying to give the workers good aesthetic satisfaction, would not stage something you could see in any flea-bitten sideshow [*balagan*],[2] and thinking that at an evening devoted to E. Sazonov we would not hear the banalities so frequent in the sideshows, we decided to attend. But what we found did nothing to illuminate the name of this people's freedom fighter. On the contrary, the feet of the dancers from the Lin Theater and the others who performed debased this name and trampled it in the mud. For example, Madame Garina, an artist from the Moscow Zimin Theater, appeared on the stage and began performing "folk songs" that called up the basest of human feelings, emphasized by a great deal of smiling and grimacing and gesturing and winking. After this "folk" artist, the "poet" R. L. Adolgoim came out on stage and started reciting his "Letter to Wilhelm." The title alone gives you a good notion of what kind of "poetry" this was, not yielding in the least to the very basest works of the boulevard press. After all they saw, many comrades were mightily indignant over the performance of such things, and not wanting to create a scandal at a comradely evening, they decided to go see the comrades who organized the evening, in order to find out what was going on, but they also could do nothing to stop it. As we were leaving them, though, we witnessed something incredible. Two of the dancers from the Lin Theater, arms akimbo and hands pressed into their sides, grimacing and twitching their shoulders, were performing a "lubok"[3] dance—truly something beneath anything you would associate with the lubok you see in the sideshows. Finally, unable to bear this mockery of the name of our popular hero, E. Sazonov, and the poetry and culture of mankind, we declared our protest then and there, in the hall. Have members of the S.R. party actually reached the point of such philistinism that they are capable of presenting the popular masses with such banality and vulgarity? Have they actually reached the point where they let the lofty name of the people's fighter E. Sazonov be disgraced by such performances by citizen artists as the performance of R. Adelgoim, Garina, and the others? If so, then what would E. Sazonov, whose name you intended to honor, say? We hope, though, that our comrades in our common work have not stooped to such base cultural demands and from now on will be more selective and cautious. And to all those who wish to help spread knowledge, culture, and poetry to the working masses, don't think that the workers are so ignorant and undiscriminating that they can be stuffed with dancing and with yellow [cheap and crass] poetry like "Letter to Wilhelm." No, the undeveloped but keen instinct inherent in every man tells the workers where the beauty of culture leaves off and the sideshows begin. Everything marvelous that human culture gives him he soaks up, and everything cheap and tasteless [*zhelto-balagannoe*] is cast aside, like a useless rag, with a protest.

N. Aleksandrov
A. Bodrov

1. Yegor Sergeevich Sazonov (1879–1910) was a well-known activist in the Russian Socialist Revolutionary Party. Expelled from Moscow University for his participation in the student movement and first arrested in 1902 for radical activities, he was banished to Siberia in 1903 but escaped and fled abroad. Returning secretly to Russia, he participated in 1904 in the assassination of Minister of Internal Affairs V. Plehve, for which he was sentenced to an indefinite term of imprisonment at hard labor. He committed suicide while in prison.

2. A *balagan* was a temporary building—the word itself meant shed or barn—put up for theatrical presentations to popular audiences, especially at fairs.

3. In its primary and most common meaning, the *lubok* was a cheap popular print, originally one from a woodcut but later mass-produced commercially. By analogy, lubok literature (or, in this less common usage, lubok performance) was defined as literature (or performance) that was vulgar and lacking artistic merit, catering to the lowest cultural tastes of popular audiences.

· 62 ·

Resolution by the cultural commission of the Berg factory, Tver, 17 August 1917.

Resolution Passed at the General Meetings of 3 and [illegible] August 1917 by the Cultural-Educational Commission Under the Executive Committee of the Soviet of Workers' Deputies of the Factory of the Rozhdestvensky Manufacturing Company of P. V. Berg in Tver.

While setting as the goal of our activities the improvement of the intellectual, moral, and social-political level of the working masses, and considering the political freedom won by the revolution to be an inalienable right of the people, an essential condition for their cultural rebirth and their struggle for social liberation,

the Cultural-Educational Commission of the Soviet of Workers' Deputies of the Berg factory in Tver declares its protest

against the restoration of the death penalty, the most shameful "legal institution" of murder of man by man, that legacy of barbarism which corrupts the consciousness of our people, and

we protest the restoration of the "punitive forced labor [*katorzhnye*] laws" of the overthrown tsarist system, which violate the freedoms of speech, press, unions, and assembly and the inviolability of the person and his residence, benefits obtained by the blood and sufferings of generations, and we protest restrictions on voting rights, the restoration of censorship, administrative arrests, searches, and incarceration in jails and prisons erected by the autocracy, which lives on in our memory in shame.[1]

Condemning the repressions that stand as a barrier to the education and organization of the working masses and that crush under their heavy weight the most revolutionary strata [of workers], and protesting the restoration of the "policy of blood and iron" that reigned in "the old days of autocracy,"

the Cultural-Educational Commission

brands with scorn the insolent and low pogromist slander and defamation that are being raised against the revolutionary democracy in the attempt, the interests of counterrevolution, to blacken and smother the spread of the shining days of international unity and solidarity of mankind,

and sends its greetings to all the fighters persecuted for the ideas of the International,[2] which has been resurrected in the streams of Blood of the World War, and to everyone waging the selfless fight against the hydra of imperialism and for world justice, for the happiness, freedom, and peace of the whole world.

Tver, 17 August 1917

1. From mid-July to early August, the Provisional Government passed a series of emergency measures that included restoration of the death penalty at the front, military censorship, administrative arrest and deportation of those who threatened internal security, hard labor for acts of violence against the state or possessing arms for such use, and administrative prohibition or closing of public meetings that threatened the state.

2. The Socialist International was the main association of the world's socialist parties. The Second International existed from 1889 to 1914, when most of the member parties split over issues raised by the outbreak of World War I.

· 63 ·

Resolution by the workers of the Erikson Telephone Factory, Petrograd, printed in the Bolshevik newspaper *Proletarii* (Proletarian), 18 August 1917.

We, the workers of the Erikson factory, at a general meeting of twenty-five hundred people, heard a report on the activities of the Provisional Government and the Central Executive Committee and reached the following conclusion:

1) That the Provisional Government, by helping the dictatorship of the counterrevolutionary bourgeoisie, has been engaged during the time of its existence in bringing about the restoration of the old order;

2) That the policy of the Provisional Government is an inevitable consequence of its compromise with the counterrevolutionary bourgeoisie and can lead to nothing but the destruction of the gains of the revolution;

3) That the policy of the Provisional Government that is leading to the surrender to the bourgeoisie of all the freedoms won by the revolution was made possible only thanks to the policy of the Soviet majority, which supports this government; by rejecting power, the Soviet majority condemned itself to political fragmentation and to even greater isolation from the workers, soldiers, and peasants.

For these reasons, the general meeting of workers of the Erikson factory believes that the revolution's salvation and development onto an international scale are feasible only if we reject the policy of compromise with the bourgeoisie and organize a truly revolutionary authority that rests on the workers and the soldiers and the peasant poor—that is, the kind of authority that would be a dictatorship aimed against the counterrevolutionary bourgeoisie.

· 64 ·

Resolution of a general meeting of the union of forestry workers, Dubovki, Saratov Province, 27 August 1917.

Resolution
of the Union of Forestry Workers
Dubovki settlement, Saratov Province, Tsarytsin Uezd
We, the workers of the Union of Forestry Workers, having discussed all aspects of the death penalty, the State Duma, and the State Council[1] at a general meeting on 27 August 1917, have come to the following conclusion and resolved: In a free country, the death penalty is impermissible, for what is most precious to a man is his life. For hundreds of years we have been fighting the old government, fighting the vampires and these barbaric laws; much blood has been shed, many of our comrades have perished over this at the hands of the despots, yet that for which our comrades rotted in prisons has not come to pass. The new government repealed this barbaric law for a few hours, but then it was reinstated; therefore, on this great day of the half-year anniversary of the Russian revolution we protest at the top of our voices against the death penalty and against those who reinstated it.

We demand that the nest of the State Duma and the State Council, woven from the gang of counterrevolutionary scoundrels, be disbanded and the guilty parties arrested and put on trial.

Carthage must be destroyed!!! The Duma must die!!!

The resolution was passed unanimously.

Chairman, G. Artemiev
Secretary, V. Terentiev

1. The State Council was the upper house in the semiconstitutional system established in Russia in 1906. Half its members were elected by major corporative groups in Russian society—provincial rural assemblies (zemstvos), the nobility, merchants and industrialists, the clergy, the Academy of Sciences and the universities, and the Finnish Diet. The rest were appointed by the tsar and included many of Russia's oldest aristocratic families. Proposals that it be formally disbanded were widely discussed in the late summer of 1917.

· 65 ·

Telegram to the Provisional Government from workers and employees
at the Georgievsky Company Sugar Factory, Petrograd, 6 September 1917.

A meeting of all factory and office workers without exception at the Georgievsky Company Sugar Factory discussed the situation in the country that has resulted from the actions of General Kornilov[1] and is deeply upset that our homeland has suffered this grave calamity of domestic breakdown which has radically intensified the already unbearably grave situation for the homeland and for the Provisional Government and has issued the following resolution expressing its absolute readiness to do everything in its power to support the Provisional Government and placing itself at its complete disposal we have utter confidence that only a unitary power in the person of the Provisional Government can save the homeland and the gains of the revolution and that it will not allow a return to the past and thus assured we continue each in his own place to work calmly and with full energy for the good of the homeland—Workers of the Georgievsky Company Sugar Factory.

1. On 26 August, General Kornilov began moving troops against the capital to establish a military dictatorship under his command.

· 66 ·

Resolution of all the political factions of the Slutsk Soviet, Minsk Province,
September 1917 (received 20 September).

Resolution of the Slutsk Soviet of S.W.P.D. [Soldiers', Workers', and Peasants' Deputies] approved by all factions (S.D. and S.R.) unanimously.

Having heard the comrades' reports on the current situation and taking into consideration the gravity of the situation resulting from General Kornilov's counterrevolutionary attempt at mutiny, which represented in essence an aspiration by the propertied classes to seize power, and being aware that the roots of this aspiration are to be found in all bourgeois groupings and parties, whose representatives belong to the Provisional Government, we demand:

1) The creation of a single Revolutionary authority coming from the depths of the revolutionary democracy, resting on it, and responsible to its central organs.

2) In order to avoid further compromises with counterrevolutionary privileged [*tsenzovye*] elements, a total rejection of any compromises or coalitions with the bourgeoisie.

3) The repeal of the death penalty and an immediate revolutionary class trial against the mutineers.

4) The most energetic struggle possible against the counterrevolution, while retaining the Committees for the Salvation of the Revolution[1] and their emergency powers.

5) The immediate disbanding of the State Duma and the State Council and the closing of the union of officers of the army and the navy[2] as a blatantly counterrevolutionary organization.

6) The total democratization of the army, to be brought about with the assistance of the troop committees.

7) The convocation of the Constituent Assembly as scheduled and without delays.

8) The restoration of the freedom of assembly and freedom of the press and the banning of the counterrevolutionary press.

9) The taking of the most decisive steps to achieve a democratic peace without annexations or indemnities and, on the principle of self-determination, an immediate review of the secret agreements concluded by the tsarist government and the total abolition of secret cabinets in foreign policy.

10) The immediate release of our comrade freedom fighters from the prisons they were cast into and the handing over to trial of their slanderers.

[seal of the Executive Committee
of the Soviet of Workers', Soldiers', and
Peasants' Deputies of Slutsk]

Secretary, [signature]

1. To help organize the struggle against Kornilov's forces, the Soviet Executive Committee created, on 28 August, a special Committee for the Struggle Against Counterrevolution, which included representatives of Mensheviks, Socialist Revolutionaries, and Bolsheviks, as well as of soviets and trade unions. The committee took control of distributing arms, protecting food supplies, and organizing popular organizations to resist Kornilov. Similar committees were formed throughout the country, usually by local soviets. These local committees were known variously as revolutionary committees, military-revolutionary committees, and, very often, committees for the salvation of the revolution.

2. A strongly conservative organization, created among Russian military men after the February revolution of 1917. The union supported the idea of a military takeover in

Russia and the establishment of an authoritarian regime, to which end it endorsed Kornilov's mutiny.

Soldiers

· 67 ·

Letter to the Soviet from the soldier Yurchenko, in the trenches
at the front, 8 July 1917.

Letter from the Trenches
To the comrades of the Soviet of Soldiers' and Workers' Deputies of Petrograd

Comrade soldiers,

I most humbly ask you to inform us in the trenches how long this pointless war is going to continue, and also whether the bourgeoisie is going to keep trying to pull the wool over our eyes for very long, because hundreds and thousands of men are dying practically every day, and for what? They say it's for freedom. But is the German really trying to infringe on our freedom? No, on the contrary, this is just something made up by the bourgeois ministers, who tell us we have to strengthen freedom, but at the same time they're killing people in this offensive of theirs and what can come of that? When the army is on the attack, the ministers rejoice and, when they aren't, cry the most innocent tears. Why don't they take a look at the mothers who are weeping over their sons who have fallen on the field of battle for English and French capital?

"Comrades, enough blood!" the Provisional Government was bellowing not so long ago, but now they are doing just the opposite. In short, I am finishing up my letter, but I repeat that we have had enough blood, enough killing of innocent people. Enough! It's time to put an end to the war. We will hold freedom in our hands as long as we're alive, but if we're gone, if they keep killing us in this idiotic offensive, then the common people are not going to see freedom because there will be freedom only for the bourgeoisie and the people are going to be back pining away under the heavy fist of the bourgeoisie.

And so, comrades, peace now. Let us see our life, for we have forgotten it in these three years of war.

Come on, comrades, peace now [*skoree mir*],
Peace now
And nothing but peace!

> Soldier of the 5th Army, 19th Corps, 183rd Division, 729th Novo-Ufimsky Regiment, 7th Company, jr. non-com. [junior non-commissioned officer], Yurchenko

· 68 ·

Letter to the Bolshevik party from two soldiers
on the southwestern front, 8 July 1917.

8 July 1917

Comrade Bolsheviks!

We, your comrades on the southwestern front, most humbly ask you to respond to our request and send us *your program*, which, unfortunately, we do not have yet because no matter who we send to get literature, no one ever brings any back. We consider the program of your Bolshevik party the most just. Everyone keeps denying it and saying that the Bolsheviks are counterrevolutionaries, but we, your comrades, see from your speeches in the newspaper that everyone respects known as *Pravda* that there is nothing here but benefit for us peasants and workers, and nothing harmful. But our leadership, which is still from the old regime, keeps trying to shove a stick into the wheel of our cart, which is traveling along the road of truth. And we, your comrades, are against the shedding of excess blood, which is now being spilled in streams here on the southwestern front, and against an offensive, which we also do not see bringing any benefit other than sacrifices, losses, and injury, but unfortunately there are very few of us, but my comrades and I hope that many of our men, who still understand too little, will join us; and in view of this we need the program of your Bolshevik party like a fish needs water or a man air, and time is passing and we, your politically conscious comrades, need to sow and sow and sow. One more thing, dear comrades, we ask that you tell us whether or not you have a trade union in your party[1] and how much the membership dues are. We also report that we can get your party's newspapers only with great effort, so we barely got hold of your newspaper *Pravda* in Stanislavov, and at the sight of it in our hands our old-regime leadership, like the old "pharaohs" [police],[2] jumped back three paces and asked us not to read newspapers like that any more. But we, your comrades, want to have your program because the time of the Constituent Assembly is already near, and we need to sow in order to reap a good harvest.

> With respect for you, your comrades, noncommissioned officers, Nikolai Solovyov and Ivan Baronin.
> Address: Active army, 309th Military Transport, 62nd Driver Battalion, N. Solovyov. Please send it in a closed package.

We are sending you forty kopeks for your program.

1. The question is further indication of the limited understanding of the Bolshevik party, and, for that matter, of Russian political parties generally, though the mistake is

made more understandable by the fact that most trade unions in Russia had been organized by members of socialist parties.

2. *Faraony*, or pharaohs, was a contemptuous popular name for the police.

· 69 ·

Resolution on the July Days by the soldiers of the 22nd
Railroad Battalion, 9 July 1917.

Resolution

Proclaimed by the 22nd Railroad Battalion on the occasion of the armed uprising in Petrograd on 3–4 July 1917.

We express our unconditional confidence in the Provisional Government and the soviets of soldiers', workers', peasants', and cossacks'[1] deputies. To Minister Kerensky we express our regret over the insult inflicted on him in words and in the press and ask him to continue to serve the homeland and Russian democracy just as selflessly as he has up until now.[2] We express our protest against all the comrades and political parties leading wittingly and unwittingly to counterrevolution and anarchy, such as the Bolsheviks and the Black Hundreds active under the flag of Bolshevism and the rest setting up every possible kind of republic, armed demonstrations, and those producing terror and violence against free citizens. We ask the Provisional Government and the soviets of soldiers', workers', and peasants' deputies to bring the most decisive measures of influence to bear on all the above-named parties and individuals; should the need arise, we are prepared to support people's minister Kerensky and the Provisional Government with all the means at our disposal; we ask the Provisional Government to transfer all governmental and public-political institutions and, when possible, defense enterprises from Petrograd to Moscow—the heart of Russia, being a truly Russian (and not half-German) city, healthier in political respects.[3] We ask the Provisional Government to get the Soviets of Soldiers', Workers', Peasants', and Cossacks' Deputies to unite and work jointly when possible and become part of the central Executive Committee and, in general, the Democratic parliament (the soviet of soldiers', peasants' and workers' deputies) has to accept without exception representatives of all the organized classes of the population proportionally. No one should have any advantage, because every citizen has to help decide our Homeland's fate; we must not take tsarism as our example—listen to some and shut the others up—this cannot be allowed to happen in a free country. We ask the War Minister to let all troop units freely express their opinions about the war and about politics, and if the majority turn out to be on the side of Lenin and his supporters, then we agree to submit to the majority and to recognize them as the authority, and then let them lead Russia down whatever path they choose. But if the majority are on the side of our comrade freedom fighter Kerensky, which means our side, then they have to submit to the majority without a murmur, and if not, then everyone who doesn't want to recognize the right of the majority should be considered enemies of freedom, the revolution, and the Homeland, lackeys of the old order and Wilhelm; apply the severest measures of punishment to them up to and including hard labor and deportation out of Russia after the conclusion of peace.

Truly signed:
Chairman of the general meeting of the battalion, Sublieutenant Polkovsky, and secretary of the battalion committee, Chvertko.
Certified true copy:
For the secretary of the battalion committee, Larchik
To the Executive Committee of the All-Russian Congress of Soldiers', Workers', and Peasants' Deputies, copy to the editorial offices of *Izvestiia* of the Petrograd Soviet of Soldiers' and Workers' Deputies and to the Executive Committee of the 5th Army
Dispatched
For the chairman, member of the battalion committee, [signature]
9 July 1917
No. 372
For the secretary, Larchik

1. Soviets of Cossacks' Deputies formed in the Don, Kuban, and Terek regions in February 1917.

2. Presumably a reference to the criticisms that accompanied the Bolshevik attempt to overthrow his government. This may also be a confused reference to news of the bomb attack against Kerensky on 6 June that partly wrecked his train. Or, it may be an even more confused reference to the huge press campaign at that time accusing Lenin of being a German agent.

3. Many Russians spoke of having "two capitals"—the old capital of Muscovite Russia and the new capital built by Peter I in early 1700s. These two cities were also long viewed by many as political and cultural symbols: St. Petersburg, Peter the Great's deliberate, geometric, and visibly European city, as a symbol of rationality and order, of innovation and reform, and of imperial power; and Moscow, a city laid out less in accordance with reason than with nature and history, as a symbol of Russia's ancient traditions and especially (with its hundreds of churches and monasteries) of Russia's religious spirit. Many described it as a distinction between Russia's "mind" (St. Petersburg) and its "heart" (Moscow). Political traditionalists often voiced contempt for St. Petersburg as a false and un-Russian city. St. Petersburg was given the more Slavic-sounding name Petrograd during the war.

· 70 ·

Resolution from soldiers of the 2nd Caucasus Engineering Regiment,
July 1917 (received 21 July).

Resolution
of the 2nd Caucasus Engineering Regiment

1. Since the entire democracy of the Great Russian people in the person of the All-Russian Soviet of Peasants' Deputies and the All-Russian Congress of Soviets of Workers' and Soldiers' Deputies has stated that at the present time our army must retain its full battle strength and must be prepared not only for defense but also for an offensive, and since the matter of an offensive has been decided by the military leadership appointed by the Provisional Government, then any refusal to carry out military orders that demoralizes the army is a direct crime against the entire people of Great Russia, the revolution and freedom. In particular, the multiple refusals of the 2nd Caucasus Grenadier Division to carry out military instructions and orders is a blatant violation of the will of the revolutionary Russian people; it shows disrespect for its interests and directly slanders these, and all this puts a shameful stain on it that will remain there forever in our eyes and that history will never erase.

2. After three centuries of battling the tsarist regime for their freedom and civil rights, the great Russian people have finally achieved these rights and have loudly proclaimed them to the whole world, having permanently ended persecution of the free expression of ideas and having abolished the death penalty—that shame of mankind. Despite this, the 703rd Regiment of the 2nd Caucasus Grenadier Division has made itself an accomplice in the greatest crime against freedom and the revolution. It has allowed its ranks to commit a series of tortures and murders of our citizens over nothing but freedom of speech. Within its ranks there are ignorant men who have trampled upon all the Great human and civil rights; they have dragged speakers off tribunes and even beaten up those who suffered under the old regime for trying to attain freedom. Liberated by the labors and concerns of these people from the age-old eyes of tsarism, these soldiers have made themselves the hangmen of their own liberators. In particular, the beating of comrade deputy SOKOLOV,[1] who fought so hard for freedom, has caused our cup of patience to overflow. We cannot look calmly at the savage acts of a handful of citizens, brigands, we cannot tolerate them in our military milieu and cannot understand how the 703rd Suramsky Regiment can tolerate them, thereby unwittingly making itself accomplice to their crimes. We brand with shame this ignorant handful of murderers and hope that the 703rd Regiment itself will support us. We propose immediately discovering the direct participants in all the crimes committed in the 703rd Regiment and arresting them and handing them

over for trial without mercy or leniency. We will not and cannot allow ignorant people who beat freedom fighters to death in free Russia to go unpunished.

Committee of the 2nd Caucasus Engineering Regiment
[Added by hand] Our most humble request to the editors of the respected newspaper *Zemlia i volia*[2] not to refuse to run this resolution in the next issue.

Secretary, Botsnov

1. Nikolai Dmitrievich Sokolov was a radical lawyer and Menshevik. In 1917, he was a founder of the Petrograd Soviet and a member of its Executive Committee. He helped soldiers draft the famous Order No. 1, the charter of soldiers' rights. On 21 June 1917, Sokolov and several other members of the Executive Committee of the Petrograd Soviet of Workers' and Soldiers' Deputies were beaten and arrested by soldiers during their visit to the 703rd Suramsky Infantry Regiment of the 2nd Caucasian Grenadier Division, when they tried, at the assignment of the Soviet and the war minister, to convince these soldiers to return to battle.
2. The daily newspaper of the Socialist Revolutionary Party, published in Petrograd from March to October 1917.

· 71 ·

Resolution by a general meeting of soldiers and officers of the 3rd Company of the Ust-Dvinsk Fortress Artillery, Gulf of Riga, 27 July 1917.

At a general session of the 3rd Company of the Ust-Dvinsk Fortress Artillery, on 27 July 1917, after discussing the introduction of the death penalty in the active army during wartime,

We have resolved unanimously that we soldiers and officers of the 3rd Company of the Ust-Dvinsk Fortress Artillery protest the death penalty, which was introduced only in the active army. And for this reason we demand that the death penalty be extended not only to the active army but also to those traitors to the Homeland who have already sold half of the Russian State and have not been punished to this day, even though the free people have demanded more than once that they be punished. So let the shameful death penalty, which they introduced not only for traitors and betrayers of the Homeland but also for our comrades who were following the path of truth and justice, be applied to those traitors to the Homeland, too. We reiterate: those contemptible oppressors of the people should be punished, such as, for example, beginning with the house of Romanov and ending with its lackeys, Sukhomlinov, Shtiurmer, Protopopov, Frederiks,[1] and so on, and also those betrayers and traitors who are encroaching on the cause of the Revolution and Freedom and on the organs of democracy we have authorized should be punished, such as, for example: Purishkevich and Maslennikov,[2] who call the Soviet of W., S., and P. Deputies a gang of criminals and rogues.

We also protest the closing of the editorial offices of newspapers of leftist orientation, which are opening our eyes in many ways and are writing only the honest truth. Whereas those bourgeois newspapers are blatantly conducting counterrevolutionary propaganda, and for some reason they are not being closed down, and those bourgeois newspapers for some reason get to have full freedom of speech and press. Whereas newspapers of leftist tendencies have no freedom of speech or press. And we demand that if the editorial offices of the leftist newspapers are closed, then the rightist newspapers should be closed as well.

So You Want the Truth!

Where is it, brothers? Where is the truth?

It must be somewhere.

We also ask why they are resurrecting the dead, such as, for example: the State Duma and Council. After all, that is a government organ of autocracy, which has already collapsed along with the rotted-out autocratic order of our oppressors; and they have been swept away by the Revolutionary wave of the Free people, which is why we demand that the Soviet of W., S., and P. Deputies lean very hard on these dead organs of the oppressors and crush them so that they don't rise up again—there's no place for them in a free country, nor should there be. Down with the State Duma and Council. For these are the prerevolutionary headquarters that are keeping the democratic order from coming to life and preventing the speedy convocation of the Constituent Assembly. For this reason we demand that the Provisional Government quickly convene the Constituent Assembly and bring democratic ideas into life.

Chairman, Andreev

Secretary, Shcherbin

[Note added by hand]

Mr. Editor

We ask that you place our resolution in your respected newspaper *Rabochaia gazeta*.[3]

1. Boris Vladimirovich Shtiurmer (1848–1917) was a tsarist minister during World War I and a close associate of Rasputin. He was regarded as one of the most irresponsible and corrupt tsarist officials at that time and was arrested after the February revolution. Aleksandr Dmitrievich Protopopov (1866–1918) was an industrialist and landowner, hereditary nobleman, member of the Octobrist party, deputy to the third State Duma, and deputy chairman of the fourth State Duma. Owing in large part to Rasputin's endorsement, he was appointed acting minister of the interior on 16 September 1916 and full minister on 20 December 1916. He was a member of Nicholas and Alexandra's trusted inner circle. Count Vladimir Borisovich Frederiks (1838–

1927) was a major landowner, member of the State Council, adjutant general in Nicholas II's imperial suite, minister of the imperial court and estates (beginning in 1897), chancellor of the Russian imperial and tsarist orders, head of the imperial household, and one of Nicholas II's most trusted associates. During the February revolution he was deported from staff headquarters by orders of the Provisional Government and then arrested.

2. Vladimir Mitrofanovich Purishkevich (1870–1920) was a deputy from Bessarabia to the second, third, and fourth State Dumas and a leader of the Duma's political Right. In 1916, he was one of the initiators of the assassination of Rasputin. After the February revolution, he argued for restoration of the monarchy. A. M. Maslennikov was a Progressist member of the fourth State Duma. On 18 July 1917, both men participated in the meeting of members of the former Duma to discuss how the Duma might "save Russia," at which they openly chastised the Soviet leaders (Maslennikov was reprimanded by the meeting's chairman for using unnecessarily "strong expressions") and advocated calling the Duma back into session to form a new government.

3. The newspaper of the Menshevik party, published in Petrograd from March to November 1917.

· 72 ·

Letter to the minister-president of the Provisional Government
from Staff Sergeant (*Fel'dfebel'*) Safonov, July or August 1917.

It has become obvious to everyone that humane treatment of politically unaware people in the rear and in the army is harmful, and decisive measures are necessary, and any deviation from these amounts to betrayal of the fatherland, which must come first before freedom. There must not be any party disturbances in this instance in view of Russia's imminent collapse. How can there be any discussion of the death penalty and discipline when there are willfulness and anarchy [*proizvol*][1] all around us? Let a few dozen traitors hang, so that thousands can be saved from treason, the enemy, and anarchy.

Staff Sergeant Safonov[2]

1. *Proizvol* normally refers to willful and arbitrary authority. The term was often used in criticism of tsarist politics. Here, however, it refers to a more universal willfulness, with the implication of a transfer of autocratic arbitrariness to the masses of ordinary people.

2. The style of the text and of the handwriting suggests that the author was a relatively uneducated individual, notwithstanding his rank, which was that of a senior non-commissioned officer (*unter-offitser*). Many lower-class Russians rose rapidly through the ranks in 1917 because of the devastating depletion of personnel during wartime.

· 73 ·

Letter to the Central Executive Committee of Soviets from the soldiers' committee of the 129th Bessarabian Infantry, received 5 August 1917.

Comrades!

We, the soldiers of the 129th Bessarab.[ian] Inf.[antry] Reg.[iment], ask you, the Provisional Government, to rescue Russia from the bloody Slaughter. The way it needs to be saved is by making a speedy peace, and then there will be calm and quiet. This offensive has become loathsome to all the soldiers. Like Kerensky, you ordered an offensive on the western front, but here this attack has led to nothing but ruin. You don't achieve peace by attacking, and we, all the soldiers, refuse to attack and cause bloodshed: our corps as well as the 21st corps and the Siberian regiments and the Latvian battalions—we all stand firm on the same point. If you want to save Russia and yourselves, then all we ask you to do is make peace quickly. The strength is in us, the soldiers, in the poor class. If you defend the poor class, then there will be a democratic republic, but if you defend the interests of the capitalists, then Russia is lost. We'll strangle all the capitalists and you with them. Hold on to the peasant soldier and make a speedy peace—that's the only way to save Russia. If you continue the war, you'll let the Germans into Russia, and for us it will be Siberia with the Japanese.[1] So there it is for you, brief and to the point. You don't scare us with your instructions about the death penalty and iron discipline. We have tasted the sweet and now we won't take the bitter. And how did Brusilov especially, that bloodthirsty leech, slip away? He deserves death and we'll kill him all the same. And so, comrades, we ask you to make peace quickly, or else Russia is done for. What are you doing trying to deceive the soldiers? Anyway, it's hard to deceive us!

Author of the letter, P. Gurianov 6th company
For the committee chairman, E. Petrov

1. This sentence was omitted from the published version of the document in the major Soviet collection of documents on the revolution, *Revoliutsionnoe dvizhenie v Rossii v iiule 1917 g.* (Moscow, 1959), 436.

· 74 ·

Letter-essay to "Comrade Citizens" from soldier A. Kuchlavok, approved by the regiment, received 7 August 1917.

Comrade Editor, do not refuse to run this piece of writing in your newspaper [*Izvestiia*].

Letter to the editor
COMRADE CITIZENS

We brothers in spirit wish to share with you our opinions about the troubles our country is going through, the heart aches from the injustice of what has been happening during this difficult time, and to pour out what has accumulated in our hearts, so here having consulted among ourselves we have decided to tell our brothers what we have been seeing and hearing like spiders making a web for flies. Our moist mother earth is groaning, sensing the collapse of our dear country, those living on it are weeping bitterly and sobbing, and the evil hydras, the disturbers of peaceful life, are celebrating, sucking the people's blood, enjoying luxury—this is what is happening in Russia. The heart is grieving within the meek working people, they rule them like animals, and receive honor for this, innocent blood is flowing, and the people bear it with their limitless patience. When will this hellish patience come to an end? Comrades, do not place your hopes in princes or the sons of man because there is no salvation in them, it is time for us to close ranks amongst ourselves, let us close our ranks solid and open our minds, which our leaders have clouded, and our eyes, into which they have thrown dirt, our leaders who set out to lead us forward but turned out to be blind and frivolous, and if a blind man leads an ignorant man, then both are bound to fall into a ditch: we will not surrender to be enslaved to the blind leaders who promised us luxury the likes of which we had never seen or heard of, and for their promise, which proved empty, carried away millions of lives to the grave. Our grandfathers, our fathers, we and our sons have fought and everyone has tried to achieve a better life, but alas we have achieved nothing. Just take an example from history about whether or not war ever enriched the laboring people and you realize that no, war has brought us many calamities, cripples and orphans, but to the capitalist rulers it has brought honor and enrichment, that we can see that there are people for slaughter and beatings and spreading hatred of one against the other but there aren't any for a quiet and peaceful life. Take the example of the reigns of the Romanovs, who taught us only to fight to defend the homeland but instead of defending the homeland we got enslavement for ourselves and comfort for them. An ignorant man enjoys certain rights over animals, but he works with them inseparably and looks after the animal as he does himself, but the Bourgeois is also a man with the same dignities, but for some reason he sets himself apart, to take an example from the soldier's life, one and the same people united and went off to defend a certain freedom, but how do they unite the one who works without putting his hands down and is content with seventy kop[eks] a day and the one who extracts a life of luxury and gets ten to twenty rubles a day—is his stomach really ten to twenty times bigger? The revolution has accomplished its business: right away it turned off the road the old regime was going down, that camp of stuffed, greasy, gluttonous living, but very soon after it returned to that same rut as before under the monarchist order, where the same animals cart the unbearable, torturous weight, the same wolves govern us only in sheep's clothing and the same words are spoken and promises made about the good life but no it is not for us that they want a good life but for themselves, us they want to shove into the water and the trenches and themselves to climb up onto thrones,[1] and instead of a good life we are getting enslavement and mockery: they made promises to us while they themselves were sitting on the thrones where the executioners and murderers used to sit and set about their affairs, and we gave them a life of luxury and saved them from hardships. They express gratitude like the wolf who said to the crane: Wasn't it enough that I didn't bite off your head when it was in my teeth?[2] Such also are our benefactors. For we received a stone instead of bread, and instead of the promised golden rain we got a hail of steel bullets that knocked down a tenth part of the country and infected the rest with malice, envy, and hatred. Now another Savior of the world must be born, to save the people from all the calamities in the making here on earth and to put an end to these bloody days, so that no beast of any kind living on the earth created not by princes and rulers but by God-given nature is wiped out, for God is an invisible being inhabiting whoever possesses a conscience and tells us to live in friendship, but no there are evil people who sow strife among us and poison us one against another pushing us to murder, who wish for others what they would not wish for themselves. There were people who said at a meeting of the State Duma back in 1916: put government in the hands of the socialists, we will put an end to this carnage, conclude a peace that is advantageous to the whole people, we will put an end to the bloodshed from which the earth moans with the tears and blood of innocent people; and we believed, we put our faith in this word, and the people unleashed their granite might, did their deed, overthrew the old executioners and traitors, but alas it proved in vain, those socialist well-wishers turned out to be wolves in sheep's clothing, they occupied the same posts and were infected with the same filth that was in the old regime. And so, fellow working people, let us close our ranks more solidly, let us unite as one to destroy the weeds that are destroying our healthy shoots, pick out from among us all the persons leading us to ruin, who refuse to listen to the wails and lamentations of our wives, mothers, and children, who keep repeating: Did we care for you and groom you that such a portion should befall you, that scarcely before the sun could shine on you, our breadwinners, you were covered by the gray earth? Who will lead our children into the world?[3] They will live like beasts, our betrayers will torment them in every way because anyone who leads us onto the path of truth will be put to death, but anyone who leads us to the slaughter and to all kinds of crime receives honor and glory, reward, and honor. Whoever does the most to divert us from the true and just path receives honor and praise.

Can murder really be the only way to achieve a free life? No, by murder they achieve not freedom, but rather ruin for the entire people, malicious delight in others' misfortunes and strife: one achieves brotherly love not by murder but by peaceful means, and who can achieve this peace?—only a people who have known misfortune. Have the capitalists sitting in their luxurious palaces and thinking only about their own profits suffered? On the contrary they now have more luxuries and keep saying that we should wage the war to a victorious conclusion. Where is that end of victory, how many years will it take to bring it about, even if we are victorious, how many lives must perish and what must the country be led to for this? Already our wives and children, fathers and mothers are going barefoot and naked, what is next? The rulers don't care about our life at all, they are like the animal that having stuffed itself on acorns and then started tearing up the roots of the oak; when the raven said to it from the oak, "Ingrate, don't you see, this is harming the tree, it could dry up," in reply the animal said, "Let it dry up, that doesn't bother me in the slightest just so I have my acorns,"[4] and so with our rulers and capitalists, they don't care in the least about the people's calamities, they just want to obtain an honorable peace, honor and glory, and for us, humiliation and enslavement. What good is it to me if we conquer the whole world, ravage, pillage, and burn everything we accomplished through our own sweat and blood? We derive no benefit from this but only losses and calamities, as is evident from the history of previous wars, and so comrades we need to band together and find the limit to this slaughter of the human race, to stand up for what we think is right, so that the people elected as delegates to the peace talks are experienced and have endured many misfortunes and have sympathy for the misfortunes of the people, who are at the brink of ruin, but don't send anyone who represents the camp of the full-bellied capitalists and their personal interests.

Everyone promises us the Kingdom of Heaven but they themselves run away from it, they promise us life everlasting, but for themselves luxury in this life. They know no bounds to their own luxury, they wrote us the words "land and liberty" and they were not wrong that we get the land, for it covers the corpses of the dead. When will we get land and liberty if the war is unending, and the people's life hangs by a thread—who will need land if there is no one to work it? They say our children, but what children will there be to leave it to if our children are perishing by the thousands and there is no end in sight to all this death? Why are they postponing the conference[5] and the Constituent Assembly if not to seize the people in their pincers and then, whatever the capitalists say is what will be. Who can after the sweet willingly taste the bitter? No one except out of necessity. How can our enemies surrender to us if where they live life is much better than we have here? Can they fall into this kind of enslavement, into the kind of governance there was in Russia? Is this such a good example that Russia is considered the breadbasket of the world but the Russian people have to die of hunger? No, they are prepared to die but not to fall into the hands of an incompetent government. The rulers are dreaming up various punishments and death penalties for us, but for their own followers, who have betrayed millions of innocent victims, the death penalty has been repealed, and security reinforced, so that nobody can offend them. They tell us the politicals stood up for the people, that they rotted in the prisons and that lots of them were hanged. No, they did not stand up for the people but for their own personal interests: they only relied on our strength, they got luxury for themselves through our sweat because the muzhik toiled without cease, sometimes day and night, and so he will continue to toil, and if he doesn't work he'll die of hunger. All they say is untrue. We work for them, sacrifice our life. An animal works for us under the whip but works alongside us, and this is for the good of man, but our leaders and teachers are working off of our strength, though they themselves don't lift a finger for that work, they wage war behind walls but not with us. It is not the soldiers who want to wage the war to a victorious conclusion, but all the rulers who themselves are sitting in luxurious palaces. If you ask in any village whether the people want to continue the war, no one agrees, the only one who agrees is the one who has steeped himself in the teaching of the rulers and became deceived by empty promises—after all there are people like the one who when they are preparing the rope that will hang him, and they are saying that anyone who speaks of peace should be hanged, would themselves approve this, saying, "Bravo, that's right," and suddenly he himself would be hanged by the same rope, or his son, who could not stand it any more, or his wife. Those people are insane who can't tell bad from good, who want something for others that they don't want for themselves. Were we really created just for suffering and the capitalists for a life of luxury? The word capitalist means that same landowner who earned not by his own labor and the ruler-priests who with money earned by our blood and sweat erected stone palaces without doing anything and receiving incalculable sums of money, they are trying not to take up the plow of the muzhik who works for his oppressors. The muzhik they rob and oppress but he endures it and the muzhik has patience without limits: let the muzhik provide the bread and money and everything there is, but for the muzhik there are not even the basic necessities, the muzhik goes naked and barefoot but still they pull the skin off him. The capitalist sits and just laughs and takes his rewards and an incalculable salary, he has bread, he has money, he has clothing, he has everything and he rejoices in his soul, though he amassed much of his wealth through falsehood. Comrades, it is time, time for us to unite so that the beloved sun can shine down upon us, at least peek through the clouds, and dispel that darkness into which our teachers cast us. Let us take our example from the southern front. Who made this confusion? The officers, but the soldier is guilty. In his letter to Nicholas, General Gurko wrote that we were loyally serving the old regime only secretly but solidly, so why didn't they hand him over first for torture and then for the death penalty? Because the same wolves in sheep's clothing are ruling us. They used to say that the war was foisted off on us by Nicholas. Nicholas has been overthrown, so who is foisting the war on us now? His secret henchmen [*oprichniki*], who are constantly trying to persuade the man who could lead the people onto the path of truth but is frivolous and immediately became tempted by their flattery.[6] So comrades it's better for us to follow the good example of our enemy than that of a feeble friend, because brotherhood lies not in friends but in good actions. If the enemy does a good deed for us then he's a friend and a brother to us. And so comrades:[7]

> all around are falsehood and bondage
> the tormented people are silent,
> has the time not come comrades
> of freedom now to speak,
> of plain and honest freedom,
> of the freedom of honest work,
> of freedom strong and mighty;
> the time has come to forge,
> not the freedom we were promised
> by the rulers of the land,
> the freedom to which we gave,
> our fathers and our sons,
> but to forge for ourselves a freedom,
> burning with the joy of life,
> and amaze our beloved Russia,
> our land of the mighty hero.[8]
> They gave us the free word,
> and the word was with God,
> And the word was God,[9]
> but as there is no God among the butchers,
> and there is no freedom among people,
> because they promise us freedom
> while all torment one another,
> so let us not have
> the son slay the father
> or brother kill brother
> for every man wants to live,
> life is precious to all,
> even when it is poor,
> but unrighteous death is terrible.
> Let us end this all in peace,

> let us live as a family,
> recalling tragic times,
> the world catastrophe,
> what the butchers wrought,
> and whosoever shares our thoughts
> take up your labor,
> live peacefully, live happily,
> and to you Godspeed.

This appeal was approved in its entirety by a general meeting of the regiment.

Writer, A. Kuchlavok

1. Probably a reference to Kerensky, who, after becoming prime minister in July, moved into the Winter Palace, where he occupied the suite of Alexander III.

2. A reference to Ivan Krylov's well-known fable about a crane that helped a wolf that was choking on a bone.

3. The preceding passage is written in the style of a *plach*, a traditional rural funeral lament sung by women. Especially when the loss is of a son or husband, a breadwinner, the lament speaks of the calamities that will result.

4. The allusion is to Krylov's fable "The Pig Under the Oak."

5. Presumably the Second All-Russian Congress of Soviets, which, when finally held in late October, resulted in a quite different political majority in the Soviet, one favoring soviet power.

6. He is probably referring again to Kerensky.

7. The remainder of this appeal is written as verse, with rhyme and meter (often imperfect), though the lines of the original are not broken except by commas. This translation reverses the poetic form: breaking the phrases into verse lines but not preserving the rhyme or rhythm that indicated these breaks in the original Russian.

8. Bogatyrs, legendary heroes of Russian folk epics.

9. A quotation from John 1:1: "In the beginning was the Word, and the Word was with God, and the Word was God."

· 75 ·

Letter to the Central Executive Committee of Soviets on behalf
of positional soldiers, 9 August 1917.

———————

Comrade Soldiers and Workers,

All of us positional troops[1] ask you as our comrades to explain to us who these Bolsheviks are and what party they belong to because we don't know them or their opinion.

Our provisional government has come out very much against the Bolsheviks. But we, positional soldiers, don't find any fault with them at all. Before, we were against the Bolsheviks. But now after waiting so long for what was promised, because the provisional government promised during the very first days to give the poor people their freedom but then didn't.

We are little by little going over entirely to the side of the Bolsheviks. But in order for us to find out exactly about the Bolsheviks, we are turning to you, comrades, as our advisers—explain all this to us, but in order to explain it to us, we ask you send us your delegates or explain in the newspaper of the Soviet of W. S. and P. Deputies.

> With respect, all the positional Soldiers
> 9 August 1917
> Active army
> Sirebrov, Soldier

1. Soldiers occupying fixed strategic positions along a solid and extended defensive line, a method widely used by the Russian army in World War I.

· 76 ·

Letter to the Central Executive Committee of Soviets
from a soldier at the front, 9 August 1917.

1917—9 August

I, a soldier, while in the trenches, read the newspapers and listen to the conversations of the soldiers. This is what the soldier says: they write discipline, war, punishments, drills, that the soldier is stupid. All that is what your bourgeois newspaper writes, and in your alliance with the Provisional Government, orders are issued that have no right to be issued, for the country is free, and all of you are friends of the English and French rich. You would like to win certain advantages for these two states, and then something will come your way from the capitalists at the cost of the people. You are not worthy of being Russians. When you talk, you always say, "Everyone is a fool," and, bugging out your eyes, you spitefully shout, "The homeland is in danger!" Go on and shout all you want, you bourgeois, and Kerenskys, and Chernovs, and Skobelevs, all of you. The time to pay up will come, though. Know that the whole of the people are at the front, and they are waiting to see what happens, what sort of benefactors you are—you didn't reproach anyone, but you're no better yourselves, and here, when the cup of sorrow fills to the brim because of you the same as it did because of Nicky II, then watch out, all of you. It'll be worse for you than for Nicholas, because the tsar was an enemy and nothing good is expected from an enemy, but from you, as friends, the people expected good. But alas, even though we'll have to go on fighting until winter, if there's no peace, then watch out. We'll show you "no annexations," "to victory," and "no indemnities."[1] Don't think that discipline silences soldiers. But you write with your tongue hanging out that the soldier is ready, will agree to anything. Nicholas used to say the same, but it worked out just the opposite—the workers seized him, and the soldiers are going to get you. . . . They're lying to you, and you make things up to others—in short, you lie about freedom and things like that. We drove out one gang headed up by the tsar, and now another has settled in, with Kerensky at the head. Here's a soldier's opinion for you. You'll say it's a provocateur writing. No, I'm your friend, but I'm warning you, but you go look for yourselves, then you'll see, all the soldiers' committees already can do nothing. You took away their power because they stood up for the soldiers; in other words, you, the bourgeois, pretended to be populists [*narodniki*].[2] You want to turn the country into a wasteland. You're taking the bread away from our wives, the bread they earned with their tears. You are enemies of the people! Down with all of you! I am a soldier, and I love my God and my homeland. You are traitors to Russia. You have betrayed Russia to England and France.

1. A rough characterization of the Soviet policy toward the war using often repeated phrases.

2. *Narodniki* was a term used to describe socialists who devoted themselves to the cause of the people (*narod*), especially the peasants. Specifically, it referred to a late nineteenth-century movement of non-Marxist socialists in Russia, though it often was applied more loosely to people who sympathized with the cause of the common people.

· 77 ·

Appeal to the soldiers of the telegraph company, 7th Engineering Regiment, from the soldiers' committee of the telegraph company, 13 August 1917.

Appeal from the Telegraph Company Committee
to the Soldiers of the Telegraph Company, 7th Engineering Regiment
We members of the Telegraph Company Committee, 7th Engineering Regiment, in a session held on 13 August, ending our terms as deputies, after having considered our three months of activity in connection with the circumstances born of the new democratic life, have found that the honor and well-being of the army consists only in unity and in sensible progress along the paths indicated by the law of justice, and therefore we appeal with a pure heart to everyone for whom a free and sensible life is dear, to everyone who in the chains of slavery saw his death and in the sunlight of freedom saw his resurrection.

COMRADES! If thousands of slaves were freed from the yoke of slavery and a whole society was formed from them and they were asked, "What do you need?" they would reply, "Freedom and order." "Fine, here's your freedom . . . now, establish order, since freedom can exist only on condition of order, and the more order is violated, the less freedom is really freedom." But if someone asked, "What is order? Doesn't everyone imagine it differently?" "Order should be precisely of that kind which would guarantee freedom, and if it deviates from the obligation to observe freedom's interests, it is no longer order."

COMRADES! We don't think any of us would deny that we too need freedom and order, and if anyone accepts only freedom while rejecting order, then he necessarily is an unworthy member of the society that wishes to be free. Our life consists of striving for freedom, and if we know that life can be sensible and happy only when freedom has been placed at its base, then we also must know that there can be freedom only when at its base lies a sensible order, and that any order is sensible, when, without violating the principle of freedom, it gives us a law that leads us toward the good and shows each of us his place in the march down the road to that good. Many of us are mistaken in saying there is no freedom if we aren't allowed to do what we want. . . . Saying this, they are considering only themselves personally and not taking into account the freedom of someone else, which they might be violating by exercising their own personal will. Besides, the person who does not violate other people's interests, and consequently does not encroach on other people's liberty, demonstrates to us precisely that order we are talking about. So that willful anarchy [*samoproizvol*] will not destroy freedom, we and everyone for whom this freedom is precious must call each and every person to order. It is pointless to think that under freedom there should not be any kind of order; by thinking this way, we are passing a death sentence on what we are supposed to be defending. And the more order there is, and the stricter it is, then the more stable freedom will be, the more tranquil, the easier it will be for society and each individual member of it to live.

COMRADES! Not so long ago our army was a slave army and at the same time the embodiment of disorder. Now it is free—and it is order that should support the army's freedom—and if we don't make an effort to support this order, freedom itself will die in the army. But how could anyone who has tasted the sweet ever wish for the bitter? Not that long ago we became members of a free army, but we are familiar with every aspect of that freedom, and if anyone ever got a notion to take it away from us, we would soon prefer death over falling back into harsh slavery. We cherish our freedom. In the name of this freedom we must exert all our powers to create and support the order on which our freedom rests.

COMRADES! We have been too frightened by the word "discipline" to treat it fairly. Of course, we have considered discipline to be only the most savage and immoral manifestation of "the powers that be," and the notions of discipline that were formed in the prerevolutionary era still fill our imagination and we can't free ourselves from them. This word alone evokes a sense of revulsion; but after all, the word "discipline" is not as frightening as it seems to our terrified imaginations. Discipline is nothing but the very order we have been talking about. We must understand the word "discipline" as order, not tyranny. And if we admit that order is essential in an army, then the strictest discipline will only strengthen our power and might, which will keep anyone from stealing the freedom we won over long, nightmarish years. And if we grimace at having this discipline foisted upon us, then let us make sure no one foists it upon us but that it itself arises from our own sensible attitude toward the duty laid upon us. It is very easy to treat our duty sensibly if we can understand the full significance of the situation we are living through. But if we give it all a wave of the hand and understand freedom in the sense of our own personal good, we will be extending our hands to the blacksmith-reactionary who watches us by the minute for a chance to put back on us those chains that we cast off so recently and with such effort. In order to reinforce our freedom, and remembering that in unity there is strength, we have become organized and resolved [to create] committees to keep watch over our interests. But in order for the committees to be what they should be, we need a different attitude toward them, we need to have confidence in them, we need to support them. All of us make up the milieu that created these organizations, and we must trust in them because we ourselves cannot help trusting in them. These are not the gendarmes our oppressor assigned to watch us but guards we have assigned to watch the host of our oppressor, which like a thief is always creeping up toward our bivouac. This black host can sneak up on us only when we let down our guard and disunite and when our sentry falls asleep. But we shall remember that if we lose our freedom, we lose everything we have always strived for—and this will give us an infusion of courage and strength.

And so, comrades, we need more order, a more conscious attitude toward duty and, most important, more attention to and confidence in our organizations. We face new elections for the committees for a new six-month term now, and at precisely this moment we ask you to demonstrate more involvement in this matter. Remember that by electing your own representatives you are putting them into a serious and important post safeguarding for you everything that matters deeply to us. . . . A post that safeguards our freedom and happiness. . . . And the sentries who must stand at this post must be committees one can rely on and trust. On this day, election day,[1] down with all personal, narrowly egotistical scores! Let us forget old quarrels with one person or another! Let us obey our minds and hearts, let them tell us whether this person is worthy of standing guard over our common interests . . . and if he is worthy, then let him be that guard, for we need guards who can tell us in a moment of danger: "Here come our enemies, but before they can put the chains on those who put us in this post, they will have to step over our dead bodies."

Chairman of the company committee of the telegraph company, soldier I. Borzenko

Members of the soldiers' committee [seven signatures]

Secretary of the soldiers, Bachurin

1. For a new soldiers' committee.

· 78 ·

Letter to Kerensky from soldiers at the front, 18 August 1917.

Mr. War Minister!

We, soldiers from various regiments, warn you as minister in advance that we are going to stay in the trenches at the front and repel the enemy, and maybe even attack, but only until the first days of baneful autumn, by which time we ask you to end the war and its bloodshed at any cost (there will be honor and glory in this for you). If this is not done, then believe us when we say that we will take our weapons and head out for our own hearths to save our fathers, mothers, wives, and children from death by starvation (which is nigh). And if we cannot save them, then we'd rather die with them in our native lands than be killed, poisoned, or frozen to death somewhere and cast into the earth like a dog.

Remember that all your threats about the death penalty and discipline and the eloquent words of orators will cease to have any effect on us then—it will be too late. You know we are all tired, both at the front and in the rear, and we cannot endure another autumn and winter, nor do we have any wish to.

For a second time we ask you, Mr. War Minister, put an end to the slaughter. Only by doing this can you keep the enemy from penetrating deep inside Russia and save us both from this invasion and from starvation.

Soldiers

· 79 ·

Poem sent to *Izvestiia* by the soldier P. Anoshkin, in the active army, received 16 August 1917.

Endure this, oh Soldier, our cripple,
This bloody and damnable war.

From hunger you've suffered aplenty,
And your body is glutted with cold.
Three years now they have been drinking
Your blood running weary inside.
And again now they wish to bestir you
To fight on in this blood-spilling war.
Remember the tenth of July,
In this year nineteen seventeen.
Outside of Dvinsk we were trampled—
Poor Soldiers, this was no dream.
Behind them they left many cripples,
And many left orphans as well.
Watch after them now, oh Russia,
These unlucky fatherless young.
But who will we say now is guilty
When the settling of scores has begun?
The damnable bourgeois, those scoundrels,
To the gallows we'll send one and all.

    Soldier of the active army
    P. Anoshkin
We most humbly ask you, Mr. Editor, to find room for our piece in your newspaper.

· 80 ·

Letter to the Socialist Revolutionary newspaper *Delo naroda* from I. Morozov, artillery soldier at Vyborg Fortress, end of August 1917.

————————

The Vyborg Tragedy
(Letter from a Soldier)

Dear Comrade Editor,

I hereby inform you, as an eyewitness, about the details of the incident at Vyborg on 29 August.

Here in Vyborg, where in the first days the revolution proceeded without a drop of blood, where there were no arguments or scandal, where the monarchy was smashed by peaceful means, everything has gone backward: blood was spilled on Abossky Bridge, and it turned the gulf's waves crimson.

My God, what a picture! I cannot describe what I lived through that day. Right before my very eyes a horror occurred that truly frightens me and makes my heart ache. In compliance with Resolution 42 of the committees of the army and of the Vyborg garrison, three generals and one colonel were arrested. They were placed in the main guardhouse, near the bridge. A small group of soldiers that had gathered there began to grow.

At first, the soldiers just argued, but then they demanded that the arrested men be handed over to them as traitors to freedom and the homeland. The committee approved measures to prevent reprisals; delegates began arriving in automobiles, trying to convince and prevail upon the comrade soldiers, but the latter would not listen to the delegates' plea and forgot even that they had put their trust in the members of the soviet. Suddenly, the crowd gave a heave and burst into the guardhouse building. The arrested men were pulled and dragged out one after another, punched in the face and head and at random with fists, feet, and gun butts. They all begged for mercy, but there was none to be had from the comrades. It was pitiful to watch the way Vasiliev the general was dragged over the pavement: he was covered with blood and asked for nothing, just kept crossing himself. They dragged and carried them onto the bridge, where they threw them into the water. Then the storm began and there was a settling of personal scores as well.

In all, about twelve men suffered, and of them, most were innocent, for which, comrades, we feel ashamed. Now we have stained ourselves with an ineradicable stain. I am aware that they wanted to crush Kornilov's lackeys and weaken them, but no one will achieve anything doing it this way.

For us, this is a disgrace and a shame.

Artillery, Vyborg Fortress, I. Morozov

· 81 ·

Resolution of the soldiers' committee of the 92nd Transport Battalion,
1 September 1917.

Resolution
Committee of the 456th Military Transport, 92nd Transport Battalion,
on the current situation, 1 September 1917
Everywhere and all around we are pursued by a voice that is like the desperate, choking, frenzied scream of a drowning man. There are many people running around the lake, disturbed, trying to save the dying person. Some are ready to throw themselves impulsively into the arms of death and wrest back its victim. Others have joined the general chorus; with great ferocity they fall upon the first group, restraining them from such an intention. A third group also shouts about saving the dying man

but stands hesitating, waiting for a miraculous salvation. As if bewitched by the general cry for rescue, they do not notice that within this crowd there are people who are making every effort to paralyze the will of the first group. They themselves cannot take substantive measures to save the victim; they don't even have the courage to free the first group to take action. Meanwhile the victim is perishing, choking.

The homeland and the revolution are in danger! Like a thundering tocsin this rings out across the land. Each and every citizen is aware that freedom is in danger, but decisive measures have yet to be undertaken. There have been so many words, so much shouting and debating over how to save the homeland, but there has been no effort to put those words into action; they have never gone beyond words; there has been no deed. People seem to be taking up the cause of the homeland's salvation, but their deeds, their energy, and their strength have broken apart on the bulwark of the bourgeoisie. Democracy is sacrificing everything in the name of saving the country and the revolution, neither sparing its forces nor begrudging its wealth, and giving the invaluable gift of nature—life. But a tiny class has wrapped its tentacles around these efforts, and it gloats as it destroys them, preventing them from having any effect. All the work of democracy has been reduced to naught—all its efforts were in vain.

What is the group we call the bourgeoisie doing? After all, the democracy has not ejected it from the ranks of those fighting the sinister threats. Quite the contrary, they have turned to it countless times as one of the "living forces of the country," to render aid in the cause of revolution. The revolution has been going on for more than half a year. This time ought to teach us to look at things for what they are. We have seen all the activity of the bourgeois. But now it is time to realize that all their work came down to counterrevolution, and thus that they led the country to its ruin. All their intentions were aimed specifically at wrecking the revolution, so we would be no better off than when we started.

Comrades! It is time for us to wake up! After all, we are not helpless children; no one should need to watch over us. It is time to shake off the spell of the bourgeoisie; it is time to discard it like an oozing scab, so that it doesn't do any more damage to the revolution. We shouldn't look for the revolution's savior in the bourgeoisie. Their road is the road to the ruin of revolutionary democracy. The well-to-do class has shown that it is incapable of giving up its personal prosperity or refusing power. After all, Christ said: It is easier for a camel to go through the eye of a needle, than for a rich man to give up his money.[1] To retain its power and capital, it does not shy away from resorting to all manner of nefarious means. It commits the country to devastation by our bitterest enemies, it squanders our life like some trifle, and it produces disaster wherever it turns. How much harm it has done to the revolution already! Its mad dance will soon crush us and the country unless we manage to come to our senses quickly and stop it. It is waging a deathly battle with the revolution at every step, taking cover behind fine words. The bourgeoisie has not quit shouting about saving the revolution; it shouts the way the thief in the crowd shouts, "Stop him!" Its criminal deeds loom like a black cloud behind these words.

Enough of cleverly woven words! Enough of trying to pull the wool over our eyes. We are laying our lives on the altar of the country's defense, and just as boldly and victoriously must we bear the precious and holy slogans of liberty, equality, and fraternity. The revolution cannot continue this pact with our blood enemies. The working people and the exploiters are on different paths. We cannot make peace with counterrevolutionaries. They are leading us to our ruin. The country and the revolution can be saved only by those to whom they are truly precious; only the laboring revolutionary people will save them. The people can rely only on itself and must not extend a comradely hand to the hated enemy. It is time to shake off these "saviors of the revolution," who have stuck to the body of the country like leeches. The enemies of the working people must not be allowed to keep them from disposing of their own destiny, arranging their own life; these web-weaving spiders must not be allowed to darken the great horizon of the revolution. If they do not yield to the people, the people must sweep them aside with one mighty motion. But if we don't wipe them out, we must not be complacent in the future about the fate of the country and the revolution.

Nor should any of our leaders forget that without us for strength, support, and a buttress, they could not lead the country to salvation. They should stop relying on the "powerful of this world." There is in this country no stronger or firmer force than the force of that mighty giant, THE PEOPLE. And the people will not stand for walking together with our enemies.

Our leader comrade KERENSKY should heed our voice and issue a call not to the "Moscow conference,"[2] but instead, addressing the soldiers and sailors of the revolutionary troops, say his mighty word: "Gather together to save the country and take up this cause without delay, for the cause cannot wait."

Time does not wait. We need unification. Recent events have shown us that there is no solidarity or unified spirit even within our ranks. There have been traitors to the revolution who have followed the homeland's traitors. The traitors have managed to disrupt our ranks. They started this work long ago, and it has had its effect in the fact that conflict arose between different units: the infantry rose up against the artillery, the cavalry against the navy, and so on. A total collapse of the entire army was imminent. The counterrevolutionaries, hoping we had broken up into separate groups and relying on treacherous regiments, moved against the revolution.[3] Maybe their uprising will be put down, but we can at any moment expect a new outbreak of this kind of conspiracy. Even if we arm ourselves from head to foot, we will lack one weapon: strong and powerful organization. Although a huge part of the army is against this plot, it will take great efforts to crush it. This is clear because the criminal uprising is supported by its own troops. And at the needed moment the revolutionary authority cannot rely on a strong armed force that could crush the counterrevolution mercilessly at the slightest provocation.

This is why we must immediately prepare to create a mighty SOCIAL REVOLUTIONARY VOLUNTEER MILITIA [*DRUZHINA*].

In trying to achieve this, we need to smash every obstacle along the way so that the will of the people remains uppermost. This voluntary militia must unite the whole army into a single revolutionary army. It must be made up of one or two politically conscious soldiers from each unit equal to a company, of soldiers prepared to sacrifice their life for the revolution, for LAND and LIBERTY, without hesitation. It must also include representatives of the labor army: workers, peasants, and railway workers. This militia must be provided with full battle equipment. It should not disband until the country is in complete safety. The revolutionary militia must work hand in hand with the Central Exec. Comm. of the Soviet of Work., S., and Peas. Deputies. Its principal tasks should be:

1. Eradicating counterrevolution, both in the army and in the rear.

2. Ascertaining the political reliability of the entire officer corps and continuing to do so in the future; reviewing the entire list of the general staff and getting rid of all counterrevolutionary elements, as well as taking up the reduction of the officer corps in noncombat units.

3. Monitoring the army's battle-readiness and the correct progress of military actions.

4. Expanding cultural-educational work in the army to help develop the army's organization.

5. Monitoring the stockpiling of weapons and ammunition, as well as the supply and distribution of same at the front.

6. Monitoring the working capacity of transport and taking measures to restore it.

7. Observing troops in the rear.

8. Carrying out all measures concerning the land question and food in order to ease the life of the population. In general, carrying out all measures aimed at saving the country.

9. Controlling all production. Monopolizing all essential output.

The entire militia should be stationed in one place, at the country's center of governance, being itself the center of the country's entire armed forces. Units equal to a regiment or larger must be in constant communications with the militia and supply information familiarizing them with the current life of the unit. This will unquestionably give the army the opportunity to present a unified whole.

People may say that this will entail immense expenditure. Such words can come only out of the mouths of people trying to destroy the revolution and the country. Since we are here locally, we are already bringing the treasury our expenditures. Is this money really worth more in some other place? ([Footnote in original:] If this is not enough, then we can assign the salary of several generals from the general staff, superfluous officials, and officers who are still draining the people's treasury for naught.) People may say that this will strip the front. But we have so many troops in the rear that could replace the men who join the militia.

Only this voluntary militia can help save the revolution and the country, and no one else. We cannot trust the country's entire fate to a few individuals any more. This militia is a mighty weapon of the people against all enemies encroaching on our freedom. It can eradicate any counterrevolution and bring the country safely to the Constituent Assembly and a democratic federative republic.

If this militia is guarding the revolution, we can all stand calmly at the battle sites and defend our country with our own bodies against the foreign enemy. We cannot defend the country under the command of the general staff. We don't trust them any more. We see them as blatant counterrevolutionaries. They are ruining us. This has been proven by the events of recent days. How can anyone think that we can't get along without these strategists? The generals have proven themselves to be unfit for military command in a revolutionary army. Under the old regime they specialized not in strategy but in careers and personal gain. The revolution has completely stifled them. The excess trash has to be cleared out. But the general staff is not only trash but a camp obviously hostile to us. Thanks to their concerns and distortion of facts, all kinds of misfortunes in the country have been blamed on the common soldiers; the death penalty has been introduced—aimed only against soldiers. The entire counterrevolutionary officer corps has been left outside this law. A revolutionary army should not have an unjust court. We demand the immediate punishment of traitors to the freedom and homeland so precious to us.

So let us start, comrades who hold the homeland and freedom dear! It is time to cast off the nightmare that has befallen us.

We must put an end to the hostility between the socialist camps. The incriminations must stop. Our forces are being dissipated in this squabbling. We summon all socialist leaders to work, to unification, before we lose our faith in you.

There is but one revolutionary path for the salvation of the Revolution.

Chairman of the sold.[iers'] committee, Karimov
Secretary, sold.[ier] Nikolai

1. The original text, of course, was "It is easier for a camel to go through the eye of a needle, than for a rich man to enter the Kingdom of God" (Mark 10:25).

2. The State Conference was held in Moscow from 12 to 14 August. The call for the Moscow conference was issued 13 July by the interim Provisional Government headed by Kerensky after the July Days. Representatives of all organized political, civic, and business groups in Russia were invited to hear addresses by representatives of the government and to express their views on the current situation.

3. A reference to the Kornilov "mutiny."

· 82 ·

Letter to the Central Executive Committee of Soviets from soldiers
at the Caucasus front, 16 September 1917.

Comrade soldiers and gentlemen free Citizens,

Some of you are not aware of the wretched life that has been suffered by the man in the trenches who has been sitting there for three years. Few of you who have sat in the rear the whole time have heard the voice of the tormented man or know what he is saying.

You are heroes of the rear, and it is easy for you in the rear to talk and draw up a resolution about how we need to attack. If you would only think about how much hot blood would be spilled, how many lives broken, how many cripples there would be, and how they would curse you while you were alive and there would be no place for your bones. Wherever I go,[1] the tortured soldier feels the same. When the soldiers, who have suffered, have heard about an offensive, they have said: We used to have bloody Nikolka,[2] and now we have a bloody government. You know yourselves that Nikolka was bloody. He took the wrong road, which led to his downfall, so you, Provisional Government, you'd better not follow that same road Nikolka traveled, or the same could happen to you. You think the people are ignorant, that you can fool them; well, the people may be ignorant and taken for dung because they were shut up with a bayonet and not allowed to say anything but "Yes, sir" and "No, sir," but now that we have freedom of speech and freedom of assembly, when we gather in groups, we discuss this question or that, and we are perfectly capable of figuring out who is readying the noose for the working man's neck.

You may be offended at hearing a voice like this from the trenches, but don't forget that sitting in the trenches is a man just like you, for we know very well that when you take a leech into your hands, it doesn't drink your blood right away but first only gets its suckers into you and then, when you give it your full confidence, it bites down and starts sucking your blood.

Reporting, comrade soldiers from the Caucasus front
Soldiers: Tronshin, Vetkin, Karpukhin, Repin, Trofimov

1. Though the letter was signed by a group of soldiers, this lingering first-person phrase reminds us of the individual voices that were sometimes endorsed as a collective expression of opinion.

2. A combination of a contemptuous nickname for Nicholas II and the political epithet "Nicholas the Bloody."

· 83 ·

Poem sent to *Izvestiia* by a wounded soldier, Ilya Ladanov, received 22 September 1917.

A Soldier's Life

As I lie on my cot full of thought
How my time on this earth should be spent,
How my life has been lost in the trenches,
   How the blood from my veins has been spilled.
I have drained every drop of my strength
For my homeland that is so dear.
And once all my wounds have healed over,
It's to the trenches I'm bound, I fear.
   This life is beyond my endurance,
   The lies that are circling all round,
   The soldier's good name has been slandered—
   Live such a life if you can.
Unfortunate, yes, are the soldiers,
But what do they say about us?
We'd better check up on the generals
To see what they're cooking up.

Staff Sergeant Ilya Ladanov

Mr. Editor:

Please print my uneducated verse in your respected newspaper. I'm lying in recovery in the infirmary and I'm terribly insulted at how they're slandering us for no good reason.

· 84 ·

Appeals to the country and the soldiers from the Soviet of Soldiers' Deputies
of the 12th Army, printed in *Izvestiia,* 7 October 1917.

Appeal to the Country from the
Soviet of Soldiers' Deputies of the 12th Army

The Sov. Sold. Dep. of the 12th Army has decided to address the following appeal to the country.

The Soviet of Sold. Deputies of the 12th Army, having met on 3 October in an hour when a new blow threatens to strike at the northern front, and having discussed the issues concerning the situation in the country and the army, in the name of all the soldiers and officers, and in fulfillment of the will of the entire army, addresses this final, decisive word to the country, the people, and the government.

All that has been gained by the revolutionary people, the entire future of our tormented country, is at stake. A fury of wild, blind movements and pogroms is inundating the country. Against the backdrop of this movement of ignorant, politically unaware strata of the people—who emerged from the foundations of the old life and were gripped by the general torturous dissatisfaction—impotence and disorder have vividly manifested themselves among the organized strata of democracy. The revolutionary authority does nothing. The entire country, all its strata, are caught up in the imminent demise of the economy and the state. The basic demands for a revolutionary program which are especially precious to the people are not being met. The country has no active, coordinated domestic policy. Self-interest is holding on tenaciously among the country's propertied classes. However, the blind indifference, the absence of alarm or a general public consciousness, and the criminal concentration on their own group interests are beginning to penetrate deeply into the working strata of the population. Economic collapse is mounting, and so is counterrevolution. The revolution and the country are on the brink of danger. In this black hour the army finds itself on the eve of new trials, abandoned by the country. The German navy and the army of German imperialism are about to inflict a new blow, and when we call upon the soldiers of our army to fight to their last drop of blood, we know that we are appealing to ill-clothed, half-starved men whom the country has forgotten. There is no immediate way out of this war. Wilhelm's regiments are advancing on us, and we must not waste a minute before defending ourselves. We declare before the entire people: this cannot go on any longer. Someone who is dying, someone who has sacrificed everything and is going to his death, has a right to make demands, and his demands should be met. By way of fulfilling the will of the army that selected us, we demand:

1) The government of the Russian republic must take emergency mea-

sures to raise and resolve basic issues in the life of the people, especially the laboring peasantry. The land must be handed over to the land committees or the newly elected volost zemstvos[1] even before a decision is reached by the Constituent Assembly.

2) The government of the Republic should make every effort to keep up its work toward the speediest conclusion of peace.

3) The government and all organizations of the Revolutionary people must make every effort to stop the pogroms in the country immediately. Revolutionary order must be restored immediately, using the means and influence of these organizations. Bread must go to the army, warm clothing to the army, fodder to the army. The village must urgently be supplied with products of the city. Those who selfishly do not give their grain stores to the exhausted soldiers now should be declared criminals, as should those who by their inaction delay the work of transport and supply.

4) Reinforcements must be sent to the army. Every extra soldier in the rear is a criminal! Every idle, full-bellied, carousing soldier in the reserve units is a criminal! The army sends its indignation down upon those who in this terrible hour refuse to go to the front. The army's patience has been exhausted. Enough of this disgrace. Send reinforcements to the army, and fast! Reinforcements to the army, trained reinforcements! We don't need any of those base cowards or pathetic riffraff that the rear is bestowing on us.

Soldiers of the rear! We demand that you stop your scandalous behavior [*bezobrazie*]. There should not be a single hour without action, discipline, and training—otherwise a curse on you, traitors to the revolution! The soldiers' organization of the rear must come to our aid quickly in this matter!

5) All strata and all classes of the country must give everything to the army, which has to defend you in this moment of utmost danger! Sacrifice everything, depriving yourself more and more! Give the army everything they need to fight! Material sacrifices, your labor, all your energy, this is what we demand from you, from the entire country.

6) Bearing its cross and scattering the fields of ongoing battles now with new corpses, the army of the Russian Republic demands everything from the country. The day and hour have come when delay is criminal. The soldier demands reassurance in the fatal hour of battle about his country's destiny, the revolutionary order and the work of the authorities in the country, he demands in this hour that the country show its concern and see that he is dressed, fed, and reassured about the fate of his family. With this final and decisive word, the Soviet of Soldiers' Deputies, in the name of the soldiers and officers now going into battle, appeals to the country and the people and expects the country to take the path of all-out struggle against imminent ruin, to unite all our powers and immediately come to the aid of its defending army.

Appeal to Soldiers
from the Soviet of Soldiers' Deputies
of the 12th Army

Comrades and brothers! We whom you have chosen appeal to you in a difficult moment in life. The army lacks so much. Winter is coming. Dissatisfaction and disenchantment are mounting among the soldier masses. And now the Germans are about to strike a new blow and send Wilhelm's blinded troops against revolutionary Russia. Comrades! At this moment, in the name of the entire army, we have raised our voice, appealing to the country. We have demanded that the country, the people, the authorities, give and do everything the army needs to defend the country and the revolution. Let our voice resound throughout the country, arouse all vital forces, and send them to the salvation of the revolution and to the aid of the battling soldier masses at the front.

Comrades! In our appeal we demanded that all democracy and the government struggle energetically to bring about a speedy conclusion to the war. Understand, brothers, that this peace will not come to us at the point of the German army's bayonets, that no matter how hard it is for us now, no matter how weary we are, we have to fight because they are attacking us, we have to keep on defending ourselves with all the power of our despair and all the love we feel for our free country. The country needs peace, but right now, at this moment, there is no peace! And therefore, brothers, summon up your last forces, kill the disappointment and weakness in your soul, and give all you have without hesitation for the country's defense! The country has to help us. We have demanded this, and we ourselves are here honestly performing our revolutionary duty. We all know what we are defending. Try to convince the fainthearted and despairing who talk about how the revolution is nothing and we don't need land and liberty but only peace.

Revolutionary soldiers, if your future and your children's future, your land, and your newly won liberty are precious to you, you must be defenders of the country, despite your weariness, despite all obstacles, despite the harsh conditions of war, for the Germans are not waiting.

Comrade soldiers! Do not give in to calls for dissension and hatred toward the commanding officers. We must keep the army unified and strong! Be united with your officers and all the citizens who are dying in masses on the fields of battle and whose blood is indelibly marking their service in the interests of the revolutionary people and the Russian republic. In times of travail, everyone must stand firm, have faith in your powers, fight faint hearts and panic, and permit no hesitation whatsoever in carrying out orders.

Comrade soldiers and officers! Right now there is no peace. Right now Wilhelm's regiments are all advancing on us as one man in defense of German imperialism. Remember that the hour of life and death for the revolution is upon us!

1. Zemstvos were provincial and district self-governing institutions from 1864 to 1918, responsible for education, road building, health care, and improvement of agricultural technique. At the turn of the century, they had become organizing centers for Russian liberalism and the source of demands for a more representative national government. In March 1917 the Provisional Government created the zemstvo at the township (*volost*) level and extended zemstvos to all parts of the country. Unlike their prerevolutionary ancestors, zemstvos in 1917 generally excluded nobles and large landowners and hence were considered popular democratic organizations.

· 85 ·

Letter to *Izvestiia* from a soldier and member of the Petrograd soviet, received 4 October 1917.

[Added by hand] Please print this

Letter
from a member of the Sov. of Work. and Sold. Dep.

Nearly Murder

I, Skvortsov, stopped in for some tea at the 11th Company, No. 15. An orchestra was playing there, and a drunken soldier came out on stage armed with a revolver and a saber and started singing all kinds of drivel unworthy not just of a soldier but of someone who has lost everything, and, as if that were not enough, when he stepped off the stage he started collecting money. I decided to ask him, "Comrade, I don't have any money to give you, but say, is that what they gave you that gun for?" And he answered straight back in my face, "Damn troublemaker! I'm gonna shoot you!" and he reached for his revolver, but his comrade, who was also drunk, grabbed him, and there was a whole scandal. There were lots of drunks, and he kept shouting, "I'm gonna kill him, and nothing'll happen to me." Seeing the danger, I decided to go to the police and the commandant, so I took ten soldiers with me over to where we saw a whole group of drunks singing songs. The soldiers surrounded the table and those drunks raised a hue and cry. Some were shouting, "Beat him!" and others, "We'll take care of him!" and so on. They refused to leave the tearoom at our suggestion, and the soldiers who were with me, seeing the inevitability of a conflict situation, suggested I leave with them to save me from a beating. I couldn't get any more soldiers, since the commandant only had thirty in all, so we left and everything stayed the same there with all the commotion and songs. I have to point out that in Narva district[1] this phenomenon is quite commonplace, there have been open drunkenness, prostitution, theft, and even murders, and such foul dens number about thirty.

Comrades, while it's not too late to save the revolution, I am proposing that the Petro. Sov. and all public organizations take the most decisive measures, or else it will be too late. By the way, I should point out that a few days ago here a member of the Soviet was robbed and a murder was committed right before his very eyes.

The police are never at their posts here, and no one knows what they're doing. Comrades, pay serious attention to the threat to the revolution latent in all this; we need decisive and immediate struggle.

Member of the Petrograd Soviet

1. Located in the southwest section of the city, the Narva district had a heavy concentration of industrial workers and was one of the poorest in the city.

· 86 ·

Appeal to the Provisional Government from soldiers at the front,
early October 1917.[1]

Appeal No. 1

We soldiers at the front have been in the trenches for more than three years now. There is severe hunger here at the front. We get 1 lb. of bread and 1 oz. of meat.[2] We walk around in tatters, like beggars. At night we sit by the barbed wire for six hours at a stretch. We have lost the last shreds of our health, while at home our families are going hungry on their two *sotkas* of land.[3] We soldiers at the front ask you comrades of the Provisional Government to put a speedy end to the war. It would be good for you comrades of the Provisional Government to do the fighting. When you drink and eat [you get] whatever your heart desires, and bullets and rockets aren't whining over your head, while we soldiers at the front sit by the wire fence at night and in the day we have to stand in the trench—even if you get a few hours of rest every day, the lice never give you any peace. Once more we demand a speedy peace from you the Provisional Government, and if you don't try to do this, Comrade Kerensky, then in the near future we are going to throw down our rifles and leave the front for the rear and destroy you, the Bourgeoisie. You need war and money, but we need life. Once more we demand a speedy peace. For now, that is your primary task. We ask you to carry out our decision. If not, it will be our sword and your head from your shoulders.

The active army

1. Dated by content and placement in the archive file.
2. In the original, one *funt* and five *zolotniki*.
3. A sotka is a linear measure marking a hundred *sazhens* (seven hundred feet) along

roads. It was not normally used as a measure of land but here might indicate the extent of lands in a village as marked out along a road.

· 87 ·

Instruction (*nakaz*) to the delegates to the Second All-Russian Congress of Soviets from the Congress of Soldiers' Representatives, 6th Army Corps, 18 October 1917.

Instruction to the delegates to the All-Russian Congress of Soviets of Workers', Soldiers', and Peasants' Deputies,

passed at the congress of the 6th Army Corps, by a majority of 303, with 4 against and 15 abstentions.

Every extra day of the continued existence of the coalition government, which was established using every trick in the book behind the people's back through the conciliationist machinations of leaders who have not justified the people's hopes, brings the country closer to ruin. The country needs a firm and democratic authority founded on and responsible to the popular masses. Only such a democratic authority can ensure a proper convocation of the Constituent Assembly and safeguard it from any attempts to sabotage it or break it up. Only this kind of authority can undertake real measures in the struggle against complete economic collapse and bring us closer to peace. We have had enough words, rhetoric, and parliamentary sleight-of-hand! We consider the All-Russian Congress of Soviets of Workers', Soldiers', and Peasants' Deputies to be the sole organ reflecting the will and voice of the people. We consider it political suicide for it to refuse power. We are sure that all effective elements of democracy both in the rear and at the front are prepared to be like a wall in defense of their representative organs. Only aloofness from public life, only the demagoguery of certain foolish leaders, only the influence of the slanderous bourgeois press can explain the absence at this congress of representatives of several sections at the front. In the name of the men who have suffered so much in the trenches, in the name of the men over whom has loomed the terrible specter of a fourth winter campaign, which would sap all our energy and all the fullness of our revolutionary fervor, we call on the Congress of Soviets, over the heads of the revolution's deserters and the conciliators and over the hysterical cries of the political shriekers [*klikushi*],[1] to take all the fullness of power into its own hands and give Russia its long-awaited revolutionary order.

> Chairman of the corps congress, Ensign Karaian
> Secretary, Tiabov

18 October 1917
Act.[ive] army

1. *Klikushi*, or "shriekers," was a term applied to village women whom peasants considered to be possessed by demons, though notions of female hysteria gradually replaced the traditional explanation.

· 88 ·

Resolution of the soldiers' committee at the front, 2nd Company,
11th Siberian Rifle Regiment, received 23 October 1917.

Resolution of the 2nd Company, 11th Sib.[erian] Rif.[le] Regiment

In view of the present situation at the front and in the country, we soldiers of the said unit earnestly implore the comrade soldiers who are in the deep rear, and are enjoying a peaceful life, and are not enduring the deprivations that men are suffering here in the damp trenches, your comrades. Comrades! Russia is on the brink of ruin. Help us, this is Your Homeland, and our freedom is going to die along with it.

Once again the same lot will befall us that our grandfathers and fathers suffered for three hundred years from our tyrants, who mocked us.

Comrades! Forget your personal scores, forget everything in the name of our tortured and injured homeland. Close ranks into a unified whole and come to our aid. Comrade soldiers! Our ranks keep thinning, so fill them out. Otherwise, there will be only a handful of us. We are spilling our blood under the onslaught of the German beasts. The enemy spares nothing, he poisons us with his gases and does everything he possibly can to destroy Russia and with it Freedom. Comrade Workers! It may be that healthy and strong men are concealed in your midst, so we beg of you not to conceal those cowards but despise them, drive them this way into the trenches—their places can be taken by weaker men who have already given half their life in the name of the Homeland.

We earnestly implore everyone who holds the Homeland and Freedom dear. Despise and drive to us those soldiers who are now in the rear. We will consider every soldier who hesitates an enemy of our homeland. Never never will the front-liners forgive those scoundrels who have not followed their conscience. Then we will force those pathetic cowards to do it. After all, history will never forgive you; rather, it will record your betrayal, and not only will we despise you, but so will all free peoples.

Committee chairman, Vasiliev
Secretary, Chibrikin

· 89 ·

Letter to *Izvestiia* from Mikhail Savin and the committee
of wounded soldiers, mid-October 1917.

We wounded soldiers, forty men in all, are now recuperating in the infirmary set up in Azov-Don Commercial Bank No. 83. All of us come from the ignorant masses and have been practically forgotten by everyone. No one will come see us or enlighten our ignorant souls. It is almost eight months since our long-awaited freedom came to Russia, but most of us are not up to date on this matter. We are simply unable to make sense of party affairs, we don't have any of their programs, and we don't know who we should follow. We don't have books, we don't have anything. All we get to hear is a few words from our director Mr. Basias, who has been informing us partially about the revolutionary cause. Here in the infirmary we have a senior doctor, Mr. Verter, who thinks it's disgraceful to speak to us. There are also sixteen wounded officers, who are strangers to us, and we cannot get into a conversation with them, since they all despise us.

Comrades! I beg of you! Send us and come see us yourselves with your comrades. Bring us your slogans, come see us, we are waiting for you, send us your speakers. Sow the seed in our hearts, set us on a pure path we can follow unimpeded.

Chairman of the soldiers' committee,
Senior noncommissioned officer Mikhail Savin

Peasants

· 90 ·

Letter to the All-Russian Central Executive Committee of Soviets
from the peasant Ivan Pastukhov, Vologda Province, received 7 July 1917.

Citizens of our Great Russia, workers' and soldiers' deputies,

We, the peasants of Vologda Province, beg you to help our families in their time of Need since we, their fathers, were drafted into military service and got sick in the service: some have rheumatism, some typhus, any and every kind of sickness; we can't work at all, the hayfield goes uncultivated, there is no life-sustaining food at all, and all because of the war.

Comrades, we beg of you, end this bloody drama as soon as possible. It isn't a war—it's the extermination of the people. The people's cause, the way people used to say before, has been abandoned, tsarism is again starting to poke through our young freedom. We beg of you again, comrades, w.[orkers'] and s.[oldiers'] d.[eputies], make peace right away. Otherwise we will die of hunger, without Bread or sugar, and they're sending nothing at all to our remote North. High prices have overtaken everything. This war benefits only the bourgeoisie, and over these three years the land, our poor soldiers' land, has gone desolate or unplowed.

It's time to end this bloody work because now we also have to fight our own enemy [in] Russia—the bourgeoisie. Each of us would like to live in a free Russia, but we got our freedom first and have had to go to our death for freedom.

We also ask the Soviet of W. and S. D. why at the beginning of freedom the Death penalty and life imprisonment were abolished, but [now] the death penalty is back again. More than enough of our men have died by the death penalty in these three years of war run by Nicholas Romanov.

We peasants beg of the Soviet of W. S. D. to start doing something about the Constituent Assembly as soon as possible. For some reason you keep putting it off. It is necessary to destroy the capitalists as quickly as possible.

Also heed our request. For the Moscow Military District there are no soldiers more than thirty-five years old at the front line, but we have many in their forties. Owing to old age, none of them can bear the weight of war the way they did before they were thirty-five. You need to let everyone go from the service because the autocrat Kerensky is carrying out the program of Nicholas Romanov.

Down with the war, down with the bourgeoisie, down with hard labor and the death penalty!

Peasant Ivan A. Pastukhov

· 91 ·

Resolution of Gagarin Volost assembly of peasants,
Kostroma Province, 9 July 1917.

On the 9th day of July, 1917, the citizens of Gagarin Volost, Vetluzhsk Uezd, Kostroma Province, on this date, at a volost assembly of 303 people, discussed the sad events that took place on the 3rd of this July in Petrograd and unanimously

Resolved
1) To recognize all the speeches of Lenin and those who agree with him as a symptom of counterrevolution, and so ask the Provisional Govern-

ment [and] the Soviets of Workers', Soldiers', and Peasants' Deputies to take the most decisive measures to eliminate anarchy and all those individuals who are causing the breakdown in strengthening our hard-won freedom.

2) We the working peasantry can tell that the Bolsheviks of Social Democracy are pursuing only selfish goals and do not want to be a friend and comrade to the working peasantry, and since this is so, then we in turn declare that we can get along without them, but they will die of hunger without us—we are not going to give them grain or meat or fuel until they recognize a single firm authority in the person of the Provisional Government and abandon their aspirations to take power.

3) Even if we are deprived of manufactured goods, even if we return to a primitive state with respect to these goods, we will not extend a helping hand to those who are destroying our slogans "Land and Liberty."

4) To those soldiers who have joined Lenin's ranks consciously, be they sons or brothers, we send our curse, and upon their return to the homeland those traitors and betrayers of the homeland will meet with our contempt. Enough of thinking that we cannot make sense of this matter of state, because for us it is quite clear: without victory over the external enemy, freedom will not be won, and without the latter there is no land or liberty.

5) We call on the entire working peasantry to close ranks tightly in the struggle for freedom, land, and liberty and to declare loudly that we, the many millions of peasants, will never allow this banner to drop from our hands; better death than a return to the nightmarish past. We must all unite under a common banner on which is written: Long live the democratic republic! Long live the Provisional Government leading the people to this republic! Long live the great citizen of the Russian land A. F. Kerensky. Copies of this resolution shall be sent out to all the volosts of Vetulzhsk Uezd. [Signing] this resolution, the citizens of Gagarin Volost.

[303 signatures]

· 92 ·

Letter to Kerensky from Ivan Shabrov, Ryazan Province, 13 July 1917.

Aleksandr Fyodorovich!

In the name of the revolution's salvation, I am allowing myself to take a few minutes of your time.

The revolutionary Provisional Government has already been presented with all dictatorial rights and given all the fullness of firm authority. The difficult moment we are living through, complicated by the events in Petrograd and the catastrophe at the front, demands that firm and powerful authority be invested in the provincial organs of the revolutionary government as well: the province and uezd commissars and the military chiefs. And here is why:

In the provinces there is total collapse. If the capitals and major cities remain at the pinnacle of the revolution's tasks, the countryside is sliding back down. Popular peasant ignorance does a bad job of figuring out ideological constructions and slogans. All it knows is the shirt on its own back, and it lives only for today, which gives peasants a chance to scrape together another ruble, but they never even take a peek into the distant tomorrow. There is a lot of grain in the countryside, but it is being concealed from any inventory. In the countryside there are masses of runaway soldiers and deserters. Even now, more and more new soldiers have been showing up here with furlough tickets (forgeries, I think), even though you categorically banned leaves in June. There is no one to fight these phenomena and nothing to fight them with. The military authorities are obviously powerless, for they don't send patrols to the villages to arrest deserters, and the rural militia is unarmed (quite literally) and terrorized by the soldier-traitors. To this must be added provocation and bribery on the part of supporters of the fallen regime. The executive and food committees in the countryside were selected haphazardly, and people wound up on them who were either indecisive or known to be from the counterrevolutionary camp, and often unscrupulous as well. Bribery is flourishing all over. In short, the situation in the countryside is not favorable. It's not favorable on the R.R. or at the post office or the telegraph office either. Here people talk a lot about their rights but are silent when it comes to their responsibilities, and things are done any which way and every day it's getting worse. Still, these are the things you can see. The revolutionary centers have only vague notions of the countryside, but meanwhile the countryside will have the decisive word in the revolution: to be or not to be?

En route from a distant corner of Yenesei Province to a village in Ryazan Province,[1] I looked and listened very closely. Total collapse. Firm revolutionary authorities must be established in the provinces. The truth must be told: the people were ill prepared for this revolution, they have a poor concept of freedom, and most often misinterpret it, to the detriment of the revolution and statehood; therefore, they don't recognize discipline that isn't welded together with bare knuckles and an iron fist, they won't submit to anything, and reasonable arguments have no effect on them. It's embarrassing and painful to say, but it must be said: in order now to save the revolution from defeat and Russia from a restoration of the tsarist regime, we must immediately show the insurgent people—who have been in slavery for so long and have blinded themselves with their perverted understanding of freedom—the revolutionary stick, that is, force, which is the only thing they will bow to or follow. I call upon you, as the head of the Rev. Gov. and as a man and revolutionary I trust, to start immediately down the path of firm authority in the provinces. It is essential to appoint men with bright minds and firm wills immediately as province and uezd commissars, granting them broad rights and authority. Besides uezd commissars, also appoint volost ones with the same rights and authority. Instruct military commanders to take measures immediately to arrest deserters and remove them from the countryside for introducing degeneracy and decay into the countryside. Instruct them to send military units to assist the commissars, should the latter request it. History will vindicate and bless these measures, for only a decisive and centralized revolutionary authority can save the revolution and Russia now.

In full awareness of my responsibility for what I am saying,

Amnestied participant in the uprising in the 2nd Rostov Grenadier Regiment in December in Moscow, former soldier of the 12th Company, this is a peasant from Karlovka village, Ryazan Province, Sapozh.[kovsk Uezd],

Ivan Yakovlevich Shabrov
Karlovka
13 July 1917

1. In other words, from deep in Siberia to the heartland of European Russia.

· 93 ·

Letter to the Bolshevik newspaper *Rabochii i soldat*[1] from Timofei Gurov, an injured noncommissioned officer, 9 August 1917.

Comrade workers and soldiers!

Help me sort out the following matter. Yesterday I heard a discussion about land, about how we have to defend it to the end from the Germans and also how after the war, by decision of the Constituent Assembly, it will go to the peasants for compensation, which they are kindly stretching out for us over many long years.

This is when I thought: Here I am with two-thirds of an acre of land, while some landowners have thousands of acres.[2] Who is defending them? Well, it's people like me. Am I really supposed to sacrifice my life for someone else's wealth?

Isn't this cruel mockery?

For three and a half years I was in active service; since the very beginning of mobilization I've been tossed around the trenches, enduring hunger, cold, and want.

And here I am deprived of everything. This is insulting. After all, you know you're benefiting someone, that someone is getting rich, while your own home is desolate and empty.

So let them pay me back for all their profits, all those people I defended. Let them give us the land that we bought with our blood.

> 143rd Dorogobuzhsky Regiment, injured 10 July,
> senior noncommissioned officer Timofei Gurov

1. *Rabochii i soldat* (Worker and soldier) was the daily newspaper of the Bolshevik party in Petrograd from July to August 1917. It succeeded *Pravda*, which was closed by the government when Bolsheviks were blamed for the July Days.

2. The original is "twenty-four sazhens of land" (one sazhen equals seven feet; for land this is a squared measurement) compared with "thousands of desiatinas" (one *desiatina* is equal to twenty-four square sazhens).

· 94 ·

Report addressed to Kerensky from peasants in Valdaisk Uezd,
Novgorod Province, 19 August 1917.

To Minister A. F. Kerensky
Report from the provinces
from the peasants of Valdaisk Uezd, Zhabinsk Volost
from the local district [*raion*] committee at Firovo Station, N.[ovgorod] R.[ailroad]. Three thousand residents, on the basis of which we possess the legal competence for our opinion for this report, together with the delegate we have empowered, Ivan Yefimovich Lebedev, held a discussion at a general meeting. We resolved to send our representative I. Lebedev with this report personally.

1st. For everything, for your Activity, our respected one, for your sincere devotion to the idea of a [better] life for the people, we are sincerely devoted to you; and we are deeply confident that your tasks among the people will be carried out in full. You can believe that the power and will of the people's reason are behind you; we will tell you boldly and proudly and confidently that anyone who is against you is against the people; our confidence is in you and Comrade Agriculture Minister Chernov, our honor and our glory and our support in everything and the people's victory and your fulfilling your task; we have always believed in you, the power of the people, and you are our Heroes [*Bogatyrs*] strengthening our freedoms. Land and liberty to all the working people. Only here do we find life, salvation, and the kingdom of heaven on earth for the people. You are our friends you are our saviors and we trust you and our hope is in you for the salvation of the working population of Russia and our confidence is in you. You can believe that no power will ever shake us as long as we live. You and us, together and united.

2nd. We report our resolution. The ideas of the Kadets who speak to us and on our account travel out in threesomes and pairs, and what do they promise us? They started out in the first place saying tsarist, cabinet, and monastery land should be for the people, 2nd the landowners bankers manufacturers and factory owners should have their lands, 3rd we tell them:

All the land must go to the working people; instead, you gentlemen Kadets are getting a nobleman's stable ready for us, to sleep on bast mats, to fight with birch branches. Down with the Kadets, and get them away from the working people. They don't have our trust and never will.

3rd. Educational goals. An unrestricted clergy of and from the people.

4th. Volost zemstvos are independent. District [*raion*] committees considered as Local Oversight Committees.

5th. Together with the peasants, a Constituent Assembly in one chamber and a popular representative of the head and honor of the working people.

6th. Wage military action to victory and glory for Russia.

7th. Lenin and his agents must be punished by the people's justice along with Mr. Miliukov.

8th. Send all the old police starting with the town guards constables police officers gendarmes governors up to the Romanovs to the front lines of the drum fire and in the future we won't have any faith in them, or in any of the popular institutions now and in the future.

9th. We hereby empower the district [*raion*] committee located at the Fir.[ovo] Station N.[ovgorod] R.[ailroad] and the representative of the report Lebedev by signature of the chairman of the committee and the village elder Potap Alekseev.

19 August 1917 P. Kirillov

· 95 ·

Declaration to the Provisional Government from a village assembly, Tambov Province, 21 August 1917.

To the Provisional Government
from the citizens of Stenshino village
Butyrsk Volost, Lipetsk Uezd, Tambov Province

Declaration

We, the citizens of the village of Stenshino, Butyrsk Volost, Lipetsk Uezd, Tambov Province, gathered for an assembly [*skhod*] on 21 August of this year and discussed the difficult situation in our homeland and arrived at the conclusion that we, all the citizens, are bound to make every effort to support all the undertakings of the Provisional Government leading up to and including the Constituent Assembly. We declare:

that we shall give all our grain to the front and the needy population, but we definitely remember that the land is for all the people and that a final long-awaited resolution of the land question must be made by national decision, the decision of the Constituent Assembly.

Until it is conclusively decided and while the confusion over land mounts, impatience over our landlessness mounts, too. We insist before the Provisional Government that it not slow it down but immediately issue the already completed Draft Provisional Land Law.

Only by this measure, we think, can the Provisional Government make sure the peasantry works calmly until the Constituent Assembly.

> Chairman, Ivan Shanynev
> Secretary, Ivan Veretin
> Members of the assembly: [signatures follow: twenty-seven men and one woman]

· 96 ·

Petition to the Ministry of Agriculture from Andrei Kulagin,
peasant in Penza Province, received 21 August 1917.[1]

To the Ministry of Agriculture
From a peasant of Penza Province and Uezd,
Kuchug-Por, Arkhangelsk Volost,
Village of Kuchek, Andrei Dmitriev Kulagin

Petition

First of all, I beg the Ministry to take pity on Russia, to rescue her from ruin, to put an end to the unauthorized seizures and the illegal decrees of the Province and Uezd Committees and the various Congresses. All this is leading Russia to total economic ruin and collapse. I consider the Party of the Social Rev.[olutionaries] the guilty one in all this.

Then I beg you to do what you can to try to protect property because without property no one can live in any State. That is, especially in the land respect, because even now the poor cultivation of the land can be seen and no one is even talking about fertilizing. The winter wheat has been sown badly. You can't tell the winter wheat from the unplowed land. Even the most resolute farmers want to abandon this trade and do something else.

> Peas.[ant] Andrei Kulagin

1. Evidently, this petition, which presented a rare, but for the government attractive, peasant argument, was taken seriously. It bears stamps of receipt by the Ministry of Agriculture (21 August), the Inspectorate (*revizionnyi otdel*) of the Committee for Land Affairs (25 August), and the Economic Section of the Main Land Committee (26 August 1917).

· 97 ·

"Man and the Land," letter-essay by Semyon Martynov, a peasant
from Orel Province, August 1917.[1]

Man and the Land

The land we share is our mother; she feeds us; she gives us shelter; she makes us happy and lovingly warms us; from the moment of our birth until we take our final rest in eternal sleep on her maternal breast, she is constantly cherishing us with her tender embraces. And now, despite this, people are talking about selling her, and truly, in our corrupt, venal age land is put on the market for appraisal and so-called sale. But selling land created by the Heavenly Creator is a barbaric absurdity. The principal error here lies in the crude and monstrous assertion that the land, which God gave to all people so that they could feed themselves, could be anyone's private property. This is just as much an act of violence as slavery. Land is the *common and equal legacy of all people* and so cannot be the object of private ownership by individual persons. All people from the very outset and *before any legal act* own the land—that is, they have the right to be allotted land where nature and accident have put them. The bodies of men and women, and even more so their souls, should not be bought or sold, and the same goes for land, water, and air, because these things are the essential conditions for the support of people's bodies and souls. Ownership of land, as property, is one of the most unnatural of crimes. The repulsiveness of this crime goes unnoticed by us, the poor, only because in our immoral world this crime is deemed a right according to human laws. *Remember and do not forget* that you do not have *any right whatsoever* to the land, that you are a servant of that principle which gave you life, and so you have only obligations to fulfill the teaching of Christ. The land belongs to almighty God, as His creation, and to all the sons of man, as His heirs in equal part, just as we give it to our heirs in equal part for working on it, or to those who would work it with their own hands. It is the property not of any one generation but of all past, present, and future generations who work it and who will work it, each with their own hands, in order to feed themselves, and not according to the whim of the so-called private owners of the land. These people descend, for the sake of satisfying their own animal needs, to the level of cattle, while those people by whose labor an abundance of wealth is created struggle in poverty. Each person, upon being born into the world, does not bring any property with him into the world, and also no one being born is designated to own private land. Where did they ever come up with such barbaric rights to private ownership of the Lord's land? Current land rights cannot be said to be legal. Let anyone who thinks so look through the chronicles. Assault, deceit, power, cunning—here are the sources from which these rights stem. After all, there are people in the world who, having renounced all divine and natural laws, have created laws for themselves and obey them strictly, such as, for example, thieves and others. And now, on the basis of just such laws, immoral people have turned up who, not without great sin, are participating in the seizure, sale, purchase, reinforcement, and management of privately owned land. If a person acquires property he did not produce, he necessarily acquires it at the expense of those who did produce it. By acquiring private ownership of land in this way, you are forcing the majority of people to be and consider themselves unhappy. What kind of happiness can there be that is acquired to the detriment of others' happiness? Alexander of Macedonia and all the authorities of the past lived by a lie alone and *based their happiness on the unhappiness of others.* He [such a person] is conscious in himself of the impossibility of producing anything good and so assures himself that everything he produces is good. Don't dream that you might benefit from anything that goes together with betrayal, dishonesty, hatred, malice, arrogance, hypocrisy, or any kind of deed that requires a curtain or a closed door. *And whatever you stop at is where you will remain.* Simple justice does not allow private land ownership, because if one part of the earth's surface can fairly be the property of a single individual and can be held by him for his personal gain and use, as a thing over which he has an exclusive right, then other parts of the earth's surface can easily be made into the same kind of property, and the entire earth's surface might possibly be made into the same and so the globe would become private property, and then there would not be land for future generations to feed themselves. Look from the standpoint of an observer of nature at a landless person, at a being who has the opportunity and ability to exploit the land and is forced by necessity to exploit it but at the same time is illegally deprived of his right to land. This is as unnatural as a bird without air or a fish without water. The worst thief is not the one who takes what he needs but the one who keeps the most inalienable property—the land, which is essential if people are to be able to feed themselves—away from people. Private ownership of land never arose from natural relations among men but always appeared in history as a consequence of seizure and theft and is such an extreme absurdity, such a crude injustice, such a blatant squandering of productive forces and a barrier to the most profitable exploitation of natural wealth, so much the opposite of sensible public policy, and such a

brake on any true improvement in the daily life of mankind that it is tolerated only because the government is gagging the majority of the poor people so that they can't express their own desires and needs. Did God ever
give something to one without giving the same to the other? Would the Father of All exclude any of His children from participating in the land
legacy? Are all the private landowners His natural sons and everyone else
the stepchildren of some other father? You who demand the exclusive
right to hold land in private ownership, show your brothers, who were
born with the same rights as you, the testament according to which God
bequeathed the land to you as private property but deprived your other
brothers of their land inheritance. He did not give anyone such a law that
allowed people the right to sell and buy His land. Moral men are ashamed
of property as is used for idle whims and as a result of which millions of
your brothers and sisters struggle in poverty and go hungry, and they, the
landowners, should burn with shame as soon as the word "theft" is mentioned. Better to accrue wealth for yourself that thieves cannot steal, that
tyrants would not dare encroach upon, that will remain with you even after your death, that will never be diminished and will never rot—this is a
good and justice. A shipwrecked sailor has been cast onto our shore. Does
he have the same natural right as we, on the same basis as we, to occupy a
bit of the land in order to feed himself by his own labor? This right would
seem to be beyond question. But meanwhile, how many people are born
on our planet Earth whom the people living on it refuse this right to land?
Since I was born on earth, to take from it what I need for feeding myself
but not for luxury, then I have the right to demand my share for myself.
Tell me, where is it? I will take pleasure in it as a loan given while I am
alive—your share was stolen by selfish men for private ownership! Go
work for them and they will give you a crust of bread, and if they hear the
word "theft," they'll put you in prison. While recognizing land as private
property, people are worn out by work and hunger, deprived of all the joys
and charms of life, doomed to ignorance and an impoverished existence
and led to crimes and suicide, seemingly apart from anyone's will but by
force of an apparently fateful necessity that is no one's fault. This war,
which is a government-sanctioned crime, is taking away the sole worker in
the family, one without land, and driving him out under the pretext of war
to defend the rich and privately owned land, but they don't drive any private landowners to war—they say there's no law. They hang men, send
men into hard labor, put them in prison, and kill them in war because
there is a law, but for private landowners to perform compulsory military
service there is no law? But laws don't surface from the water or grow up
out of the earth or fall down from the sky, rather they are written in pen,
on paper, by people. And in this way people are killed, according to the
law, so that they won't demand land for feeding themselves. Like any injustice, the injustice of private land ownership is inevitably linked to the

many injustices and evil deeds required for its protection. If the state is administered on the principles of reason, then one should be ashamed if there are people without land; if the state is not administered on the principles of reason, then one should be ashamed of land ownership because it did not arise out of the natural relations among men. *I earnestly implore you to print this in the newspapers for people to know.*

> Citizen of Durovka village, Uspensk Volost, Maloarkhangelsk Uezd, Orel Province, Semyon Vasilievich Martynov, Uspensk Postal Department, Orel Province.

1. Dated by content and placement in the archive files and in relation to a second essay by Martynov, on religion, received by the government and numbered after this one. That essay refers to a press article of 19 August 1917. GARF, f. 1778, op. 1, d. 234, l. 91.

· 98 ·

Letter to Kerensky from G. Korotkov, a worker in the provincial town of Slaviansk, Kharkov Province, 26 August 1917.

To Mr. War Minister Kerensky

I will be brief, Mr. War Minister.

I consider it my sacred duty to inform you that the Provisional Government should expect a new counterrevolution. The mood among the popular masses is decidedly counterrevolutionary in view of the failure in battle of the Russian Army. The peasants arriving in the town of Slaviansk say openly that only the tsar can save Russia and bring all the food prices down; they are extremely embittered against the bourgeoisie and the workers, who are constantly engaged in party struggle; they are embittered against the soldiers, who to their disgrace have fled from the Germans. . . . Judging from all this, for the salvation of freedom and the revolution, we need—temporarily of course—a dictator with unlimited authority. We need, in the name of our Homeland's salvation, to put down strikes by force and get the defense factories going; we need to introduce iron discipline into the army by force, otherwise Russia will perish on account of the ignorance of her sons!

P.S. Once you have read this all the way through, Mr. War Minister, you may think I am right-wing, like Purishkevich and so on. No! I am a simple worker who sympathizes with the pop.[ular] soc.[ialists], but above all I am a *citizen of Russia.*

> G. Korotkov
> Slaviansk, 26 August 1917

· 99 ·

Telegram to Kerensky from the "working peasantry" of Botsmanovo-Ivanovsk
Volost, 2 September 1917.[1]

———————

Honored Aleksandr Fyodorovich in this ominous hour Russia is living
through the working peasantry hastens to declare that it will be with you
to the end do not let power slip from your hands the peasants believe in
you alone let all the socialist ministers you lead remain at their posts be
brave and steadfast be merciless and stern with enemies of the people—
only you can save Russia and lead her out into the light into the path of
liberty equality and fraternity all you have to do is call on us and we will
rise up as one in a unified host under the banner of revolution and die for
freedom—Arefiev on behalf of the peasants of Botsmanovo-Ivanovsk
Volost.

     1. Dated by position in the archive folder.

· 100 ·

Resolution by a general meeting of peasants,
Petrograd Province, 17 October 1917.

———————

We, the peasants of the 3rd electoral precinct, Osminsk Volost, Gdovsk
Uezd, Petrograd Province, gathered for a general meeting on 17 October
of this year and discussed the difficult moment for our Homeland that we
are now experiencing.

The old men, women, and children left behind in the countryside are
worn out by the horror going on at the present time. The insane war continues and our sons are dying fighting a foreign enemy to satisfy the whim
of a tiny little handful of men—the capitalists. Our economy is collapsing
because we have no strength left to labor amid such troubles. We face the
imminent danger of going barefoot; there is no leather for boots, no cloth,
no iron, no equipment for cultivating the land; whenever an opportunity
does arise to buy something, then it is only at insane prices.

The situation poses the gravest danger to the whole state. Meanwhile,
the bourgeois Provisional Government has proven itself utterly incapable
of carrying out the people's will. In seven months of revolution this government has allowed the capitalists to close factories and plants intentionally and thereby condemn to starvation workers who are already suffering
from malnourishment; it has allowed the organization of counterrevolutionary forces that, led by General Kornilov, have come out openly against
the gains of the Revolution. By an act of 18 June, it threw an army worn

out by a three-year war under the blows of that brigand Wilhelm and his henchmen and vilely coerced the Russian army, which understood things, to attack by threatening them with the disgraceful death penalty. The Provisional Government has released all the criminals against the people, the former henchmen of the tsarist autocracy, who go about freely spreading all manner of foul fabrications against the revolution. The Provisional Government has allowed the above-cited blatant encroachments on freedom on the part of the gentlemen capitalists, despite the fact that the revolutionary people have tried with all their might to fight this kind of violence.

In view of all that has been said, we henceforth and forever will not trust any longer an authority that is not responsible to the people, and we demand that the All-Russian Congress of Soviets of W., S., and P. D. take power into its own hands both in the center and in the provinces. The Soviet must immediately exercise all its powers to carry out the will of the revolutionary people, who dictated the following back in the very first days of the revolution:

1. Immediately propose to all the countries warring with us, as well as to our allies, an honest democratic peace without any seizures of foreign lands or indemnities of any kind, so that all nations can live freely without being enslaved by anyone.

2. Immediately declare all the land public and hand it over for disposal by the volost land committees.

3. Immediately institute state control over capital and production, as well as the distribution of provisions.

4. Immediately assess taxes on the propertied classes for the benefit of the state.

5. Immediately take energetic measures to provision the countryside, which at the present time is in need of kerosene, cloth, leather, iron, and nails, as well as grain, to cover the shortfall.

6. Immediately turn the profoundest attention to the people's schools, as well as to the teachers, who at present are in the direst straits; short on funds, the schools are emptying out, and the teachers must starve.

7. The rights of the cooperatives must be expanded with respect to provisioning the countryside with food products and manufactured farm goods, as well as with the export of foodstuffs to the towns from the countryside, thereby eliminating the middlemen speculators between the producer and the consumer.

8. Immediately repeal the death penalty, which brings shame upon revolutionary Russia before the revolutionary democracy of the entire world.

The resolution was passed unanimously by the assembly on 17 October.

Chairman of the assembly, A. P. Vorobyov
Secretary, A. Ryndin

· 101 ·

Plea to the soldiers from Iskeevsk Volost, October 1917.

Comrade Soldiers!
Our Husbands and Children!

Unpleasant and grievous rumors are reaching our villages saying that many comrades are abandoning their posts without leave and are abandoning their comrades, the defenders of our dear free homeland, at their positions. Our dear defenders! Close ranks and form a single unbroken ring and an impenetrable armor for the salvation of our dear Homeland and of us, your aged fathers, wives, and mothers, who are being shielded by your mighty breast. Much blood has been spilled for free Russia. Can it be that we, newly citizens, will not be able to enjoy the freedom that was wrested away? Can it be that the long-awaited new dawn of our free life is going to be hidden away from us forever?

Comrade soldiers! Husbands and children! We beg of you! You have suffered much in the damp trenches, and many of you have spilled your precious blood. We implore you! Do not abandon your comrades in the trenches until the international conflict is settled and you win full freedom for our great Russia, whose fate rests on you. All our most vital interests are in your mighty hands!

Accurate: for the chairman of the Iskeevsk Volost committee, his assistant A. Filonov

· 102 ·

Pyotr Oreshin, a "Song of Freedom,"[1] printed in the Socialist Revolutionary paper *Delo naroda*, 17 September 1917.

Unfurled are the banners of scarlet
    As broad as the dawning of day . . .
On the meadow and gully and summit
    An intolerable grief has been laid.

The hut of each miracle reaper,
    Has plunged into longing, alarm—
'Neath our sun, our dear sun, flaming deeper
    Our roads in their misery yearn.

No stars, but ingots of gold,
    Roses that seem there to burn . . .

In the daytime—tortures so cruel
 And grief and tears without end.

All the thoughts and intentions we cherish—
 Are they not just an ocean of blood?
The more beautiful our liberty, the more lavish,
 The harsher the men of the crowd.

Streaming pathways of crimson,
 Swift rivers of blood flowing red . . .
Will we not be slaves and bondsmen—
 Forever and after we're dead?

Like nighttime in violet the dark fields
 Are alive with noises and sighs . . .
Horseshoes clattering, crashing down byroads—
 And twinkling stars in the sky.

No! Neither slaves are we nor bondsmen,
 The children of freedom are we . . .
Leading down pathways of scarlet,
 All the peoples of our land to be free.

Was it not in our own crowded hovels
 That the tablets of Christ safe were kept . . .
In the fields, like deserts untraveled,
 Was it not then we who wept?

1. This is the last of three "songs of freedom" (*pesni svobody*) by Oreshin appearing together in this issue.

· 103 ·

Ivan Loginov, "To a Worker Friend," printed in the socialist
newspaper *Rabotnitsa*, 25 September 1917.

———————

To a Worker Friend
Don't be sad, dear friend of mine,
That life has been so hard and cruel.
Through common work there'll come a time,
When build we shall a temple new.
When build we shall a new free temple
Where there'll be no place for gods
That ever made the nations tremble

Those many centuries long and broad.
There shall come a time of building
The Temple of Labor—it will be called,
There'll be no trace in it left lingering
Of the bourgeois's former tranquil calm.
Believe, my friend, in what draws nigh—
Our happiness lies ahead . . .
Cast aside your mournful sigh
And carry on your ever braver tread.

PART 3

Soviets in Power:
From the October Revolution to the
Closing of the Constituent Assembly

Yes, we are living through a storm of dark passions. . . . All that is vile and despicable on earth has been and is being done by us, and all that is beautiful and intelligent, for which we are striving, lives within us. . . . Yes, yes, we live up to our necks in blood and filth; thick fogs of detestable vulgarity [*poshlost'*] surround us and are blinding many. Yes, at times it seems that this vulgarity will poison and stifle all the beautiful dreams to which we have given birth in labor and torment, all the torches we have lit on the way to rebirth. But a human being is, nevertheless, a human being, and ultimately only that which is human triumphs.

MAXIM GORKY, 24 December 1917

The willingness of the Bolsheviks to establish a one-party government in the wake of the fall of the Provisional Government not only offended many socialists and liberals but convinced many observers that the new regime could not possibly survive longer than a few weeks or even days. On 26 October, after failing to convince left-wing Socialist Revolutionaries to join the government, the Bolsheviks proposed to the Congress of Soviets a new cabinet composed entirely of Bolsheviks, with Lenin as chairman. The congress, abandoned by most other parties, agreed. The new government was to be called the Council (Soviet) of People's Commissars (Sovnarkom)—a name Lenin reportedly liked: it "smells of revolution."[1] The obstacles to political survival were daunting. Not only did the new government face the immediate necessities of getting Russia safely out of the war and restoring the collapsing economy, but it had to create effective political rule in a country in which Bolsheviks were not the majority party. Predictions of failure, not without undertones of satisfaction, were widespread. The independent socialist newspaper *Novaia zhizn'* (New life) argued that the Bolsheviks were too "detached and isolated" to succeed for long. In their view, only a broad alliance of all the revolutionary groups in the country could hope to defend soviet power against the certain opposition of "the propertied classes." The Bolshevik desire to rule alone would "in very short time lead to collapse."[2] Other socialist papers predicted the same or worse. Faced with certain opposition outside of Petrograd, the Bolsheviks would soon discover that they were merely "caliphs for the hour," *Narodnoe slovo* (People's word) argued, and forecast that the Bolshevik "coup d'état" would turn out to be only another "stage" on Russia's "thorny path," to be filled with "new torments and trials."[3] The Soviet's own newspaper *Izvestiia*, commenting on its final day before being put under Bolshevik control, also suggested that a Bolshevik government would lead only to failure and to the "bloodshed and pogroms" of "civil war."[4] Liberals thought the same. An editorial in the Kadet newspaper *Rech'*, on the day before it was shut down by the government, portrayed Bolshevik power as only a new turn on the country's "road to Golgotha" and argued that the pressing and complex problems the country faced could "not be gotten rid of by the cheap rhetoric and idle talk of meetings" or by "deceitful and unrealizable promises."[5]

The Bolshevik leadership recognized the challenges ahead and approached them with a variety of solutions. Partly, they viewed the Russian revolution and its fate in transnational terms. Lenin and other leading Bolsheviks repeatedly described the purpose of the October revolution as being partly to inspire revolution in Western Europe, and spoke of international revolution as essential to their own success. They were not blind to the obstacles they faced as a radical socialist workers' party trying to hold power and construct socialism in a largely peasant country surrounded by hostile states. They believed that revolution in advanced industrial countries would end their isolation and make Russia part of a cooperative international socialist environment which would ensure both survival and progress. The success of "proletarian" power in Russia, Lenin argued at a Bolshevik party conference in April 1917, was "only possible through world revolution."[6] Throughout 1917, the Bolsheviks watched for any sign of social unrest in Germany, Austria, Britain, and France, and seem to have believed that revolution in those countries was imminent.[7] By early 1918, when it was clear that the revolution there had been, at the very least, delayed, Lenin was still arguing that "salvation" from all the difficulties they faced lay in "an all-European revolution." This had been part of the reasoning in October, he recalled: "If we took matters into the hands of the Bolshevik party alone, we took this upon ourselves because we were certain that the revolution was maturing in all countries." And though it was now clear that that hope had been too sanguine, the logic of the argument remained valid: "It is an absolute truth that without a German revolution we are doomed." At the same time, Lenin insisted, while waiting for this coming salvation, the Bolsheviks had to rely on their own resources to resolve the many "difficulties."[8]

In dealing with these difficulties, Lenin and other leading Bolsheviks drew upon a complex and even inconsistent set of ideas about revolutionary power. These contradictions in Bolshevik political thinking helped in turn to shape the contradictory popular responses to October that we see in the documents presented here. To simplify a bit: on the one side stood ideals of popular creativity and power, of the revolution's power to unleash ordinary people's desire to control their own lives and build a new socialist society; on the other side stood a belief in the necessity of strong leadership and control, of discipline and dictatorship. Many scholars have argued that there was no contradiction when Bolsheviks spoke of and encouraged popular activism and local control. Their purposes, it is argued, were simply utilitarian—or cynical. In this view, libertarian discourse and the encouragement of popular power were, especially for Lenin, nothing more than a means "to destroy the old political system and thus clear the way for the establishment of his own party's dictatorship."[9] Many contemporaries, including some socialists, shared this judgment. As we try to interpret Bolshevik political thinking, we must bear in mind, first, that Bolshevism was not yet identical with Leninism. Many party members and even many party leaders—a number of whom would in time organize openly in opposition to Leninist authoritarianism—were sincerely committed to libertarian notions of popular power and democracy. One must also recognize that even Lenin may have been a less monolithic and consistent thinker than he has commonly been portrayed as being.[10]

Lenin often reiterated Marxist arguments about the need for the proletariat to "smash" the state that the exploiting classes had created in their own interests and replace it with forms of revolutionary power in which large numbers of people could participate at different times, so that no one could become a bureaucrat, and in which the interests of the lower-class majority would be represented through their own direct involvement in administration.[11] Throughout 1917, Lenin frequently argued, both in public and within his party, that a socialist government in Russia would succeed in the face of so many obvious obstacles because it would release the "energy, initiative, and decisiveness" of the people, which could perform "miracles." In response to critics who, on the eve of the Bolshevik insurrection, argued that the party was too small to govern Russia, he maintained that, on the contrary, Soviet power would be able to "draw the working people, draw the poor, into the daily work of state administration," and so, unlike the bourgeoisie, would be able to boast a "state apparatus of one million people" who would serve not for "fat sums" received every month but "for the sake of high ideals." The most important thing, he asserted, was "to imbue the oppressed and the working people with confidence in their own strength." Otherwise, Lenin said, "Russia cannot be saved from collapse and ruin."[12] In the first weeks and months after October, Lenin frequently appealed to people to realize this ideal. In early November, for example, he appealed to "all working people" (*trudiashchiesia*—a term denoting workers, poor peasants, and common soldiers) to "remember that you yourselves are now administering the state. . . . Take matters into your own hands from below, waiting for no one."[13] In the months following, he continued to speak of the need to unleash "the enterprise, energy, and bold initiative of the masses of the population" and to insist that the key to the success of Soviet power lay in "the independent creative work of the majority of the population, especially the majority of the working people, as makers of history."[14]

At the same time, Lenin and other Bolshevik leaders were absolutely convinced of the necessity of strong leadership and control, at least in the hands of a party that had the consciousness and vision to lead the country toward its socialist future. Bolshevik authoritarianism, in other words, was not simply a response to the difficult circumstances of maintaining power in Russia in late 1917 and after (though it was that too). It was an intrinsic part of Bolshevik, and especially Leninist, ideology. Well before coming to power in 1917, Lenin liked to remind people that Bolsheviks were "not anarchists." Indeed, notions of "dictatorship" were already an explicit part of Bolshevik thinking about revolutionary government. This was, to be sure, envisioned as a dictatorship by the common people against "exploiters." It was an idea of dictatorship, however, that did not hesitate to embrace the most coercive methods, including mass arrests, terror, and summary executions.[15] Even in his pamphlet *State and Revolution*, with its talk of smashing the old political apparatus and drawing the masses into governance, Lenin recognized, quoting Engels, that "a revolution is the most authoritarian thing there is," and spoke of the need for a revolutionary state to use "coercion" and enforce "strict, iron discipline."[16] These arguments, of course, were consistent with Lenin's most influential work on revolutionary strategy, *What Is to Be Done?* (1902), which established as the basic outlook of Bolshevism distrust of merely "spontaneous" ideals and actions by the working class, in favor of strategic reliance on an elite vanguard of the most conscious and disciplined revolutionaries.

After his coming to power, Lenin's public statements were filled with the vocabulary of authoritarian rule: control, suppression, coercion, discipline, dictatorship. And, for good measure, these nouns were usually complemented by appropriate adjectives: it had to be "ruthless suppression," "iron discipline," and so on.[17] Although this repression was mainly to be directed against the "rich exploiters," it was also to target "enemies" whose otherness was primarily political and moral rather than social. "Crooks, idlers, and hooligans" were to be suppressed, Lenin urged, though he also spoke of imprisoning workers inclined to "shirk their work," of "shooting on the spot one out of ten idlers," of using "an iron hand" to put down all "elements of disintegration" in society, and of the need, within industry, "in the interests of socialism," for the "absolute subordination of the masses . . . to the unified will of the leaders of the labor process."[18]

The first acts of the new Bolshevik government were in accord with this dualistic orientation toward revolutionary power. On the one hand, the government immediately set out to realize a revolutionary program of libertarian emancipation, as summarized in the proclamation of Soviet power by the Congress of Soviets: to propose "immediate democratic peace" to all nations, to safeguard the transfer of land to the control of peasants' committees, to defend soldiers' rights and introduce "complete democratization" into the army, to establish workers' control in industry, to supply the cities with bread and the villages with essential products, to guarantee to all nationalities in Russia the "right of self-determination," to ensure the timely convocation of the Constituent Assembly, and to transfer "all local authority" into the hands of local soviets of workers', soldiers', and peasants' deputies.[19] With these goals in mind, the congress approved several key decrees. Capital punishment at the front was abolished. All persons arrested for "political crimes" were to be set free. Local power was taken out of the hands of the commissars of the Provisional Government and transferred to local soviets. Most important, the congress passed two decrees, both read to the meeting by Lenin, proclaiming Soviet policies on peace and land.[20]

The Decree on Peace—more a proclamation to the peoples of the world than a proper law—proposed that all the nations agree to a "just and democratic peace" without indemnities or annexations of territory, that all nationalities feeling themselves to be oppressed as nations be given the right to decide through democratic elections whether they desired to establish independent states, and that an armistice be signed immediately, while peace negotiations were under way. The proclamation called on the common people of Europe to pressure their countries to agree to peace, while at the same time assuring governments that this proclamation was not an ultimatum and that Russia was ready to consider any terms in negotiating for peace. Finally, in a gesture clearly meant to indicate that the new leaders of Russia did not intend to do things in accordance with the traditions of the old world, Russia declared its intent to reveal the texts of all secret treaties—indeed, these immediately began appearing as a regular feature in the Soviet press—and to conduct all future diplomacy "openly before all peoples."[21]

The Decree on the Land abolished, without compensation, "land ownership by the gentry" and transferred all lands belonging to the gentry, royalty, monasteries, and the Church to peasant land committees and peasant soviets. Although it was left to the Constituent Assembly to decide a final policy on land reform, the decree recommended in the meantime as a guide for land reform a detailed "instruction" (*nakaz*) that had been drawn up and published in August by the All-Russian Soviet of Peasants' Deputies. Based on peasant petitions, this nakaz recommended abolition of all private land, the end of the use of hired agricultural labor, and the distribution of all farmland to citizens willing to work it with their own families. The amount of land that peasants received would be determined, in conformity with rural tradition, according to household need in conjunction with available family labor and would be periodically redistributed on the same basis.[22] Some Bolsheviks voiced reservations about adopting wholesale a decree drawn up by the Socialist Revolutionaries, especially since it was at odds with the Bolshevik preference for state rather than peasant control of land. Lenin's answer was blunt and revealing: "So what? Who cares who drafted it? As a democratic government, we cannot ignore the resolutions of the lower strata of the people, even though we may not agree with them."[23]

In the weeks immediately following the congress, the government enacted further measures evidently aimed at emancipating and empowering common people. On 26 or 27 October, Lenin drafted a proposal on "workers' control," which was elaborated and approved by the Soviet Executive Committee on 14 November. The decree endorsed a dramatic openness in workplace management: workers were by law guaranteed complete access to all information about the finances and administration of their enterprise and to all supplies and equipment; workers were given the right to inspect correspondence by owners or managers; and commercial "trade secrets" were outlawed. The decree also endorsed the rights of workers to make decisions about factory life that (subject only to the decisions of higher level councils of workers' control) were binding on management, though the decree was vague about what decisions workers' control organs had the right to make. This ambiguity left plenty of room in the following months for differing interpretations and practices.[24]

On 2 November, over the signatures of Joseph Dzhugashvili-Stalin (commissar for nationalities) and Lenin, the government declared that along with the emancipation of peasants, soldiers, and workers from the arbitrary authority of landlords, officers, and capitalists, it was time to free the "peoples of Russia who . . . are suffering under oppression and arbitrary rule." Voicing confidence that "an honest and solid union" of the peoples of Russia could be formed, the government declared that all future policies would be guided by the principles of "equality and sovereignty" of different peoples, the right to freedom of self-determination, "including to the point of separation and the establishment of an independent state," abolition of all privileges and limitations based on nationality or religion, and the "free development" of all national and ethnic groups living in Russia.[25]

On 10 November, the government abolished all legal designations of civic inequality, such as estates, titles, and ranks. All people were to be designated identically as "citizens of the Russian Republic." All properties of estate organizations (clubs for the gentry, for example, or merchant guilds) were to be transferred to local municipal or rural governments.[26] On 24 November, all existing juridical institutions were abolished, to be replaced by "courts established on the basis of democratic elections."[27] On 16 December, the government did away with all ranks and titles in the army (as well as marks of hierarchy such as decorations and the practice of saluting), declared that "full power within any military unit" was in the hands of its soldiers' committees and soviets, and required that all officers be democratically elected.[28] Finally, on 4 January 1918, the Soviet Executive Committee approved the "Declaration of the Rights of Working and Exploited People," which was to be presented for approval to the Constituent Assembly.

The declaration sought to encapsulate all these emancipatory acts in a single statement.[29]

Side by side with these measures of liberation and empowerment, the authoritarian tendencies in Bolshevik rule were also immediately visible, and they grew steadily in the months and years that followed. The first step, as already noted, was the establishment of a single-party government—controversial even among some Bolsheviks. There was certainly reason for concern. As many of the documents in this collection make clear, popular discontent with the Provisional Government and with the compromises of the moderate socialists could not be equated with support for Bolshevism. Even support for the Bolshevik program of soviet power, immediate peace, land, and workers' control was not identical to embracing Bolshevik ideology itself, much less Leninism—which, in any case, was little known or understood outside of small circles of longtime activists. As the documents here remind us, large numbers of lower-class Russians (perhaps most) approved the Bolshevik seizure of power in October as an act to establish soviet power, which meant the united authority of the whole "democracy," of the entire narod—in other words, of all the socialist parties. That was, after all, what the Bolsheviks themselves had been publicly advocating. Exclusive Bolshevik power, many critics now argued, not only violated the spirit and intent of the revolution but was a dangerous act that could only divide and weaken the forces of democracy as they prepared to face the armies already organizing on the right. And even if they survived that fight, it was thought, the Bolsheviks by themselves would not have the strength to establish the long desired "kingdom of labor and freedom."[30] This argument was already to be heard at the Second Congress of Soviets, especially from Menshevik-Internationalists. This argument would be heard increasingly in the following weeks, as organized opposition to Bolshevik power arose.

Opposition appeared quickly. Already in the final days of October, Kerensky began to move troops against the capital, military school cadets mutinied, armed battles broke out in Moscow when the local Bolsheviks tried to take power, the Cossack general Aleksei Kaledin declared full Cossack power in the Don region and began organizing military action against the new government, civil servants in huge numbers refused to work for the new government (or even to let newly appointed Bolshevik officials into their offices), and the All-Russian Committee to Save the Country and the Revolution formed to unite the major moderate-left civic organizations opposed to the Bolshevik "coup" (including representatives of city dumas, the preparliament, the old Soviet Executive Committee, the Peasants' Soviet, and the central committees of the Mensheviks and Socialist Revolutionaries). On 29 October, an appeal from various left-wing socialists (including Left S.R.'s and Menshevik-Internationalists) appeared in Maxim Gorky's newspaper *Novaia zhizn'*, calling for a united front so that the revolution would not be "drowned in the blood of soldiers, workers, and peasants."[31] On the same day, the Central Executive Committee of the All-Russian Union of Railroad Employees and Workers, known by its Russian acronym, Vikzhel, issued an ultimatum threatening a national strike unless the two sides halted all use of force—described as a "fratricidal war" that threatened to lead to "civil war." The Vikzhel regarded the use of force, especially against fellow socialists, not only as morally wrong but as likely to benefit counterrevolution, and demanded open negotiations with other socialist parties to form an all-socialist government.[32] Many factories and soldiers' committees around the country also passed resolutions supporting the call for an all-socialist government.[33] Finally, Bolshevik moderates like Grigory Zinoviev and Lev Kamenev (who was delegated by the Soviet to negotiate with the Vikzhel) also expressed a preference for a multiparty socialist government.

Under these pressures, but especially to avoid a crippling railroad strike at a time when the government was faced with a growing military threat, the Bolshevik leadership began discussions with other parties. Within a few days, however, once Kerensky's military movement and others against them were crushed, interest in coalition waned. On 4 November, Lenin warned party members that continued opposition to the majority policy on power would lead to their expulsion from the party. Several leading Bolsheviks, including Kamenev and Zinoviev, resigned from the Central Committee in protest, as did five Bolshevik people's commissars. Determined to fight the course of their own party, they made their protests public; letters from them appeared on 5 November in the Soviet newspaper *Izvestiia* (where they evidently also had support) criticizing one-party government as a policy that was "destructive," contrary to the will of the majority of workers and soldiers, sustainable only through "political terror," and likely to result "in the destruction of the revolution and the country."[34] Although the interparty conference hosted by the Vikzhel continued to negotiate the terms for forming a new coalition government, conflicts and disputes grew, and no agreement resulted.[35] Nonetheless, arguments for an all-socialist government continued to be heard, for example, at the Congress of Peasant Soviets that met in Petrograd from 10 to 15 November

1917, though in the end the congress endorsed the current government and agreed to merge with the workers' and soldiers' Soviet.

The Bolsheviks could hardly ignore the widespread sentiment for coalition government, though it is clear that they hoped to avoid it. Part of their answer was to defuse the criticism—and to attract peasant support—by negotiating an agreement in early December with the Left S.R.'s (who in late November had established a formal party of their own) that the latter would enter the government in a minority position. As a result, seven Left S.R.'s joined the government as people's commissars on 12 December, where they hoped to moderate Bolshevik tendencies toward one-party rule and authoritarianism. Left S.R. commissars, especially the commissar of justice, Isaak Steinberg, tried to limit what they viewed as Bolshevik violations of civil rights and the tendency to govern without requiring the sanction of the Soviet Executive Committee. This modest coalition government lasted only until March 1918, however, when the Left S.R.'s resigned from the government (formally to protest the terms of the peace treaty with Germany) and joined the opposition to Bolshevik rule. Cooperation with the Left S.R.'s was part of the Bolshevik answer to criticism; mostly, though, the Bolsheviks responded with the certainty that it was in the best interests of the revolution for them to lead and with a willingness to silence those who disagreed and to suppress those who challenged their authority.

One of the first laws of the new government—issued by the Sovnarkom and signed by Lenin without first seeking Soviet approval—was the Decree on the Press of 27 October. On the 26th, a number of "bourgeois" papers, but many socialist papers as well, were "confiscated" and their presses closed by order of the Military Revolutionary Committee (the Bolshevik-led committee of the Petrograd soviet that had been in charge of the seizure of power) or by comparable organizations in Moscow and other cities.[36] The formal decree, whose effect was defined as temporary, until "normal conditions of social life" returned to the country, was a wide-ranging attack on the press. The decree itself opened argumentatively, with the observation that many people were already complaining that the socialist principle of a free press was being violated by the new government, but then countered that in a capitalist society the principle of the free press was a "liberal cloak" masking the freedom of the propertied classes to "poison and sow confusion in the minds of the masses." At this critical moment when the new workers' and peasants' government was just being established, it was essential to take "a weapon no less dangerous than bombs and machine guns" out of the hands of the bourgeois enemy. Echoing the sentiments of lower-class Russians and the language often used to express them during the preceding months, the decree justified the measures already taken as necessary to "suppress the torrent of filth and slander with which the green and yellow press would gladly have drowned the young victory of the people." The decree replaced the administrative shutdown of newspapers with a process controlled entirely by the Sovnarkom and subject to review by the courts. Still, the categories justifying closure were broad: "inciting to open resistance or disobedience" to the workers' and peasants' government, "sowing sedition through a clearly slanderous perversion of the facts, or encouraging deeds of a criminal character."[37]

Even many members of the Soviet Executive Committee were opposed to this measure. A Left S.R. member characterized Bolshevik justifications of press censorship as "Hottentot ethics," in which it was wrong for you to steal my wife (that is, for the Provisional Government to close down the Bolshevik press) but right for me to steal your wife (to close down bourgeois papers). Another argued that this course of action reflected a false belief that socialism could be introduced by force; in truth, however, "socialism is not only a struggle for material prosperity but for the highest moral values of mankind, . . . not the truth of a hungry stomach, but the higher truth of the liberation of the human person." Despite these arguments, though by a divided vote of 34 to 24, the Soviet leadership agreed on 4 November to approve the measure and even to go one step further: to authorize the confiscation of all private printing presses and paper stock, which local soviets were then to distribute to approved political parties and groups.[38] In the face of continued opposition, including from moderate Bolsheviks, the decision was not immediately put into effect and the press decree was applied sparingly. Also, in practice, many of the non-Bolshevik papers that were shut down were allowed to reappear under new names. At the same time, the pressure on the press continued. To undermine the financial basis of private publishing, on 7 November all private advertising was banned except in papers published by soviets, as was "disguised" advertising in the form of paid articles or reports.[39] When a number of socialist papers protested this decision by including paid advertising even when they had not done so before, they were temporarily closed.[40] Still, alternative opinion had not yet been silenced altogether. The government—faced with widespread hostility to restrictions on the free press (evident in many of the documents presented here), continuing dissent within the Bolshevik party on questions of democratic rights, and the negotiations and agreement with Left S.R.'s to enter the Sovnarkom—hesitated to silence all opposition voices.

The opposition focused its hopes on the coming Constituent Assembly. Since long before 1917, the idea of a national democratic election, in which men and women of all classes would come together as equals to create a body that would finally establish a legitimate and fully democratic new order in Russia, had been treated as a nearly sacred ideal, and it was pursued all the more fervently throughout the revolutionary year. The entire Left, including many moderate Bolsheviks, was deeply committed to it and had regularly blamed the bourgeoisie, which inevitably found itself in the minority, for delaying its realization. Indeed, rumors that the Provisional Government was planning on delaying or canceling the Constituent Assembly had furnished one of the Bolsheviks' justifications for the need to seize state power. Thus, the very day after the new Soviet government was formed, on 27 October, Lenin officially confirmed that elections to the Constituent Assembly would be held as scheduled on 12 November.[41] Official statements about the assembly remained as committed and avid as ever, though, it has to be noted, support was conditional on what it must do: "The Constituent Assembly is the master of the Russian land. It must decide questions of land reform, of the war, and of the disposition of all of the wealth of the nation. The Constituent Assembly must right the historical wrongs against millions of peasants . . . [and] protect the working class from exploitation."[42] Lenin himself was still more hesitant— even before coming to power. On the one hand, he argued, in an article in the summer of 1917, that only Soviet power could ensure that the assembly would be allowed to meet, and he expressed confidence that the populace, which had moved continually leftward, would choose a leftist majority. At the same time, he warned, as he had for many years, of the dangers of "constitutional illusions" and insisted that the "course and outcome of the class struggle" were more important than the Constituent Assembly.[43] He and others continued to hint at what this might mean. On the eve of the election, for example, some Bolsheviks were maintaining that "the masses have never suffered from parliamentary cretinism" and warning that the party did not regard the assembly as a "fetish"; therefore, "if the Constituent Assembly should go against the will of the people, the question of a new insurrection would arise."[44]

In competing for seats in the Constituent Assembly, all the major parties active in 1917 were authorized, under rules established by the Provisional Government, to put forward electoral lists. Dozens of parties competed nationwide, though many were only local. Still, electoral choices abounded—nineteen parties were on the ballot in Petrograd, for example. The major groups competing for seats included Kadets, Socialist Revolutionaries (usually with no separate listing for Left S.R.'s, since the party split occurred after the elections had already been planned, though in some places dissident Left S.R. lists were fielded), Mensheviks (in some places split between "internationalists," headed by Yuly Martov, and "defensists"), Bolsheviks, and a variety of smaller socialist, nationalist, feminist, Cossack, and religious parties. The campaign itself was impassioned and even bitter. Bolsheviks warned against the danger of letting the bourgeoisie steal the revolution, while the Kadets, for instance, warned in return that it was "a serious sin against the country" to vote for the Bolsheviks, who were nothing more than "power grabbers," "murderers," and "destroyers of freedom."[45]

Polling took place throughout the country over the next few weeks, first in Petrograd and then Moscow, and subsequently throughout the country (though not in Poland or other regions under German occupation, and in a number of areas votes were incomplete or left uncounted). As the tally of votes slowly rolled in, two things became clear: socialism had triumphed as an ideal, and the Bolsheviks would not have a majority. The success of socialists was impressive. Of more than forty million votes cast, the Socialist Revolutionaries (not including the scattered dissenting Left S.R. lists) won 38 percent of the vote (and the Ukrainian S.R.'s won another 8 percent), the Bolsheviks 24 percent, the Mensheviks 3 percent, and other socialist parties another 3 percent, giving all socialists combined approximately 75 percent of the total vote. Nationalist parties (Muslim, Armenian, German, Jewish, and others, some of which had a socialist orientation) won approximately 8 percent of the total. The liberal Kadets polled less than 5 percent. Other nonsocialists (including rightists and conservatives) won only another 3 percent. These results also meant, however, that the Bolsheviks, with barely a quarter of the total vote, could hardly justify retaining monopoly control over the government on any electoral basis. Their gains were impressive, to be sure, especially in certain key areas: the northern industrial regions, large cities, and the army. In Vladimir Province, for example, located in the central industrial region, the Bolsheviks won 56 percent of the vote. They also won large majorities among the troops at the northern and western fronts. In Petrograd and Moscow, the Bolsheviks won 45 percent and 48 percent, respectively, of the total votes.[46]

As 28 November, the date scheduled for the opening of the Constituent Assembly, drew near, the Bolshevik government acted to limit the potential damage. Hoping for changes in the composition of the assembly, on 21 November the government authorized the recall of all elected deputies from representative bodies, including the Constituent Assembly, as long as half of the electors favored the step. As a concrete measure, city councils (dumas) in Petrograd, Moscow, and Saratov were closed, and new elections scheduled. On 23 November, a Red Guard detachment forced its way into the offices of the electoral commission for the Constituent Assembly, arrested its members, and took them to government headquarters at the Smolny Institute, where they were interrogated for several days and then replaced by a Bolshevik official, Moisei Uritsky. A few days later, with elections in some parts of the country still going on, the government ordered that the opening of the assembly be delayed until a quorum of four hundred certified deputies (half the expected members) could gather in the capital and stipulated additionally that the assembly could be opened only by a person "empowered by the Council of People's Commissars."[47] Meanwhile, the government and party press vigorously and repeatedly warned the public of the deceitfulness of self-proclaimed "defenders" of the assembly whose real goal was to reverse the revolutionary overthrow of the bourgeoisie, and insisted on the government's own commitment to opening the assembly as promised.[48]

The opposition, in the meantime, was preparing to confront the Bolsheviks. Former members of the deposed Provisional Government met on 16 November and affirmed that the assembly must open on the 28th. On the 23rd, a coalition of non-Bolshevik socialist parties and "democratic organizations" (unions, cooperatives, army committees, and the like) met and established the Petrograd Union for the Defense of the Constituent Assembly. The union proclaimed the Constituent Assembly the "last hope of the Russian revolution" and warned that the Bolsheviks intended to prevent it from taking its proper place at the head of the nation. Proclaiming 28 November, the planned date for the opening of the assembly, a "national holiday," the union joined other organizations in calling for a great march to the Tauride Palace, where the assembly was scheduled to meet.[49] On that day, thousands of people—including striking civil servants, students, professionals, officers, printing workers, some factory workers, and others—marched to the palace (the government claimed fewer than ten thousand were present, whereas the organizers counted more than two hundred thousand). Speeches were made. Recently elected deputies who had marched with the crowd convinced the guards to let them into the palace, where, since a quorum was lacking (only about fifty delegates, mostly S.R.'s, were in attendance), they held an unofficial meeting of the assembly. They resolved to meet daily until enough delegates arrived for an official meeting.[50]

The Bolshevik government, still insisting that rumors about its plans to disperse the assembly were lies, responded swiftly. The palace was surrounded by soldiers and sailors with strict orders to allow no demonstrations near the palace, to allow entrance only to deputies with official passes, and to permit no meeting of the assembly until a quorum was present.[51] The government also took the offensive. Noting that the armed forces of generals Kornilov, Kaledin, and others had already begun to fight against the Soviet government, and suggesting that the Kadets were helping to organize and finance this counterrevolution, the Sovnarkom accused the Kadets of threatening the cause of peace and the "conquests of the revolution" under the cover of the Constituent Assembly. The government further insisted, in the same declaration of 28 November, that those who claimed that "the Sovnarkom opposes the Constituent Assembly" were lying; rather, the Kadets were trying to open the assembly before a quorum had gathered, in order "to make the voice of a few dozen bourgeois deputies sound like the voice of the Constituent Assembly," a deceit that was intended to cloak an uprising. In response, the government officially declared the Kadet party to be a "party of enemies of the people" and ordered the Kadet leaders arrested and other Kadets put under surveillance.[52] In effect, the party was outlawed. When Left S.R.'s and Menshevik-Internationalists criticized this decree at a meeting of the Soviet Executive Committee on 2 December, Trotsky advised them to prepare themselves for a still rougher fight against counterrevolution. This was only "mild terror" by comparison with what would be necessary as the class war heated up in the coming months. Soon, Trotsky warned dramatically, "not prison but the guillotine will be ready for our enemies."[53]

This was indeed only the beginning of a wide-ranging effort to suppress all "enemies of the people"—a phrase that began to be heard more and more often toward the end of 1917, both in official statements and in popular resolutions and letters. For this purpose, on 5 December, the Sovnarkom established an important new arm of direct state power: the All-Russian Extraordinary Commission for the Struggle Against Counterrevolution and Sabotage, known by its abbreviated name as the Cheka or Vecheka. Earlier steps had already been taken in the same direction. On 24 November, when abolishing all existing courts, the government had announced that soviets would establish in their place "revolutionary tribunals" charged with the "struggle against counterrevolutionary forces and against sabotage by bureaucrats and state employees" and with combating "profiteering, embezzlement, sabotage, and other such abuses."[54] The Cheka was to exist parallel to these organs, though under the direct authority of the Council of People's Commissars rather than of the soviets, its members were to be appointed rather than elected, and it was to include not only investigatory and organizational sections but also a "fighting section" (which, in several months' time, would become the major executive arm of the "Red terror"). The Cheka was charged with investigating all forms of counterrevolution and sabotage, from strikes and other "sabotage" by civil servants to armed struggle against the government, and with supervising "the press, saboteurs, strikers, and Socialist Revolutionaries of the Right."[55] In the weeks following, the arrested Kadets were joined in the Peter and Paul Fortress by a number of prominent Socialist Revolutionaries, including deputies to the Constituent Assembly, who were accused of helping the Kadets in their attempted "armed uprising" against the government on 28 November. In addition, orders were prepared by the Cheka for the arrest of such prominent Mensheviks and S.R.'s as Irakly Tsereteli, Viktor Chernov, and Fyodor Dan.[56]

Meanwhile, a final confrontation over the Constituent Assembly was approaching. On 12 December the Bolshevik party's "Theses on the Constituent Assembly" (written by Lenin but printed with no byline) appeared in the Bolshevik party newspaper, *Pravda*. The arguments were ominous: the electoral lists were out of date (especially since the split in the S.R. party), the "will of the people" (especially among peasants) had already shifted further to the left since the elections had taken place, and, in any case, the soviets, as institutions expressing the power of the laboring classes, were a "higher form of democracy" than a bourgeois democratic republic.[57] Such arguments would have surprised no one who had been listening to what the government and party had been saying in recent weeks (and they might even have recognized Lenin's hand, for he had been making similar arguments for weeks). At a meeting of the Soviet Executive Committee on 1 December, for example, Lenin had explained that the Constituent

Assembly could be thought to express the "will of the people" only if viewed abstractly, apart from the "class struggle" and the rising "civil war," which necessitated suppressing the counterrevolutionary resistance of the oppressors.[58] On the following day, at a meeting of the second Congress of Peasants' Deputies, Lenin had argued that the soviets, as class institutions, were "a hundred times superior to the Constituent Assembly."[59] At the same time, the Soviet newspaper *Izvestiia* had been regularly putting forward the argument that "democracies never unconditionally bow before representative assemblies," and that "the Russian laboring classes cannot and will not hand over their rights and their power to any parliament, even if it calls itself the Constituent Assembly." The true "sovereign of the Russian land," according to this view, was not the assembly "but the laboring people itself," which would recognize the authority of the assembly "only insofar as it carries out the will of the working people, serves their interests, and defends their conquests."[60] The handwriting spelling out the fate of the Constituent Assembly was already clearly on the wall.

The Constituent Assembly was finally scheduled to convene on 5 January. In the days leading up to the opening, the Union for the Defense of the Constituent Assembly called for peaceful demonstrations on that day under the slogan, "All Power to the Constituent Assembly!" Only such a truly national body, "uniting the whole of the people," it was argued, could achieve the essential goals of the revolution: lasting peace and an end to economic breakdown and hunger.[61] In response, the government issued a stern admonition: reporting that the "Extraordinary Commission for the Security of Petrograd had received information" that counterrevolutionaries, including Kaledin and Kerensky, were planning an armed attack on Soviet power on 5 January, the government declared the city to be under a state of siege and ordered the population not to participate in any rallies, meetings, or marches. Warning was further given that all disorders, and especially any attempts by counterrevolutionaries to approach the Smolny Institute (the headquarters of the Bolshevik government) or the Tauride Palace, where the Constituent Assembly was to meet, would be met by armed force.[62] The Petrograd soviet also appealed to workers, soldiers, and "honest citizens" to keep off the streets, for counterrevolutionaries were planning bloodshed. As for the slogan "All Power to the Constituent Assembly," it was derided as only a cover for giving "all power to the bourgeoisie."[63] Adding to the tension of these days—and to the plausibility of Bolshevik warnings about counterrevolution—was an attempt by an unknown assailant on 1 January to assassinate Lenin (he was unhurt, though a visiting Swiss socialist, Fritz Platten, riding beside Lenin in the car, was shot and injured). To ensure order, the government filled the streets of the city on 5 January with soldiers and sailors. The opposition warned that preparations were under way for a "great crime" against the "will of the people," for shutting down the Constituent Assembly, and it called upon "workers, soldiers, and citizens" to ignore the "shameful" lies of the government and to come out into the streets in peaceful defense of freedom.[64] Some members of the S.R. party proposed that people be prepared to fight with arms, but that recommendation was rejected. This was, after all, to be an act of moral defiance against those who had seized power by force.[65]

On the morning of the 5th, crowds began marching, as planned, from various points in the city toward Mars Field, the burial site of those who had fallen in the February revolution and the symbolic center of so many meetings and demonstrations during 1917. The crowds may have numbered as many as fifty thousand people. Many carried red banners. This was not, however, the mass showing that the opposition had hoped for. The soldiers stayed away altogether. Workers took part, but most of the participants were evidently white-collar employers, civil servants, professionals, and students. Many women were also among the marchers. At several points throughout the city, the crowds met with gunfire—from troops blocking their way or from machine guns mounted on rooftops. As demonstrators fled in panic, soldiers sometimes jeered at them, as "bourgeois" and "saboteurs," and tore up or burned their banners. Hospitals reported fifteen dead and dozens wounded, both men and women.[66]

When the Constituent Assembly opened in the old State Duma chamber at 4:00 p.m. on 5 January, the tone was contentious and contemptuous. Bolsheviks and their socialist and liberal opponents interrupted each other with insults, whistling, and derisive laughter. Additional disruption issued from the galleries, which were filled with pro-Bolshevik workers, soldiers, and sailors. Lenin sat in the former government loge, where "he gave the impression of a general at the moment before the start of a decisive battle."[67] Indeed, all sides treated the meeting more as a combative gathering of opposing political forces than as a serious attempt to constitute a new state order. The Bolsheviks introduced their Declaration of the Rights of Working and Exploited People, which had appeared the previous day in *Pravda* and *Izvestiia* after having been approved by the Soviet Executive Committee. The declaration was a ringing endorsement of Soviet power and of rapid progress toward socialism in Russia and throughout the world. In the name of achieving a society without social classes and freed of all "exploitation of man by man," the Constituent Assembly was asked to approve the decrees already passed by the government: the abolition of private ownership of land and the transfer of all land to those who worked it, workers' control in industry, as a first step toward the end of private ownership, the transfer of banks to the state, the disarming of the propertied classes and the arming of working people, immediate democratic peace, and a complete break with the "barbarous policy of bourgeois civilization" that, it was argued, dominated and exploited millions of toilers in Asia, in colonies, and in small countries. Finally, making explicit the irrelevance of the assembly implied by the call for it to approve all the government's actions, the declaration required the Constituent Assembly to formalize its own powerlessness: to devote itself to the task of formulating general principles for establishing a socialist society and a federation of soviet republics but to vest all state power in the soviets.[68]

After the declaration was read, by Yakov Sverdlov on behalf of the Soviet Executive Committee, almost the entire assembly stood to sing the socialist anthem, "The Internationale." At first glance, this would appear to have been a moment of great unity (even the liberal Kadets stood up, though they did not sing). But, as many recognized, the song carried different, even opposing, meanings for different groups of socialists. Some were clearly singing in protest against the others, a combative stance made explicit when Viktor Chernov (the leader of the S.R.'s, soon to be elected chairman of the assembly) gestured toward the Bolsheviks when the song reached the words "but if thunder should strike a pack of hounds and hangmen."[69] When the singing ended, opponents hurled clashing slogans across the room at each other. Then the speeches began: often long and idealistic, sometimes accusatory and even insulting, and constantly interrupted by shouts, whistling, laughter, and applause. The Bolsheviks were accused of making hollow promises and of usurping power. The S.R.'s and other socialists were accused of "abstract" thinking, or worse: of allying themselves with the class enemy.

When the declaration was brought to a vote, everyone understood that the decision above all concerned support for the current government and its policies. The answer was clear: 146 members, mainly Bolsheviks, voted in favor, and 237 voted against. When the meeting resumed at 1:00 a.m., after a brief recess, the Bolshevik delegation read what amounted to a death sentence against the Constituent Assembly (though they preferred to speak of the assembly as having "committing suicide" by refusing to endorse the government's program). Condemning the assembly as dominated by a "counterrevolutionary majority" that served the interests of the bourgeoisie against those of workers, peasants, and soldiers and that reflected only the "revolution's past," the Bolsheviks announced that they would withdraw and let the Soviet government decide what to do with the remains of the assembly. Before the meeting ended at 4:40 a.m., the Left S.R.'s had walked out as well. The remaining majority, mostly S.R.'s, was determined to go down with at least a symbolic assertion of socialist principles, and so quickly passed declarations in favor of radical land reform and a democratic peace. Only after the assembly had been informed that "the guard [was] tired" and deputies had been threatened with force if they kept talking did they finally agree to adjourn. When the deputies tried to resume the session at the Tauride Palace that afternoon, they were refused entry and informed that the assembly had been dissolved by order of the Council of People's Commissars.[70] Headlines in the Bolshevik newspaper *Pravda* that accompanied the announcement of the order were unrelenting in their condemnation of the Constituent Assembly as the tool of bankers, capitalists, landlords, and other "enemies of the people," which paid lip service to popular demands for land, peace, and workers' control in order to "fasten a noose around the neck of socialist power and the revolution."[71] Meanwhile, several opposition papers, notably *Delo naroda*, the paper of the S.R. party, were temporarily closed or at least silenced: armed guards (oprichniki, critics called them, using the old socialist term of opprobrium for the tsarist political police)[72] were posted beside the presses to prevent their publication.[73] Overall, however, knowing how divided the population was, the government wisely preferred to weather the modest storm of protest rather than overreact by silencing all critical voices.

Protests were certainly heard. In the days following, many voiced discontent and anger over the violence of 5 January and the closing of the Constituent Assembly. Some of these voices are heard in the documents that follow. The violence shocked many. However much contempt many people already felt for the Bolsheviks, few seem to have expected them to fire on unarmed people marching in the name of the long-idealized Constituent Assembly. "For almost a hundred years the finest Russians have lived by the idea of a Constituent Assembly," Maxim Gorky wrote at the time. "In the struggle for this idea, thousands of the intelligentsia and tens of thousands of workers and peasants have perished in prisons, in exile, and at hard labor, on the gallows and by soldiers' bullets. . . . And now the 'People's Commissars' have given orders to shoot the democracy that demonstrated in honor of this idea."[74] Similar sentiments were expressed in resolutions passed at meetings at factories and trade unions, by various political organizations, and in statements by individuals, including some Bolsheviks.[75] Comparisons of the violence on 5 January 1918 with Bloody Sunday, 9 January 1905, when tsarist troops brutally attacked unarmed workers demonstrating in the streets of St. Petersburg, were inevitable. The comparison was especially explicit during the funeral procession held on the anniversary of Bloody Sunday, 9 January 1918, for the "victims of the Smolny autocrats" who had fallen "for people's power" (*narodovlastie*). The bodies were even buried in the same cemetery where the dead of Bloody Sunday lay.[76]

For many contemporaries, and for many historians as well, the closing of the Constituent Assembly and the violent suppression of its supporters was a more significant moment in the history of the revolution than the October seizure of power itself. The October revolution had formally been about soviet power—which many at the time understood broadly as power for the parties and classes known as the democracy. The actions of the government in early January, however, defined the revolution in more restricted terms as power in the hands of a unified, disciplined, and radical authority. As Lenin was later said to have described the decision, "the dispersal of the Constituent Assembly by Soviet power is the complete and open liquidation of formal democracy in the name of revolutionary dictatorship."[77] In the view (partly wishful) of many non-Bolshevik socialists, this was the moment, as Bloody Sunday in 1905 had been before it, when many workers and others who had supported the Bolsheviks "awoke and sobered up," seeing clearly, now that they were freed from their thrall to "Bolshevik demagogy,"[78] the dangerous path down which the Bolsheviks were leading the country and the revolution. Some historians have similarly described this as the moment when the "smoke screen" concealing the Bolsheviks' real intentions was cleared away.[79]

And yet no popular upheaval took place against Bolshevik power. The fate of the Constituent Assembly may have helped convince some socialists to support the opposition during the coming civil war, but most, given the huge ideological gap between them and the conservative and nationalist leaders of the White movement, would reject such an alliance. Similarly, few workers or peasants would support the opposition in the civil war, however discontented they were with Bolshevik policies. As documents here remind us, large numbers of Russians supported the Bolsheviks as most likely to back their pursuit of their own hopes and interests. Even for those who did not approve of Bolshevik rule, it was one thing to condemn the Bolsheviks as usurpers, autocrats, and enemies of true socialism and democracy, and quite another to take up arms against a socialist state. Perhaps also, after years of upheaval and unfulfilled promises, many people had become, as some historians have suggested, cynical and indifferent toward politics and politicians.[80] People were also evidently confused and uncertain in the face of complex and contradictory political events. No less, as throughout the months of revolution, much of the population was preoccupied with the more immediate struggles for power that were continuing in various arenas in their lives: in factories, in military barracks, at the front, in the villages.

It was of enormous importance to people that the new government unhesitatingly endorsed this ongoing social revolution. Workers' control, army democracy, the redistribution of land to the toilers, and autonomy and independence for nationalities within the empire were all explicitly authorized and encouraged. To be sure, disillusionment with the social results of October was growing, as production continued to decline and food shortages worsened. We hear some of these voices of discontent in the documents that follow. For now, though, much of the population seemed to feel, or at least hope, that Soviet power offered the best support for their own particular struggles, and perhaps even for their visions of a better future. Observers interpreted the often brutal social conflicts of these days variously. Some believed that the actions of workers, peasants, and soldiers in these months amounted to nothing more than anarchic plunder of the rich, or hooliganistic and vengeful violence. To others, they represented a direct assertion of rights and dignity, a fight for justice and freedom, or at least revenge for the oppressions and indignities of the past. In many ways, it was a matter of both social perspective and moral values whether these were struggles with "iron hands" for a "world new and beautiful,"[81] or "senseless and merciless" violence born of the "boundless hatred of ideas and of people" that had accumulated over the centuries.[82] These opposite understandings also reflected the contradictions and ambiguities of the times, even of the revolution as a whole. As Maxim Gorky wrote at the end of 1917, "In these days of revolt, blood, and hostility, days that are terrifying for many people, one should not forget that, through great torments and unbearable trials, we are marching toward the rebirth of man. . . . Yes, now, at this very moment when people, deafened by the preaching of equality and brotherhood, are robbing their neighbor in the streets, stripping him bare . . . in these days of monstrous contradiction a new Russia is being born."[83]

Workers

· 104 ·

Resolution of the workers of the Kushnerev Printing Works, Moscow, 1 November 1917.[1]

The workers of the Kushnerev Printing Works,[2] at a general factory meeting, discussed the current political situation and resolved the following:

The situation we are living through right now brings to mind the terrible days of the last "autocrat." Freedom of the press and assembly, the inviolability of the individual and his place of residence, the freedom to strike and assemble, universal suffrage—everything we fought and died for—has been destroyed and desecrated by those we call our comrades.

The notorious slogan "All power to the soviets" has for all intents and purposes been transformed into the power of the Bolsheviks.

We have not yet recovered from yesterday's horror; the scenes of devastation, fratricide, violence, and tyranny have not yet been blotted from our memory. Today, as yesterday, we are living in anticipation of a rout of our factories and workshops, dependent on the will of those who, relying on the ignorant, politically unaware masses, on bayonets and cannons, lead us too down the path of adventurism, the path of ruin for our country, the path of ruin for our newly won freedom, for which we paid the high price of centuries of slavery.

To armed demonstration, which brought total disorganization to the ranks of the proletariat and which has brought us face to face with starvation and anarchy, and which cleared the way for the counterrevolution that is nearly upon us, yesterday's victors are adding the ineradicable shame of surrendering to the mercy of another conqueror, announcing peace negotiations with him and meeting with a worthy reply even from such a usurper of human rights even as Wilhelm Hohenzollern.

Bearing in mind all that has been said, we dare not, we must not, allow the socialist "autocrats" to experiment on that which is dear to us, that which is holy to us, and we must remind these newly appeared "pleasers of the worker and peasant poor" of the great commandments of our teachers Marx, Engels, and Plekhanov, the same Plekhanov whom, yesterday, Social Democrats so crudely and criminally insulted.[3]

Knowing the designs of the Bolsheviks, we must clearly and specifically demand that they—as well as we—recognize the Constituent Assembly, as soon as it convenes, as the sole spokesman for the people's will, and until then that we put an immediate halt to all those violations of the law whose indignant witnesses we have been.

Recognizing the need to organize a unified authority, we declare that until the Constituent Assembly opens, there must be unity among all of the revolutionary democracy.

1. Dated by content.

2. Although printing workers were divided politically in their attitudes toward the Bolshevik-led seizure of power, the majority tended to be sympathetic to the Mensheviks and opposed to the October revolution. The Kushnerev plant was known for its long history of labor activism.

3. On 31 October 1917, a detail of soldiers and sailors from the local soviet in Tsarskoe Selo, the Petrograd suburb in which lived Georgy Plekhanov (generally considered the "father" of Russian Marxism), burst into his home, as part of a wide-scale search for hidden arms and counterrevolutionaries. The next day Plekhanov's paper *Yedinstvo* and other newspapers described the event, laying the blame on the Bolshevik party.

· 105 ·

Resolution of the workers of the Baltic Shipbuilding Works,
Petrograd, 2 November 1917.

Resolution
of the Workers of the Baltic Shipbuilding and Machine Works
of the Department of the Navy
2 November 1917
(Received from a delegation of thirty people)

We, the workers of the Baltic Shipbuilding Works, having gathered for a general factory meeting on 2 November of this year and discussed the current difficult situation in the country, find that the policy of compromise with the bourgeoisie and the creation of coalition governments has led the country and the revolution to ruin. With every passing day, this power has been losing confidence and authority among the broad masses of the labor democracy and the army.

Although seizure of this power by a single political party would be an incorrect step, at this time, when an overthrow has been accomplished and become fact, the departure of several political parties from the congress is a step that cannot be justified either. So because of everything laid out above, we have reached a split between the democracies into two hostile camps, which has led to fratricidal war. Seeing the full horror of civil war, we decisively and insistently demand the immediate cessation of this bloody nightmare and the creation of a unified socialist authority based on understandings and mutual concessions by all the socialist parties, from the comrade Bolsheviks to the popular socialists, inclusive, and once it is united, the democracy will put up an energetic resistance as a united front to the counterrevolution being brought about by Kaledin[1] and company.

The new power must first carry out the following urgent tasks:

1. Approval of the decree on land.[2]

2. Immediate proposal of a democratic peace to all warring countries.

3. Control over production and distribution.

4. The convocation of the Constituent Assembly as scheduled. In conclusion, we say that responsibility for any further shedding of blood falls on the heads of those leaders of political parties who out of party ambition refuse to agree to mutual concessions for the sake of saving the country and the revolution.

Approved unanimously; opposed 1 [*sic*].

Chairman, Palitsa
Secretary, Kostiuk
Chairman, Afanasiev
Secretary, T. Nikiforov

1. Aleksei Maksimovich Kaledin (1861–1918), a former tsarist general, was relieved of command in May 1917, owing to a conflict with the minister of war, Kerensky. In June 1917, he was elected ataman (chief) of the Don Cossack military government. After October, he organized and commanded Cossack forces to oppose Soviet power.

2. The Decree on Land, approved by the Second Congress of Soviets on 26 October but subject to final decision by the Constituent Assembly, abolished private property in land and confiscated without compensation all private, crown, and Church lands. Local land committees and peasant soviets were authorized to distribute lands "to those who would cultivate it."

· 106 ·

Letter to the Central Executive Committee of Soviets from a group of Putilov factory workers, Petrograd, received 5 December 1917.

Comrades

Yesterday we wrote a letter saying that you have earned yourselves enemies in the person of the workers by being more concerned about the bourgeoisie than about the lower class of workers and peasants. For the second month, workers have failed to receive their pound of sugar, but you are giving it to the bourgeois confectioners who make sugar into all kinds of candies at ten rubles a pound. As if a poor worker could buy that. You go by a store, and the eye sees, but the tooth is out of luck.[1] Say a holiday is coming up, you look in the food stores, they have sausage. You ask how much does a pound cost? Eight rubles, so make yourself scarce and get lost. I happened to ask about a piece of clothing that used to cost fifty rubles. Now it's twelve hundred rubles. How can you compare that with our salary increases? And you want to take away our last kopek. If you have six three-[ruble] notes, you give him one. You're putting the worker and peasant on the same level as the bourgeois. If some soldier's wife has a hundred rubles, and you give her twenty rubles, she cannot even buy boots with that sort of money. You should first worry about food and shoes and clothing to make it cheaper. The bourgeois have earned millions, they have stored up goods [bought] at cheap prices, and now they're grabbing twenty times as much. You ought to be worrying about the problems of everyday life [*byt*], and take your percentage by the thousands and not the hundreds, from the rich and not the poor. The power is in your hands, don't make yourselves enemies of the people. Requisition footwear and clothing and food reserves from the rich.

Your comrades from the Putilov works

1. A Russian proverb (*Oko vidit da zub neimet*).

· 107 ·

Resolution of workers and employees of the Bogomdarovannyi mine,
Yenisei Province, to the Commission on Elections
to the Constituent Assembly,[1] 10 December 1917.

Resolution on attitudes toward the Constituent Assembly,
passed on 10 December 1917 at a meeting of workers
and employees at the Bogomdarovannyi mine,
Achinsk Uezd, two hundred people present.
Bearing in mind that the Russian proletariat, in fraternal alliance with the soldiers, threw down from its shoulders the centuries-old yoke of tyrannical autocracy in a mighty surge, that by its revolutionary movement and for the sake of building a new life, a new kingdom of labor and freedom, it continues to wipe off the face of the Russian earth everything, all the barriers and obstacles, that held it in the chains of ignorance, poverty, and slavery. At this very difficult time our Constituent Assembly, to which all the fullness of power should be transferred, is going to have to perform a great task. The Constituent Assembly must establish a new or-

der in our country. It must write new laws for all Russian citizens, the kind of laws that can break down class barriers, rid the workers of their oppressors, give the peasants enough land, and bring the entire country a just peace. Therefore the entire country, especially we workers and employees of the Bogomdarovannyi mine, are looking forward to the Constituent Assembly, where all the socialist parties must join forces to implement the laws listed above, and we also suggest to all the socialist parties that they follow closely the work of the Constituent Assembly, which must be conducted in the interests of the working masses.

> Chairman of the assembly, I. Rudenko
> Secretary, A. Yermolaev

1. Elections to the Constituent Assembly were held starting on 12 November. The assembly met, for a single day, on 5 January.

· 108 ·

Letter to Lenin from "a former Bolshevik," Rostov-on-Don, 19 December 1917.

———————

To Comrade V. I. Lenin
Chairman of the Council of People's Commissars![1]
I will be brief. At first I believed in you because you promised good things for us—real peace, bread, and freedom. I thought you wouldn't destroy the homeland. But instead of what you promised, you sold Russia out, gave us no bread, and established a Nicholas kind of freedom. May you be thrice cursed and know that the wave of popular vengeance will reach you and you who have destroyed Russia will perish. Don't think I'm one of those so-called "patriots." No, you'd better tell us what we workers are going to do when there is unemployment and the Germans or someone else brings in cheap goods. We are going to turn into Chinamen, aren't we? May you be cursed once more because soon I'm going to be starving. You sold Russia to the Germans and are spilling our brothers' blood all over the country under the command of German officers.

I curse you and all your comrades in the Council of Usurpers and Betrayers of our native land.

> Rostov-on-Don, 19 December 1917
> A former Bolshevik

1. The Council of People's Commissars, or Sovnarkom, was the new ministerial cabinet formed after the Bolsheviks took power. The members were initially all Bolsheviks, though some members of the Left Socialist Revolutionary Party agreed to enter the government in early December.

· 109 ·

Letter to *Pravda* from Frants Kontaka, a worker at the Obukhov
Metal Works, Petrograd, printed 3 January 1918.

The Revolution of 25 October and the Obukhov Plant

Ever since the counterrevolutionary conspiracy between Kornilov and
Kerensky, the Obukhov workers have seen clearly who their friend is and
who their enemy. The mass of more politically conscious workers has
turned sharply away from the party of appeasers and followed the party of
the revolutionary proletariat, for the majority see in it the defender of the
interests of the urban and rural poor and of the entire working people.
Particularly apparent was the fall of the parties of the S.R.-Menshevik
bloc, when in one issue of *Izvestiia* their leaders compared the Soviets to
barracks and Kerensky's Preparliament to a new building and advised
workers to move into this new housing, cleverly constructed by the leaders
of the parties of appeasement and National enslavement, and to leave the
Soviets, like temporary barracks, to the whim of fate. The workers did not
fall into this trap, and at the new elections for the Executive Committee of
the Sov. of Work. Dep. neither Mensheviks nor S.R.'s got a single seat,[1]
and after this no one would dare reproach the Obukhov workers for lag-
ging behind or being unorganized or inconsistent—all the resolutions that
came out during this period at the general factory meetings demanded all
power to the Soviets. When on 25 October the final decisive struggle began between labor and capital, when the overthrown idol of the Mensheviks and S.R.'s ran away,[2] the Obukhov workers were the first to come out
with weapons in hand and take up battle positions and occupy the approaches to Petrograd and were prepared to stand on guard for the revolution to their last drop of blood and to fight the traitors and betrayers of
the workers, soldiers, and peasants.

Those same parties that laid claim to primacy during the eight long
months before the October revolution were anything but passive during
the days of the great battle for power. No, they continued their vile provocational work and made every effort to incite one section of the workers
against the other, broke up factorywide meetings, and issued absurd resolutions from the minority, thereby slowing the course and development of
the revolution and trying to steer it in a completely different direction.

In this trying and crucial time, though, the masses did not follow them,
and they will not follow enemies of the people; the workers no longer have
confidence in them; they will be alone; we are not going their way.

Worker from the Obukhov plant
Frants Kontaka

1. Actually, the new Executive Committee, formed at the Second Congress of Soviets on 26 October, consisted of sixty-two Bolsheviks, twenty-nine Left S.R.'s, six Menshevik-Internationalists, and four representatives of smaller leftist parties. Though other parties were among the deputies to the congress, most Mensheviks and S.R.'s had walked out in protest against the October seizure of power.

2. On 25 October, before the Winter Palace was stormed and the cabinet arrested, Kerensky had fled, allegedly in disguise, in a car seized from the U.S. Embassy and flying the American flag, in order to find and rally loyal troops.

· 110 ·

Resolution of the workers of the Petrograd Military Horseshoe Factory,
4 January 1918.

Resolution of the Workers of the Petrograd Military Horseshoe Factory of 4 January 1918

We, the workers of the Petrograd Military Horseshoe Factory, having gathered, on this date, for a general meeting, and having listened to a report from Constituent Assembly member Comrade Sosnovsky[1] on the current situation, have resolved, in the interests of the working people, to defend Soviet power and the People's Commissars to our last drop of blood. The rifles in the hands of our Red Guards will not flinch.

With regard to the attempt on the life of Chairman of the Soviet of People's Commissars Comrade Lenin,[2] we declare that this vile action is nothing but an attack by improper means on the people's Soviet power of the workers, soldiers, and peasants, and we brand with shame and contempt the villain who raised his knife against our dear comrade.

All power to the Soviets. Long live socialism!

Chairman of the general meeting, [signature]

1. Lev Semyonovich Sosnovsky (1886–1937), a journalist, had been a member of the Russian Social Democratic party since 1904. After the February revolution, he served on the presidium of the All-Russian Central Executive Committee and directed the Agitation and Propaganda Department of the Bolshevik party Central Committee. He was elected to the Constituent Assembly in January 1918.

2. On 1 January 1918, an unidentified assailant fired at Lenin while he was riding in his car. A passenger, a Swiss Communist, was slightly wounded. Lenin was not harmed.

· 111 ·

Resolutions sent to *Pravda* by "The Working Masses on the Disbanding
of the Constituent Assembly," 7 January 1918.

The Working Masses on the Disbanding of the Constituent Assembly
On 7 January, a general meeting of the workers from the Skorokhod
Factory resolved to welcome the actions of the Workers' and Peasants'
Government with respect to the Constituent Assembly.

The workers of the "Old Parviainen" factory welcome the departure of
the Bolshevik and Left S.R. factions from the Constituent Assembly and
the decree to disband it, which was presided over by those who voted
for the death penalty for the utterly exhausted soldiers.

The 14th Don Cossack Regiment, having gathered in its full comple-
ment on 7 January, deems proper the decree to disband the Constituent
Assembly. We are the sons of the free Don, the Cossacks declare, and we
promise the Soviet of People's Commissars, as the authority selected from
the 2nd All-Russian Congress of Soviets, our full support in its struggle
against counterrevolution, no matter where or who it comes from.

The general meeting of the 3rd Bicycle Battalion commends the party of
Bolsheviks and Left S.R.'s on leaving the Constituent Assembly. The bicy-
clists declare that they will not stop short of the use of armed force to defend Soviet power.

The combined Helsingfors and Petrograd detachments of revolutionary
sailors declare that not one of them will lay down his arms until all power
is in the hands of the working people. Down with the Constituent Assembly. Long live Soviet Power.

Similar resolutions were adopted by the men and women workers of the
cen.[tral] fac.[tory] of the N.[orthern] J.[oint]-s.[tock] Co. Zh. K. (six hundred people), by the sailors of the Guards Crew, by the workers of the Ar-
tur Koppel factory, by the garrison soviet of the Peter and Paul Fortress, by
a meeting of the Bolsheviks and Left S.R.'s from the Department for the
Printing of State Papers, by a general meeting of the ship of the line *Volia*,
by a general meeting of workers from the Zelenev and Zilim works, by the
soldiers' detachment of the officers' pilot school, by the workers and employees of the Iorgan Crucible Works Company, by the workers of the
Shtuder sawmill, and by a general meeting of fellow-countrymen societies
[*zemliacheskie organizatsiia*] of these united provinces: Tver, Kostroma,
Arkhangelsk, Vitebsk, Smolensk, Viatka, Ryazan, Yaroslavl, Kaluga, Vladimir, Vilna, Nizhegorod, Tula, Mogilev, Novgorod, Pskov, Olonets, Minsk,
and Voronezh, and of Gdovsk Uezd, Petrograd Prov.[ince], and many
others.

· 112 ·

Letter to Trotsky, shortly after 5 January 1918.[1]

To Citizen Trotsky[2]

I am sending you a New Year's greeting from the whole Russian people. God damn you to hell! The blood of these innocent victims cries out to God! What did the worker-demonstrators who were marching peacefully today down Petrograd's streets ever do to you? Why did you fire on them? You used to shout that "Pharaohs!" [cops] fired from the roofs of buildings. So how will your names be written down in the history of the Russian revolution? Who do you think you are? Where did you come from? Bandits! Know this: Before three months are out you will break your neck! You have disarmed all the citizens and left them without any way of defending themselves against the bandits, who you send to rob and kill innocent "persons"! Vengeance is at hand, though! Soon, very soon, you will see that God is still alive and will not forget his own! Murderers and thieves, you broke your promise to the people. You are stealing the people's money, you want to get away with sacksful. So know this! The very first one the Germans hang will be Ulianov-Lenin[3] and the second will be his secretary that yid [*zhid*] Bronshtein-Trotsky. The Russian people have no wish to be under the yoke of the yids. This shall never be! Remember these words three months from now when you are sitting in prison. Then you will have visits from the ghosts of those unfortunate innocent dead from 5 January!

Prison and death on a pillar of shame—that will be your fate in 1918. These are not empty words. This is the voice of destiny. Remember, in three months your destiny will be fulfilled. You are not the people's chosen. You are impostors [*samozvantsy*].[4] You deserve to be hanged, state criminals.

---

1. Dated by content—a response to the events of 5 January; stamped received 10 January.

2. Lev Trotsky was commissar (minister) of foreign affairs and head of the Russian delegation to the peace talks with Germany at Brest-Litovsk. Born Lev Bronshtein, he was the only person of Jewish background on the Sovnarkom. His Jewish ethnicity made him a particular target of attacks on the government.

3. Lenin, the leader of the Bolsheviks, was born Vladimir Ilich Ulianov.

4. Often translated as "pretenders," the term refers to false claimants to the right to rule.

· 113 ·

Letter to the Central Executive Committee of Soviets from F. Petrov,
between 5 and 11 January 1918.[1]

How long are you aggressors going to go on crucifying freedom? When
will there be an end to the killings and executions? The peasants and workers protest against you, and *you impostors* [*samozvantsy*] have the nerve to
call yourselves a worker-peasant government. You are selling out and betraying us. You are killing off everything holy, you are against popular
power. You have routed the entire people, you do not have the faith of the
people, we ask you to get away from here and go back to where you came
from. We don't need this kind of socialism—we need order, we need complete freedom of speech and press and the inviolability of the individual
and his place of residence. Where are the promises you made, you who demanded that a Constituent Assembly be called immediately? You deceived
us, you disbanded the assembly. Even Nicholas the Bloody was afraid to
disband the first State Duma. So why did you have to put blinders on the
workers' eyes? We may not be literate, but now we see where our enemies
and where our friends are. Our friends have been degraded, on 5 January
they were killed. You may write saying that they aren't the people, but that
means we aren't human beings and you are no government for us. We
won't have anything to do with a government like that; we need peace inside the country and out. Peace without annexations or indemnities and
democratic so that there are no conquered or conquerors. Let the German
people, the workers, extend a hand to us, not the generals. We don't recognize generals and we aren't about to start. The workers of Russia should
talk only with the workers of Germany. What do we need a war in Ukraine
for? We're not afraid of General Kaledin: we managed to remove him. We
removed Nicholas, but we don't need blood or Kaledin. So know that the
peasants do not want blood. But if you want it, then I advise you to have a
duel instead, for at least then the people's blood will remain untouched. Because, as the saying goes, when masters quarrel, it's the slaves who get it in
the face.[2] We demand that you give us back the Constituent Assembly, all
power must belong to the people, we don't trust any party members, down
with all parties, long live the Constituent Assembly.

F. Petrov
Eternal memory to the fallen and curses on the tyrants, whoever they are.

1. Dated by content. Received by the Executive Committee 11 January 1918.
2. *A to [kogda] pany ssoriatsia a u kholopov chuby letiat* (When the *pany* quarrel it's
the slaves' forelocks that'll fly). The original (full of misspellings that have been corrected here) is a Ukrainian saying. *Pany* is Ukrainian for landlords (borrowing from the
Polish, but also because many landowners in Ukraine were of Polish origin). *Chuby* are
the long forelocks that Ukrainian Cossacks wore on their otherwise bald heads.

Soldiers

· 114 ·

Resolution of soldiers of the Preobrazhensky reserves, Petrograd,
printed in *Izvestiia*, 2 November 1917.

After discussing the current political situation, which has provoked
bloodshed in the center of Petrograd and its outlying districts, the General
Assembly of company and detachment committees of the Preobrazhensky
Guards Reserve Regiment has resolved:

1) To propose to all the central committees of all the revolutionary socialist parties to join the Military Revolutionary Committee, which thus
would become the spokesman for the will of the workers, peasants, and
soldiers.

2) We demand that the right-wing socialist parties break any compromises with the bourgeoisie and not seek salvation in a coalition with them,
since the former Provisional Government led by Kerensky proved incapable of keeping power in its own hands, for that kind of power henceforth would only be an act of violence against the workers, peasants, and
soldiers.

3) Down with coalition with the bourgeoisie! Long live revolutionary
socialist authority in the person of the Military Revolutionary Committee
and the second All-Russian Soviet of Workers', Peasants', and Soldiers'
Deputies. Only this kind of authority can bring about a speedy and just
peace, land to the laborers, and control over production and lead the
country up until the Constituent Assembly as scheduled. Long live full accord among the socialists of all parties.

· 115 ·

Resolution of the soldiers of the Reserve Electrotechnical Battalion,
printed in *Izvestiia*, 2 November 1917.

Resolution

We, the soldiers from the detachment of the regimental radio-station
formations of the Reserve Electrotechnical Battalion, gathered on 2 November for a general meeting, heard the report made by our representative
to the Petrograd Soviet of Workers' and Soldiers' Deputies, Comrade Kul-
chitsky, on the current situation and welcome fervently all the resolutions
of the second All-Russian Congress of Soviets of Workers' and Soldiers'

Deputies and the recently formed popular government of Workers and Peasants, the Government of People's Commissars.

We declare that although we are not all Bolsheviks, all of us stand as one for the unified program of actions and will follow without hesitation this party, which will move decisively and relentlessly toward the stated goal of total emancipation for all laborers.

We will sweep aside anyone who stands in the way.

We have the deepest contempt for all the pitiful compromiser-defensivists who left the Congress and brand them with the disgrace of betraying the cause of the people's revolution.

The decrees on peace, land, and control over production can be wrested away from us only along with our hearts.

Power to the Soviets and only the Soviets everywhere, both in the center and in the provinces.

We will not stand for any adulteration of the Soviets by bogus democrats and obvious Kadets.

We demand immediate publication of secret treaties and a swift and harsh revolutionary court-martial against all the traitors to the people, the counterrevolutionaries.

We fervently welcome the party of the Bolsheviks as the sole party that is leading us, at long last, to full power for the people. We fervently welcome Comrade Lenin as our sole true steadfast leader who has always moved straight toward the stated goal, toward the good of the working people.

Down with compromisers.

Down with hesitations.

Stand fast.

Onward to peace, freedom, and socialism.

Passed by an overwhelming majority of votes.

[signatures]

· 116 ·

Resolution of the Regimental Committee of the 20th
Siberian Rifles, 6 November 1917.

———————

Resolution on the Current Situation Passed Unanimously
Excerpt from the minutes
Of the sessions of the Regimental Committee of the 20th Siberian Rifle Regiment of 6 November 1917, No. 45.

The continuing Civil War, to which no end is in sight, will leave the army now in the trenches in a desperate position. The specter of death from starvation and cold already looms over the army. The soul of each and every soldier is gripped by horror at the thought of his starving family. Anger fills his heart when he reads that his father and mother, his wife and children, are perishing in the fire of fratricidal war, are perishing inside the country while he is defending his country from the enemy with his own body. The soldier in the trenches loses heart and becomes dispirited, seeing his increasingly thinning ranks but no arriving reinforcements.

We consider the Civil War and lack of reinforcements, bread, forage, uniforms, and military supplies tantamount to the most treacherous stab in the back, and bearing in mind that we cannot remain impartial witnesses any longer to the senseless slaughter and anarchy in the rear, we demand:

1. The immediate cessation of the Civil War and the establishment of revolutionary order in the rear.

2. The creation of a unified socialist Ministry made up of representatives from all the socialist parties.

3. The immediate conclusion of peace.

4. Convocation of the Constituent Assembly according to schedule.

We declare that our patience will soon be exhausted, and woe to the insane leaders of the Civil War when the army abandons its trenches and sets out in search of those guilty of the ruin of the country and the Revolution.

> Chairman, Ensign Yudin
> Secretary, Koshkin

· 117 ·

Appeal from the Extraordinary Congress of soldiers' committees of the 12th Army, 17–21 November 1917.[1]

The Army's Appeal

The Extraordinary Congress of the Great Soviet of the 12th Army, in the name of the inhabitants of those damp holes in the earth, the gray soldiers in the trenches, who have been worn out by bloody slaughter, starvation, and the cold of winter, in the name of the hundreds of thousands of sons of labor who have been wrested from their plows and lathes, from their native huts and families, by the greedy plunderer-exploiters, and in the name of those who have been shedding blood for more than three years and dying of scurvy and cold, sends its fraternal greetings to "Red Petrograd," its revolutionary fighters who are dying but not surrendering for the liberation of labor, and to the workers of Petrograd, the Red sailors of the Baltic Fleet and the revolutionary garrison that rose up against the government of national betrayal, falsehood, and treachery, against the lackeys and cliques of capital.

We soldiers in the trenches, who have assembled for this Congress and who have been falsely accused and slandered by people from the former but now overthrown reign of deceit, who are sowing separation and dissension in the great family of labor, address a fiery summons to all laborers who still believe the petty bourgeois socialist traitors (Soc.[ialist] Rev.[olutionaries] and Mensheviks), various traitors like Kerensky, Avksentiev, Voytinsky, Gots,[2] and so on, to cast off the intoxication of deceit and join the solid ranks of those fighting for the liberation of labor and in a single, orderly phalanx, in a mighty surge, to start down the path of building a new, free, workers' Russia and realizing the great and shining ideals of labor.

In the convulsive torments of the tortured people, in the streams of its blood that have washed over the immense fields in the death throes of its final efforts, the mighty chain of capital, which shackled laboring Russia for centuries, was broken and the vivid summer lightning of liberation was born.

The dawn is at hand. So we must not let the black clouds of obscurantism fill it with darkness. All of those from the labor family who are still blinded by lies and hypocrisy, who have been unable to understand where the fighting people are, are raising their hand against their tormented brother by their very failure to see. Come to your senses! Do not spill innocent blood on the resplendent garment of the newborn freedom of labor. Let the blood of your brothers fallen at the front, those burial mounds assembled from the bones of trench soldiers in the name of the vampires of labor, flattened by torrential rains and swept by blizzards of snow, and the scarlet blood that has yet to cool off from the revolution, spilled by those who rose up outside Petrograd and Moscow for the cause of brotherhood and of the liberation of labor, be a lesson to you.

Red Petrograd and you, Baltic sailors! The hearts of the trench soldiers of the 12th Army are with you!

Their hearts, with yours, are beating in alarm over possibly losing the gains we all share.

There is no going back—onward!

In this holy struggle we will support you with all the means available, without harming the front.

Long live the Second Proletarian Peasant Revolution!

Long live the power of the Soviets and the people's commissars!

Long live socialism!

1. According to *Izvestiia*, no. 228 (17 November 1917): 6, the congress opened on 17 November, with a Left S.R. and Bolshevik majority—unlike the 28–29 October meeting, which was evenly divided between supporters and opponents of the Bolshevik seizure of power.

2. Nikolai Dmitrievich Avksentiev (1878–1943) and Abram Rafailovich Gots (1882–1940) were leaders of the Socialist Revolutionary Party. Vladimir Savelevich Voytinsky (1885–1960) was a Bolshevik until April 1917, when he joined the Mensheviks. As members of the Central Executive Committee of Soviets, the three were key organizers of the Menshevik-S.R. bloc in the Soviet and in the Provisional Government. They actively opposed Bolshevik power.

· 118 ·

Appeal from the soldiers' committee of the 1st Cavalry Corps,
printed in *Izvestiia*, 30 November 1917.

Comrade Soldiers!

In the great hour of our All-National Holiday, when all power over the People's Russian Land has been transferred into the hands of the People themselves, when the right of self-governance has been transferred to the People, when there are no more slaves or masters, when the long-awaited and Great hour has arrived for the realization of the Great slogan *Liberty, Equality, and Fraternity*, we call on you, our Comrade Soldiers of the 1st Cavalry Corps, to defend with your own bodies the Freedom the People have won and not let our enemies do violence to it again.

We know who our enemies are, and they cannot hide from us behind any political slogans or in any political parties. They are always cursed among our People, always worthy of the People's punishment. Long live the power of the newly awakened People!

The sweeter speeches of our enemies will not lull us to sleep or lead us further into the abyss of slavery, poverty, and depersonalization [*bezlichie*]. The soldiers' might is getting stronger, the workers' power will get stronger, and the peasants' truth [*pravda*] is getting stronger.

Let us turn our backs on the nightmare of countless resolutions: they will not feed the Russian people or shelter our hungry, impoverished families.

There must not be two ideas; we must not have two solutions. The corps must not have contradictory resolutions but rather one common idea, one common decision, one common resolution: Give the People *Peace, Land, Bread, and Liberty*.

No matter who holds power, we will be unswerving in our demands, and we will be on guard for the interests of the Russian People.

We will not retreat a single step from our demands and our work. As we have steered, so we will keep steering down that channel through which the People, Peace, Land, and Liberty must come sailing in.

We have no need of loud, eloquent speeches and words about Freedom, Democracy, and Socialists. What we need is *Genuine Freedom, Genuine Democracy, and Genuine Socialists*.

We have been harangued by speakers quite enough and have read quite enough different resolutions. Now is the time to try some Bread.

We have shed enough blood in our Homeland: it is not the princes or the barons or the counts and capitalists who are lying around on the streets after the battle but our Russian muzhik, peasant, soldier, or worker lying in blood, having left his children orphans.

Enough blood. It's time for us brothers to put our long-suffering Russian Land in order, our blood-red but at long last free Russia.

Our People's heroes must find support among the entire People.

Their work will go well if the People themselves support them in their Holy work.

We are not seeking a grand palace or piles of gold, we are not seeking luxury for ourselves but bread, that simple black Bread without which our children and brothers will starve to death.

Remember, Comrades, that of all our former rulers, the ones who came closest of all to the essential question of our Peace, Land, Bread, and Liberty are our current People's Heroes, our current rulers, LENIN and TROTSKY. We don't need men who only talk about Freedom but do not give it to the People. Men like that are like men who preach senselessly to the hungry man about the high moral significance of labor but do not give him bread.

The People need deeds, not words.

In its individual units and in its whole, the Corps Committee, like all the other Corps Committees, will fight for the People's Right, fight for the life of the People, untiringly continue to battle our People's common enemy, Slavery and Want, and looks forward to the triumph and strengthening of Freedom and will fight for Peace, Bread, Land, and Liberty.

Corps committee of the 1st Cavalry Corps.

· 119 ·

Appeal to soldiers from the soldiers' committee of the Volynsky Reserve Guards Regiment, Petrograd, printed in *Izvestiia*, 3 December 1917.

Appeal

from the regimental committee of the Volynsky Reserve Guards Regiment

Comrade soldiers! Some sad events have taken place in recent days. The soldiers stormed and smashed up wine cellars, got drunk themselves, and then got their comrade soldiers drunk who hadn't participated in the plundering. Comrades, if drunkenness in and of itself is harmful, then right now, when we are only beginning to live a new life, it is doubly dangerous.

The tsarist Government tried to keep the people in ignorance and so kept them drunk intentionally. Now, comrades, this should not and cannot be. We must state firmly that there can be no return to the past. We soldiers who swore to protect and defend freedom and the revolution with our very bodies are ourselves drowning them in wine.

Comrades! Think about this.

Freedom is in danger!

Russia may perish with it, and so may all of us. Are we soldiers, the hope and buttress of freedom and the revolution, actually going to behave like Judas and betray everything that is precious and holy to us for a bottle of wine? It's not too late, comrades. It is within our powers to put a halt to this sad and shameful calamity. And we must put a halt to this disgrace, this outrage. In the name of Russia and the freedom that is so precious to us, we must shout to everyone trying to lead us astray, Hands off! Comrades, restrain everyone who is tempting you, trading in wine, and getting the people drunk. Try to influence your comrades, try to show everyone how dangerous and ruinous this disgrace is for the safety of Freedom and Russia!

The Regimental Committee of the Volynsky Reserve Guards Regiment appeals to all its comrade soldiers from Red Petrograd.

The Regimental Committee trusts and hopes that its appeal will not be a lone voice in the wilderness. It trusts that the comrade soldiers will not drown Freedom and the Revolution in wine.

For the chairman of the committee, [signature]
For the regimental adjutant sublieutenant, [signature].

· 120 ·

Instruction from the soldiers' committee of the 22nd Infantry Division
at the front to the committee's delegate to the All-Russian
Extraordinary Congress of Peasants' Deputies, 2 January 1918.

Instruction

To our delegate of the 22nd Inf.[antry] Division to the All-Russian Extraordinary Congress of Peasants' Deputies.

§ 1.
On Power

We, soldiers in the trenches, demand full support for the power of the Soviets of P., W., and S. Deputies, in the person of the Council of People's Commissars, which has started down the path of decisive struggle for PEACE and the just demands of the popular working masses.

To all those who are opposing the power of the working people, to all the saboteurs and counterrevolutionaries putting the brakes on the cause of peace and provoking fratricidal civil war inside the country, we soldiers in the trenches send our contempt and curse.

We demand that the most decisive and merciless measures be taken in the struggle against counterrevolution, no matter where it starts.

§ 2.
On the Constituent Assembly

To all those who are shouting, All power to the Constituent Assembly, we soldiers in the trenches categorically declare that we will recognize and support the power of the Constituent Assembly only when it manifests the true will of the working people. All the decrees issued by the Council of People's Commissars, such as on PEACE, LAND, Workers' control over production, the Nationalization of banks and others, must be passed in full. Otherwise, the assembly must be immediately disbanded by the will of the Soviets of P., W., and S. Deputies.

§ 3.
On War and Peace

On the issue of war and peace, the most sensitive for us soldiers in the trenches, we declare: Three years of tsarist policy and eight months of appeasement policy have led the army to absolute wrack and ruin. The harsh trench life with all its adversities has completely undermined our last reserves of strength. And if the front has not been completely abandoned yet, then that is only because the peace negotiations begun by Soviet Power have brought to the easily swayed masses hope for a speedy end to the war. Any delay, to say nothing of any interruption in the peace negotiations, if only for the briefest of times, will result in the most grievous and catastrophic consequences. Taking into consideration all of the above, we warn that the sole salvation of the country and the revolution lies in the immediate conclusion of peace.

§ 4.
On the Formation of the Red Guards

Regarding the telegram from the Supreme Commander in Chief on the formation of the Red Guards, we consider it essential to state that the formation of a mighty new army such as the Supreme Commander in Chief proposes assembling is impossible, for the country and the army have been exhausted to their last extremity by the unparalleled harsh conditions of these three and a half years of war and carnage. By separating out the most politically conscious elements, one could create spiritually strong but numerically small detachments that, in view of the magnitude of the tasks imposed on them, could offer up no force themselves. Only an immediate peace—that is the sole possible source of salvation from the threat of terrible catastrophe.

Chairman of the divisional committee of the 22nd Inf.[antry]
Division, [signature]
Secretary, [signature]
2 January 1918. Active army.

· 121 ·

Letter from a soldier in Petrograd to Lenin, 6 January 1918.

-----

6 January 1918

Bastard! What the hell are you doing? How long are you going to keep on degrading the Russian people? After all, it's because of you they killed the former minister A. I. Shingarev and F. F. Kokoshkin,[1] and so many other innocent victims. Because of you, they might kill even other former ministers belonging to the S.R. party because you call them counterrevolutionaries and even monarchists, for example, you called Gots, who is a respected comrade, a monarchist in the newspaper *Pravda,* and you also called Chernov, Avksentiev, and others who spent several years at hard labor counterrevolutionaries. And you, you Bolshevik gang leader hired either by Nicholas II or by Wilhelm II, are waging this pogrom propaganda against men who may have done time with you in exile.

Scoundrel! A curse on you from the politically conscious Russian proletariat, the conscious ones and not the kind who are following you—that is, the Red Guards, the tally clerks, who, when they are called to military service, all hide at the factories and now are killing not just the Kadets but practically their own father, the way the soldiers did in 1905 when they killed their own, or the way the police and gendarmes did in '17. That's who they're more like. They're not pursuing the ideas of socialism because they don't understand them (if they did they wouldn't act this way) but because they get paid a good salary both at the factory and in the Red Guards. But not all the workers are like that—there are very politically aware ones and the soldiers—again not all of them—are like that but only former policemen, constables, gendarmes and the very very ignorant ones who under the old regime tramped with hay on one foot and straw on the other because they couldn't tell their right foot from their left and they are pursuing not the ideas of socialism that you advocate but to be able to lie on their cots in the barracks and do absolutely nothing not even be asked to sweep the floor, which is already piled with several inches of filth. And so the entire proletariat of Russia is following you, by count fewer than are against you, but they are only physically or rather technically stronger than the majority, and that is what you're abusing when you disbanded the Constit. Assembly the way Nicholas II disbanded the St.[ate] Duma. You point out that counterrevolutionaries gathered there.[2] You lie, scoundrel, there wasn't a single counterrevol. and if there was then it was you, the Bolsheviks, which you proved by your actions when you encroached on the gains of the revolution: you are shutting down newspapers, even socialist ones, arresting socialists, committing violence and deceiving the people; you promised loads but did none of it. You are deceivers! In fact, even if they had elected Black Hundreds to it, that would have been the will of the people and you have no right at all to go against the majority of the people, against their will. After all you're not a fool but a person with an education and you can understand that the majority of Russia's population doesn't want you. Go and organize a vote on it if you're an honest man [to find out] who is for you and who against. . . .[3]

1. Andrei Ivanovich Shingarev (1869–1918) and Fyodor Fyodorovich Kokoshkin (1871–1918) were leading members of the liberal Kadet party and deputies to the prerevolutionary Dumas. In 1917, Shingarev, a physician by profession, was minister of agriculture (March–April 1917) and minister of finance (May–July 1917), and was elected to the Constituent Assembly. Kokoshkin, a law professor, was named controller of the state budget in the second coalition government (July–August 1917). Both were arrested in November 1917 for antisoviet activity. While hospitalized in January 1918, both were killed by rioting soldiers and sailors.

2. Lenin referred to the "counterrevolutionary majority of the Constituent Assembly" in his Declaration of the RSDRP (Bolshevik) Group at the Constituent Assembly Meeting, 5 January 1918.

3. Letter continues in this vein. This is the only document in the collection not presented in full.

· 122 ·

Letter from the front to Lenin, received 15 January 1918.

Letter from the front

Comrade Lenin: It's been four whole days since we've had a glimpse of bread, we are walking around naked and barefoot. Yet still there's no peace and none is expected. Comrade Lenin, did you really seize power so that you could drag the war out three more years? Comrade Lenin, where is your conscience, where are the words you promised: peace bread land and liberty in three days' time? Did you promise all that just so you could seize power? And then what? But no, you don't want to fulfill your obligation. Now, this is all lies. If you don't keep your promises by 1 February, then you're going to get what Dukhonin got:[1] you'll drop like a fly. If you've picked up the reins then go ahead and drive, and if you can't, then, honey, you can take a flying fuck to hell, or as we say in Siberia, you're a goddamned motherfucker, son of an Irkutsk cunt, who'd like to sell us out to the Germans.[2] No, you won't be selling us out: don't forget that we Siberians are all convicts.

1. Nikolai Nikolaevich Dukhonin (1876–1917), a lieutenant-general, was chief of staff for the southwestern and western fronts from June to September 1917, and chief of staff at supreme headquarters beginning in September 1917. When the Bolsheviks took power, Kerensky, before fleeing, named him supreme commander in chief. Dukhonin tried to keep the army neutral in the political debate. The Bolsheviks labeled him an enemy of the people and arrested him in December 1917. He was killed by soldiers and sailors as he was being taken to Petrograd.

2. This string of profanity is what many lower-class Russians called, often with admiration, three-story cussing.

Peasants

· 123 ·

Resolution to the Main Land Committee in Petrograd from a village gathering in Kherson Province, 9 November 1917.

Resolution

We, the undersigned citizens of the Novo-Grigorievsk Community of Kazankovsk Volost, Elisavetgrad Uezd, Kherson Province, assembled in 1917 on the ninth day of November in a village gathering and discussed our difficult situation concerning the land and resolved! The peasants have not worked their own land for a long time, not having any, but they have worked for the noble landowners, the rich—and then they fertilize other people's soil with their own sweat and blood, yet the fruits of our labors are enjoyed by the parasite landowners and not us, the poor peasants. It is impossible to go on this way! The land has to belong to those who work it. While calmly awaiting a complete resolution of the land question by the Constituent Assembly, we cannot look on indifferently as our wives, children, and mothers, who are without even a scrap of land, drag out a half-starved existence. Our fathers, sons, and brothers have been shedding their blood for a free Homeland for more than three years, and their families have been enduring terrible want. Therefore we demand the immediate transfer of all the land into the hands of the land committees, which will distribute the land among the needy, to which the Novo-Grigorievsk village committee attests.

Committee members, E. Litvinenko, A. Tsymbal
Committee chairman, F. Rudenko
For the secretary, Ya. Dofmin

· 124 ·

Resolution from a county [*uezd*] "peasant congress," 22 November 1917.

Resolution
of the uezd peasant congress, passed at a general meeting
on 22 November 1917

Having discussed the issue of distilling home brew, the congress finds it
to be a serious crime against the army and the country, to distill hundreds
of thousands of pounds of grain for home brew, while our brothers in the
trenches and in the factories are dying by the hundreds from malnutrition.
Therefore the congress has resolved to order all peasants in the provinces
to stop making this diabolical liquid, in which freedom and the revolution
may well drown.

Those who distill after this declaration shall be considered enemies of
the people and put in prison for up to six months or fined up to five thousand rubles, and those who get themselves drunk shall be put in prison for
up to three months or be subject to a monetary fine of up to one thousand
rubles.

Chairman, Z. Uspensky
Secretary, P. Nechaev

· 125 ·

Instruction (*nakaz*) to the Constituent Assembly from representatives of peasant
communities, Voronezh Province, 27 November 1917.

Instruction
to the Constituent Assembly

Composed by Representatives of the communities of Kazinsk Volost,
Zadonsk Uezd, Voronezh Province, who gathered on 27 November 1917,
at the summons of local volost Representative V. Pamsin.

We peasant laborers have resolved:

with a summons to all peasants to form a strong ring around the banner
"Land and Liberty" [*Zemlia i Volia*].

1. End the war immediately. We assign the conclusion of a peace treaty
to the All-National Constituent Assembly, then suggest to all the warring
nations that a cease-fire be concluded on all fronts, both the Russian and
also those of the allied powers, without moving troops—that is, without
attacking the weak.

2. In the future Russian Democratic Republic there must not be any re-

strictions on the sovereignty of the people; the working people must act on their own behalf. This working people will clear a path for itself toward a shining future, when there will be no tears or hatred or blood or fratricidal wars on earth.

3. Transfer all the manor, merchant, monastery, church, appanage, and cabinet, as well as privately owned, lands to the people, and give the working peasants land use in equal ownership without compensation.

4. All minerals, ores, oil, coal, salt, and so on, as well as timber and bodies of water of national significance, should transfer to national use. All small rivers, lakes, and others should transfer to the use of rural communes [*obshchiny*], on condition that they administer them through local organs of self-government.

5. All agricultural inventories from the confiscated lands, both animals and objects, depending on their size and significance, shall transfer to the exclusive use of the state or the commune, without compensation, as shall any structures.

6. If in individual locations the fund of available land turns out to be insufficient to satisfy the entire local population, then the excess population shall be subject to resettlement; the state must take upon itself the resettlement as well as the costs, the provision of agricultural inventories, and so on.

7. Broad local self-government.

8. Inviolability of the person and of his place of residence.

9. No restriction on freedom, conscience, speech, assemblies, strikes, unions, or the press.

10. Freedom of movement for enterprises.

11. Right of the population to receive an education in its native language, and the provision of the schools necessary for this at the expense of the government and the organs of self-government.

12. Right of each individual to proceed against a guilty official in court in the customary manner.

13. Election of judges by the people.

14. Replacement of permanent troops with a universal people's militia.

15. Separation of church from state, and school from church.

16. Free, compulsory, and universal vocational training for all children of both sexes, provision to poor children of food, clothing, and textbooks (study guides) and equipment at state expense.

17. A repeal of indirect taxes and the establishment of progressive taxes on income and inheritance.

18. Repeal of all payments and obligations connected with the estate status of the peasants and the destruction of debt obligations having a slavery-like character.

19. Satisfaction of the peasants' basic needs.

[Signatures follow]

· 126 ·

Instruction to the Constituent Assembly from citizens of Viazhishchensk Volost, Petrograd Province, 31 December 1917.

Instruction

To the chairman of the Constituent Assembly from the citizens of Viazhishchensk Volost, Gdovsk Uezd, Petrograd Province, a total of five hundred people, who attended the meeting on 31 December 1917, *resolved*: to demand from the Constituent Assembly the following:

1) Power must be soviet democratic power, both in the center and the provinces. The Constituent Assembly, as the highest organ, must implement everything the oppressed people supports. Whoever is in power and does not obey the oppressed people will be supporting the oppressors and will be immediately barred from membership and declared counterrevolutionary, and we demand from the electoral district a more democratic order and that they exclude the Kadets.

2) Strengthen and implement the decree on land passed by the Congress of Soviets of Soldiers', Workers', and Peasants' Deputies on 26 October 1917, and do not honor any payments whatsoever under decree §§ 1, 2, 3, and 4. Everything must transfer free of charge to the benefit of the people, and proceed with the remaining §§ without alteration.[1] Repeal resettlement; subject to resettlement are the account keepers and well-to-do peasants whom society would recognize as depraved members and deserters. Soldiers may be resettled only at their own request.

3) Pass the most energetic measures to eliminate Kaledin's band of brigands. Bring the greatest pressure to bear on the bourgeois Ukrainian Rada,[2] which is facilitating the adventurers and bandits who are waging campaigns against Soviet power. Put an end to the fratricidal [war] of the bandits, Kaledinites, Kornilovites, Kerenskyites, Dutovites and Co.;[3] take measures to put down, arrest, and hand the main authors of the fratricidal war over to the strictest revolutionary court.

4) Demand strict support for the decree on peace passed by the second All-Russian Congress of Soviets of Soldiers', Workers', and Peasants' Deputies on 26 October 1917. Any members of the meeting who are against this should be arrested immediately and sent to one of the revolutionary regiments for the formation of separate battalions and dispatched to the front without being supplied with any form of clothing and armed with sticks, as happened at the River San[4] in 1915. Maintain continuous oversight from the rear to avert desertion. The meeting considers it essential to promulgate as soon as possible the decree on the arrest of individuals, in both the center and the provinces, where such people are found to be advocating a continuation of the war or a new one with the Allies. Designate a place for the heroes who have been in the trenches to form up for dispatch to the rear.

5) Take up immediately the most energetic work in the plants and factories where they manufacture agricultural equipment and the peasants' basic necessities, such as plows, harrows, axles, scythes, iron, nails, sickles, manufactured items, and so on, without regard for the eight-hour workday. The more productivity improves, the more prices for items will fall. The above-mentioned output must be distributed at the demand of citizens and only to cooperative shops, and under no circumstances to private traders. Citizens who do not have the funds to acquire equipment for cultivating the land should be given such in installments from the state fund.

6) Repeal all payments on the land, taxes must be taken from income and be progressive, starting at no less than one thousand rubles.

7) Repeal the insurance payment on deeds, and make this tax progressive as well, starting at no less than five hundred rubles. Give out money in the event of fire, calculated so that each victim can build himself a structure without going into debt or selling off any livestock, and so forth, prematurely, which did occur among the peasantry under the old regime, which is what led the peasantry into poverty. No taxes on peasant structures, livestock, agricult. equipment, and so on, can be assessed from income. Income may be from earnings and sales.

8) Maintain medical institutions under the volost with doctors and beds without disturbing the uezd facility, which should be more organized, have a structure, lighting, heating, and a staff of medical personnel, at state expense. The work of the latter must be on democratic principles.

9) To satisfy the poor, work out a pension subsidy now on which one could live easily and thereby end the difficult status of the homeless.

10) Because of the yoke of the Romanovs they have endured, the peasants could not acquire agricultural structures, so the Meeting came out unanimously in favor of working toward brotherhood and equality, by demanding that building material be released free of charge from government reserves. Issue the soldiers a monetary subsidy equal to this cost.

11) Maintenance of administrations, institutions, and employees must be taken on by the state. There can be no improvements in the day-to-day and financial matters if those are provided for by the peasants.

12) Road repairs and swamp draining must be taken on by the state. Set about this work immediately, for there are no passable roads at all in the volost. The swamps are flooding several hay meadows and fields.

13) Immediately select a commission at the expense of the producers in both the center and the provinces to verify their productivity and management and the stealing and looting that have been committed during the present war. Where such are discovered, hand them over immediately to the revolutionary court-martial.

14) Full compensation to ill and wounded fighters and their families for the predatory war; the Meeting expresses its total lack of confidence in the old-regime medical boards that examined the warriors [*voiny*] and con-

siders it its duty to declare that special medical boards should be appointed immediately and should include more politically conscious doctors as well as members from the wounded warriors proportionately for both. Files of all the soldiers participating in the current war must be considered. Pay must be monthly, specifically a) to those who have lost all capacity to work, 200 rubles, b) half the ability to work, 160 rubles, c) one-third, 120 rubles, d) one-fourth, 80 rubles—and those who have suffered wounds, illness, contusions, and asphyxiation during service that did not entail a decline in ability to work, 25 rubles, e) a killed husband's wife who has full ability to work should receive 60 rubles a month. If the wife of a killed man is ill, proceed according to §a). A killed man's wife who has remarried loses her subsidy. Children up to the age of eight years get a payment of 20 rubles; and after eight years, the same as students. f) A father and mother who lost a son in the war and do not have other sons living with them must be compensated according to [sections] a, b, c, d; g) the payment must be issued as of the day the soldier incurs the wound, contusion, asphyxiation, illness, or death; h) for warriors who have lost all ability to work there must be shelters, charitably arranged, with all the comforts and staff if those who have suffered wish to be there.

15) Agronomists must work in each volost with the consent of the citizens. For which a certain amount of land must be set aside for trial and instruction in the correct management of peasant farms. The maintenance of the latter is at treasury expense.

16) Full freedom of speech and the press, gatherings, meetings, assemblies, unions, and strikes. (Total inviolability of the person, in both the center and the provinces, for inflicting humiliation by an action, no matter in what form it was inflicted.)[5]

17) As soon as possible, promulgate the most merciless section of the decree for individuals committing various types of robberies, assaults, and raids on citizens or inappropriate anarchistic tricks that cause panic among the population, as well as for individuals engaged in speculation and looting. Only this way will the population be reassured.

18) Strict and just [workers'] control over plants, factories, and mines, on the railroads and steamships, and so forth, over their productivity: cut leaders off from predatory profits and improve work productivity in production, thereby helping the exhausted population out of the impasse in which the country now finds itself. Arrest those sabotaging productivity and hand them over to a strict revolutionary court.

19) Levy merciless progressive taxes on capitalists, starting at five thousand rubles, in order to return our rubles that they stole, which they've been collecting for three hundred years, and especially in the current war, and in this way help the population start a new and just life.

20) Carry out a complete confiscation of the palaces of the Romanov clan as well as their valuables and capital, wherever they are, and put everything into the state fund.

21) Immediately carry out a universal requisitioning of privately owned commercial industry and trade and turn everything into cooperatives. Under requisitioning, prices must be minimal—that is, no higher than they were in 1914; make a monetary payment only for the monthly upkeep of the owners and their families. All production henceforth, until the population's needs have been met, must be sold through a ration card system, in both the center and the provinces, with an exception made for soldiers.

22) Melt down all monuments, with the exception of writers', and reforge them into sickles, scythes, plows, and the like.

23) Separate the church from the state and the schools from the church. The churches then must be maintained at the expense of parishioners. The construction of school buildings, lighting, heating, textbooks, teachers, and so on, must be paid for out of the treasury.

24) Universal education for both sexes. Start of studies at eight years, ending at sixteen years, except for those wishing to continue further. Each student must from now on be issued an annual subsidy for the academic year both for food and for expenses, in both the center and the provinces, out of the state fund.

25) Provide a subsidy for the peasantry out of the state fund in the event of a failed harvest or the decline or illness of livestock, for the value of the loss.

26) Repeal all excise taxes and indirect taxes. Trade in output should be free.

27) Introduction of universal labor obligation. Press the selfish exploiters [*shkurodery*]⁶ to the lathes, joiner's benches, mines, and other dirty jobs, and by no means allow them into any institutions or establishments.

28) Confiscate any privately owned automobiles, carriages, harnesses, and horses. Organize a carrier industry for the benefit of the State.

29) Requisition all gold and silver items now, wherever they are, and melt them down for coins; this will improve the ruble's rate of exchange.

30) Immediately after the demobilization of the army, set about the installation of a telegraph-telephone network for communications, especially between the volost and the uezd and the uezd and the provincial center, which will improve work productivity in organizations.

31) For the unification and enlightenment of the peasantry, immediately set about constructing a building at the volost level for assemblies, meetings, unions, and so on, for there are no such buildings; equip the building with a movie theater; the cost of this must come out of the state fund.

32) When pregnant, women must have an equal right to a subsidy with those working in plants, factories, and so forth.

33) It is required that individual members of the peasantry adhere strictly to the instructions and demands of the peasantry, without taking one step back, and that everything possible be done to improve the living conditions for the land-poor peasantry and make them equal with other

peasants and workers. We consider it impermissible that until now land-poor peasants have worked from eighteen to twenty hours a day. Use all our powers and funds to improve their day-to-day material and financial status. The Meeting expressed the opinion that it will support representatives who are advocates for the oppressed people—up to and including using weapons against individuals who dare speak out in favor of the former oppression.

Long live Socialism
> Freedom
> Soviet power
> the peace of nations
> the Constituent Assembly
> the International

We will support the present instruction with all the powers and means at the volost's disposal. We ask our comrades to join us. Send it to the uezd and Petrograd Soviet of Workers' and Peasants' Deputies and the Revolutionary Committee. Ask the socialist newspapers to reprint it.

Passed unanimously.

Chairman, F. Anisimov

Resolution of the General Meeting of citizens of Viazhishchensk Volost 31 December 1917	Demand an immediate Convocation of the Constituent Assembly

Chairman of the general meeting of the citizens of Viazhishchensk Volost, F. Anisimov

1. The Decree on Land was in four sections. The first three sections abolished private ownership, placed land holdings at the disposal of local land committees and peasant soviets, and declared any violence during the transfer process or damage to confiscated property a crime. The fourth stipulated that, until a final decision by the Constituent Assembly, the guide to implementing the decree should be the peasant mandate compiled by the *Izvestiia* of the All-Russian Soviet of Peasants' Deputies on the basis of 242 local peasant mandates and published on 19 August 1917. Included with the Decree on Land, these are the "remaining §§" referred to.

2. After the February revolution of 1917 a Central Rada (equivalent to the Russian Soviet) was organized in Kiev by the Society of Ukrainian Progressives and various Ukrainian socialists. It functioned as a semi-independent Ukrainian government from March 1917 to April 1918. After October, the Rada tried to resist Bolshevik attempts to assert Soviet authority in Ukraine.

3. Aleksandr Ilich Dutov (1864–1921) was elected chairman of the All-Russian Cossack Congress in Petrograd in June 1917. He supported General Kornilov's demands for stronger central leadership. After the October revolution, he became the leader of the antisoviet Cossack forces in the Ural region.

4. Located at the northern border of Galicia, now in Poland. After German soldiers crossed the San River in May 1915, the "great retreat" of the Russian army began.

5. This appears to be an example of what Russian linguists call "speech phantomization" (see the afterword), in which the speaker has adopted words or phrases (here, "inviolability of the person") without fully understanding their established meaning and hence misuses them. Like much of this document, this section is awkward in its determined use of the educated public discourse of the time, especially the language of the press. Still, the sense that these phrases concerned protecting individuals from insult was essentially correct.

6. *Shkurodery* (pronounced shkurodyory) is a slang expression drawing on the phrase *drat' shkuru s kogo* (to pull the skin off someone—i.e., to exploit him) and *shkurnik* (one who selfishly thinks only about his or her own skin).

· 127 ·

Letter to Lenin from five peasants, Moscow Province, received 7 January 1918.

Happy New Year, proud leader of the Russian proletariat! We, a group of peasants from Moscow Province, Dmitrovsk Uezd, send you curses for the fact that you benefactors have been taking us to the end of our tether, to the point that we don't have a bit of grain left. It's time to come to your senses, criminals, time to take a look and see what the unhappy peasant has come to. We reach out piteously to the authorities—who aren't there. We are surrounded by violence, robbery, killings, bribery, and our babies are already swelling up from hunger and crying: Dear Papa, give us some bread. Our view of everything is that you should do everything you advocated and this means more education. Your "decrees" don't make any sense to the countryside: we have the same trouble figuring them out as we did the manifesto on peasant liberty.[1] So look, comrades, it's time for you to get wise and hear our cry and refuse power if you are smart people, since you poorly know our ignorant countryside. For beware: if we ever get out of our heavy peasant coats, it won't bode well for you. But too bad, for then it will be too late, there won't be anyone else to blame before the people.

Down with the aggressors

Down with the dirty Guards [*griaznaia Gvardiia*][2]

Down with the bitch and bandit deputies [*sobach'ikh i razboinich'ikh deputatov*][3]

All power to our gray farmers and to the Constituent Assembly.

A group of peasants, real ones, of course, and not bourgeois, Shcherbakov, Petrov, Plotnikov, Kalitkin, Afasiev

1. In February 1861, the tsarist government issued a manifesto announcing the end of serfdom in Russia, though with all sorts of restrictions on peasant liberty, mandatory redemption payments for receiving only part of the land peasants had long worked, and a "two-year waiting period" during which nothing would change. Many peasants

found the terms difficult to fathom, not only because they were so complicated but also because they were so far from what peasants understood "freedom" to mean.

2. A pun on "Red Guards" (*Krasnaia gvardiia*).

3. A pun on "Soviet of Workers' and Soldiers' Deputies" (*Sovet rabochikh i sol-datskikh deputatov*).

· 128 ·

Letter, written in red ink, to the Bolshevik leaders from a peasant,
Orel Province, 10 January 1918.

TO YOU!

Rulers, plunderers, rapists, destroyers, usurpers, oppressors of Mother Russia, citizens Lenin, Trotsky, Uritsky, Zinoviev, Spiridonova, Antonov, Lunacharsky, Krylenko, and Co.[1]

Allow me to ask you how long you are going to go on degrading Russia's millions, its tormented and exhausted people. Instead of peace, you signed an armistice with the enemy, and this gave our opponent a painful advantage, and you declared war on Russia. You moved the troops you had tricked to the Russian-Russian front and started a fratricidal war. Your mercenary Red Guards are looting, murdering, and raping everywhere they go. A fire has consumed all our dear Mother Russia. Rail transport is idle, as are the plants and factories; the entire population has woken up to find itself in the most pathetic situation, without bread or kerosene or any of the other essentials, unclothed and unshod in unheated houses. In short: hungry and cold. Nonetheless you continue to torment us. That's right, you, Citizen Lenin! With your oprichniki you are like King Herod who would not spare fourteen thousand infants just to exterminate the Great Socialist Jesus Christ among them.[2] You are like Judas who sold Christ for thirty pieces of silver. But Herod took only baby boys from their mothers, whereas you are taking everyone—no one is safe from you. You have orphaned millions of small children and left old folks without their children. Judas at least felt guilty and hanged himself, but even though you sold Russia much dearer, not one of you has hanged himself. You promised to open the Constituent Assembly right away, so it could decide Russia's fate, but just as Herod ordered male infants killed so that he would not be pulled from the throne, so you, in order not to be taken from power, are trying to disband the Constituent Assembly and arrest the people's representatives. On the fourth of January[3] the Constituent Assembly opened, and you did everything you could to stifle it, you wouldn't let Tsereteli, a member of the Const. Assem., give his speech, you shouted at him from your seat, "Butcher!" though that has nothing to do with him, but the Ensign Krylenko[4] could only shout, Butcher! It's you who are the butchers, you usurpers, butcher Lenin, butcher Trotsky, butcher Ensign Krylenko, you're all butchers, but not this member of the Const. Assem. Tsereteli, who has been fighting for the people's freedom all his life. You have strangled the entire press, and freedom with it, you have wiped out the best freedom fighters, you have destroyed all Russia. Think it over, you butchers, you hirelings of the Kaiser. Isn't your turn about up, too? For all you are doing, we, politically aware Great Russians, are sending you butchers, you hirelings of the Kaiser, our curse. May you be damned, you accursed one, you bloodthirsty butchers, you hirelings of the Kaiser— don't think you're in the clear, because the Russian people will sober up and that will be the end of you. I'm writing in red ink to show that you are bloodthirsty. And you, Krylenko, I've been at the front and was wounded, and I slap your right cheek and spit into your shameless eyes. Damn you, you butcher! I'm writing these curses, a Great Russian native of Orel Province, peasant of Mtsensk Uezd.

10 January 1918

1. Leaders of the Bolshevik party and of the Soviet government after October 1917. Vladimir Ilich Lenin (1870–1924), born V. I. Ulianov, was the founder and leader of the Bolshevik party and, as chairman of the Council of People's Commissars (Sovnarkom), the first leader of the new Soviet state. Leon Trotsky (Lev Davidovich Bronshtein, 1879–1940) was a former Menshevik and independent socialist who joined the Bolshevik party in July 1917. Elected chairman of the Petrograd Soviet in September, he played a decisive role in planning and organizing the Bolshevik seizure of power. He was named people's commissar for foreign affairs in the new Soviet government. Moisei Solomonovich Uritsky (1873–1918) was also a former Menshevik who, together with other members of Trotsky's political organization in 1917, joined the Bolshevik party in July. He was elected a member of the Bolshevik Central Committee in August, served in the People's Commissariat for Internal Affairs, and played a leading role in suppressing the Constituent Assembly in January 1918. Grigory Yevseevich Zinoviev (born Radomyslsky) (1883–1936) was a close associate of Lenin and a Bolshevik from the faction's formation in 1903. He was elected chairman of the Petrograd soviet in December 1917. Maria Aleksandrovna Spiridonova (1884–1941) was a leader of the left wing of the S.R. party, a member of the Petrograd Soviet and of the Executive Committee of All-Russian Soviet of Peasants' Deputies, and the Bolshevik–Left S.R. candidate for chair of the Constituent Assembly. Vladimir Aleksandrovich Antonov-Ovseenko (1884–1938) directed the capture of the Winter Palace and the arrest of the Provisional Government. After October 1917, he was appointed commissar for military affairs of the Petrograd district. As a member of the collective responsible for military and naval affairs, he sat on the Council of People's Commissars. Anatoly Vasilievich Lunacharsky (1875–1933), a Bolshevik on and off beginning in 1903, was named people's commissar for enlightenment in October 1917. Nikolai Vasilievich Krylenko (1885–1938), a former student and soldier and longtime Bolshevik activist, was a member of the All-Russian Central Executive Committee after February 1917 and a member of Committee of Military and Naval Affairs of the Council of People's Commissars after October. On November 9, he was appointed supreme commander in chief.

2. Matthew 2:16. Seeking to rid himself of the one prophesied to have been born king of the Jews, Herod gave orders to kill all the boys in Bethlehem and its vicinity who were two years of age or less. The number is legendary not scriptural, nor is it realistic, given the small population of Bethlehem.

3. Actually, on 5 January.

4. When he left the military in 1913, Krylenko had the rank of ensign in the reserves. At the assembly's opening session on 5 January 1918, Tsereteli delivered a speech in which he attacked the Bolsheviks for planning to dissolve that body and called for the preservation of democratic institutions as the only hope for Russia and the revolution.

· 129 ·

Resolution to the Constituent Assembly from peasants,
Kursk Province, 13 January 1918.

Resolution

We, the Citizens of the Village of Troitsk, Streletsk Volost, Starooskolsk Uezd, Kursk Province, having gathered during these great and historic days—the days of the beginning of the work of our long-awaited Constituent Assembly—and discussed the significance of the historical moment we are now living through, have resolved: To welcome the Constituent Assembly in the person of its members, who were chosen by the entire people and who have been authorized to express the people's will. Right now, all our intentions and hopes are focused on the Constituent Assembly, the sole authorized master of the Russian land. The whole fullness of state power at this time must belong only to the Constituent Assembly. Dear representatives, we peasants are expecting from you the speediest possible stable democratic peace and the speediest possible implementation by the democratic republic of the speediest possible transfer of all lands—manor, cabinet, appanage, monastery, church, and other—to the working people, without compensation, on the basis of equalized workers' landownership, and we hope that the people's representatives will be able to rally the Citizens of the Russian republic into a unified whole and give the working people true freedom, land, and liberty.

Long live the Constituent Assembly.

Long live Peace, Land, and Liberty.

Troitsk Executive Committee chairman, Sichevnikov
Secretary, Krestonev

13 January 1918

· 130 ·

Pyotr Oreshin, "What Chasms to Us Have Opened,"
printed in *Delo naroda*, 24 December 1917.

What chasms to us have opened,
At what distance lies our fate . . .
Is it not from under tombstones
That our wakened dreams escape?

Fits of love and joy abound,
Fiery soul and shoulders strong—
Can I keep them handsome, proud
For today and ages long?

What shall I say in the world to come
To the shadows, to my countrymen? . . .
How much broader, more immense
The sunset over fields now golden.

I walk through the gates flung wide
In the gloom of times untold,
On the wings of flight eternal—
Into a dream unique, unspoiled.

Our joyful death will unloose the ties
That bind my soul where torments teem,
And the earth, beneath the heavens' skies,
The earth's firmament, will be a dream.

· 131 ·

Vladimir Kirillov,[1] "To the Proletariat," printed in the proletarian
culture journal *Griadushchee* (The future), January 1918.

To the Proletariat

Oh, many-faced Master of the World!
Whose faith is Reason, whose strength is Work.
All the dreams of the heart, all the strings of my lyre
    In harmony sing
    To the might you bring
    It is to You I sing.

Beneath a dark smock, in a breast so stern
You bear the Sun of New Life
    You—the first thunder
    Of coming spring.
Always stormy, always calling.
    In you alone
    The sole vindication
    For all the privation
    And the Search's tribulation.

When the rumble of your rebellion
And your flashing sword of Red
Through the smoke glinting
    Strikes our enemies down—
Killing, destroying,
And so a world new and
    Beautiful it creates,
The deaf sky
You won't ask
    For a crust of bread.
You believe in the power
    Of iron hands.
Your prayers
Are just battle hymns
    To a Life without cares.

    In its movement,
    Its aspiration,
    Shining Genius
      Lights the world.

    All those killed,
In the name of Sun and the name of Light,
    With you have merged.
    In you lies the answer
    The revenge they await,
    The dreams of the crucified,
    Through ages anathematized,
      Blossom in your wake.

Go! Thunder out a stormy roiling
    In the spring so tender
      Across the world—howl!
The sacred news of Liberation,

Bring them without hesitation,
The sound of chains as they fall.

1. Vladimir Timofeevich Kirillov (1890–1943) was a self-taught worker-writer born into a peasant family in Smolensk Province. After attending a year of primary school, he worked variously as a bootmaking apprentice, sailor, and folk musician (even playing briefly in a music hall in New York). Drafted in 1914, he remained on active duty until 1917. He was frequently involved in political activity after 1905, for which he was arrested and exiled. He began writing poems and stories in 1910.

· 132 ·

Aksen-Achkasov (Ilya Sadofiev),[1] "We Go On,"
printed in *Griadushchee*, January 1918.

We Go On

Smashing through all obstacles
All barriers, we go on.
Revelations new and details
To the world we will make known.
 The might of the summons
 The sweetness of battle
 The gust of the whirlwind
 The faith and the joy,
In our breast we have cherished
In our fiery young breast.
 In the power
 Of happiness, passion,
 Of Liberty Bright,
 Our Destiny Red . . .
  Ahead:
To greet the Morn, Sun, and Day . . .
The masterful, clear, and crimson day.

Thorny the path, the cliffs high—
We have lit the flame in summons
Glowing is the dawning scarlet,
Fading is death's silhouette.
 Night's cover
 We tear
 So the workers
 Will hear.

Meetings and speeches,
Battles now joined . . .
The joy of impoverished
So sleepy and pale

Villages . . .
Keep your faith burning
In your soul creative,
In iron and in granite
We will trample the flowers.

1. Ilya Ivanovich Sadofiev (1889–1965), a worker-poet, was born to migrant workers who regularly moved between St. Petersburg and Tula. He worked as a shepherd, farmhand, and factory worker, often changing jobs and sometimes living on the streets. A brief village education was followed by workers' night courses in St. Petersburg. He began to write at the age of ten and was involved in radical politics in 1905 and after. His poems appeared regularly in the Bolshevik newspaper *Pravda*. After October 1917, Sadofiev became a deputy to the Petrograd Soviet and a leading figure in the "proletarian culture" movement.

Afterword:
Style in Lower-Class Writing in 1917

Ekaterina Betekhtina

An examination of the discursive style of letters and other texts from 1917 and early 1918 is as essential to understanding their meaning as is a consideration of content. Indeed, it is often precisely the language of the documents in this collection that best reveals who the authors of the texts were and who they wanted to appear to be, what values they held, and what was especially important to them. The documents in this collection can be divided into five basic types: 1) resolutions and decisions of various workers' and soldiers' meetings and of peasant assemblies (сходы); 2) appeals from workers, soldiers, and peasants to the government and to their compatriots; 3) letters from citizens to the popular political press, especially the Soviet newspaper *Izvestiia*; 4) letters to ruling bodies (such as the Provisional Government or the Central Executive Committee of Soviets) and also to leading political figures; and 5) poems by lower-class writers.

Resolutions from Meetings

An orientation toward formal, official language is one of the most important stylistic features of the first type of document (decisions from meetings). Indeed, resolutions were undoubtedly composed and styled by their authors as official documents, and this orientation determined their precise structure. It usually consists of two parts: the first, or introductory, section describes the occasion for the meeting and sets forth the date, place, and sometimes the political context for the meeting, and the second part contains the actual content of the resolution.

The introductory section is often full of bureaucratic clichés characteristic of official documents, as in the following example:

Мы *ниже подписавшиеся* граждане дерев. Осничково и Андреево быв сего *числа* на общем собрании и обсуждали вопрос Государственного Строя и Земельного; а также и все нужды нашего общесетва и *единогласно постановили.*[1]

We, *the undersigned* citizens of Osnichkovo and Andreevo, having attended a general meeting on this date, discussed the question of State Order and the Land, and also all the needs of our society and *unanimously resolved.* (Document 44)

The syntax of the introductory section, which usually consists of one long sentence, is often noticeably weighed down by an abundance of subordinate clauses and numerous detached constructions (indeed, virtually every resolution begins with an gerundial[2] construction). To some degree, this structure is probably an attempt to condense the content of a long text, especially to set forth an appraisal of the current political situation while remaining within the framework of the introductory section or sentence.[3] But an equally important function of the detached construction, and particularly of the gerundial construction, is to raise the "communicative tension of the utterance."[4] Thanks to its expressiveness and ability to enhance the dynamism of language, the gerundial construction evidently particularly appealed to the authors of resolutions and decisions, because it allowed them to express the fervency of popular emotion while staying within the framework of the prestigious formal linguistic style.

Nonetheless, the proletarian authors' low level of education and their consequent inexperience with formal written language are apparent. Frequently a sentence, saturated to the limits with information, and complicated by numerous subordinate clauses and detached constructions, has no main predicate whatsoever:

Гневно *протестуя* против большевиков и их лидера Ленина, которые недоверяют Временному Правительству и хотят забрать власть в свои руки, как это видно из их слов, *сказано* на Всероссийском Съезде Рабочих и Солдатских Депутатов и *получившим* полное поражение по всем пунктам [от] нашего уважаемого Военнаго Министра Керенскаго.

Furiously *protesting* against the Bolsheviks and their leader Lenin, who do not trust the Provisional Government and want to take power into their own hands, as is obvious from their words *spoken* at the All-

Russian Congress of Workers' and Soldiers' Deputies, which *suffered* total defeat on all the points from our respected War Minister Kerensky. (Document 17)

In this case, the function of the predicate in the main clause is fulfilled by the gerund "protesting" (протестуя).[5] Grammatically inexperienced authors often interpret the adverbial participle (here "furiously protesting") as a type of predicate that is much more expressively charged than an ordinary verbal or nominal predicate. Similar substitutions, as well as strings of detached constructions, one on top of another, constitute the most prominent syntactic feature not only of the resolutions but also of other documents collected in this book. Of course, the poems provide an exception, for they use different methods of achieving expressive effect.

The introductory section of the resolutions usually ends with the words постановили, вынесли резолюцию, or заявляем ("[we] have resolved," "[we] have passed the resolution," "[we] announce"). The writers then proceed to enumerate the points of the resolution. This second part, which is most important and substantial with regard to content, is often introduced by subordinate clauses with the conjunction что, by imperative infinitive constructions (for example, in Document 10), or by transitions to slogans (especially in the resolutions of general meetings—for example, Document 18). Frequently, visual methods of expressively arranging the text are used: each sentence or each infinitive phrase begins on a new line.

An orientation toward formal style is present in this second section also; however, instead of bureaucratic clichés, here we encounter a social-political lexicon characteristic of the language of front-page newspaper articles and political pamphlets (for example, in Document 10). Here we often find foreign words used: организовать, реквизировать, бойкотировать (to organize, to requisition, to boycott); bookish expressions: предметы потребления, твердые цены, продукты продовольствия, широкие массы, реставрация прежнего строя (objects of consumption, fixed prices, staples, the broad masses, restoration of the previous system); and substitution of verbs for verb-noun combinations, which adds a "weightier" and more literary feel to the expression: произвести захват (to effect a capture) for захватить (to capture), выражать протест (to express a protest) for протестовать (to protest), and so forth. Writers of resolutions also commonly strive for maximum concentration of content. Owing to the authors' inexperience, however, this condensed form of expression often makes the resolutions difficult to understand. The reason for the difficulty is purely syntactical: the overuse of subordinate clauses and detached constructions, the abundance of deverbals, and the stringing together of genitive and instrumental cases hinder easy comprehension.

More so than the resolutions from workers' meetings, the resolutions of peasant assemblies (приговоры—literally, "decisions" or "verdicts") mainly treated issues that had a direct impact on peasant life (for example, Documents 46, 48, 49). Above all, this meant the issue of land. Peasants' demands also tend to be relatively simple and concrete and, from a linguistic point of view, less marked by an inclination toward formal language than the resolutions from workers' meetings. Greater informality is especially characteristic of the second part of the peasants' resolutions, in which a neutral lexicon prevails, though one also encounters such bookish phrases as наемный рабочий труд, предмет купли и продажи, решение вопроса во всем его объеме, федеративно-автономное управление (hired labor, object of buying and selling, determination of a question in all respects, federal-autonomous government), as well as formal agricultural terms: покосы, пахотность, душевой надел (mowing, arability, allotment per head).

Syntactically, the peasants' decisions are marked by a much greater "transparency" or structural clarity. Here we find neither the abundance of detached constructions nor the strings of deverbals in the genitive and instrumental cases that are characteristic of the resolutions from workers' meetings. It would appear that many workers were convinced, as they were encouraged to think by Marxist activists, that the proletariat represented the leading class in the revolution—the status of the conquerors and defenders of freedom—and that they strove to conform to this image by writing as if they were participants in the administration of government and in the formation of its foreign and domestic policies. Their resolutions functioned as a type of official decision and thus were written in a weighty "state" (that is to say, formal or official) language.[6] The main goal of the peasant authors, by contrast, was to achieve the greatest possible comprehension on the part of the reader, which in their eyes was fundamental to the rapid fulfillment of their demands. Elucidation and repetition are the linguistic means used to achieve that purpose. In their desire to be absolutely clear, the peasants try to clarify each term they use, each phrase they think might be interpreted ambiguously. Thus a bookish expression or term is explained by a colloquial or neutral phrase: "учение должно быть за счет государства, т.е. на всем готовом" ("the time spent in study should be at the expense of the state—that is, full room and board"); "пахотность, то есть пахотная земля" ("arability, that is arable land"—Document 46).[7] Often in these resolutions or decisions (приговоры) a "ladder of synonyms" or gradation is used (incidentally, this was also Vladimir Lenin's favorite speech device): the repetition of words and expressions similar in meaning, which are called upon "to clarify meaning, to portray a phenomenon thoroughly and emotionally."[8] The peasant authors' use of a ladder of synonyms in the endeavor to be explicit sometimes, however, has the opposite result: the text, oversaturated with derivationally or semantically related words that, nonetheless, do not form a gradation in a series of homogeneous parts of the sentence, seems verbose and unclear:

> [Мы] выносим [в протокол] нужды всего народа, в чем мы нуждаемся, какая наша нужда, [а также то] что народ требует себе лучшей доли.

> [We] express the needs of the entire people—that is what we need, what kind of need we have, [and also] that the people demand for themselves a better share. (Document 48)[9]

The peasants' lower level of education, as compared with the workers', also explains the almost complete absence of punctuation in their resolutions and the abundance of nonstandard forms: for instance, подписуемся, об нас, между нуждающими, and expressions which arise through a contamination of certain bookish expressions, such as частные богачи-спекулянты ("частная собственность" + "богачи" + "спекулянты") [private rich men–black marketeers (private property + rich man + black marketeer)], or насильственная власть ("насильственные меры" + "власть, как аппарат насилия") [forcible power (forcible means + power as an apparatus of violence)].

Appeals

Unlike the resolutions of the workers' and soldiers' meetings, appeals drafted at protest meetings do not exhibit a clear compositional structure; nor are they oriented toward official style. Rather, they are characterized by pathos and by solemn, lofty rhetorical phrases: вся будущность истерзанной страны, час жизни и смерти революции настал, братоубийственная война, освобождение народа русского ныне свершилось ("the entire future of our tormented country," "the hour of life and death for the revolution is upon us," "fratricidal war," "the liberation of the Russian people has now been accomplished"), and so forth. Similar phrases contain emotionally assertive components and create solemn and passionate connotations:

> Сбросить с себя угар обмана и присоединиться к сомкнутым рядам борющагося за освобождение труда и единой, стройной фалангой, в мощном порыве, идти вперед по пути строительства новой, свободной, трудящейся России, к воплощению в жизнь великих и светлых идеалов труда.

> To cast off the intoxication of deceit and join the solid ranks of those fighting for the liberation of labor and in a single, orderly phalanx, in a mighty surge, to start down the path of building a new, free workers' Russia and realizing the great and shining ideals of labor. (Document 117)

The effect of solemnity or loftiness is strengthened by the use of Old Church Slavicisms, which are characteristic of the high style in Russian (for instance, ныне, свершиться, or "now, to occur") and of biblical expressions: сильные мира сего, несущая свой крест армия, все как один человек, кровь наших братьев взывает к нам (the mighty of this world, the army bearing its cross, all as one person, the blood of our brothers calls out to us).

The basic function of an appeal is that of a call to action. This tone is set in the forms of address at the beginning of the text: Граждане земли русской! Товарищи и братья! Товарищи крестьяне, отцы наши и братья! Товарищи солдаты, Мужья наши и Дети! Товарищи рабочие и воины Петрограда! (Citizens of the Russian land! Comrades and brothers! Comrade peasants, our fathers and brothers! Comrade soldiers, our Husbands and Children! Comrade workers and warriors of Petrograd!) For soldiers' appeals such forms of address as the following are also characteristic: Боевые товарищи! Славные богатыри! Свободные воины! Славные солдаты! (Fighting comrades! Glorious bogatyrs! Free warriors! Glorious soldiers!) The bombastic effect and emotional intensity spring from expressive inversion of the word order and from the use of novel, socially significant forms of address, which had not yet lost their semantic meaning through overuse (Граждане! Товарищи! [Citizens! Comrades!]), emphatically positive appellations and epithets (герои, богатыри, славные, свободные [heroes, bogatyrs, glorious, free]), as well as terms of kinship, which always bear positive connotations.

The high note of address is further maintained by hypercharacteristic epithets in the body of the appeal: кровопролитный, героический, беспросветный, великий, неудержимый, райски-радостный (bloody, heroic, pitch dark, great, irrepressible, heavenly-joyful), and so forth. For instance:

> В судорожных муках истерзанного народа, в потоках его крови, залившей необъятные поля в предсмертном напряжении его последних усилий, порвалась могучая цепь капитала, веками заковывавшая трудящуюся Россию и родилась яркая зарница освобождения.

> In the convulsive torments of the tortured people, in the streams of its blood that have washed over the immense fields in the death throes of its final efforts, the mighty chain of capital, which shackled laboring Russia for centuries, was broken and the vivid summer lightning of liberation was born. (Document 117)

In some curious instances a new expressive epithet arises from a metaphorical or metonymical displacement and begins to be used separately from it, creating entirely new expressive units. The adjective серый ("gray") may serve as an example. We see a metonymic transfer of the expression серые шинели ("gray overcoats") to mean "soldiers," for the soldiers of the tsarist army wore gray overcoats.[10] The adjective "gray" also has figurative meanings in Russian: "dull" and "joyless": серый день (a gray day), and, most relevant here, "ordinary," "uneducated," "uncultured": серость, серый человек (grayness, a gray person). The contamination of the figurative meanings of the adjective "gray" and the epithet from the metonymic phrase "gray" (= soldier's) gave birth to a new meaning: "unfortunate, famous for being long-suffering" in new phrases that include the component "gray" and have the general meaning of "soldier": серые солдаты, серые окопники, серые рабы, серый герой, серый русский мужик (gray soldiers, gray trenchmen, gray slaves, gray hero, gray Russian peasant), and so on:

> Вспомните, товарищи о тех, кто в окопах, под угрозой смерти, увечья или тяжкого плена, всего себя отдает родине и не за 200 или 300 руб., а за 75 копеек в месяц! *Серый русский мужик* сидит в окопах и молча, без унизительных в такое время торгов, делает свое великое дело. Но настанет пора, пройдет над миром кровавая буря, вернется *серый герой* в родные деревни, села и города, и предъявит счет, длинный счет, писанный кровью миллионов своих братьев, и работникам тыла придется тот счет оплачивать.

> Remember those who are in the trenches, comrades, under the threat of death, injury, or harsh captivity, who are sacrificing themselves for

their homeland, and not for two or three hundred rubles but for seventy-five kopeks a month! *The gray Russian muzhik [peasant] is* sitting in the trenches and, without trying to make any kind of deals, which would be degrading at such a time, doing his great deed without a murmur. The time will come, though, when a bloody storm will pass over the world, *the gray hero* will return to his native villages, settlements, and towns, and he will present a bill, a long bill, written in the blood of millions of his brothers, and the workers in the rear will have to pay that bill. (Document 25)

A powerful emotional effect characterizes the lexicon of opinion and judgment used widely in the appeals: смута, бойня, трудящийся люд, немецкие полчища, презренные угнетатели народа (turmoil, carnage, laboring people, German hordes, despicable oppressors of the people). Metaphor plays an equally important role in the creation of the emotionally judgmental coloration of the texts of the appeals:

Не усыпят нас более слащавые речи врагов наших и не сведут они нас более в пропасть рабства, нищеты и безличия.

The sweeter speeches of our enemies will not lull us to sleep or lead us further into the abyss of slavery, poverty, and depersonalization. (Document 118)

Освобождение народа русского ныне свершилось. Над родиной засияло солнце свободы.

The liberation of the Russian people has now been accomplished. The sun of freedom has started to shine over our homeland. (Document 23)

Близок рассвет. И нужно не дать темным тучам мракобесия заполнить его тьмой.

The dawn is at hand. So we must not let the black clouds of obscurantism fill it with darkness. (Document 117)

Metaphors in the appeals do not always have a literary quality, however. Often the images can be traced back to folk speech:

Мы сидим в окопах, мы не видим свету, а все слухи слышим из тылу пущены. На наши плечи камни сложены. Товарищи, . . . мы все больные, мы без сил. Товарищи солдаты и рабочие, помогите нам!

We are sitting in the trenches and without light or happiness, and we hear all the rumors let loose from the rear. Stones have been placed on our shoulders. . . . We are all sick, we have no strength left. Comrade soldiers and workers, help us. (Document 33)

The stone, as a symbol of melancholy, illness, powerlessness, and grief, appears widely in folk phraseology, as in phrases like камень на сердце, камень с души свалился, камень на шее (a stone on the heart, a stone has fallen from one's soul, a stone around the neck). In Russian folklore, the stone often appears with the traditional epithet горюч (wretched, woeful).[11] The mythological Firebird (Жар-птица), a creature from another, purer, and more just world, a terrible and beautiful image with fiery blood-red plumage, becomes in the appeals a symbol of freedom and a new life:

> Где новая жизнь—та райски-радостная огненно-красная птица, которая заманчиво пролетела над нашей страной и скрылась . . . точно обманув нас?

> Where is the new life, that heavenly-joyous, fiery-red bird that flew so temptingly over our country and then hid—as if to trick us? (Document 57)

Metaphorical vulgarisms are used to convey negative connotations:

> Видим мы также, как *шакалы* из Государственной Думы и Государственного Совета протягивают свои *грязные лапы,* чтобы задушить свободу.

> We also see *the jackals* from the State Duma and the State Council reaching out with their *filthy paws* to strangle freedom. (Document 36)

Set expressions are also widely used in the appeals. These include the already mentioned biblical expressions and colloquial idioms: темные личности, мертвая хватка, дорожить собственной шкурой, выезжать на чужих плечах, теплое место (dark and suspicious persons, dead grip, saving your own skin, riding on other people's shoulders, a cozy corner), as well as a large number of expressions drawing on educated forms of speech. Here one should particularly single out social-political clichés: работа административного толка, бюрократически мертвые формы, призывать к решительному разрыву с политикой, самым решительным образом протестовать (против чего/настаивать на чем) (work of the administrative type, bureaucratically dead forms, to call for a decisive break with a policy, to protest against something/to insist on something in the most decisive manner), and so forth.

At times the low educational level of the authors of the appeals, as well as their understandable lack of experience in creating this type of document, is evident. We see confused logic and varied grammatical abuses, contamination of bookish expressions that have not been completely mastered, and a tendency to mix literary constructions with common vulgarisms. Such usage no doubt struck educated Russian readers even then as quaint and even humorous. The stylistic and "objective-logical" discrepancies, though, which attest to the authors' inexperience, in no way detract from the general effectiveness of the appeals. They can even add a certain color and serve as a guarantor of the authors' artlessness and sincerity.[12]

The pathos of the appeals results also from the use of certain expressive syntactic constructions, such as inversions (though this device does not translate into English):

> Освобождение *народа русского* свершилось.

> *Отцы наши* и братья!

> The liberation of the *Russian people* [reversed in Russian] has been accomplished.

> *Our fathers* [reversed] and brothers!

Powerful means of heightening the expressive power of the text, such as the rhetorical question, are used widely, frequently in the form of an anaphora (a repeated word or expression at the beginning of successive phrases). This device, as is well known, is "an effective means of activating the attention of the reader, increasing the expressiveness of the speech with the help of the logical placement of the necessary word."[13]

> Остановитесь! Что вы делаете? *Вы хотите* оставить нашу армию без хлеба, без мяса, без фуража? *Хотите,* чтобы нас голодных здесь немцы голыми руками взяли? *Вы хотите* погубить нашу Родину и свою свободу? *Вы хотите,* чтобы у нас был опять царь Николай со старыми порядками, с розгами, с виселицами, с карательными отрядами, со стражниками, с ингушами? *Хотите,* чтобы у вас вместо земли и воли была голь да маета хуже прежнего?

> Stop! What are you doing? *Do you want* to leave our army without bread, meat, or fodder? *Do you want* the Germans to capture us with their bare hands right here as we starve? *Do you want* to wreck our Homeland and your own freedom? *Do you want* us to have Tsar Nicholas back with the old ways, the birch rods, the gallows, the penal detachments, the guards, the Ingush? Instead of land and liberty, *do you want* poverty and misery worse even than before? (Document 45)

An obligatory compositional element of the appeal is to conclude with a call to action. Sometimes the whole text of the appeal consists largely of slogans. A characteristic feature of these exhortative constructions is the exclamatory ellipsis:

Вся власть С. Р. и К. Д.!

Против разоружения рабочих!

Хлеба! Мира! Свободы!

All power to the Soviet of Workers', Soldiers', and Peasants' Deputies!

Against the disarming of the workers!

Bread! Peace! Freedom! (Document 18)

The visual presentation of the appeals is also often expressive: large type may be used, or each sentence may begin on a new line. All the linguistic methods employed in the appeals are subordinate to their main function: to issue a call to action.

Letters from Citizens to the Press

The letters of workers, soldiers, and peasants to the periodical press are similarly characterized by a strong appeal to the reader's emotions, which is created in this case less by bombastic phrases than by a mixture of bookish language and a colloquial, emotional-judgmental lexicon. Letters to newspapers as a rule contain frank judgments, slogans, and didactic conclusions. Their linguistic structure contains critical reflections (emotional commentary) side by side with narration:

А все те, кто пожелает помогать насаждению знаний, культуры и поэзии рабочих масс [*sic*], пусть не думает, что рабочие настолько темны и неразборчивы, что их можно пичкать плясками и желтой поэзией, вроде "писем к Вильгельму". Нет, неразвитой, но чуткий инстинкт, заложенный в каждом человеке, подсказывает рабочим, где кончается красота культуры и начинается балаганьщина и все прекрасное, что ему дает культура человечества, он впитывает в себя, а все желто-балаганное, как ненужную ветошь, с протестом отбрасывает в сторону.

And to all those who wish to help spread knowledge, culture, and poetry to the working masses, don't think that the workers are so ignorant and undiscriminating that they can be stuffed with dancing and with yellow [cheap and crass] poetry like "Letter to Wilhelm." No, the undeveloped but keen instinct inherent in every man tells the workers where the beauty of culture leaves off and the sideshows begin. Everything marvelous that human culture gives him he soaks up, and everything cheap and tasteless is cast aside, like a useless rag, with a protest. (Document 61)

The letters of workers and soldiers are oriented toward a literary style to a greater degree than the letters of peasants, as is evident in the characteristic use of a social or journalistic style: понимать серьезность переживаемого момента, защищать интересы свободной России, обратить внимание на кроющуюся в чем опасность для революции, последняя и решительная схватка труда с капиталлом (to understand the seriousness of the time we are living through, to defend the interests of a free Russia, to pay attention to the hidden danger for the revolution, the last and decisive skirmish of labor and capital), and so on. Very often, however, colloquial features are juxtaposed with these phrases.[14] The combination is particularly evident in letters written in the first person:

> Мы изнемогаем, истерзаны, больны и после долгих месяцев окопной жизни не имеем смены! ... Пусть те *крикуны,* которые требуют войны до победного конца, сменят нас здесь.

> We are exhausted, mutilated, and sick, and after long months of trench life we have no relief. . . . Let those *loudmouths* who are demanding war to the victorious conclusion relieve us here. (Document 35)

> *Боже мой, какая картина!* Не могу описать, что я в тот день пережил.

> *My God, what a picture*! I cannot describe what I lived through that day. (Document 80)

The frequent use of diminutive forms, as well as rhyme—both lost in translation—is characteristic of Russian folk speech:

> Когда сидишь на позиции в серых и грязных окопах в передовой линии, в соприкосновении с противником грудь с грудью, и, иногда выглянешь из *окопчика* в сторону противника, то *сердце невольно кровью обольется, а именно потому, что не дождешься* того времени, когда поступит приказ о наступлении или же о мире.

> When you're sitting at your position in the dirty gray trenches on the front line, chest to chest with your foe, and once in a while you peek out of your little trench at your opponent, *your heart involuntarily surges with blood, because you can't wait* for the order to attack or else about peace. (Document 37)

> Мы не *Анархисты* и не *монархисты,* не Николай II и не *Гришки* Распутины, и *не Алисы-Кулисы,* а мы позиционные солдаты, *окопные крысы.*

We are not *Anarchists* or *monarchists*, not Nicholas II or *Grishka* Rasputin, and not *Alisy-Kulisy*. We are position soldiers, *trench rats*! (Document 37)

The syntax of the letters also combines elements of the colloquial and the bookish. Colloquial features include the conjunctions а, да, и to begin a sentence: И вот, товарищи! А кто это такие? А потом началась буря (And here, comrades! And who are they? And then the storm began); the use of modal particles, conjunctions, and adverbs— еще, только, вот (still, only, here): А вот и скажем! (And here we will say!); and a widespread use of direct speech. Features of bookish syntax include detached constructions with complex prepositions— несмотря на (in spite of); the widespread use of participial and gerundial constructions; and the use of anaphoristic constructions:

Когда же 25 октября завязалась последняя решительная схватка труда с капиталом, *когда* низверженный кумир меньшевиков и эсеров бежал.

When on 25 October the final decisive struggle began between labor and capital, *when* the overthrown idol of the Mensheviks and S.R.'s ran away. (Document 109)

Overall, a definite lack of stylistic harmony is readily observable in the letters, whose writers experienced the desire to sound "weighty," to formalize their language, and to modify it according to the style of newspaper editorials, as they sought to create an authoritative impression. Very often, owing to the letter writers' general lack of education, the effect was quite the opposite. At times, the thoughtless copying of expressions could sound absurd, in such clumsy expressions as *дать рабочим хорошее эстетическое удовольствие* (to give the workers good aesthetic satisfaction), помогать *насаждению знаний, культуры и поэзии* (to help spread knowledge, culture, and poetry), нет хороших театров, где можно было бы *отдохнуть душою от повседневных работ* (there are practically no good theaters where one can find rest for the soul from one's daily work), all in Document 61. In the first example the adjective хороший (good) is inappropriate because neither the adjective эстетический (aesthetic) nor the noun удовольствие (satisfaction) requires any positive modification. The verb дать (to give) is incompatible with the noun удовольствие (satisfaction) and should be replaced by доставлять (to deliver.) In the second example the verb насаждать (to spread) normally has negative connotations—for instance, in насаждать ненависть (to spread hatred)—and is not usually followed by positive objects. In the third example the expression отдохнуть душою (to rest one's soul) is normally used only in the figurative sense "to receive pleasure, to enjoy." Here the author intends the primary meaning of the word отдохнуть (to rest): отдохнуть от повседневных работ (to rest from one's daily work), a usage that nullifies the phrase's figurative meaning in addition to introducing a stylistic dissonance into the whole sentence.

In other cases, however, bookish expressions are used creatively and effectively. A. Kuchlavok's letter-essay (Document 74), which he wrote in the name of the soldiers of his regiment, is an example of writing in which literary and colloquial elements can coexist harmoniously, mutually enriching and amplifying one another. Unlike most worker and soldier authors, Kuchlavok used less a journalistic style than a literary, even high, style. His letter is full of biblical expressions and allusions: Не надейтесь на князи и сыны человеческия, вожди слепые, волки в овечьей шкуре, царство небесное, получить камень вместо хлеба (Do not place your hopes on princes or the sons of man, the blind leading the blind, wolves in sheep's clothing, the Kingdom of Heaven, to receive a stone instead of bread, and so forth). He uses these expressions, as well as expressions drawn from literature, easily and naturally:

> Ведь мы *получили вместо хлеба камень,* а вместо обещанного *золотого дождя* получили тучи стальных пуль от которых пала 10-я часть страны.

> For we *received a stone instead of bread*, and instead of the promised *golden rain* we got a hail of steel bullets that knocked down a tenth part of the country. [This and all following quotations from Kuchlavok's letter are Document 74]

Biblical allusions often appear in this essay as in other writings: the author expands an expression by reminding the reader of a biblical parable, and thus clarifying the meaning of a phrase:

> [Наши вожди], которые взялись вести в перед но оказались слепыми и легкомысленными, *а если слепой темнаго ведет, то оба упадут в ров:* недадимся *вождям слепым* в порабощение.

> Our leaders who set out to lead us forward but turned out to be blind and frivolous, *and if a blind man leads an ignorant man, then both are bound to fall into a ditch*: we will not surrender to be enslaved to the blind leaders.

At times no actual reference to a literary source is present, leaving only explication of a presumably familiar literary plot, as in this allusion to Ivan Krylov's fable "The Pig Under the Oak":

Правители не заботятся об нашей жизни они подобны животн., которое наевшись желудей у дуба подрывать корни стала, как говорит ему ворон с дуба[: ']небдагодарная ведь это дереву вредит оно засохнуть может['], но животное в ответ сказало[: ']пусть сохнет ничуть меня не тревожит мне лишь бы желуди были['].

The rulers don't care about our life at all, they are like the animal that having stuffed itself on acorns then started tearing up the roots of the oak; when the raven said to it from the oak, ["]Ingrate, don't you see, this is harming the tree, it could dry up,["] in reply the animal said, ["]Let it dry up, that doesn't bother me in the slightest just so I have my acorns.["]

Kuchlavok's language is marked by the richness of visual imagery that typifies folk language. When using clearly learned words and expressions, the author often reworks them creatively, adapting them to his natural colloquial style, or rather to the style of the storyteller, of the traditional narrator of folktales. This may be seen, for example, in the word гидра (hydra), which appears so frequently in newspapers of that era: гидра капитализма, гидра империализма (the hydra of capitalism, the hydra of imperialism). Kuchlavok accurately picks up on the negative connotations of the word and skillfully includes them in his tale of the sufferings of the Russian land. In this way the word is no longer a journalistic cliché; in a sense it experiences a second mythologization and its lost expressiveness returns:

Стонет мать земля сырая, горько плачут и рыдают живущие на ней, торжествуют *гидры злые* мирной жизни возмутители, кровью народа упиваясь, роскошью наслаждаясь так творится в России.

Our moist mother earth is groaning, . . . those living on it are weeping bitterly and sobbing, and the *evil hydras*, the disturbers of peaceful life, are celebrating, sucking the people's blood, enjoying luxury—this is what is happening in Russia.

Despite the numerous literary expressions, Kuchlavok's language nonetheless remains essentially that of the common folk. The colloquial flavor results from the use of such typical devices as inversion: льется кровь невинная и терпит народ своим беспредельным терпением (innocent blood [reversed in the Russian] is flowing and the people bear it with their limitless patience), or развернул народ свою мощь гранитную (the people unleashed their granite might [adjective and noun reversed]). Question-and-answer constructions also occur: Неужели только убийством можно достичь свободной жизни—нет, не свободы убийством достигают, а погибели для всего народа

(Can murder really be the only way to achieve a free life? No, by murder they do not achieve freedom but rather ruin for the entire people).
Also testifying to Kuchlavok's essentially popular style are numerous
folk expressions: тянуть лямку (to toil), драть последнюю шкуру (to
pull the last skin off); proverbs: в него хлеб в него деньги в него
одежда все *пей душа и веселися* (he has bread, he has money, he has
clothing, he has everything—and he *rejoices in his soul*); folk formu-
las: мать-земля сырая (the moist mother earth), палаты каменные
(stone palaces); and references to plots drawn from folklore:

> Они же в благодарность говорят как волк журавлю сказал, что раз-
> ве тебе мало награды, что головы не откусил, когда она в зубах
> была, так и наши благодетели.

> They express gratitude like the wolf who said to the crane: Wasn't it
> enough that I didn't bite off your head when it was in my teeth? Such
> also are our benefactors.

Especially interesting is Kuchlavok's imitation of the traditional peasant lament for the dead—the juxtaposition of the biblical плевел
(weeds) and the bureaucratic лиц (person) is also notable here:

> И так товарищи трудовые сомкнем ряды свои плотнее, объедини-
> мся дружнее, для уничтожения *плевел* заглушаюших наши ха-
> рошие всходы, выбрать из своей среды всех *лиц* ведущих нас к
> погибели, которые не слышут воплей и причитаний наших жен,
> матерей и детей, которые твердят, *натоли мы вас холили и чесали*
> *чтобы такая Вам доля припала, что и солнышко еше не светило, как*
> *Вас наших кормильцев сера земля прикрыла.*

> And so, fellow working people, let us close our ranks more solidly, let
> us unite as one to destroy the weeds that are destroying our healthy
> shoots, pick out from among us all the persons leading us to ruin, who
> refuse to listen to the wails and lamentations of our wives, mothers,
> and children, who keep repeating: Did we care for you and groom you
> so that such a portion should befall you, that scarcely before the sun
> could shine on you, our breadwinners, you were covered by the gray
> earth?

  Kuchlavok probably did not have much formal education, as is indicated by the absence of consistent punctuation, as well as by the numerous departures from orthographic and literary norms, such as phonetic spellings (хароший, дирут, недадимся) and his regular use of
dialectal forms (хотит, слухать, в него = у него). His letter is notable,
however, for the originality of its style and the absence of cliché. It ends

with a poem whose form is imperfect, but whose every word conveys passion and sincerity.

Kuchlavok's letter is not the only manifestation of intellectual and stylistic individuality in the public writings of lower-class Russians in 1917. Among peasants, too, educated and gifted individuals took up the pen—for example, S. M. Martynov, in his letter-essay "Man and Land" (Document 97), which is written in a literary language containing a great number of bookish expressions, participles, and gerunds. This is much more the exception than the rule, however; the vast majority of peasant letters are written in a predominantly colloquial style. Features of this style include colloquial expressions—они все поют свое (They keep singing the same old tune), а дело все трут да мнут (We never seem to get anywhere), как с нас драли и рвали лесная стража (The forest guards continue to fleece and claw us); endearing diminutives—накосить травки (to mow the *grass* [a diminutive in Russian]), пропустить в газетке (to publish in the *newspaper*); incomplete and inverted sentences; and so forth. Frequent departures from the norms of spelling and the rules of punctuation also occur, especially phonetic spellings (чювтсвительно, жывет, *ече* [еще], славами, ничево). This particularly applies to the spelling of foreign words: *едиодскую* [идиотскую] расправу, вынимая *леворвер* [револьвер]. Substandard forms also appear: *становить протокол*, [стража] *упражняется ходить* по огородам, никакой *помощи* никто не хочет *сделать* друг другу.

Also telling are instances of "speech phantomization,"[15] which occurs when the author has confused notions of the words and expressions he is using. Thus, the author of one letter "categorically declares" ("категорически заявляет") that in his village "there are no provocateurs" ("провокаторов нет") and, lamenting the general ignorance and backwardness of his village, appeals to the editors of the newspaper *Izvestiia*:

> Товарищи солдаты, прошу я вас *высылайте сюда провокаторов,* потому что одному мне солдату не справиться. . . . Высылайте безплатно сюда газету из своей редакции, объединяйте темный народ.

> Comrade soldiers, I beg you *to send provocateurs* because I can't deal with this alone. . . . Send a newspaper here from your offices free of charge, unite the ignorant people. (Document 44)

Evidently, the author meant агитаторы or прокламаторы (propagandists), not провокаторы (provocateurs). Undoubtedly, he had often heard these words or seen them in the newspapers but did not completely understand their meanings. Here the orientation toward formal language—in other words, trying to write "like the newspapers"—underscored the author's own lack of education.

Letters to Powerful Institutions and Individuals

The inclination to use colloquial language is evident to an even greater degree in letters to institutions of power and to leading political figures. This is no mere coincidence, for in this case the authors are addressing not the public in general, but a specific individual or a specific group of people; thus, they can allow themselves a more relaxed and personal style.

Of course, a significant number of such letters were written in formal language, too. On the whole, these are letters and telegrams in support of the policies of the Provisional Government or some other official agency or individual (see, for example, Documents 19, 59, 65). A stylistic tendency toward formal language is also noticeable in various types of instructions and proposals (about, for example, what the young Russian republic should be like, the formation of a people's militia, and so on) addressed to administrative agencies. Frequently these proposals resemble resolutions in both style and content; however, the first section of the proposals is rarely an introduction in the formal or bureaucratic sense but rather includes salutations and words in support of the corresponding agency or politician (see Documents 92, 94, 95).

Petitions written in neutral or colloquial language (which may include the occasional use of journalistic clichés) can be placed in a separate group. Many of them are actually labeled ПРОШЕНИЕ (PETITION), and their introductions and conclusions are often constructed according to the demands of the old epistolary-bureaucratic etiquette (which can be historically traced to the Old Church Slavic tradition):[16] expressions of humility toward the addressee, wishes for health and prosperity, requests for attention, and so forth:

> *Покорнейше просим* Петроградский народный комитет совета солдатских и рабочих депутатов, *обратить на сие ваше благосклонное внимание.*

> *We most humbly request* that the Petrograd People's Committee of the Soviet of Soldiers' and Workers' Deputies *turn its favorable attention to this.* (Document 12)

Мы, солдаты, *имеем честь покорно просить* Вас и Вашего распоряжения, как можно поскорее заключить мир.

We soldiers have the *honor of humbly asking* you for your order to conclude peace as quickly as possible. (Document 30)

A great number of petitions are from soldiers asking for an end to the war. Gradually the requests become demands. At first the soldiers attempt to restrain themselves, and the style of their petitions remains neutral, though the tone of the letters may indicate a suppressed threat:

Господин военный министр! Мы, солдаты разных полков, заранее предупреждаем Вас как министра, что мы будем сидеть в окопах на фронте и сдерживать врага . . . лишь до первых дней губительной осени, к которому времени и просим Вас во чтобы то ни стало закончить войну и это кровопролитие.

Mr. War Minister! We, soldiers from various regiments, warn you as minister in advance that we are going to stay in the trenches at the front and repel the enemy . . . only until the first days of baneful autumn, by which time we ask you to end the war and the bloodshed at any cost. (Document 78)

Later the threats become more insistent and, possibly without deliberately intending to, the authors slip from a neutral style into colloquial speech or even slang:

Еще раз требуем скорейшего мира. . . . Просим это решение выполнить. *Если не выполните наш меч а ваша голова с плеч.*

Once more we demand a speedy peace. . . . We ask you to carry out our decision. *If not, it will be our sword and your head from your shoulders.* (Document 86)

Если будете защищать интересы капиталистов, то погибла Россия. *Всех придушим капиталистов, и вас вместе.* Держитесь за крестьян-солдат и делайте скорый мир, и вот один выход спасти Россию.

If you defend the interests of the capitalists, then Russia is lost. *We'll throttle [a slang word is used here for "to kill"] all the capitalists and you with them.* Hold on to the peasant soldier and make a speedy peace—that's the only way to save Russia. (Document 73)

Letters from those disappointed with the policies of the government or of some political party may be full of curses and rough language:

Сволочь что же ты делаешь, до каких-же ты пор будешь издеваться над русским народом. . . . *Мерзавеч проклятие тебе* от сознательного Российскаго пролетариата!

Bastard! What the hell are you doing? How long are you going to keep degrading the Russian people? . . . *Scoundrel! A curse on you* from the politically conscious Russian proletariat! (Document 121)

К ВАМ! Правители, *грабители, насильники, разорители, узурпато- ры, угнетатели* матушки России, гражданин Ленин, Троцкий, Урицкий, Зиновьев, Спиридонова, Антонов, Луначарский, Кры- ленко и Ко. . . . *будьте вы прокляты анафемы палачи кровожадные* наемники кайзера, вы не думайте—отрезвится русский народ и придет вам конец.

TO YOU! Rulers, plunderers, rapists, destroyers, usurpers, oppressors of Mother Russia, citizens Lenin, Trotsky, Uritsky, Zinoviev, Spiri- donova, Antonov, Lunacharsky, Krylenko, and Co. . . . *May you be damned, you accursed one, you bloodthirsty butchers*, you hirelings of the Kaiser—don't think you're in the clear, because the Russian people will sober up and that will be the end of you. (Document 128)

The bookish word узурпаторы "usurpers" appears side by side with the folk and religious curse анафема "accursed one," and the more printable мерзавец (scoundrel) appears beside the less presentable сволочь (bastard). The more heated the situation, the more expressive the language becomes, and the writers do not shrink from using taboo words:

Товарищ Ленин: а где же ваша совесть, где же ваши слова, что вы обещали: в три дня мир хлеб земля и воля. Вы для таво все эта обещали чтобы взять власть. А потом как[?] А долг свой исполнять не хотите, нет. Эта все враки. Если вы не выполните своих обещаний до 1 февраля то будит вам то что Духонину: погибнишь как муха. Если взяли вожжи то правте, а если не можете то летика ты, свет, на хуй, по сибирски сказать к ебеной матери, ты, еб твою мать, иркутская блядь, хотишь нас немцам продать.

Comrade Lenin, where is your conscience, where are the words you promised: peace bread land and liberty in three days' time? Did you promise all that just so you could seize power? And then what? But no, you don't want to fulfill your obligation. These are all lies. If you don't keep your promises by 1 February, then you're going to get what Dukhonin got: you'll drop like a fly. If you've picked up the reins, then go ahead and drive, and if you can't, then you can take a flying fuck to hell, or as we say in Siberia, you're a goddamned motherfucker, son of an Irkutsk cunt, who'd like to sell us out to the Germans. (Document 122)

This illustration demonstrates how the author's growing emotion alters the style by degrees. In the beginning, though negative connotations are present in the letter, Lenin is addressed formally as вы (the second person plural) and the text maintains a neutral style. Gradually, the sentences become more abrupt: А потом как[?] А долг свой исполнять не хотите, нет. Эта все враки (And then what? But no, you don't want to fulfill your obligation. These are all lies.). The first instance of vulgar language, враки (lies), appears. Then the author sharply switches to the familiar form of address ты (second person singular), followed by an open threat: погибнишь как муха (You'll drop like a fly). Finally, no longer able to restrain himself, the author resorts to obscenity, the most expressive type of abusive language in Russian (its expressiveness being due first of all to its taboo status in public discourse).

Most of these letters do not use vulgarisms to express negative evaluations of events. In his critical letter about the October revolution, an anonymous peasant includes not only numerous literary expressions but also historical allusions:

> Последуйте примеру Минина и Князя Пожарского: когда было наше отечество в опасности, они дали клич народу и спасли этим свое Отечество Москву и всю Русь Святую, если же вы посмеете выразить протест Правительству то мы вам не дадим доверия и не дадим денег.

> You should follow the example of Minin and Prince Pozharsky: when our Fatherland was in danger, they sent a call to the people and thus saved their Fatherland Moscow and all Holy Rus, so if you dare to express a protest against the Government, we will not give you our confidence or any money. (Document 41)

Veiled literary allusions are also used in his letter—and, again, as in Kuchlavok's letter (Document 74), the reference is to Krylov's fable "The Pig Under the Oak."

> Вы рабочия покрыли себя позором пролитой крови солдата гражданина, на вас останется черное пятно неповинной крови, вот поистене [*sic*] неблагодарная *свиня* [*sic*] *подубом вековым наевшись желудей досыта* носом подрывает дуб от котораго была сыта и осчастливлена.

> You workers have covered yourselves in shame by spilling the blood of the soldier-citizen, and the black mark of innocent blood will remain on you, indeed you are like that ungrateful pig that, *foraging under a*

venerable oak, stuffed its belly full to bursting and is now with its snout digging up the very oak that made it full and happy. (Document 41)

On the whole it should be noted that a significant number of writings by plebeian authors in 1917 demonstrate a striving to achieve creative mastery of literary style and means of expression. Many letters are in essence philosophical essays, and others contain pieces of poetry that are sometimes on quite an accomplished level.

Poetry

The poetic tradition of self-taught worker-poets can partly be traced back to workers' folklore. Many of these poems (especially those which are weakest from a literary standpoint) bear a strong similarity to workers' songs, which were "as a rule written in the form of a mournful monologue."[17] This is how Ilya Ladanov describes his lot as a soldier:

> Утратил я всю силушку
> За родину сваю
> А, раны как залечут,
> Опять в окоп пойду
> Здесь жить моей нет мочи
> Здесь везде и всюду ложь
> На солдата здесь клевещут!
> Вот и живи как хошь.

I exhausted all my strength for my motherland. Ah, when my wounds heal, to the trenches I'll go again. To live like this is beyond my strength. All around are only lies. Here the soldier is slandered. I can't go on like this! (Document 83)[18]

Motifs from folklore also slip in, with such expressions as утратил силушку (exhausting my strength) and жить нет мочи (to live like this is beyond my strength).

In describing the folklore of workers' songs, Anikin and Kruglov note that "in the songs a collective image of workers is drawn. In the first verses of the songs the pronouns 'we,' 'our,' and 'us' ring out emphatically."[19] To a great degree this characterization also holds true of many of the poems in this collection.

> Какия бездны *нам* раскрыты,
> Какия дали суждены.

What chasms to us are opened, what distances have been fated. (Document 130)

> Разрушая все преграды,
> Все препоны, *мы* идем

Breaking down all barriers, all obstacles, we go (Document 132)

The last example comes from the poem "We Go," by Aksen-Achkasov (the pseudonym of the worker Ilya Sadofiev). The themes and marchlike rhythm of the poem (Полог ночи/ Разрываем/ И рабочих/ Призываем—"We break down the cover of night and call upon the workers") connect it with a type of workers' song that several researchers[20] have labeled the march-song, which "was prominent in revolutionary activity and occupied a special position in the repertoire of mayovkas [illegal prerevolutionary May Day meetings] and demonstrations."[21]

At the same time, however, songs and verses of literary origin exerted a strong influence on the poetry of the self-taught worker-poets, as on workers' folklore itself. Poems and songs of professional poets frequently served as a basis for the creation of new workers' songs. Indeed, based as they were on widely known texts, rhythms, and melodies, they were much better memorized and remembered. The self-taught poets did not reject this tradition either. Thus the peasant Mikula specifically indicates that his "Russian folk hymn" should be set to the music of the famous "Kol' slaven" (Document 3), and in the lines of Demian Semyonov's "To the Fallen Freedom Fighters" (Document 4) the influence of the famous anonymous song "Вы жертвою пали в борьбе роковой" (You fell victim in the fateful battle) is obvious:

> Много товарищей *жертвою пали*—
> С деспота все же сорвали венец

Many comrades *fell victim*—But they tore the crown away from the despot.

The poetry of self-taught worker-poets is often deeply metaphorical, and among its most characteristic features is religious symbolism. In general, in worker poetry during the years before and immediately after 1917, "the religious idiom heard among these lower-class writers was mainly metaphoric and symbolic, not literal. Christian terminology, imagery, and narratives were fundamental but were typically divorced from theistic belief. . . . Biblical and hagiographic elements were freely combined with other sacred and mythic symbols and tales."[22]

> Не в наших ли хижинах тесных
> Христовы скрижали?
> В полях, как в пустынях безвестных,
> Не мы ли рыдали?

Weren't Christ's sacred texts [literally, "tablets"] in our crowded shacks? In the fields, as in unknown deserts, did we not weep? (Document 102)

Both the phrase Христовы скрижали (Christ's sacred texts/tablets) and the allusion to the biblical narrative of the Jews' long and wearisome wanderings in the desert in search of the promised land and a new life—в полях, как в пустынях безвестных, не мы ли рыдали? (In the fields, as in unknown deserts, did we not weep?)—seem to allude to Scripture. Yet nowhere in the Bible are Christ's "sacred tablets" mentioned—this is a completely new image, though echoing and reworking older ones.[23]

One also encounters in workers' poetry the motif of the temple as the proletariat's holy of holies:

> Посягнет кто на храм твой священный,
> Кто посмеет его осквернить?
> Нет никто, ты герой, ты титаник великий,
> Все и всё пред тобой замолчит

Who will trespass upon your holy temple, who will dare to defile it? No one, you hero, you great Titan. Everyone and everything will fall silent before you. (Document 5)

Again, however, we are not dealing with an established religious symbol. This is not the temple in Jerusalem or Christ's heavenly temple. The proletariat is creating a new world, and with it a new sacred symbolism. This temple is the atheistic Temple of Labor, a symbol of the new order, of a world without rich or poor, of universal happiness and prosperity:

> Будет время, общей силой
> Мы воздвигнем новый храм.
> Мы воздвигнем храм свободный,
> Где не будет тех богов
> Пред которыми народы
> Трепетали ряд веков.
> *Время будущего строя*

Назовем мы Храм Труда,
Буржуазного покоя
В нем не будет и следа.
Верь в грядущее, друг милый,—
Наше счастье впереди . . .
Брось навеки вид унылый
И смелей вперед иди.

There will come a time when through our common strength we will raise a new temple. We will raise a temple of freedom where there will not be those gods before whom the people trembled for centuries. *The time of the new order we will call the Temple of Labor*. In it, there will not even be a trace of bourgeois tranquillity. Believe in the future, dear friend—our happiness lies ahead. . . . Cast off forever your dejected appearance and go forward bravely. (Document 103)

The torturous search for the promised land, the expectation of a New Man, and the building of a temple are all essentially metaphors for the general idea of a new life or salvation, a common feature of workers' poetry.

Salvation, deliverance from suffering, in these poems "often came on wings—a potent symbol of transcendent power and freedom with roots equally in Christian tradition and other mythic cultures."[24] Newer sources for the mythologization of flight included the works of Nietzsche, whose ideas strongly influenced the worldview of such revolutionary poets and writers as Maxim Gorky (see "Song of the Falcon" and "Song of the Stormy Petrel," among others).[25] The struggle for a new life gives wings to human beings and makes them free, subject neither to earthly pulls nor to earthly cares:

Кафтан долой! . . . Лечу я по полю
На крыльях огненных времен.

Down with the caftan! . . . I am flying over the field on the fiery wings of the ages. (Document 52)

Иду в раскрытыя ворота,
Во мглу безчисленных времен,
На крыльях вечного полета—
В неповторяющийся сон.

I am going through the open gate in the darkness of countless ages, on the wings of eternal flight, to a unique dream. (Document 130)

In the metaphorical world of folk tradition, winged salvation was often represented by the mythological Жар-птица—the Firebird. A poem about the revolutionary rising of peasants and the coming of the new, free life concludes:

> Бросают зло в пучину черную
> Свой медный крик колокола.
> Не Жар-ли птица Русь просторную
> Крылом кровавым обняла?

The bell throws fiercely its bronze cry into the black gulf. Is it not the Firebird that has embraced vast Rus with her bloody wing? (Document 52)

The Firebird, a well-known figure in Russian folklore, the protagonist's longed-for prey, is a bird with golden plumage which shines so brightly that it is impossible to look at it. "The golden coloring of the Firebird is connected with the fact that it comes from another ('thirtieth') kingdom, in which everything gold-colored originates. Another connection exists, between the Firebird and metaphorical images that emblematize fire."[26]

> Мечется золото-пламя
> Машет багряным крылом.
> Братцы, не воля-ль над нами?
> Братцы, куда мы идем?

The gold flame quivers and flaps its crimson wing. Brothers, isn't that freedom above us? Brothers, where are we going? (Document 51)

The personification and cult of fire doubtless grew from varied roots: fire as a companion and helper in the struggle against predatory animals, fire as a symbol of home and hearth, and so on. During the dramatic revolutionary era, fire became metaphorically important above all as an image of purifying and healing power,[27] though at the same time it appeared as a terrible and dangerous element. As was typical of the apocalyptic attitude of those years, salvation was seen as possible only through renunciation of the past, even through its complete destruction. Thus, the radical Russian version of "La Marseillaise" declared, "Отречемся от старого мира,/ Отряхнем его прах с наших ног!" (We will renounce the old world; we will shake its dust off our feet!), and the Russian "Internationale" declared, "Весь мир насилья мы разрушим/ До основанья, а затем/ Мы наш, мы новый мир построим:/ Кто был ничем тот станет всем!" (We will raze the whole world of violence to its foundations and then we will build a new world. Those who were nothing will become everything!).[28] We see similar images in workers' poems of the Russian revolution:

За темным лесом пышет зарево,
Хохочет радостный набат . . .
Ах, не дворцы ли государевы
Под небом северным горят?

Beyond the dark forest, the glow of fire blazes, the joyful alarm laughs. Ah, aren't those our sovereign's palaces burning under the northern sky? (Document 52)

Those who wish to enter the new world should experience purification by fire and cleansing through blood, for "the law requires that nearly everything be cleansed with blood, and without the shedding of blood there is no forgiveness" (Hebrews 9:22).

Все думы и помыслы наши—
Не море ли крови?
Чем воля богаче и краше,
Тем люди суровей.
Дымятся бягряно-лиловы
Кровавые реки.

All our thoughts and intentions—are they not a sea of blood? The richer and more beautiful freedom is, the sterner people are. The steam rises from the bloody red-purple rivers. (Document 102)

Разверни свои сильные плечи
Кто возмутит твой кровью купленный путь?

Turn your strong shoulders. Who will disturb your path paid for with blood? (Document 5)

Even the Firebird "embraced vast Rus with her bloody wing" (Document 52).

The conjunction of the images of fire and blood is logical; both are connected with sacrifice and purification. They are united in our consciousness also through the color red, which is "the most significant [color] for humankind."[29] The color red and its various shades (crimson, scarlet, and so on) predominate in the worker-poet's palette because red is the color of the revolutionary banner, and the color of purifying fire and redemptive blood:

Когда гремит твое возстанье
И меч твой Красный
В дыму сверкая,
Врагов разит,—
Он убивая и разрушая
Иной прекрасный
Мир творит.

When your rebellion thunders, and your Red sword, shining through the smoke, strikes down the enemies, as it kills and destroys, it creates another, beautiful world. (Document 131)

The crimson dawn, symbol of the beginning of a new day, is a harbinger of that "other, beautiful world." The worker-poets often compare dawn to the red proletarian banners:

> Развернуты *алые стяги*
> Широкие *зори.*

Unfurled *scarlet banners*—the wide *dawns.* (Document 102)

At the same time, dawn is compared with fire, inflaming the sky and devouring its blue covering:

> Поля и степи за оврагами
> *Раздули розовую мглу . . .*
> Крестьяне *с огненными стягами*
> Идут по вольному селу . . .
>
> Земля и воля—краше золота
> Земля и воля—наш девиз . . .
> Степная даль ножом распорота,
> *Горят остатки синих риз.*

Fields and steppes beyond ravines have fanned the *flames of rosy haze.* The peasants with *fiery banners* are walking through the free village. Land and liberty are more beautiful than gold. Land and liberty is our motto. The steppe distance is ripped by a knife. *The remains of dark blue chasubles burn.* (Document 52—ellipses in the original)

The image of the new and happy life itself is painted by the worker-poet in reddish hues:

> Мы во власти
> Страсти, счастья,
> Светлой Воли,
> *Красной доли.*

We are in the power of passion, of happiness, of bright freedom, of *red [beautiful] fate.*[30] (Document 132)

In her research on the symbols of color and the universality of audience perception, Anna Wierzbicka has suggested the term "macro-red" to describe a range in which red predominates but in which yellow and orange also figure, because it is associated with "brightness."[31] The color gold could also be added because, as Propp points out, "golden coloring is synonymous with fieriness" in Russian folklore."[32] (285). Indeed, the second most frequently mentioned color in these poems (after red) is gold, which is often perceived as a shade of fiery-red:

> Вспыхнуло золото-пламя
> Вспыхнуло в небе ночном . . .
> Мечется золото-пламя,
> Машет багряным крылом.

The gold-flame blazed up, blazed up in the night sky . . . The gold-flame quivers and waves its crimson wing. (Document 52—ellipses in the original)

As mentioned earlier, golden coloring is also a hallmark of the thirtieth heavenly kingdom, symbolizing the next world, the world beyond, where souls go after death and where there are no tears, no grief, no hunger, no exhausting labor. It is notable that in this poetry "the coming of the new age was expected to unite the dead with the living."[33] This may happen when the lyrical persona of the poem arrives in a golden kingdom—the kingdom of the dead:

> Что расскажу в нездешнем мире
> Теням-сородичам моим?
> Все необъятнее, все шире
> Закат над полем золотым
>
> Иду в раскрытые ворота,
> Во мглу безчисленных времен,
> На крыльях вечнаго полета—
> В неповторяющийся сон.

What will I tell the shades of my kinsmen in the unearthly world? The sunset over the golden field is becoming wider and more immense. I am going through the open gate in the darkness of countless ages, on the wings of eternal flight, toward a unique dream. (Document 130)

This golden thirtieth kingdom is simultaneously the kingdom of the sun, for the golden objects in the thirtieth kingdom are the color of the sun.[34] The sun as a symbol of salvation, of the new and eternal, sin-free, and happy world also figures in workers' poetry. (Note also the theme of uniting the living and the dead in the following example.)

> Под темной блузой, в груди суровой
> Ты носишь Солнце Жизни Новой
> Все, кто убиты,
> Во имя Солнца, во имя Света
> с Тобою слиты.

Under a dark smock, in your stern chest, you wear the Sun of a New
Life . . . All who are killed in the name of the Sun, in the name of the
Light are united with you. (Document 131—ellipses in the original)

The fairy-tale hero who enters the kingdom of the sun must overcome
numerous obstacles that stand in his way and therefore cannot be an
ordinary person; he must be a hero in the fullest sense of the world.
And the poet who sings of the worker building a New World perceives
him with a significant degree of romantic mysticism: Владыка мира,
Титаник великий (Lord of the world, great Titan).

In an artistic sense, the poetry of the worker-poets leaves much to be
desired: tedious passages, superfluous details, and clumsy use of literary rhythms and bookish expressions are all present. In the emotional
sense, however, these poems always achieve their goal, owing to their
sincerity, passion, and vivid exposition. The preferred trope of the
worker-poets is metaphor. Irrespective of the source of the
metaphor—biblical parable, Jewish narrative, or images from folklore—a creative rethinking occurs, an adaptation to the new revolutionary mythology.

Ordinary Russians in 1917 revealed a remarkable ability to creatively master a range of available forms and styles of expression, as
the texts collected here suggest. The revolution changed people's notions of the surrounding world and of themselves; lower-class Russians were encouraged to see themselves as the builders and rulers of
the new world. They wanted to create a new social order, new values,
and a new mythology for this world; and in creating this fresh and
beautiful world they tried to create a new language—at times skillfully, at times less so—blending together in the same crucible their
own dialect and an incompletely understood bookish lexicon, bureaucratic clichés and lofty or bombastic phrases. Whether they succeeded
is no longer important; the outcome is well known. Still, their attempt,
perhaps naive, to begin anew, their desire to rise above themselves,
their revolutionary romanticism (as we would now call it)—all these
are strikingly evident in even the most formal resolutions that lower-
class Russians drafted in 1917.

Chronology of the Revolution

Note: Until 1 February 1918, Russia used the Julian calendar, which was, at the time of the revolution, thirteen days behind the Gregorian calendar in use in the West.

1917

23 February (8 March, International Women's Day): Strikes and demonstrations in Petrograd, the capital, grow over the next few days.

26 February: Tsar Nicholas II prorogues the State Duma and orders commander of Petrograd military district to suppress disorders.

27 February (the February revolution): Garrison mutinies. The Provisional Committee of the Duma is formed by liberals from the Constitutional Democratic party (Kadets), and the Petrograd Soviet of Workers' Deputies, headed by Mensheviks and Socialist Revolutionaries (S.R.'s), is established.

28 February–2 March: Political strikes and demonstrations spread to Moscow and provincial capitals. Soviets—councils of elected workers' and soldiers' deputies, usually led by socialist party activists—form in most Russian cities.

1 March: Order No. 1 of the Petrograd Soviet.

1–2 March: Provisional Government is established after an agreement with the Petrograd Soviet. Nicholas II abdicates. In the weeks following, the government declares broad civil rights.

12 March: Death penalty is abolished.

23 March: "Funeral of the Victims of the Revolution." Ceremonial bur-

ial in Mars Field in Petrograd of "fighters for freedom" who died during the February revolution.

27 March: Under pressure from the Petrograd Soviet, the Provisional Government issues Declaration on War Aims, repudiating domination or occupation of territories.

3–4 April: Lenin returns to Petrograd from his exile in Switzerland and issues his "April Theses," which call for revolution against the "bourgeois" Provisional Government, political power to the soviets, an end to the war, nationalization of land and distribution of land to peasants, and worker control of industry through workers' councils.

20–21 April ("April Days"): Mass demonstrations by workers, soldiers, and others take place in the streets of Petrograd and Moscow, triggered by the publication of Foreign Minister Miliukov's note to the Allies, interpreted as affirming commitment to the war policies of the old government.

April–May: Peasant seizure of private land begins.

4 May: First All-Russian Congress of Peasants' Soviets convenes in Petrograd. A national Central Executive Committee is formed, headed by Socialist Revolutionaries.

5 May: First coalition government forms when socialists, representatives of the Soviet leadership, agree to enter the cabinet of the Provisional Government.

11 May: The government approves a revised version of the Declaration of the Rights of Soldiers, originally drafted by the soldiers' section of the Petrograd Soviet and published in *Izvestiia* on 15 March 1917, though, in response to complaints by senior officers, alterations were made to increase command authority slightly.

2 June: Kadet ministers resign from the government, formally over a disputed agreement to grant autonomy to Ukraine.

3–24 June: First All-Russian Congress of Workers' and Soldiers' Deputies meets in Petrograd. Elects Central Executive Committee, headed by Mensheviks and Socialist Revolutionaries.

8 June: Twenty-eight Petrograd factories shut down in protest against the government's effort to expel the Petrograd Federation of Anarchist-Communists from their Vyborg district headquarters in the seized villa of the former tsarist minister-general P. P. Durnovo.

10 June: A planned Bolshevik demonstration in Petrograd is banned by the Soviet.

18 June: Official Soviet demonstration in Petrograd is unexpectedly dominated by Bolshevik slogans: "Down with the Ten Capitalist Ministers," "All Power to the Soviets." Beginning of Russian offensive on the Austrian front. Within days, after brief success, the offensive collapses as soldiers refuse to continue fighting.

3–4 July ("July Days"): Mass armed demonstrations in Petrograd, encouraged by the Bolsheviks, demand "All Power to the Soviets."

7 July: Prime Minister Lvov resigns and asks Kerensky to form a new government.

12 July–4 August: The Provisional Government, headed by Kerensky, passes a series of directives and laws, in the effort to restore strong authority in the country, including provisions for the death penalty for military personnel at the front, administrative closure of meetings that "may constitute a danger to the war effort or to the security of the state," and arrest and deportation of individuals viewed as a threat to "internal security" or freedom.

18 July: Members of the fourth State Duma gather in the Tauride Palace (the Soviet having been moved to the Smolny Institute) to discuss how to save Russia.

25 July: Second coalition government is formed, with Kerensky as prime minister.

12–15 August: State Conference organized by the government is held in Moscow. Representatives of all political, civic, and business groups in Russia are invited to hear addresses by representatives of the government and to express their views on the current situation, which reveal broad sentiment in favor of firm authority and order as well as deep social and political divisions in the country. Many Moscow workers strike in protest.

26–30 August: Kornilov "mutiny" begins when the commander in chief of the Russian army, General Lavr Kornilov, demands (or is believed to demand) that the government give him all civil and military authority and moves troops against Petrograd.

31 August: A majority of deputies at a meeting of the Petrograd soviet approves a Bolshevik resolution for an all-socialist government excluding the bourgeoisie.

1–27 September 1917: Kerensky, as prime minister and commander in chief, heads Directory of five ministers, while seeking agreement on a new coalition government.

5 September: Bolshevik resolution on the government wins a majority vote in the Moscow soviet.

14–22 September: All-Russian Democratic Conference in Petrograd, convened by the Soviet executive committees to discuss the government question, brings together representatives of all "democratic organizations": urban and rural soviets, city dumas, soldiers' committees, trade unions, and other organizations, with contradictory results.

19 September: The Moscow soviet elects Executive Committee and new presidium with Bolshevik majorities and the Bolshevik Viktor Nogin as chairman.

25 September: Bolshevik majority in Petrograd soviet elects Bolshevik presidium and Trotsky as chairman.

27 September–25 October: Third coalition government, headed by Kerensky.

24–26 October (the October revolution): Military Revolutionary Committee, a Bolshevik-led organ of the Petrograd soviet, coordinates overthrow of the Provisional Government.

25–26 October: Second Congress of Soviets of Workers' and Soldiers' Deputies. In protest against Bolshevik seizure of power, Mensheviks and S.R.'s walk out. Congress approves transfer of state authority into its own hands and local power into the hands of local soviets of workers', soldiers', and peasants' deputies, abolishes capital punishment, issues major decrees on peace and land, and approves the formation of an all-Bolshevik government, the Council of People's Commissars (Sovnarkom), headed by Lenin.

27 October: Decree on the Press gives the Sovnarkom the power to suspend or close any publication "inciting to open resistance or disobedience" to the workers' and peasants' government or "sowing sedition by a clearly slanderous perversion of the facts."

31 October–2 November: Fighting in Moscow ends in a Bolshevik victory.

2 November: The Bolshevik party rejects demands—made by the Union of Railroad Employees and supported by several leading Bolsheviks, including Kamenev and Zinoviev—for a multiparty socialist government. Declaration of the Rights of the Peoples of Russia promises all nationalities the right to "free self-determination," including independence.

10 November: All legal designations of civic inequality, such as estates, titles, and ranks, are abolished.

12 November: Elections to Constituent Assembly begin, as scheduled by the Provisional Government. When the results are tabulated, the Bolsheviks have won most cities and garrisons but are outnumbered by Socialist Revolutionaries.

14 November: Decree on Workers' Control gives workers extensive supervisory power in industrial enterprises.

20 November: Armistice negotiations with Germany begin at Brest-Litovsk.

24 November: All existing law courts are abolished, to be replaced by "courts established on the basis of democratic elections."

28 November: Demonstrations take place in support of the Constituent Assembly, originally scheduled to meet on that day. The Constitutional Democratic party is declared to be a "party of enemies of the people" and its leaders are arrested.

7 December: Cheka is established to fight "counterrevolution and sabotage."

12 December: Left Socialist Revolutionaries (Left S.R.'s) enter the Sovnarkom (where they will remain until March 1918). Lenin's "Theses on the Constituent Assembly" justify disbanding assembly.

16 December: Decrees abolish all ranks and titles in the army, recognize the authority of soldiers' committees and councils, and require democratic election of officers.

November–December: Generals Mikhail Alekseev and Lavr Kornilov begin efforts to establish the Volunteer Army to fight against Soviet government. The Don Cossacks declare independence. First military conflicts of the civil war begin.

1918

1 January: An attempt is made to assassinate Lenin.

5 January: The Constituent Assembly meets in Petrograd. Thousands who demonstrate in support, despite the ban on demonstrations, are dispersed by force; many are killed or wounded.

6 January: The Constituent Assembly is disbanded.

Glossary

Brusilov, Aleksei Alekseevich (1853–1926). Cavalry general. During World War I, commander of the 8th Army (starting in 1914), and later commander of the southwestern front (starting in March 1916). From May to July 1917, commander in chief of the Russian armies. In 1920, entered the service of the Red Army as a military consultant and inspector of cavalry.

Chernov, Viktor Mikhailovich (1873–1952). Political activist, theoretician; one of the founders of the Socialist Revolutionary (S.R.) Party and its principal ideologist. In April 1917, elected vice president of the Petrograd Soviet. Minister of agriculture from May to August 1917. President of the Constituent Assembly in January 1918. Emigrated in 1920.

Chkheidze, Nikolai Semyonovich (1864–1926). Also known as Karlo. Menshevik leader, journalist. Deputy from Tiflis Province to the third and fourth State Dumas (1907–1912 and 1912–1917, respectively). From February to August 1917, chairman of the Executive Committee of the Petrograd Soviet of Workers' and Soldiers' Deputies; later, chairman of the First All-Russian Central Executive Committee of Soviets. Encouraged the policy of conditional support for the Provisional Government. In 1921 emigrated to Paris, where he later committed suicide.

Guchkov, Aleksandr Ivanovich (1862–1936). Major industrialist. Founder and leader of the moderate-liberal Union of 17 October (the Octobrist party). Member and chairman of the third State Duma (1907–1912) and member of the State Council from 1915. From 1915 to 1917, chairman of the Central Military Industrial Committee and member of the Special Defense Council. As a member of the Provisional

345

Committee of the State Duma, with Vasily Shulgin negotiated Nicholas
II's abdication on 2 March 1917. Served as war and navy minister in the
first Provisional Government (March–May 1917).

Gurko, Vasily Iosifovich (1864–1937). Cavalry general. After the February revolution, served briefly as commander of the western front. Was
removed after criticizing the government for the collapse of discipline.
Subsequently emigrated.

Kaledin, Aleksei Maksimovich (1861–1918). Cavalry general commanding the Russian 8th Army on the southwestern front from May 1916
until May 1917 (relieved of his command because of a conflict with War
Minister Kerensky). In June 1917, elected ataman (chief) of the military
government formed by the Don Cossacks after the February revolution. In late 1917 and early 1918, commanded Cossack forces fighting
against Red military units in the Don region. Shot himself in February
1918.

Kerensky, Aleksandr Fyodorovich (1881–1970). Lawyer and socialist
politician. Deputy to the fourth State Duma and leader of the Trudovik
(Laborist) faction. Joined the Socialist Revolutionary Party in March
1917. During the February revolution, member of the Provisional Committee of the State Duma and deputy chairman of the Petrograd Soviet
Executive Committee. Minister of justice in the Provisional Government from 2 March to 5 May 1917. War and navy minister in the first
and second coalition governments of May through September, prime
minister from 8 July through 25 October 1917, and simultaneously
commander in chief beginning 30 August. Emigrated in 1918.

Kornilov, Lavr Georgievich (1870–1918). Infantry general. After the February revolution, appointed commander of the Petrograd military district by the Provisional Government. On 18 July 1917 promoted to
supreme commander in chief. On 26 August began moving troops
against the capital to establish a military dictatorship under his command. The Kornilov "mutiny" was suppressed with the help of armed
worker Red Guards and loyal soldiers. Removed from his post and arrested on 29 August. Commander of White forces during the civil war.
Killed at Yekaterinodar on 31 March 1918, during the first Kuban campaign.

Lenin, Vladimir Ilich (pseudonym of V. I. Ulianov, 1870–1924). Lawyer
by training and professional revolutionary by vocation, active in the socialist underground in Russia from the 1890s on. After his arrest and
exile to Siberia in the late 1890s, spent most of the next two decades in
Western Europe, helped organize the Russian Social Democratic Workers' Party, and led his own faction, the Bolsheviks, after 1903. Returned
to Russia, as did many other amnestied political exiles, soon after the
February revolution (in April). After October 1917, as chairman of the

Council of People's Commissars (Sovnarkom), served as the first leader of the new Soviet state. After a series of strokes, died in 1924.

Miliukov, Pavel Nikolaevich (1859–1943). Historian, professor, political activist, publicist. One of the organizers of the left-liberal Constitutional Democratic (Kadet) party, chairman of its Central Committee from 1907, and editor of the newspaper *Rech'*. Member of the third and fourth State Dumas. During the February revolution, advocated preserving the monarchy. Foreign minister in the first cabinet of the Provisional Government (until 2 May 1917). Emigrated at the end of 1918.

Peshekhonov, Aleksei Vasilievich (1867–1933). Statistician, populist journalist. Son of a village priest; received seminary education. One of the founders and leaders of the Popular Socialist Party (1906–1918). After the February revolution, member of the Executive Committee of the Petrograd Soviet. Minister of food supply in the first and second coalition governments (May–August 1917). Emigrated in 1922.

Rasputin (born Novykh), **Grigory Yefimovich** (1864–1916). Born a peasant in Tobolsk Province, Siberia. As a "seer" and "healer," gained considerable influence at court but through his boasting and debauchery tarnished the reputation of the imperial family. Killed in December 1916 by Prince Feliks Yusupov, Vladimir Purishkevich, and Grand Duke Dmitry Pavlovich.

Rodzianko, Mikhail Vladimirovich (1859–1924). Landowner in Yekaterinoslav Province, one of the leaders of the moderate-liberal Octobrist party, member of the State Council from 1906 to 1907, deputy to the third State Duma and chairman of the fourth (1907–1917). Leader of the Provisional Committee of the State Duma during the February revolution.

Skobelev, Matvei Ivanovich (1885–1939). Menshevik leader. Deputy from the Caucasus to the fourth State Duma (1912–1917). After the February revolution, became a member of the Executive Committee of the Petrograd Soviet. Appointed labor minister by the Provisional Government from May to August 1917. Emigrated to the West in 1920.

Trotsky, Lev (pseudonym of Lev [Leon] Davidovich Bronshtein, 1879–1940). Became involved in political protests while still a student and in the 1890s was active in trying to teach and organize workers, mainly in southern Russia. Arrested and exiled to Siberia, from which he escaped in 1902. Joined Lenin, Plekhanov, and other Social Democratic exiles in Western Europe. Tended to ally with Mensheviks after the party split in 1903, yet retained considerable independence in his political positions in these years and later. Elected chairman of the St. Petersburg Soviet of Workers' Deputies after returning to Russia in January 1905. Arrested in December 1905, and again exiled, but also again fled to Western Europe and North America. Returned to Russia in early May 1917, be-

coming one of the leaders of the "interdistrict committee" of united social-democratic internationalists. Joined the Bolsheviks in July. Elected
chairman of the Petrograd soviet in September. Played a decisive role in
planning and organizing the Bolshevik seizure of power. In the first Soviet government, named people's commissar for foreign affairs.

Tsereteli (often Tseretelli in the press and in these documents), **Irakly
Georgievich** (1881–1959). Political activist, Menshevik. Deputy to the
second State Duma (1907). Exiled to Siberia in June 1907. Returned to
Petrograd in March 1917 and became the most influential Menshevik
leader of the Petrograd Soviet. Minister of post and telegraph from May
to July 1917. Emigrated in 1921.

INSTITUTIONS AND TERMS

Bolsheviks. *See* Russian Social Democratic Workers' Party.

Central Executive Committee of Soviets, All-Russian (VTsIK). Established in June 1917 at the First All-Russian Congress of Workers' and
Soldiers' Deputies.

Congresses of Workers' and Soldiers' Deputies. The First All-Russian
Congress, held in Petrograd 3–24 June 1917, brought together representatives of soviets and of the leading leftist political parties from
throughout the country. The primary questions discussed at the congress, which was headed by Mensheviks and Socialist Revolutionaries,
were the war and the relationship of the soviets to the government. The
congress also established a new national Soviet executive body, the All-
Russian Central Executive Committee of Soviets (VTsIK). The Mensheviks and S.R.'s walked out of the Second All-Russian Congress, held in
Petrograd 25–26 October, in protest against the Bolshevik seizure of
power. The congress then approved transfer of state authority into its
own hands and of local power into the hands of local soviets of workers', soldiers', and peasants' deputies, abolished capital punishment, issued major decrees on peace and land, and approved the formation of
an all-Bolshevik government, the Council of People's Commissars,
headed by Lenin.

Constituent Assembly. The assembly was intended to be a national gathering of democratically elected representatives of all citizens to determine the course of Russian political life. The Provisional Government
endorsed this goal, though it soon found itself distracted by other demands on its attention. The government formed an electoral council to
arrange the summoning of the Constituent Assembly. The council met
in late May 1917. In August, Kerensky, then head of the Provisional
Government, set the election for 12 November. Although the Bolsheviks had come to power by then, the elections took place 12–14 No-

vember. The Constituent Assembly met on 5 January 1918, with a Socialist Revolutionary majority, and was closed immediately.

Constitutional Democratic party (Kadet party). Also known by its full formal name, the Party of the People's Freedom, it was a liberal party established in 1905, standing to the left of other liberal parties. Pavel Miliukov was one of its most prominent leaders. After the fall of the autocracy in 1917, members of the party in the Duma played a key role in forming the Provisional Government.

Council of Elders (*Sovet starost*). An elected body of workers' representatives at some large factories, whose existence was enabled by a special law of 1903. Elders were permitted to hold meetings both among themselves and with other workers. The function of the council was to serve as an intermediary between the workers and the factory administration.

Council of People's Commissars (Sovnarkom). The Sovnarkom, a new ministerial cabinet formed after the Bolsheviks took power, was ratified by the Second Congress of Soviets on 26 October. The council was to stay in power only until the Constituent Assembly established a new government. The members were initially all Bolsheviks, though seven members of the Left Socialist Revolutionary Party agreed to enter the government in early December.

Duma, State. The Duma, a national representative assembly established in 1906, was, though limited in its authority, empowered to initiate and approve legislation. Day-to-day political power remained in the hands of the ministers, whom the tsar appointed and who were not responsible to the Duma. The tsar could veto legislation, as could the State Council, half of whose members were appointed by the tsar. Much of the budget (especially for the military and foreign policy) was not under the control of the Duma. In 1907, the voting law was changed to reduce representation of the peasantry, urban workers, and national minorities and to increase that of the gentry. The Duma was prorogued by Nicholas II on 26 February 1917, though not dissolved. On 27 February 1917, a private meeting of leaders from the Duma established a provisional committee "to restore order and to deal with institutions and individuals." On 1 March, the provisional committee reached an agreement with the Petrograd Soviet to allow the formation of the Provisional Government. In midsummer, moves were under way to revive the Duma's political role. On 18 July, in the Tauride Palace, a meeting of members of the fourth State Duma was organized by members of the Provisional Committee of the State Duma to discuss how the Duma might "save Russia."

Kadet party. *See* Constitutional Democratic party.

Kulak. Literally, "fist." A wealthy peasant who was seen as exploiting others.

Mensheviks. *See* Russian Social Democratic Workers' Party.

Peasant commune (*obshchina* or *mir*). A long-standing institution of peasant self-administration. Run by the heads of all peasant households in a village or in combined villages, it collected taxes, decided who would go to the army, gave permission to those wishing to leave for the city, enforced community norms (defining and punishing violations of traditional rules of conduct, including in personal life), and, most important, regulating peasants' relations to the land. Although Russian peasants worked the land not collectively, but as family households, in many communes the land—which was held and worked by individual families as strips within the various communal fields—was periodically redistributed to ensure equity among households. No less important, the commune decided how land was to be used: what was to be planted, when, and according to which methods. Already by the nineteenth century, economists had begun to blame the commune (along with strip farming) for low productivity in Russia. Politically, the commune was blamed by many government officials for rural unrest. In 1906, Prime Minister Pyotr Stolypin passed legislation allowing peasants to withdraw from the communes, though the process had advanced only slightly by 1917. On the political left, populists considered the commune the foundation for a natural peasant socialism.

Prigovor. The term was used by the assemblies of peasant communes to designate a formal resolution. Used also by the courts, it implied a legal decision.

Russian Social Democratic Workers' Party. A Marxist party established in 1898, the RSDRP (its Russian abbreviation) split in 1903, at the second party congress, into two factions: the Bolsheviks, led by Lenin, and the Mensheviks, led by Martov. The two had fundamental differences, which deepened over the years, concerning the form of the party as an organization (the Bolsheviks favored a disciplined party admitting only the most conscious activists; the Mensheviks preferred a more open and democratic organization) and over the possibilities of socialism in Russia (while the Mensheviks worried about the country's backwardness, the Bolsheviks focused on the opportunities created by uneven world development and the possibility of alternate paths to socialism, aside from the traditional Marxist notion of its emergence from developed capitalism).

Socialist Revolutionary Party. The S.R.'s were established in 1902 as the main proponent of non-Marxist socialism in Russia, often called "populism." Like earlier populists, the S.R.'s viewed the whole of the common people as the constituency for socialism, unlike the Marxists, who believed the urban proletariat to be the class that would usher in socialism. A diverse and often divided party, the S.R.'s embraced a range of positions from antiwar to pro-war, and from moderate gradualism to radical terrorism. A split in the party, first over support for the Provisional Government in the fall of 1917 and then over acceptance of the Bolshevik revolution, resulted in the formation of a Left S.R. party in November.

Soviets. Councils of deputies elected by workers and soldiers, and later by some peasants, soviets also included representatives of leftist parties, trade unions, and other organizations. They ranged in scale from neighborhood soviets to citywide councils such as the Moscow soviet. The initiative and leadership were generally in the hands of members of the socialist parties—Mensheviks, Socialist Revolutionaries, Bolsheviks—mainly intellectuals. First established during the 1905 revolution, the soviets arose again in Petrograd in February 1917, and subsequently in most Russian cities. The Petrograd Soviet, which shared the Tauride Palace with the Provisional Government, and especially its Executive Committee, functioned as a national socialist and labor political center for the Left until the First All-Russian Congress of Soviets, in early June 1917, established the All-Russian Central Executive Committee of Soviets (VTsIK). After October 1917, the Congress of Soviets, and the VTsIK between sessions, were formally the supreme organ of state power. *See also* Congresses of Workers' and Soldiers' Deputies.

Sovnarkom. *See* Council of People's Commissars.

State Council (*Gosudarstvennyi sovet*). Until 1906, the council was an appointed advisory body composed of Russia's oldest aristocratic families. Starting in 1906, the upper house, together with the Duma, participated in the new bicameral constitutional system. Half the council members were elected by major corporative groups in Russian society—provincial rural assemblies (zemstvos), the nobility, merchants and industrialists, the clergy, the Academy of Sciences and the universities, and the Finnish Diet.

State Duma. *See* Duma.

Uezd (county). An administrative district combining a number of volosts and attached to a city. Several uezds combined to form a province.

Village assembly (*skhod*). Heads of households that governed the village community or commune gathered at the skhod. *See* peasant commune.

Volost. The volost was an administrative and judicial unit combining several villages, established after the emancipation of serfs in 1861.

NEWSPAPERS AND JOURNALS MENTIONED IN DOCUMENTS

Birzhevye vedomosti (Stock exchange gazette). Daily liberal newspaper, published in St. Petersburg from 1880 to 1917. From 1902 on, the paper had a morning and an evening edition. The morning edition contained mainly business information; the evening edition featured stories of everyday life, directed at middle-class readers. In 1917, the editorial position of the paper ranged from moderate liberal to moderate socialist and was strongly anti-Bolshevik.

Delo naroda (The people's cause). The main daily political and literary newspaper of the Socialist Revolutionary Party, published in Petrograd from March 1917 to January 1918.

Den' (Day). Left-liberal daily newspaper, published in St. Petersburg from 1912 to 1917. Supported the Provisional Government. Closed October 1917.

Gazeta-kopeika (Kopek gazette). Popular daily newspaper, published in St. Petersburg from 1908 to 1918, the most famous "boulevard" paper of the time, with extensive coverage of entertainment, crime, accidents, scandals, and social issues.

Izvestiia Soveta rabochikh i soldatskikh deputatov (News of the Soviet of Workers' and Soldiers' Deputies). Official newspaper of the Petrograd Soviet and later of the All-Russian Executive Committee.

Malen'kaia gazeta (Little newspaper). Daily newspaper, published in St. Petersburg from 1914 to 1917 from the perspective of the moderate Left. Self-described as a "free socialist" newspaper that preferred to remain outside party control but identified itself as "most sympathetic" to the Socialist Revolutionary Party. Closed in July 1917.

Novaia zhizn' (New life). Independent social-democratic political and cultural newspaper, published in Petrograd, starting in April 1917. The writer Maxim Gorky was the founder and primary editor. Closed in July 1918.

Novoe vremia (New time). Major daily political and literary newspaper, published in St. Petersburg from 1868 to 1917, and edited by Aleksei Suvorin until his death in 1912. The newspaper had a reputation on the Russian Left as "reactionary." In 1917, *Novoe vremia* supported the Provisional Government. Closed in October 1917.

Petrogradskaia gazeta (Petrograd newspaper). Daily political and literary newspaper, published in St. Petersburg from 1867 to 1917. Supported the Provisional Government. Closed in October 1917.

Petrogradskie vedomosti (Petrograd gazette). Daily newspaper, published (originally as *Sankt-Peterburgskie vedomosti*) in St. Petersburg from 1728 to 1917.

Petrogradskii listok (Petrograd sheet). Daily newspaper about city life, published in St. Petersburg from 1864 to 1917 and considered Russia's first boulevard paper. In 1917 it supported the Provisional Government. Closed in October 1917.

Pravda (Truth). Newspaper of the Bolshevik party, first published in St. Petersburg between 1912 and 1914, revived on 5 March 1917. Replaced in July by *Rabochii i soldat*.

Pravitel'stvennyi vestnik (Government herald). Daily newspaper, published in St. Petersburg by the Ministry of the Interior between 1869 and 1917. In February 1917 the paper was renamed *Vestnik Vremennogo pravitel'stva*. Closed in October 1917.

Rabochaia gazeta (Workers' newspaper). Newspaper of the Menshevik party, published in Petrograd from March to November 1917.

Rabochii i soldat (Worker and soldier). Daily newspaper of the Bolshevik party in Petrograd from July to August 1917. It succeeded *Pravda*, which was closed by the government when Bolsheviks were blamed for the July Days.

Rabotnitsa (Woman worker). Weekly journal published in Petrograd by the Central Committee of the Russian Social Democratic Workers' Party. First published in 1914. Revived in May 1917.

Rech' (Speech). Daily newspaper of the Constitutional Democratic (Kadet) party, published in St. Petersburg from 1906 to 1918. Edited by P. N. Miliukov and I. V. Gessen. Closed in October 1917.

Russkaia volia (Russian will). Daily newspaper, published in Petrograd from December 1916 to October 1917. As a way of winning public opinion over to the side of autocracy, its founder, tsarist minister of the interior Aleksandr Protopopov, hired respected liberals who opposed the autocracy but supported the war to write for the paper.

Russkoe slovo (Russian word). With a circulation of more than one million in 1917, the most important daily newspaper in Moscow, with extensive coverage of national and international news. Broadly liberal in its political orientation, *Russkoe slovo* supported the Provisional Government. Closed on 27 November 1917.

Sovremennoe slovo (Modern word). Daily political, economic, and literary newspaper, calling itself a non-party democratic paper, published in St. Petersburg from 1907 to 1918.

Vechernee vremia (Evening time). Daily newspaper, published in St. Petersburg from 1911 to 1917 by the A. S. Suvorin Company. Considered a "boulevard" paper. Closed in October 1917.

Vestnik Vremennogo pravitel'stva (Provisional Government herald). *See Pravitel'stvennyi vestnik*.

Yedinstvo (Unity). Daily social-democratic newspaper, published in St. Petersburg from March to November 1917 by a small group of right-wing Mensheviks associated with Georgy Plekhanov.

Zemlia i volia (Land and liberty). Daily newspaper of the Socialist Revolutionary Party, published in Petrograd from March to October 1917.

Zhivoe slovo (Living word). Daily newspaper published in St. Petersburg from 1916 to 1917. Closed in October 1917.

Notes

INTRODUCTION

1. John Reed, *Ten Days That Shook the World* (Harmondsworth, England, 1977; orig. pub. 1919), 40.

2. *Russkie vedomosti*, 19 September (2 October) 1917, p. 3; quoted in part in Steve Smith, "Writing the History of the Russian Revolution After the Fall of Communism," *Europe-Asia Studies* 46, no. 4 (1994): 575.

3. I use the term "lower-class," as contemporary Russians did, in the deliberately vague, relative, and subjective sense, to mean people who were not elite or privileged, but who considered themselves disadvantaged and subordinate.

4. Ronald Grigor Suny, "Revision and Retreat in the Historiography of 1917: Social History and Its Critics," *Russian Review* 53, no. 2 (April 1994): 167.

5. For useful discussions of the historiography of the revolution since the 1970s, see Ronald Grigor Suny, "Toward a Social History of the October Revolution," *American Historical* Review 88, no. 1 (February 1983): 31–52; Suny, "Revision and Retreat"; Smith, "Writing the History," 563–578; Edward Acton, "The Revolution and Its Historians," in *Critical Companion to the Russian Revolution*, ed. Edward Acton, Vladimir Cherniaev, and William Rosenberg (Bloomington, Ind., 1997), 3–17.

6. Although already outdated, a relatively recent bibliography of cultural studies on prerevolutionary Russian history can be found in Stephen P. Frank and Mark D. Steinberg, eds., *Cultures in Flux: Lower-Class Values, Practices, and Resistance in Late Imperial Russia* (Princeton, N.J., 1994). A useful collection on the early Soviet period that partly marks, at least within labor history, this shift toward cultural history, is Lewis H. Siegelbaum and Ronald Grigor Suny, eds., *Making Workers Soviet: Power, Class, and Identity* (Ithaca, N.Y., 1994).

7. A. M. Selishchev, *Iazyk revoliutsionnoi epokhi* (Moscow, 1928).

8. Marc Ferro, *The Russian Revolution of February 1917* (London, 1972); Ferro, *October 1917* (London, 1980); Ronald Suny, *The Baku Commune, 1917–1918: Class and Nationality in the Russian Revolution* (Princeton, N.J., 1972); Al-

Ian K. Wildman, *The End of the Russian Imperial Army*, 2 vols. (Princeton, N.J., 1980, 1987); Tsuyoshi Hasegawa, *The February Revolution: Petrograd, 1917* (Seattle, 1981); Diane Koenker, *Moscow Workers and the 1917 Revolution* (Princeton, N.J., 1981); S. A. Smith, *Red Petrograd* (Cambridge, England, 1983); David Mandel, *The Petrograd Workers and the Fall of the Old Regime* (London, 1983); Mandel, *The Petrograd Workers and the Soviet Seizure of Power* (London, 1984); Tim McDaniel, *Autocracy, Capitalism, and Revolution in Russia* (Berkeley, Calif., 1988); Donald Raleigh, *Revolution on the Volga* (Ithaca, N.Y., 1986); Diane P. Koenker and William G. Rosenberg, *Strikes and Revolution in Russia, 1917* (Princeton, N.J. 1989). See also the articles by Marc Ferro, Leopold Haimson, Tsuyoshi Hasegawa, and William Rosenberg and the books by Oscar Anweiler, Graeme Gill, Evan Mawdsley, Norman Saul, and Rex Wade listed in the bibliography.

    9. Suny, "Revision and Retreat," 180.

   10. Smith, "Writing the History," 566.

   11. Smith, "Writing the History," 568. See also comments by conference participants in V. Iu. Cherniaev et al., eds., *Anatomiia Revoliutsii* (St. Petersburg, 1994), 176–275, 356–419, 435.

   12. Richard Stites, *Revolutionary Dreams: Utopian Vision and Experimental Life in the Russian Revolution* (New York, 1989); Orlando Figes, *A People's Tragedy: The Russian Revolution, 1891–1924* (Harmondsworth, England 1996), 346–347; Christopher Read, *From Tsar to Soviets: The Russian People and Their Revolution, 1917–1921* (New York, 1996). The most important recent works are Orlando Figes, "The Russian Revolution of 1917 and Its Language in the Village," *Russian Review* 56, no. 3 (July 1997): 323–345; Boris Kolonitskii, "'Democracy' in the Political Consciousness of the February Revolution," *Slavic Review* 57, no. 1 (Spring 1998): 95–106; and several articles in Cherniaev et al., eds., *Anatomiia Revoliutsii*, notably T. A. Abrosimova, "Sotsialisticheskaia ideia v massovom soznanii 1917 g.," 176–187; B. I. Kolonitskii, "Antiburzhuaznaia propaganda i 'antiburzhuaznoe' soznanie," 188–202 (a translation appeared in *Russian Review* in April 1994); Daiana (Diane) Koenker, "Rabochii klass v 1917 g.: sotsial'naia i politicheskaia samoidentifikatsiia," 203–216; Orlando Faidzhes (Figes), "Krestianskaia massy i ikh uchastie v politicheskikh protsessakh 1917–1918 gg.," 230–237; P. K. Kornakov, "Simvolika i ritualy revoliutsii 1917 g.," 356–365; and Orlando Figes and Boris Kolonitskii, *Interpreting the Russian Revolution: The Language and Symbols of 1917* (New Haven, Conn., 1999). The last item combines much of the previous work by the authors on these themes.

   13. See Ekaterina Betekhtina, "Style in Lower-Class Writing in 1917," which appears as the afterword to this volume. My own discussion of style has benefited greatly from her linguistic knowledge and insights.

   14. GARF, f. 6978, op. 1, d. 269, ll. 9–10.

   15. We see this use of models, for example, in large numbers of the resolutions and instructions to deputies sent throughout 1917 to the Petrograd Soviet newspaper *Izvestiia*, in June to the First Congress of Soviets, and in December to deputies to the Constituent Assembly. These can be found in huge numbers in GARF, f. 1244 (*Izvestiia*), f. 1781 (Constituent Assembly), and f. 6978 (First All-Russian Executive Committee of Soviets). See also Koenker, *Moscow Workers*, 231.

16. Betekhtina, "Style in Lower-Class Writing in 1917," Selishchev, *Iazyk revoliutsionnoi epokhi*, passim.

17. A. Selishchev, in his contemporary study of the language of the revolutionary epoch in Russia, distinguished between the "communicative" and the "emotional-expressive" functions of speech and language and noted the "enormous significance" in revolutionary times of emotional-expressive functions. Selishchev, *Iazyk revoliutsionnoi epokhi*, 121. Nikolai Sukhanov, writing about the revolution a few years later, emphasized how "incoherent" but emotionally passionate were speeches given by the great numbers of plebeians who spoke at sessions of the Petrograd Soviet. N. N. Sukhanov, *The Russian Revolution: A Personal Record* (Princeton, N.J., 1984), 236.

18. For example, GARF, f. 1244, op. 2, d. 5, ll. 41–43ob. See also Figes, *A People's Tragedy*, 346–347.

19. Throughout this introduction, references to documents in the collection are meant to be illustrative rather than comprehensive.

20. Similar statements can be found, for example, in GARF, f. 1244, op. 2, d. 10, ll. 247, 282, 310–312.

21. For example, GARF, f. 1244, op. 2, d. 35, l. 215. Many such complaints appeared in the offices of the militia—the new revolutionary police. See, for example, GARF, f. 1791, op. 2, dd. 156–157.

22. The emphasis, for example, in a report by a local soviet on a peasant woman who was prepared to donate to the government her house, fields, and crops to help the fight to defend freedom. *Izvestiia*, no. 107 (2 July 1917): 11.

23. Nikolai Sukhanov, in his contemporary *Notes on the Revolution*, described this tendency of "the peasants in their army greatcoats" to "let the bourgeoisie lead them by the nose" and to believe "all sorts of chauvinist nonsense" (Sukhanov, 202).

24. Instruction to a delegate to the Second Congress of Soviets, October 1917, GARF, f. 1235, op. 1, d. 16, ll. 41–41ob.

25. Kolonitskii, "Democracy," 103–106; Figes, "Russian Revolution and Language in the Village," 331–334; A. G. Golikov, "Fenomen Kerenskogo," *Otechestvennaia istoriia*, no. 5 (September 1992): 60–73; B. I. Kolonitskii, "Kul't A. F. Kerenskogo: Obrazy revoliutsionnoi vlasti," *The Soviet and Post-Soviet Review*, nos. 1–2 (1997): 43–65; Figes and Kolonitskii, *Interpreting*, 71–103.

26. Kolonitskii, "Democracy," 105; Figes, "Russian Revolution and Language in the Village," 331–335.

27. In addition to evidence in these texts, see also Figes, "Russian Revolution and Language in the Village," 339–344.

28. See also instructions to delegates to Second Congress of Soviets, October 1917, such as GARF, f. 1235, op. 1, d. 15, l. 24; and such letters to the Provisional Government and to the Soviet as GARF, f. 6978, op. 1, d. 264, l. 21; and f. 1778, op. 1, d. 366, l. 138.

29. See also GARF, f. 6978, op. 1, d. 244, ll. 12–13; d. 247, ll. 118–1180b; f. 1235, op. 1. d. 15, l. 24; d. 10, l. 96; op. 2, d. 14, l. 128; f. 1778, op. 1, d. 364, l. 268; f. 1244, op. 2, d. 13, ll. 75–76.

30. See the excellent discussion in Kolonitskii, "Antiburzhuaznaia propaganda," esp. 195–197.

31. Letter from a worker to the Provisional Government, July 1917, GARF, f.

1778, op. 1, d. 366, l. 138; letter from a peasant to the Soviet Executive Committee, March 1917, GARF, f. 6978, op. 1, d. 297, ll. 74–77.

32. See also, for example, letters from peasants to the Soviet Executive Committee, March 1917, GARF, f. 6978, op. 1, d. 297, ll. 74–77, 178–1780b.

33. Resolution of the Mariupol Soviet, October 1917, in GARF, f. 1235, op. 1, d. 16, ll. 17–18.

34. Letter from peasants to Kerensky, GARF, f. 1778, op. 1, d. 364, l. 268.

35. See also Kolonitskii, "Democracy."

36. *Politicheskii slovar'* (Moscow, 1917), 14, quoted in Kolonitskii, "Democracy," 100.

37. "Iz ofitserskikh pisem s fronta v 1917 g.," *Krasnyi arkhiv* 50–51 (1932): 200.

38. *Izvestiia*, no. 132 (1 August 1917): 8–9 (resolution of soldiers).

39. See also Selishchev, *Iazyk revoliutsionnoi epokhi*, 21–155; and Betekhtina, "Style in Lower-Class Writing in 1917."

40. *The Shorter Oxford English Dictionary* (Oxford, 1973).

41. "*Vnutrennee nravstennoe dostoinstvo cheloveka, doblest', chestnost', blagorodstvo dushi i chistaia sovest'.*" Vladimir Dal', ed., *Tolkovyi slovar' zhivogo velikorusskogo iazyka* (St. Petersburg, 1882), 4: 599. The common translations of *doblest'* as valor and *chestnost'* as honesty also slightly obscure the Russian sense of inward moral qualities and consciousness and of the dignity that is inseparable from these. See also B. M. Volin and D. N. Ushakov, eds., *Tolkovyi slovar' russkogo iazyka* (Moscow, 1940).

42. V. F. Shishkin, *Tak skladyvalas' revolutsionnaia moral': Istoricheskii ocherk* (Moscow, 1967); Reginald E. Zelnik, "Russian Bebels," *Russian Review*, 35, no. 3 (July 1976): 265, 272–277; Victoria E. Bonnell, *Roots of Rebellion: Workers' Politics and Organizations in St. Petersburg and Moscow, 1900–1914* (Berkeley, Calif., 1983): 43–72, 90, 102, 170–171, 183–184, 191, 264, 449, 452; McDaniel, *Autocracy, Capitalism, and Revolution in Russia*, 161, 169–174, 194–195; Leopold H. Haimson, "The Problem of Social Identities in Early Twentieth Century Russia," *Slavic Review* (Spring 1988), esp. 2–8; Mark D. Steinberg, *Moral Communities: The Culture of Class Relations in the Russian Printing Industry, 1867–1907* (Berkeley, Calif., 1992), 235–236, 242–245.

43. I discuss these themes in the culture of Russian workers more fully in "The Injured and Insurgent Self: The Moral Imagination of Russia's Lower-Class Writers," *Workers and Intelligentsia in Late Imperial Russia*, ed. Reginald Zelnik (Berkeley, Calif., 1999): 309–329; Steinberg, "Worker-Authors and the Cult of the Person," in *Cultures in Flux: Lower-Class Values, Practices and Resistance in Late Imperial Russia*, ed. Stephen Frank and Mark Steinberg (Princeton, N.J., 1994).

44. See, for example, the appeals from the Soviet Executive Committee (reprinted in many papers) in *Izvestiia*, no. 59 (6 May 1917): 1; and no. 67 (16 May 1917): 2.

45. The daily press was filled with similar appeals. See, for example, *Izvestiia*, no. 41 (15 April 1917): 3 (letter from the front); no. 64 (12 May 1917): 7 (letter from a soldier); no. 76 (27 May 1917): 8 (letter from a soldier).

46. Wildman, *The End of the Russian Imperial Army*, 188.

47. Koenker and Rosenberg, *Strikes and Revolution*, 172–174, 231–232.

48. *Izvestiia*, no. 94 (17 June 1917): 9.

49. See Joan Neuberger, *Hooliganism: Crime, Culture, and Power in St. Petersburg, 1900–1914* (Berkeley, Calif., 1993).

50. In addition to documents in this collection, there are hundreds of such texts in the formerly classified collections of "anti-Bolshevik correspondence," esp. GARF, f. 1235, op. 140, dd. 8, 10.

51. Abrosimova, "Sotsialisticheskaia ideia," 176–177; Figes, "Russian Revolution and Language in the Village," 327–329, 332, 335, 344; Kolonitskii, "Antiburzhuaznaia propaganda," 199–200; Figes and Kolonitskii, *Interpreting*, 75, 84, 145–146, 150–151; Mark Steinberg, "Workers on the Cross: Religious Imagination in the Writings of Russian Workers, 1910–1924," *Russian Review* 53, no. 2 (April 1994), 213–239.

52. Kolonitskii, "Antiburzhuaznaia propaganda," 200.

53. E.g., Jeremiah 26:15; John 8:32, 16:13.

54. Vladimir Dal', *Tolkovyi slovar' zhivogo velikorusskogo iazyka* (St. Petersburg, 1881), 2:60, 3:379. Psalm 84:12 reads, "*Istina iz zemli vozsiia, i pravda s nebese prinich*" (*Istina* springs forth from the earth, and *pravda* comes down from heaven). In the King James version of the Bible, this psalm (numbered 85:11 rather than 84:12 as in the Russian Bible) offers "truth" as the translation of what the Russians call *istina*, and "righteousness" for what appears in Russian as *pravda*. In the Hebrew Bible, truth/istina is *emes*, and righteousness/pravda is *tsedek*. The Revised Standard and New International Bibles render *istina* as "faithfulness."

PART I: LIBERTY, DESIRE, AND FRUSTRATION

1. On economic and social change in late imperial Russia, see James Bater, *St. Petersburg: Industrialisation and Change* (Montreal, 1976); David Ransel, ed., *The Family in Imperial Russia* (Urbana, Ill., 1978); Roberta Manning, *The Crisis of the Old Order in Russia* (Princeton, N.J., 1982); Joseph Bradley, *Muzhik and Muscovite: Urbanization in Late Imperial Russia* (Berkeley, Calif., 1985); Daniel Brower, *The Russian City Between Tradition and Modernity, 1850–1900* (Berkeley, Calif., 1990); Michael F. Hamm, ed., *The City in Late-Imperial Russia* (Bloomington, Ind., 1986); Stephen Frank and Mark Steinberg, eds., *Cultures in Flux: Lower-Class Values, Practices, and Resistance in Late Imperial Russia* (Princeton, N.J., 1994); as well as works listed in the notes following on particular social groups.

2. On civil society, see especially Edith Clowes, Samuel Kassow, and James West, eds., *Between Tsar and People: Educated Society and the Quest for Public Identity in Late Imperial Russia* (Princeton, N.J., 1991). On the press, literacy, and reading, see Jeffrey Brooks, *When Russia Learned to Read: Literacy and Popular Literature, 1861–1917* (Princeton, N.J., 1985), and Louise McReynolds, *The News Under Russia's Old Regime* (Princeton, N.J., 1991).

3. Robert Edelman, *Gentry Politics on the Eve of the Russian Revolution* (New Brunswick, N.J., 1980); Hans Rogger, *Jewish Policies and Right-Wing Politics in Imperial Russia* (Berkeley, Calif., 1986); D. Rawson, *Russian Rightists and the Revolution of 1905* (Cambridge, England, 1995); R. Sh. Ganelin, ed., *Natsional'naia pravaia prezhde i teper'* (St. Petersburg, 1992), vol. 1.

4. Andrew Verner, *The Crisis of the Russian Autocracy: Nicholas II and the 1905 Revolution* (Princeton, N.J., 1990); Dominic Lieven, *Nicholas II: Emperor of All the Russias* (London, 1993); Mark Steinberg, "Nicholas and Alexandra: An Intellectual Portrait," introduction to Mark Steinberg and Vladimir Khrustalev, *The Fall of the Romanovs: Political Dreams and Personal Struggles in a Time of Revolution* (New Haven, Conn., 1995); Richard Wortman, *Scenarios of Power: Myth and Ceremony in Russian Monarchy*, vol. 2 (Princeton, N.J., 2000).

5. See especially R. V. Ivanov-Razumnik, *Istoriia russkoi obshchestvennoi mysli*, 2d ed. (St. Petersburg, 1914), vols. 1–2; Nicholas Riasanovsky, *A Parting of Ways: Government and the Educated Public in Russia* (Oxford, 1976); Isaiah Berlin, *Russian Thinkers* (New York, 1978); and Andrzej Walicki, *A History of Russian Thought* (Stanford, Calif., 1979).

6. Geoffrey Hosking, *The Russian Constitutional Experiment* (New York, 1973).

7. William G. Rosenberg, *Liberals in the Russian Revolution: The Constitutional Democratic Party, 1917–1921* (Princeton, N.J., 1974).

8. Among many works exploring aspects of the history of Russian socialism, see especially Leopold H. Haimson, *The Russian Marxists and the Origins of Bolshevism* (Cambridge, Mass., 1955); Oliver Radkey, *The Agrarian Foes of Bolshevism* (New York, 1958); Abraham Ascher, *Pavel Axelrod and the Development of Menshevism* (Cambridge, Mass., 1972); Robert C. Williams, *The Other Bolsheviks* (Bloomington, Ind., 1986); Michael Melancon, *The Socialist Revolutionaries and the Russian Anti-War Movement, 1914–1917* (Columbus, Ohio, 1990).

9. Richard Stites, *The Women's Liberation Movement in Russia* (Princeton, N.J., 1978); Linda Edmondson, *Feminism in Russia, 1900–1917* (London, 1984); Barbara Clements, *Daughters of the Revolution: A History of Women in the USSR* (Arlington Heights, Ill., 1994), 1–27.

10. Studies of Russia as an empire have proliferated in recent years. See especially Daniel Brower and Edward J. Lazzerini, eds., *Russia's Orient: Imperial Borderlands and Peoples* (Bloomington, Ind., 1997), and Jane Burbank and David Ransel, eds., *Imperial Russia: New Histories for the Empire* (Bloomington, Ind., 1998).

11. There are many individual accounts of national movements in Russia. A useful overview can be found in Edward Acton, Vladimir Cherniaev, and William G. Rosenberg, eds., *A Critical Companion to the Russian Revolution, 1914–1921* (Bloomington, Ind., 1997), 659–740. See also Ronald G. Suny, *The Revenge of the Past: Nationalism, Revolution, and the Collapse of the Soviet Union* (Stanford, Calif., 1993).

12. Useful overviews of the art and literature of the period can be found in Renato Poggioli, *The Poets of Russia, 1890–1930* (Cambridge, Mass., 1960); Camilla Gray, *The Russian Experiment in Art, 1863–1922* (New York, 1962); Evelyn Bristol, *A History of Russian Poetry* (New York, 1991); Victor Terras, *A History of Russian Literature* (New Haven, Conn., 1991), chap. 8; and Bruce Lincoln, *Between Heaven and Hell: The Story of a Thousand Years of Artistic Life in Russia* (New York, 1998), chaps. 13–14.

13. Frank and Steinberg, eds., *Cultures in Flux*; McReynolds, *The News Under Russia's Old Regime*; Laura Engelstein, *The Keys to Happiness: Sex and the Search for Modernity in Fin-de-Siècle Russia* (Ithaca, N.Y., 1992); Joan Neuberger, *Hooliganism: Crime, Culture, and Power in St. Petersburg, 1900–1914*

(Berkeley, Calif., 1993); Laurie Bernstein, *Sonia's Daughters: Prostitutes and Their Regulation in Imperial Russia* (Berkeley, Calif., 1995); Roshanna Sylvester, "Crime, Masquerade, and Anxiety: The Public Creation of Middle-Class Identity in Pre-Revolutionary Odessa, 1912–1916" (Ph.D. dissertation, Department of History, Yale University, 1998).

14. Christopher Read, *Religion, Revolution and the Russian Intelligentsia, 1900–1912* (Totowa, N.J., 1979); Bernice Glatzer Rosenthal, ed., *Nietzsche in Russia* (Princeton, N.J., 1986); Richard Stites, *Russian Popular Culture* (Cambridge, England, 1992), chap. 1; Maria Carlson, *"No Religion Higher than Truth": A History of the Theosophical Movement in Russia, 1875–1922* (Princeton, N.J., 1993); Bernice Glatzer Rosenthal, ed. *The Occult in Russian and Soviet Culture* (Ithaca, N.Y., 1997); Catherine Evtuhov, *The Cross and the Sickle: Sergei Bulgakov and the Fate of Russian Religious Philosophy, 1890–1920* (Ithaca, N.Y., 1997); Laura Engelstein, *Castration and the Heavenly Kingdom: A Russian Folktale* (Ithaca, N.Y., 1999); Christine Worobec, *Bedeviled Peasants: Possession, Witchcraft, and Hysteria in Imperial Russia* (De Kalb, Ill., forthcoming). In recent years, a number of very important doctoral dissertations, notably by Vera Shevzov, Heather Coleman, and Nicholas Breyfogle, have deepened our knowledge of this religious culture.

15. The scholarly literature on peasants is now extensive. Major recent works that examine the themes just discussed (and can serve as a guide to earlier scholarship) include Frank and Steinberg, eds., *Cultures in Flux*; Christine Worobec, *Peasant Russia: Family and Community in the Post-Emancipation Period* (Princeton, N.J., 1991); Barbara Alpern Engel, *Between the Fields and the City: Women, Work, and Family in Russia, 1861–1914* (Cambridge, England, 1994); Jeffrey Burds, *Peasant Dreams and Market Politics: Labor Migration and the Russian Village* (Pittsburgh, Pa., 1998); Stephen Frank, *Crime, Cultural Conflict, and Justice in Rural Russia, 1856–1914* (Berkeley, Calif., 1999).

16. Among the many scholarly works on Russian workers, see especially Reginald Zelnik, *Labor and Society in Tsarist Russia: The Factory Workers of St. Petersburg, 1855–1870* (Stanford, Calif., 1971); Victoria Bonnell, *Roots of Rebellion: Workers' Politics and Organizations in St. Petersburg and Moscow, 1900–1914* (Berkeley, Calif., 1983); and many of the works cited in the following note.

17. On labor protest, in addition to the previously cited works of Zelnik and Bonnell, see Laura Engelstein, *Moscow, 1905* (Stanford, Calif., 1982); Gerald Surh, *1905 in St. Petersburg* (Stanford, Calif., 1989); Mark Steinberg, *Moral Communities: The Culture of Class Relations in the Russian Printing Industry, 1867–1907* (Berkeley, Calif., 1992); Charters Wynn, *Workers, Strikes, and Pogroms* (Princeton, N.J., 1992); Robert Weinberg, *The Revolution of 1905 in Odessa* (Bloomington, Ind., 1993). On peasant protest, many of the works cited in note 15 are pertinent.

18. The narrative in this section draws on a variety of scholarly accounts of the war and of the February revolution. See especially Marc Ferro, *The Russian Revolution of February 1917* (Englewood Cliffs, N.J., 1972); Norman Stone, *The Eastern Front, 1914–1917* (London, 1975); Tsuyoshi Hasegawa, *The February Revolution: Petrograd, 1917* (Seattle, Wash., 1981); W. Bruce Lincoln, *Passage Through Armageddon: The Russians in War and Revolution, 1914–1918* (New York, 1986); Richard Pipes, *The Russian Revolution* (New York, 1990); Orlando

Figes, *A People's Tragedy: The Russian Revolution, 1891–1924* (Harmondsworth, England, 1996); Rex Wade, *The Russian Revolution, 1917* (Cambridge, England, 2000).

19. Allan Wildman, *The End of the Russian Imperial Army* (Princeton, N.J., 1980), 1:76–80; Lincoln, *Passage Through Armageddon*, 41–49; Hubertus Jahn, *Patriotic Culture in Russia During World War I* (Ithaca, N.Y., 1995); Figes, *A People's Tragedy*, 257–258; Joshua Sanborn, "Drafting the Nation: Military Conscription and the Formation of a Modern Polity in Tsarist and Soviet Russia, 1905–1925" (Ph.D. dissertation, Department of History, University of Chicago, 1998): 73–81; D. Os'kin, *Zapiski soldata* (Moscow, 1929), 35–36.

20. See, for example, the letter of General Brusilov to his wife on 10 August 1914, quoted in Figes, *A People's Tragedy*, 252.

21. Wildman, *The End of the Russian Imperial Army*, 1:85–89, 99–105, 106 (quotation).

22. Peter Gatrell, *A Whole Empire Walking: Refugees in Russia During World War I* (Bloomington, Ind., 1999).

23. Figes, *A People's Tragedy*, 300.

24. "Doklad petrogradskogo okhrannogo otdeleniia osobomu otdelu departamenta politsii," October 1916, *Krasnyi arkhiv* 17 (1926), 4–35 (quotation, p. 4).

25. "Delo s doneseniiami i telefonnymi soobshcheniiami P.O.O. ob obshchestvennom dvizhenii," 2 January–26 February 1917, GARF, f. 111, op. 1, d. 669, ll. 1–386.

26. Major General Globachev (head of the Petrograd Okhrana), "Dopolnenie k doneseniiu (sovershenno-sektretno)," 26 January 1917, GARF, f. 111, op. 1, d. 669, ll. 112–113.

27. Quoted in Hasegawa, *February Revolution*, 201.

28. Letter from Anatolii Savenko (a nationalist member of the Progressive Bloc), 18 February 1917, GARF, f. 102, op. 265, d. 1070, l. 62. Letters of many other Duma deputies in mid-February (read by the police who copied down passages before sending the letters on) similarly spoke of the growing war of words amid the deepening malaise and uncertainty (GARF, f. 102, op. 265, d. 1070, ll. 60, 66, 70).

29. Hasegawa, *February Revolution*, chap. 11; Diane Koenker, *Moscow Workers and the 1917 Revolution* (Princeton, N.J., 1981), 95–97.

30. N. N. Sukhanov, *The Russian Revolution, 1917: A Personal Memoir* (Princeton, N.J.,1984), 5.

31. Letter from Alexandra to Nicholas, 25 February 1917, in Steinberg and Khrustalev, *Fall of the Romanovs*, 73.

32. Quoted by Khabalov in his testimony of 22 March 1917, in *Padenie tsarskogo rezhima: Stenograficheskie otchety doprosov i pokazanii, dannykh v 1917 g. v Chrezvychainoi Sledstvennoi Komissii Vremennogo Pravitel'stva*, ed. P. E. Shchegolev, 7 vols. (Moscow, 1924–1927), 1:190–191.

33. See, for example, the memoir by the Bolshevik V. Kaiurov, "Shest' dnei fevral'skoi revoliutsii," *Proletar'skaia revoliutsiia* 13 (1923), 165–166.

34. Act of abdication of Nicholas II, 2 March 1917, in Steinberg and Khrustalev, *Fall of the Romanovs*, 100–102.

35. Act of abdication of Mikhail Romanov, 3 March 1917, ibid., 105.

36. Robert Paul Browder and Alexander F. Kerensky, eds., *The Russian Provisional Government, 1917: Documents*, 3 vols. (Stanford, Calif., 1961) 1:45–47.

37. *Izvestiia Petrogradskogo soveta rabochikh deputatov*, no. 1 (addendum), 28 February 1917.

38. "Zhurnal [No. 1] Soveta ministrov vremennogo pravitel'stva," 2 March 1917, GARF, f. 601, op. 1, d. 2103, l. 1.

39. *Izvestiia* (Komiteta Petrogradskikh zhurnalistov), 27 February 1917.

40. N. N. Sukhanov, *The Russian Revolution: A Personal Record*, ed. and trans. Joel Carmichael (Oxford, 1955; orig. pub. in Russian in 1922), 101–108.

41. "Zhurnal [No. 1] Soveta ministrov vremennogo pravitel'stva," 2 March 1917, GARF, f. 601, op. 1, d. 2103, l. 1.

42. *Times* (London), 17 March 1917.

43. Orlando Figes and Boris Kolonitskii, *Interpreting the Russian Revolution: The Language and Symbols of 1917* (New Haven, Conn., 1999), 34; Figes, *A People's Tragedy*, 318; Sukhanov, *Russian Revolution*, 8; Wildman, *The End of the Russian Imperial Army*, 1:223.

44. *Times* (London), 17 March 1917.

45. Hasegawa, *February Revolution*, 252–253.

46. See the many memoir sources cited in B. I. Kolonitskii, "Antiburzhuaznaia propaganda i 'antiburzhuaznoe' soznanie" (a translation appeared in *Russian Review* in April 1994), in *Anatomiia Revoliutsii*, eds. V. Iu. Cherniaev et al. (St. Petersburg, 1994), 199–200.

47. *Izvestiia vybornykh osoboi armii*, no. 5 (9 April 1917), quoted in Wildman, *The End of the Russian Imperial Army*, 1:224.

48. Diary of Tatiana Gippius, 26 March 1917, quoted in Figes and Kolonitskii, *Interpreting*, 42.

49. Dalekii Drug, "Sviataia Rus'," *Malenkaia gazeta*, no. 57 (5 March 1917): 2. See other examples and citations in Kolonitskii, "Antiburzhuaznaia propaganda," 200; Figes, *A People's Tragedy*, 351–353; Figes and Kolonitskii, *Interpreting*, 42–44, 51.

50. See James von Geldern, *Bolshevik Festivals, 1917–1920* (Berkeley, Calif., 1993), chap. 1; Lynn Hunt, *Politics, Culture, and Class in the French Revolution* (Berkeley, Calif., 1984); Mona Ozouf, *Festivals and the French Revolution* (Cambridge, Mass., 1988).

51. Figes and Kolonitskii, *Interpreting*, 43–46; Figes, *A People's Tragedy*, 347–348; Kornakov, "Simvolika i ritualy revoliutsii 1917 g.," in *Anatomiia Revoliutsii*, 356–365; Richard Stites, *Revolutionary Dreams: Utopian Vision and Experimental Life in the Russian Revolution* (New York, 1989), esp. 80–83.

52. For a discussion of the cultural and political significance of funerals in modern Russian and Soviet history, see Thomas Trice, "The 'Body Politic': Russian Funerals and the Politics of Representation, 1841–1921" (Ph.D. dissertation, Department of History, University of Illinois, 1998).

53. *Izvestiia soveta rabochikh i soldatskikh deputatov*, 22–24 March 1917; *Novoe vremia*, 25 March (7 April) 1917. See also Trice, "The 'Body Politic,'" 279–286; Figes and Kolonitskii, *Interpreting*, 46–48, 75.

54. T. I. Polner, *Zhiznennyi put' kniazia Georgiia Evgenievicha L'vova* (Paris,

1932), chap. 7; Rosenberg, *Liberals*, 64–66, 84–85, 89–91; William Rosenberg, "Social Mediation and State Construction(s) in Revolutionary Russia," *Social History* 19, no. 2 (1994): 169–188.

55. B. I. Kolonitskii, "Kul'ta A. F. Kerenskogo: Obrazy revoliutsionnoi vlasti," *The Soviet and Post-Soviet Review*, nos. 1–2 (1997): 43–65. See also A. G. Golikov, "Fenomen Kerenskogo," *Otechestvennaia istoriia*, no. 5 (1992); Figes and Kolonitskii, *Interpreting*, 76–89.

56. Figes and Kolonitskii, *Interpreting*, 81. For an appreciative biography of Kerensky, see Richard Abraham, *Alexander Kerensky: The First Love of the Revolution* (New York, 1987).

57. Browder and Kerensky, eds., *The Russian Provisional Government*, vols. 1–2, passim.

58. See, for example, the first public declaration of the Provisional Government (on 6 March) and Prime Minister G. E. L'vov's interview with the press on 7 March, in Browder and Kerensky, eds., *The Russian Provisional Government*, 1:157–160; *Novoe vremia*, 8 (21) March 1917.

59. Polner, *Zhiznennyi put' kniazia G. E. L'vova*, 243–245.

60. Pitirim Sorokin, *Leaves from a Russian Diary* (New York, 1924): 14, 16; Figes, *A People's Tragedy*, 322.

61. Maxim Gorky, quoted in Sukhanov, *Russian Revolution*, 95.

62. Such incidents are described in numerous memoirs of 1917. For a summary drawing on these accounts, see Figes, *A People's Tragedy*, 315–321.

63. *Izvestiia Petrogradskogo soveta rabochikh deputatov*, no. 1 (28 February 1917): 2.

64. Sukhanov, describing views of Maxim Gorky and others, in his *Russian Revolution*, 96.

65. Sukhanov, *Russian Revolution*, 96.

66. Ziva Galili, *The Menshevik Leaders in the Russian Revolution* (Princeton, N.J., 1989), 96.

67. Diane P. Koenker and William G. Rosenberg, *Strikes and Revolution in Russia, 1917* (Princeton, N.J., 1989), chaps. 3–4; Rosenberg, "Social Mediation," 178–186; Galili, *Menshevik Leaders*, chap. 3 (quotation, p. 108); S. A. Smith, *Red Petrograd: Revolution in the Factories, 1917–1918* (Cambridge, England, 1983); chap. 3; Heather Hogan, "Conciliation Boards in Revolutionary Petrograd," *Russian History* 9, no. 1 (1982): 49–66.

68. Documents 7, 8, 9, 11.

69. Koenker and Rosenberg, *Strikes and Revolution*, chaps. 5–6; Smith, *Red Petrograd*, chaps. 4–5; Ferro, *The Russian Revolution of February 1917*, chap. 4; David Mandel, *The Petrograd Workers and the Fall of the Old Regime* (London, 1983); Tim McDaniel, *Autocracy, Capitalism, and Revolution in Russia* (Berkeley, Calif., 1988), 305–312.

70. Wildman, *The End of the Russian Imperial Army*, 1:31–36.

71. Wildman, *The End of the Russian Imperial Army*, 1:234–235, 362–370.

72. Quoted in Figes, *A People's Tragedy*, 380. See also Wildman, *The End of the Russian Imperial Army*, 1:235, 362.

73. Wildman, *The End of the Russian Imperial Army*, 1:192–196, 199, 211, 224–228; Figes and Kolonitskii, *Interpreting*, 32–33, 52–54.

74. Wildman, *The End of the Russian Imperial Army*, 1:182–188, 228–229. A full translated text of Order No. 1 appears on pages 187–188.

75. Ibid., 233.

76. Wildman, *The End of the Russian Imperial Army*, 1:332–372.

77. Document 30.

78. Wildman, *The End of the Russian Imperial Army*, 1:346.

79. Graham Gill, *Peasants and Government in the Russian Revolution* (London, 1979), 189.

80. See Browder and Kerensky, eds., *The Russian Provisional Government*, 2:582–588; Gill, *Peasants and Government*, 28–46, 189, 191; Dorothy Atkinson, *The End of the Russian Land Commune, 1905–1930* (Stanford, Calif., 1983), 149–164; Donald Raleigh, *Revolution on the Volga: 1917 in Saratov* (Ithaca, N.Y., 1986); 183–186; Orlando Figes, *Peasant Russia, Civil War: The Volga Countryside in Revolution* (Oxford, 1989), 32–46; Maureen Perrie, "The Peasants," in *Society and Politics in the Russian Revolution*, ed., Robert Service (New York, 1992), 12–23.

81. Stites, *Women's Liberation Movement*, 289–306; Edmondson, *Feminism in Russia*, 164–169; Clements, *Daughters of the Revolution*, 27–37.

82. Acton, Cherniaev, and Rosenberg, eds., *A Critical Companion to the Russian Revolution*, 659–740.

83. "Iz ofitserskikh pisem s fronta v 1917 g.," *Krasnyi arkhiv* 50–51 (1932): 200.

84. See discussion in the introduction.

85. Koenker, *Moscow Workers and the 1917 Revolution*, 233–247.

86. The text was published on the 28th and 29th in all major newspapers.

87. The text of the note, from its publication in *Rech'* on 20 April 1917, and various documents surrounding the history of the note appear in Browder and Kerensky, eds., *The Russian Provisional Government* 2:1096–1101.

88. *Izvestiia*, no. 47 (22 April 1917): 3; *Novoe vremia*, 22 April 1917.

89. V. N. Chernov, the leader of the S.R. party, became minister of agriculture; M. I. Skobolev, a Menshevik, was named labor minister; Aleksandr Kerensky, an S.R., and already in the cabinet, became war minister; P. N. Pereverzev, a Trudovik, became justice minister; I. G. Tsereteli, a Menshevik, was named minister of post and telegraphs; and A. V. Peshekhonov, founder and leader of the Popular Socialist party, was put in charge of food supply.

90. Alexander Rabinowitch, *Prelude to Revolution: The Petrograd Bolsheviks and the July 1917 Uprising* (Bloomington, Ind., 1968), 41–42, 44–47; Rabinowitch, *The Bolsheviks Come to Power* (New York, 1976), xxiv–xxv, xxix.

91. Sukhanov, *The Russian Revolution*, 372–373; Press reports cited in Browder and Kerensky, eds., *The Russian Provisional Government,* 3:1299; Wildman, *The End of the Russian Imperial Army*, vol. 2, chap. 2.

92. *Russkiia vedomosti*, no. 128 (8 June 1917): 1.

93. Sukhanov, *Russian Revolution*, 386–388; Rabinowitch, *Prelude*, 64–66.

94. For various interpretations of the Bolshevik plan, see Sukhanov, *The Russian Revolution*, 389–406; Pipes, *The Russian Revolution*, 414–417; Rabinowitch, *Prelude*, chap. 3.

95. Browder and Kerensky, eds., *The Russian Provisional Government,* 3:1312–1313.

96. *Izvestiia,* no. 88 (10 June 1917): 10.

97. *Izvestiia,* no. 92 (15 June 1917): 2.

98. Sukhanov, *The Russian Revolution,* 418.

99. *Izvestiia,* no. 96 (20 June 1917): 2–3; Sukhanov, *The Russian Revolution,* 415–418.

100. *Izvestiia,* no. 96 (20 June 1917): 1–2; *Vestnik vremennogo pravitel'stva,* no. 84 (20 June 1917): 1.

101. Documents 12, 13, 35, 48.

102. These views were stated publicly in his regular column, "Untimely Thoughts," in the newspaper *Novaia zhizn'* (New life), and privately and more forcefully, in his letters to his wife. See Maxim Gorky, *Untimely Thoughts: Essays on Revolution, Culture, and the Bolsheviks, 1917–1918* (New Haven, Conn., 1995). Some of his letters are quoted, often from their archival originals, in Figes, *A People's Tragedy,* 398–405.

103. *Rech',* no. 127 (30 May 1917): 7.

PART 2: CRISIS AND UPHEAVAL

1. Allan Wildman, *The End of the Russian Imperial Army* (Princeton, N.J., 1987), 2:95–111; summary reports from staff headquarters, 10–25 June, in *Revoliutsionnoe dvizhenie v Rossii v mae-iiune 1917 g.* (Moscow, 1959): 366–368, 377–381.

2. The incident is the subject of a protest described in Document 70.

3. *Revoliutsionnoe dvizhenie v Rossii v mae-iiune 1917 g.,* 373.

4. For accounts of the July Days on which the following discussion is partly based, see Alexander Rabinowitch, *Prelude to Revolution: The Petrograd Bolsheviks and the July 1917 Uprising* (Bloomington, Ind., 1968), chaps. 5–6; Rabinowitch, *The Bolsheviks Come to Power* (New York, 1976), chap. 1; Richard Pipes, *The Russian Revolution* (New York, 1990), 419–431; and Orlando Figes, *A People's Tragedy: The Russian Revolution, 1891–1924* (Harmondsworth, England, 1996), 423–432. Some useful contemporary sources can be found in Robert Paul Browder and Alexander F. Kerensky, eds., *The Russian Provisional Government, 1917: Documents,* 3 vols. (Stanford, Calif., 1961), 3:1335–1364. The best-known memoir is N. N. Sukhanov, *The Russian Revolution: A Personal Record,* ed. and trans. Joel Carmichael (Oxford, 1955; orig. pub. in Russian in 1922), chap. 20.

5. *Rech',* no. 155 (5 July 1917): 2.

6. Quoted in Figes, *A People's Tragedy,* 421.

7. A. Metelev, "Iiul'skoe vosstanie v Petrograde," *Proletarskaia revoliutsiia,* no. 6 (1922): 161, quoted in Rabinowitch, *Prelude to Revolution,* 160.

8. From a letter to his wife, quoted in Figes, *A People's Tragedy,* 429. See also Gorky's column "Untimely Thoughts" for 14 July 1917, in his newspaper *Novaia zhizn',* in Maxim Gorky, *Untimely Thoughts* (New Haven, Conn., 1995), 72–75.

9. Sukhanov, *Russian Revolution,* 431.

10. Pavel Miliukov, *Istoriia vtoroi russkoi revoliutsii* (Sofia, 1921), 1:243–244; Rabinowitch, *Prelude to Revolution,* 188; Pipes, *Russian Revolution,* 428–429.

11. The Petrograd soviet, after the formation of the All-Russian Soviet in June, was a local rather than a national body, though it still had exceptional influence, owing to its location in the capital.

12. *Izvestiia*, no. 108 (4 July 1917): 5.

13. *Izvestiia*, no. 108 (4 July 1917): 3–4; no. 110 (6 July 1917): 2–6.

14. Quoted in Rabinowitch, *Prelude to Revolution*, 175.

15. See especially Rabinowitch, *Prelude to Revolution*, chaps. 5–6; and Pipes, *Russian Revolution*, 419–431. Both authors acknowledge a combination of leadership and vacillation in the Bolshevik role, but Pipes insists on the evidence of a conspiracy, and Rabinowitch argues that the process was less deliberate.

16. Gorky, "Untimely Thoughts," *Novaia zhizn'*, 29 June 1917, in *Untimely Thoughts*, 67.

17. *Russkiia vedomosti*, no. 155 (9 July 1917): 4; Browder and Kerensky eds., *The Russian Provisional Government*, 3:1388.

18. *Russkoe slovo*, no. 157 (12 July 1917): 3.

19. T. I. Polner, *Zhiznennyi put' kniazia Georgiia Evgenievicha L'vova* (Paris, 1932), 258.

20. *Vestnik vremennogo pravitel'stva*, no. 100 (8 July 1917): 1, trans. in Browder and Kerensky, eds., *The Russian Provisional Government*, 3:1386–1387.

21. Browder and Kerensky, eds., *The Russian Provisional Government*, 3:1357–1358.

22. Browder and Kerensky, eds., *The Russian Provisional Government*, 2:977–988; 3:1336–1338, 1357–1364.

23. These demands were leaked to the press on 21 July. *Russkoe slovo*, no. 165 (21 July 1917): 2.

24. *Izvestiia*, no. 119 (16 July 1917): 5. See also Rabinowitch, *The Bolsheviks Come to Power*, 39–42.

25. Rabinowitch, *The Bolsheviks Come to Power*, 43.

26. For example, Document 71.

27. *Rech'*, no. 167 (19 July 1917): 3–4; *Izvestiia*, no. 121 (19 July 1917): 3–4; no. 122 (20 July 1917): 3.

28. Diane P. Koenker and William G. Rosenberg, *Strikes and Revolution in Russia, 1917* (Princeton, N.J., 1989), 240–245.

29. Browder and Kerensky, eds., *The Russian Provisional Government*, 3:1340–1341.

30. The official call appeared in the *Vestnik vremennogo pravitel'stva*, no. 103 (13 July 1917): 2. Quoted from Browder and Kerensky, eds., *The Russian Provisional Government*, 3:1450.

31. *Rech'*, no. 188 (12 August 1917): 1.

32. *Novaia zhizn'*, no. 96 (9 August 1917): 3; *Russkoe slovo*, no. 181 (9 August 1917): 3; no. 182 (10 August 1917): 2; William Rosenberg, *Liberals in the Russian Revolution* (Princeton, N.J., 1974), 210–212.

33. *Izvestiia*, no. 133 (2 August 1917): 1–2; no. 141 (11 August 1917): 4; Browder and Kerensky, eds., *The Russian Provisional Government*, 3:1451–1456; *Revoliutsionnoe dvizhenie v Rossii v avguste 1917 g.* (Moscow, 1959), 393–394.

34. Koenker and Rosenberg, *Strikes and Revolution*, 260–261.

35. *Izvestiia*, no. 143 (13 August 1917): 2.

36. *Russkoe slovo*, no. 186 (15 August 1917): 1–4; no. 187 (17 August 1917): 5–6; Browder and Kerensky, eds., *The Russian Provisional Government*, 3:1478–1515.

37. *Russkoe slovo*, no. 185 (13 August 1917): 1–2; Browder and Kerensky, eds., *The Russian Provisional Government*, 3:1457–1462.

38. *Russkoe slovo*, no. 186 (15 August 1917): 2–4; Browder and Kerensky, eds., *The Russian Provisional Government*, 3:1474–1478; Rabinowitch, *The Bolsheviks Come to Power*, 113–115; Orlando Figes and Boris Kolonitskii, *Interpreting the Russian Revolution* (London, 1999), 99–100.

39. The following account draws on reports in the contemporary press, especially *Novoe vremia* and *Izvestiia*; documents collected in Browder and Kerensky, eds., *The Russian Provisional Government*, 3:1527–1613; and scholarly accounts, especially Wildman, *The End of the Russian Imperial Army*, vol. 2, chap. 6; Rabinowitch, *The Bolsheviks Come to Power*, 117–150; Pipes, *Russian Revolution*, 441–464; and Figes, *A People's Tragedy*, 444–453.

40. For example, *Novoe vremia*, 28 August 1917, p. 1. Most Russian papers in 1917 did not appear on Mondays as a result of demands by printing workers that they have Sunday off.

41. *Revoliutsionnoe dvizhenie v Rossii v avguste 1917 g.*, 446.

42. Quoted in Rabinowitch, *The Bolsheviks Come to Power*, 127.

43. *Rabochaia gazeta*, no. 148 (31 August 1917): 1.

44. Rabinowitch, *The Bolsheviks Come to Power*, 160–162. The text of the resolution, also presented to the All-Russian Executive Committee was published in *Izvestiia*, no. 159 (1 September 1917): 2.

45. *Izvestiia*, no. 158 (31 August 1917): 3–4; no. 159 (1 September 1917): 2; no. 160 (2 September 1917): 3–4; no. 161 (3 September 1917): 5–8; Rabinowitch, *The Bolsheviks Come to Power*, 159–165; Browder and Kerensky, eds., *The Russian Provisional Government*, 3:1653–1658, 1662–1669.

46. From the previous cabinet, M. I. Tereshchenko stayed on as foreign minister and A. M. Nikitin remained minister of post and telegraph. Tereshchenko was a political independent, and Nikitin, though a Menshevik, was not involved in the party leadership in any way. Two nonparty military officials were appointed as ministers of war and navy.

47. Declaration from the Provisional Government of 1 September 1917, *Izvestiia*, no. 161 (3 September 1917): 1. The term "Directory" was not used in this initial declaration, though it became common later.

48. *Izvestiia*, no. 161 (3 September 1917): 4.

49. *Izvestiia*, nos. 171–180 (15–24 September 1917); Rabinowitch, *The Bolsheviks Come to Power*, 177–185; Browder and Kerensky, eds., *The Russian Provisional Government*, 3:1672–1695.

50. Comments from various newspapers can be found in Browder and Kerensky, eds., *The Russian Provisional Government*, 3:1717–1721.

51. *Rabochii put'*, no. 19 (24 September 1917): 3.

52. Lenin, Letter to Central Committee and to the Petrograd and Moscow party committees, 12–14 September 1917, in V. I. Lenin, *Sochineniia* (Moscow, 1952), 1:1–3.

53. Rabinowitch, *The Bolsheviks Come to Power*, chap. 11.

54. Rabinowitch, *The Bolsheviks Come to Power*, 90; Figes, *A People's Tragedy*, 458–459.

55. *Proletarii*, no. 6 (19 August 1917): 1.

56. Rabinowitch, *The Bolsheviks Come to Power*, 91–93; Rosenberg, *Liberals in the Russian Revolution*, 219–221.

57. Rabinowitch, *The Bolsheviks Come to Power*, 162.

58. *Izvestiia*, no. 181 (26 September 1917): 5–6; *Proletarii*, no. 20 (26 September 1917): 2, and no. 21 (27 September 1917): 3; Rabinowitch, *The Bolsheviks Come to Power*, 175.

59. Koenker, *Moscow Workers and the 1917 Revolution*, 136, 210–219; *Izvestiia*, no. 170 (20 September 1917): 9.

60. *Delo naroda*, no. 165 (27 September 1917): 1.

61. Rabinowitch, *The Bolsheviks Come to Power*, 291–292.

62. *Izvestiia*, no. 208 (27 October 1917): 4.

63. *Izvestiia*, no. 207 (26 October 1917): 6–7.

64. *Izvestiia*, no. 207 (26 October 1917): 5–6, no. 208 (27 October 1917): 4, and no. 209 (28 October 1917): 4; Sukhanov, *Russian Revolution*, 635–640; Leon Trotsky, *The History of the Russian Revolution* (New York, 1932), 3:311.

65. Proclamation "To All Workers, Soldiers, and Peasants," 26 October 1917. In *Izvestiia*, no. 208 (27 October 1917): 3. Also in Browder and Kerensky, eds., *The Russian Provisional Government*, 3:1797–1798.

66. As quoted above from *Rabochaia gazeta*, no. 148 (31 August 1917): 1.

67. *Russkiia vedomosti*, no. 193 (24 August 1917): 1.

68. Koenker and Rosenberg, *Strikes and Revolution*, 93, 267; Marc Ferro, *The Bolshevik Revolution* (London, 1980): 159–164; Browder and Kerensky, eds., *The Russian Provisional Government*, 2:639–640, 647–652, 655–658, 695–697, 704–707.

69. Christopher Read, *From Tsar to Soviets: The Russian People and Their Revolution* (New York, 1996), 138. See also Wildman, *The End of the Russian Imperial Army*, 2:227–228.

70. *Rech'*, no. 181 (4 August 1917): 2; *Izvestiia*, no. 138 (8 August 1917): 2.

71. Koenker and Rosenberg, *Strikes and Revolution*, 239–261.

72. Koenker and Rosenberg, *Strikes and Revolution*, chap. 9; Smith, *Red Petrograd*, 116–119; Koenker, *Moscow Workers*, chap. 8.

73. Smith, *Red Petrograd*, chaps. 6–7; David Mandel, *The Petrograd Workers and the Seizure of Power* (London, 1984), chap. 3.

74. Wildman, *The End of the Russian Imperial Army*, vol. 2, chap. 5.

75. Summary reports by headquarters, 5 August 1917, on the mood of soldiers during the last week of July, in *Revoliutsionnoe dvizhenie v Rossii v iiule 1917 g.* (Moscow, 1959), 437.

76. Wildman, *The End of the Russian Imperial Army*, 2:210.

77. Quoted in Wildman, *The End of the Russian Imperial Army*, 2:211.

78. Browder and Kerensky, eds., *The Russian Provisional Government*, 3:1581–1582, 1614–1619; Wildman, *The End of the Russian Imperial Army*, 2:202–217.

79. *Izvestiia*, no. 161 (3 September 1917): 1.

80. *Rabochaia gazeta*, no. 158 (12 September 1917): 1.

81. *Revoliutsionnoe dvizhenie v Rossii v sentiabre 1917 g.* (Moscow, 1961), 438 (quote), 453–455, 460–468; Wildman, *The End of the Russian Imperial Army*, 2:227.

82. Army intelligence report for the last two weeks of September, Belevsky Papers, Hoover Institution archives, excerpted in James Bunyan and H. H. Fisher, eds., *The Bolshevik Revolution, 1917–1918: Documents and Materials* (Stanford, Calif., 1961): 24–26.

83. Wildman, *The End of the Russian Imperial Army*, 2:267.

84. Wildman, *The End of the Russian Imperial Army*, 2:274; *Revoliutsionnoe dvizhenie v Rossii nakanune Oktiabr'skogo vooruzhennogo vostaniia (1–24 oktiabria 1917 g.)* (Moscow, 1962), 373–376, 378–379, 386, 410, 419.

85. Browder and Kerensky, eds., *The Russian Provisional Government*, 2:524–554.

86. Browder and Kerensky, eds., *The Russian Provisional Government*, 2:575–577, 588–595; Bunyan and Fisher, eds., *The Bolshevik Revolution*, 31–33; John L. H. Keep, *The Russian Revolution: A Study in Mass Mobilization* (London, 1976), 209–216; Graham Gill, *Peasants and Government in the Russian Revolution* (London, 1979), 141–169; Donald Raleigh, *Revolution on the Volga: 1917 in Saratov* (Ithaca, N.Y., 1986), 220–223, 259; Richard Stites, *Revolutionary Dreams: Utopian Vision and Experimental Life in the Russian Revolution* (New York, 1989), 62–63; Orlando Figes, *Peasant Russia, Civil War: The Volga Countryside in Revolution* (Oxford, 1989), 52–61; Maureen Perrie, "The Peasants," in *Society and Politics in the Russian Revolution*, ed., Robert Service (New York, 1992), 23–31; Ferro, *The Bolshevik Revolution*, 125–132; Figes, *A People's Tragedy*, 462–463.

87. *Volia naroda*, no. 123 (23 September 1917): 1, in Browder and Kerensky, eds., *The Russian Provisional Government*, 3:1641–1643.

88. *Izvestiia*, no. 206 (25 October 1917): 1.

PART 3: SOVIETS IN POWER

1. Leon Trotsky, *On Lenin* (London, 1971), 114; Alexander Rabinowitch, *The Bolsheviks Come to Power* (New York, 1976), 272.

2. St. Vol'skii, "Obzor pechati," *Novaia zhizn'*, no. 164 (27 October 1917): 1.

3. Quoted in *Novaia zhizn'*, no. 164 (27 October 1917): 1.

4. *Izvestiia*, no. 207 (26 October 1917): 1.

5. *Rech'*, no. 252 (26 October 1917): 1.

6. Report on current situation to the seventh conference of the Bolshevik party, 24 April 1917, V. I. Lenin, *Izbrannye proizvedeniia v chetyrekh tomakh* (Moscow, 1988), 2:171–172.

7. See discussion and many citations in Robert Service, *Lenin: A Political Life* (Bloomington, Ind., 1991), 2:241–243.

8. Lenin, political report to the seventh congress of the Bolshevik party, 6–8 March 1918, *Izbrannye proizvedeniia*, 3:108–117.

9. Orlando Figes, *A People's Tragedy: The Russian Revolution, 1891–1924* (Harmondsworth, England, 1996), 503. This is also the argument of Richard Pipes in *The Russian Revolution* (New York, 1990).

10. Studies that have emphasized Lenin's flexibility, changeability, ambiva-

lence, and uncertainty include Rabinowitch, *The Bolsheviks Come to Power,* and Service, *Lenin,* vol. 2.

11. These principles were elaborated by Lenin in his study *The State and Revolution,* which he wrote during his post–July 1917 exile.

12. Lenin, "Zapugivanie naroda burzhuaznymi strakhami," *Pravda,* no. 48 (4 May 1917): 1; "Neminuemaia katastrofa i bezmernye obshchaniia, *Pravda,* no. 59 (17 May 1917): 1; "Can the Bolsheviks Retain State Power," written in late September 1917 and published in early October. For a translation, see Robert C. Tucker, ed., *The Lenin Anthology* (New York, 1975).

13. "To the Population," 5 November 1917, *Pravda,* no. 4 (evening edition, 6 November 1917), in Lenin, *Izbrannye proizvedeniia,* 3:24.

14. Lenin, "How to Organize Competition" (24–27 December 1917, unpublished), and "The Immediate Tasks of Soviet Power" (printed in *Pravda,* no. 83 [28 April 1918]), in *Izbrannye proizvedeniia,* 3:48, 165.

15. See discussion and citations in Service, *Lenin,* 2:226–227.

16. Lenin, "State and Revolution" (August 1917), in Tucker, ed. *Lenin Anthology,* 345, 354.

17. See especially "How to Organize Competition" and "The Immediate Tasks of Soviet Power," in Lenin, *Izbrannye proizvedeniia,* 3:48–55, 162–192.

18. Lenin, "How to Organize Competition" and "The Immediate Tasks of Soviet Power," in Lenin, *Izbrannye proizvedeniia,* 3:51, 52, 54, 183, 186–187.

19. Proclamation "To All Workers, Soldiers, and Peasants" (26 October 1917), in *Izvestiia,* no. 208 (27 October 1917): 3. Also in James Bunyan and H. H. Fisher, eds., *The Bolshevik Revolution, 1917–1918: Documents and Materials* (Stanford, Calif., 1961; 1st ed. 1934). The proclamation was said to have been written by Lenin.

20. Bunyan and Fisher, eds., *The Bolshevik Revolution,* 124–132.

21. "Decree on Peace," *Izvestiia,* no. 208 (27 October 1917): 1. A translation appears in Bunyan and Fisher, eds., *The Bolshevik Revolution,* 125–128.

22. "Decree on Land," *Izvestiia,* no. 209 (28 October 1917): 1. A translation appears in Bunyan and Fisher, eds., *The Bolshevik Revolution,* 129–132.

23. "Report on the Land Decree," 16 October 1917, in Lenin, *Izbrannye proizvedeniia,* 3:12.

24. "Draft Decree on Workers' Control," 26–27 October 1917, in Lenin, *Izbrannye proizvedeniia,* 3:15–16; "Decree on Workers' Control," 14 November 1917, in *Izvestiia,* no. 227 (16 November 1917): 6. See discussions in S. A. Smith, *Red Petrograd: Revolution in the Factories, 1917–1918* (Cambridge, England, 1983), 209–216, and David Mandel, *The Petrograd Workers and the Soviet Seizure of Power* (London, 1984), 364–378.

25. "Declaration of the Rights of the Peoples of Russia," 2 November 1917, *Izvestiia,* no. 215 (3 November 1917): 4.

26. "On the Abolition of Estates and Civil Ranks," 10 November 1917, *Izvestiia,* no. 223 (12 November 1917): 6.

27. Sovnarkom decree on legal reform, 24 November 1917, in Bunyan and Fisher, eds., *The Bolshevik Revolution,* 291–292.

28. "Decree on the Elective Principle and on the Organization of Authority in the Army," *Izvestiia,* no. 254 (17 December 1917): 5.

29. *Izvestiia,* no. 2 (4 January 1918): 1. The declaration, possibly written by

Lenin, was presented to the Constituent Assembly but rejected. It was approved by the Third Congress of Soviets on 19 January and later made part of the first Soviet constitution. See the discussion that follows.

30. Document 107.

31. *Novaia zhizn'*, no. 166 (29 October 1917): 1.

32. *Novaia zhizn'*, no. 167 (30 October 1917): 2.

33. Mandel, *The Petrograd Workers and the Soviet Seizure of Power*, 323–342; Figes, *A People's Tragedy*, 496.

34. *Izvestiia*, no. 217 (5 November 1917): 4.

35. For many documents on these protests, negotiations, and conflicts (including the military threats) see Bunyan and Fisher, eds., *The Bolshevik Revolution*, 139–209. See also discussion in Rabinowitch, *The Bolsheviks Come to Power*, 308–310, and Pipes, *The Russian Revolution*, 518–520.

36. *Novaia zhizn'*, no. 164 (27 October 1917): 4.

37. "Decree on the Press," *Izvestiia*, no. 209 (28 October 1917): 2.

38. *Izvestiia*, no. 217 (6 November 1917): 4; no. 218 (7 November 1917): 3 (quotations); and extracts from press reports in Bunyan and Fisher, eds., *The Bolshevik Revolution*, 221–222.

39. *Izvestiia*, no. 219 (8 November 1917): 3.

40. *Novaia zhizn'*, no. 189 (30 November 1917): 1.

41. "Resolution on the Constituent Assembly," 27 October 1917, *Izvestiia*, no. 209 (28 October 1917): 2.

42. *Izvestiia*, no. 214 (2 November 1917): 2.

43. Lenin, "On Constitutional Illusions" (26 July 1917), printed first in *Rabochii i soldat*, no. 11 (4 August 1917) and no. 12 (5 August 1917), in V. I. Lenin, *Sochineniia* (Moscow, 1955), 25:174–187. See also Service, *Lenin*, 2:227–228.

44. Speech of V. Volodarsky at a meeting of Petrograd Bolsheviks, 8 November 1917, *Izvestiia*, no. 220 (9 November 1917): 5.

45. Bunyan and Fisher, eds., *The Bolshevik Revolution*, 345–347.

46. Oliver H. Radkey, *Russia Goes to the Polls: The Election to the All-Russian Constituent Assembly, 1917*, rev. ed. (Ithaca, N.Y., 1989); Bunyan and Fisher, eds., *The Bolshevik Revolution*, 347–348; *Novaia zhizn'*, no. 182 (16 November 1917): 4. See also Pipes, *Russian Revolution*, 541–543.

47. Bunyan and Fisher, eds., *The Bolshevik Revolution*, 349; *Izvestiia*, no. 237 (27 November 1917): 7; Nikolai N. Smirnov, "The Constituent Assembly," in Edward Acton, Vladimir Cherniaev and William G. Rosenberg, eds., *A Critical Companion to the Russian Revolution, 1914–1921* (Bloomington, Ind., 1997), 328.

48. For example, the editorial "Podozritel'nye druz'ia" (Suspicious friends), *Izvestiia*, no. 237 (27 November 1917): 1–2.

49. *Delo naroda*, no. 219 (26 November 1917): 4; *Izvestiia*, no. 238 (28 November 1917): 2; Bunyan and Fisher, eds., *The Bolshevik Revolution*, 351–354.

50. *Novaia zhizn'*, no. 189 (30 November 1917): 3; *Izvestiia*, no. 239 (29 November 1917): 2; Bunyan and Fisher, eds., *The Bolshevik Revolution*, 356–357.

51. *Novaia zhizn'*, no. 189 (30 November 1917): 3.

52. *Izvestiia*, no. 239 (29 November 1917): 1.

53. *Delo naroda*, no. 223 (3 December 1917): 4; Bunyan and Fisher, eds., *The Bolshevik Revolution*, 361–362; *Novaia zhizn'*, no. 192 (3 December 1917): 2.

54. Bunyan and Fisher, eds., *The Bolshevik Revolution*, 292; "Instruction on

Revolutionary Tribunals," *Izvestiia*, no. 238 (28 November 1917): 7. A more detailed decree was published on 19 December. Bunyan and Fisher, eds., *The Bolshevik Revolution*, 293–294.

55. Bunyan and Fisher, eds., *The Bolshevik Revolution*, 297–298; *Pravda*, no. 290 (18 December 1927): 2.

56. *Novaia zhizn'*, no. 207 (21 December 1917): 1; Bunyan and Fisher, eds., *The Bolshevik Revolution*, 366.

57. "Theses on the Constituent Assembly," *Pravda*, no. 213 (13 December 1917): 3.

58. *Pravda*, no. 207 (6 December 1917): 2; Bunyan and Fisher, eds., *The Bolshevik Revolution*, 361–362.

59. *Izvestiia*, no. 244 (6 December 1917): 6.

60. *Izvestiia*, no. 242 (2 December 1917): 1.

61. *Delo naroda*, no. 1 (3 January 1918): 2.

62. *Izvestiia*, no. 2 (4 January 1917): 1.

63. *Izvestiia*, no. 3 (5 January 1917): 1.

64. *Delo naroda*, no. 3 (5 January 1918): 2.

65. These plans are discussed in Pipes, *Russian Revolution*, 547–549.

66. *Novaia zhizn'*, no. 4 (6 January 1918): 3; *Delo naroda*, no. 4 (7 January 1918): 1, 2, 4.

67. Figes, *A People's Tragedy*, 515.

68. "Deklaratsiia prav trudiashchegosia i ekspluatiruemogo naroda," *Izvestiia*, no. 2 (4 January 1917): 1.

69. Orlando Figes and Boris Kolonitskii, *Interpreting the Russian Revolution* (New Haven, Conn., 1999): 67.

70. *Izvestiia*, no. 4 (6 January 1918): 1; no. 5 (7 January 1918): 1–2; *Delo naroda*, no. 4 (7 January 1918): 1–4; and minutes of the meeting of the Constituent Assembly, in I. S. Mal'chevskii, ed., *Vserossiiskoe uchreditel'noe sobranie* (Moscow, 1930), 3–111.

71. *Pravda*, no. 4 (6 January 1918): 1.

72. The original oprichniki, ominously dressed in black and riding on black horses, were Ivan the Terrible's special force for spreading terror against those who opposed his authority.

73. *Delo naroda*, no. 5 (12 January 1918): 1.

74. Maxim Gorky, "9 January–5 January," *Novaia zhizn'*, no. 6 (9 January 1918): 1. A translation can be found in Maxim Gorky, *Untimely Thoughts* (New Haven, Conn., 1995), 124–125.

75. See, for example, *Delo naroda*, no. 5 (12 January 1918): 3; *Delo narodnoe* [the national S.R. paper had to reregister under a new name], no. 1 (14 January 1918): 1.

76. *Novaia zhizn'*, no. 7 (11 January 1918): 2; *Delo naroda*, no. 5 (12 January 1918): 4.

77. Lev Trotsky, "Lenin and 'Democracy': On the Dispersal of the Constituent Assembly," *Pravda*, no. 91 (20 April 1924): 3. Cited in Pipes, *Russian Revolution*, 556.

78. *Delo narodnoe*, no. 1 (14 January 1918): 1.

79. Pipes, *Russian Revolution*, 556.

80. Figes, *A People's Tragedy*, 518.

81. Document 131.

82. Quotations from contemporaries in Figes, *A People's Tragedy*, 520–522.

83. Maxim Gorky, editorials on Christmas Eve and New Year's Eve in *Novaia zhizn'*, no. 210 (24 December 1917): 1, and no. 214 (31 December 1917): 1. Translations of these essays appear in Maxim Gorky, *Untimely Thoughts*, 116–120.

AFTERWORD

1. Here and in the following textual illustrations, the authors' original spelling and punctuation have been retained.

2. In this article I use "gerund" for Russian деепричастие.

3. See K. A. Rogova, *Sintaksicheskie osobennosti publitsisticheskoi rechi* (Leningrad, 1975): 66.

4. Rogova, *Sintaksicheskie osobennosti*, 64.

5. This is not accidental. Adjoining the predicate and agreeing semantically with the subject, gerundial phrases have special constructive and communicative syntactical functions that allow them to be called second-degree predicates (Rogova, *Sintaksicheskie osobennosti*, 64) or second rhemas (I. P. Raspopov, *Ocherki po istorii sintaksisa* [Voronezh, 1973], 133). Note also the incorrect agreement of participles relating to the word слов-сказано for сказанных and получившим for получивших—which also testifies to the authors' inadequate education and experience with writing.

6. Interestingly, the few peasant decisions that maintain the official style throughout (e.g., Document 91) touch upon precisely the same range of domestic and foreign policy questions as the workers' resolutions and have the same goals and stylistic orientation:

Довольно, думать об нас, *что мы не можем разобраться в этом государственном вопросе*, он для нас ясен, без победы над внешним врагом, не будет завоевана и свобода, и без последней нет земли и воли.

Enough of thinking *that we cannot make sense of this matter of state*, because for us it is quite clear: without victory over the external enemy, freedom will not be won, and without the latter there is no land or liberty.

7. At times, however, the opposite occurs: a bookish expression is used not to clarify, but to add "weight" to a colloquial expression:

[Кулаки] уступают нам, отбросы своих владений, которые им безрасчетно косить самим, т.е. *не оправдывают наетнаго рабочаго труда*.

[The kulaks] leave us the discards from their properties, which for their own use wouldn't pay for itself—that is, it does not justify hired labor. (Document 46)

8. I. P. Lysakova, *Iazyk gazety—sotsiolingvisticheskii aspect* (Leningrad, 1981), 15.

9. Later in this document two ideas are repeated in different ways over an entire page: 1) land and labor are the bases of peasant life, and 2) land can belong only to the peasant commune.

10. Note the complete expression: "Мы, ваши сыны и братья, одетые в серые солдатские шинели" (We, your sons and brothers, who wear the soldiers' gray overcoat—Document 43).

11. See, for example, the stone as a symbol of powerlessness and evil curses in the Russian folktale "Sister Alenushka and Brother Ivanushka." An evil witch throws Alenushka into a lake, and to all her brother's appeals for her to rise she answers, "Не могу, братец, горюч-камень на дно тянет!" ("I can't, brother—the woeful stone is dragging me to the bottom!" Cf. also the continuation of folkloric tradition in Gaidar's stylized fairy tale, "Goriuch-kamen,'" in which the stone symbolizes the weight of years gone by.

12. For further discussion of the concepts of breakdown in objective-logical and stylistic distribution and of the application of the term "distribution" to lexicology and phraseology, see N. L. Shadrin, *Perevod frazelogicheskikh edinits i sopostavitel'naia stilistika* (Saratov, 1991), 147–170.

13. Lysakova, *Iazyk gazety*, 15.

14. For a discussion of letters as the most important sources in the study of colloquial speech, see S. I. Kotkov and N. P. Pankratova, *Istochniki po istorii russkogo narodno-razgovornogo iazyka XII–nachala XVII veka* (Moscow, 1969).

15. For a more detailed discussion of lexical phantoms, see B. Iu. Norman, "Leksicheskie fantomy s tochki zrenia lingvistiki i kulturologii," in *Iazyk i kultura: Tretia mezhdunarodnaia konferencia—doklady* (Kiev, 1994), 53–60.

16. See S. I. Kotkov, "Materialy chastnoi perepiski kak lingvisticheskii istochnik," in Kotkov and Pankratova, *Istochniki po istorii russkogo narodno-razgovornogo iazyka*, 7.

17. V. P. Anikin and Iu. G. Kruglov, *Russkoe narodnoe poeticheskoe tvorchestvo* (Leningrad, 1987), 400.

18. In this discussion, relatively literal prose translations of the poetry appear in place of the verse renderings found in the main presentation of these texts.

19. Anikin and Kruglov, *Russkoe narodnoe poeticheskoe tvorchestvo*, 400.

20. For example, ibid., 404, and O. B. Alekseeva, *Ustnaia poeziia russkikh rabochikh: Dorevoliutsionnyi period* (Leningrad, 1971), 117–158.

21. Anikin and Kruglov, *Russkoe narodnoe poeticheskoe tvorchestvo*, 404.

22. Mark Steinberg, "Workers on the Cross: Religious Imagination in the Writings of Russian Workers, 1910–1924," *Russian Review* 53 (April 1994): 214. Steinberg has completed a forthcoming book, *Proletarian Imagination*, on themes and ideas in the poetry and other creative writings of working-class Russians.

23. Just as the Old Testament Ten Commandments from Moses' tablets became a moral (and to some degree legal) code for Jews and Christians, so Christ's "sacred tablets" are presumably a symbol of the New Testament, representing a new and therefore higher truth, and the promise of redemption.

24. Steinberg, "Workers on the Cross," 227.

25. Ibid.

26. S. A. Tokarev, ed., *Mify narodov mira: Entsiklopediia*, 2 vols. (Moscow, 1980–1982), 402.

27. Cf. the ancient ritual of cremating the dead, which exists in many cultures. Gamkrelidze and Ivanov note that in this ritual fire carried the symbolic meaning of cleansing, freeing the person's spirit, which crosses to the afterworld, to the

"meadow" or "pasture" of plenty (T. V. Gamkrilidze and V. V. Ivanov, *Indo-evropeiskii iazyk i indoevropeitsy* [Tbilisi, 1984], 832).

28. One should note, in this context, the use of biblical expressions in these lines from the most famous communist hymns: отряхнуть прах (чей/чего) с ног своих, разрушить до основанья, кто был ничем, тот станет всем (to shake the dust from one's feet; to destroy to the foundations; those who were nothing will be everything).

29. A. Wierzbicka, *Iazyk, kul'tura, poznanie* (Moscow, 1996), 273.

30. Here it should be underscored that the contemporary Russian word красный, which means "red," is related etymologically to such adjectives as красивый (beautiful) and прекрасный (excellent), a kinship that is reflected in the connotations of красный.

31. Wierzbicka, *Iazyk, kul'tura, poznanie*, 273.

32. V. Ia. Propp, *Istoricheskie korni volshebnoi skazki* (St. Petersburg, 1996), 285.

33. Steinberg, "Workers on the Cross," 229.

34. Propp, *Istoricheskie korni volshebnoi skazki*, 293. For detailed discussion of the types of kingdoms of the dead in folklore, and also of the role of the Golden, or Sun, Kingdom, see 287–297.

Bibliography

Sources of archival documents used in the collection: All materials are from the State Archive of the Russian Federation (Gosudarstvennyi arkhiv Rossiiskoi Federatsii, or GARF), especially from the following holdings:

fond 1235. Second All-Russian Central Executive Committee of Soviets (VTsIK)
  op. [opis, or inventory] 1 (October 1917)
    d. [delo, or file] 16 (instructions [*nakazy*] to delegates)
    d. 19. (provincial soviets and soldiers' committees' resolutions on current situation)
  op. 140 (former 1235 s. ch. [secret section])
f. 1244. *Izvestiia*, op. 2
f. 1778. Office of the Minister-President of the Provisional Government, op. 1
f. 1781. Constituent Assembly, op. 1
f. 1796. Main Land Committee, op. 1
f. 6978. First All-Russian Central Executive Committee of Soviets (VTsIK
  op. 1, d. 244, 247, 254, 264, 269, 296, 297 (antisoviet), 353, 354
f. 9550. Leaflets (*listovki*).

CONTEMPORARY NEWSPAPERS USED

Delo naroda (The people's cause), Petrograd.
Izvestiia Soveta rabochikh i soldatskikh deputatov (News of the Soviet of Workers' and Soldiers' Deputies), Petrograd.
Novaia zhizn' (New life), Petrograd.
Novoe vremia (New time), Petrograd.
Pravda (Truth), Petrograd.

Proletarii (The proletarian [a continuation of *Pravda*]), Petrograd.
Rabochaia gazeta (Workers' newspaper), Petrograd.
Rabochii i soldat (Worker and soldier [a continuation of *Pravda*]), Petrograd).
Rabotnitsa (Woman worker), Petrograd
Rech' (Speech), Petrograd.
Russkie vedomosti (Russian news), Petrograd.
Russkoe slovo (Russian word), Moscow.

PUBLISHED DOCUMENTARY COLLECTIONS

English Translations

Ascher, Abraham, ed. *The Mensheviks in the Russian Revolution.* Ithaca, N.Y., 1976.
Avrich, Paul, ed. *The Anarchists in the Russian Revolution.* Ithaca, N.Y., 1973.
Browder, Robert Paul, and Alexander F. Kerensky, eds. *The Russian Provisional Government, 1917: Documents.* 3 volumes. Stanford, Calif., 1961.
Bunyan, James, and H. H. Fisher, eds. *The Bolshevik Revolution, 1917–1918: Documents and Materials.* Stanford, Calif., 1961; first ed. 1934.

Russian-Language Publications

Mensheviki v 1917 godu. 3 volumes. Moscow, 1994–1995.
Perepiska sekretariata TsK RSDRP(b) s mestnymi partiinymi organizatsiiami: Sbornik dokumentov, vol. 1: *Mart–Oktiabr' 1917 g.* Moscow, 1957.
Revoliutsionnoe dvizhenie v Rossii nakanune Oktiabr'skogo vooruzhennogo vosstaniia, 1–24 oktiabria 1917 g. Moscow, 1962.
Revoliutsionnoe dvizhenie v Rossii posle sverzheniia samoderzhaviia. Moscow, 1957.
Revoliutsionnoe dvizhenie v Rossii v aprele 1917 g. Moscow, 1958.
Revoliutsionnoe dvizhenie v Rossii v avguste 1917 g. Moscow, 1959.
Revoliutsionnoe dvizhenie v Rossii v iiule 1917 g. Moscow, 1959.
Revoliutsionnoe dvizhenie v Rossii v sentiabre 1917 g. Moscow, 1961.

SELECTED BOOKS ON THE REVOLUTION

Abraham, Richard. *Alexander Kerensky: The First Love of the Revolution.* New York, 1987.
Acton, Edward, Vladimir Cherniaev, and William G. Rosenberg, eds. *A Critical Companion to the Russian Revolution, 1914–1921.* Bloomington, Ind., 1997.

Brovkin, Vladimir. *The Mensheviks After October.* Ithaca, N.Y., 1987.

Burdzhalov, E. N. *Russia's Second Revolution: The February 1917 Uprising in Petrograd.* Trans. and ed. Donald Raleigh. Bloomington, Ind., 1987.

Chamberlain, W. H. *The Russian Revolution.* 2 volumes. Princeton, N.J., 1987.

Cherniaev, V. Iu., et al., eds. *Anatomiia Revoliutsii: 1917 god v Rossii.* St. Petersburg, 1994.

Ferro, Marc. *The Bolshevik Revolution: A Social History of the Russian Revolution.* London, 1980.

———. *The Russian Revolution of February 1917.* Englewood Cliffs, N.J., 1972.

Figes, Orlando. *Peasant Russia, Civil War: The Volga Countryside in Revolution.* Oxford, 1989.

———. *A People's Tragedy: The Russian Revolution, 1891–1924.* Harmondsworth, England, 1996.

Figes, Orlando, and Boris Kolonitskii. *Interpreting the Russian Revolution: The Language and Symbols of 1917.* New Haven, Conn., 1999.

Fitzpatrick, Sheila. *The Russian Revolution, 1917–1932.* Oxford, 1982.

Florinsky, Michael. *The End of the Russian Empire.* New York, 1931.

Frankel, Edith Rogovin, Jonathan Frankel, and Baruch Knei-Paz, eds. *Revolution in Russia: Reassessments of 1917.* Cambridge, England, 1992.

Galili, Ziva. *The Menshevik Leaders in the Russian Revolution.* Princeton, N.J., 1989.

Gill, Graham. *Peasants and Government in the Russian Revolution.* London, 1979.

Gorky, Maxim. *Untimely Thoughts: Essays on Revolution, Culture, and the Bolsheviks, 1917–1918.* New Haven, Conn., 1995.

Hasegawa, Tsuyoshi. *The February Revolution: Petrograd, 1917.* Seattle, 1981.

Kaiser, Donald H., ed. *The Workers' Revolution in Russia, 1917.* Cambridge, England, 1987.

Keep, John L. H. *The Russian Revolution: A Study in Mass Mobilization.* London, 1976.

Koenker, Diane. *Moscow Workers and the 1917 Revolution.* Princeton, N.J., 1981.

Koenker, Diane P., and William G. Rosenberg. *Strikes and Revolution in Russia, 1917.* Princeton, N.J., 1989.

Kowalski, Ronald. *The Russian Revolution, 1917–1921.* London, 1997.

Lincoln, W. Bruce. *Passage Through Armageddon: The Russians in War and Revolution, 1914–1918.* New York, 1986.

McDaniel, Tim. *Autocracy, Capitalism, and Revolution in Russia.* Berkeley, Calif., 1988.

Mandel, David. *The Petrograd Workers and the Fall of the Old Regime.* London, 1983.

———. *The Petrograd Workers and the Soviet Seizure of Power.* London, 1984.

Mawdsley, Evan. *The Russian Revolution and the Baltic Fleet.* New York, 1978.

Melancon, Michael. *The Socialist Revolutionaries and the Russian Anti-War Movement, 1914–1917.* Columbus, Ohio, 1990.

Pipes, Richard. *The Russian Revolution.* New York, 1990.

Rabinowitch, Alexander. *The Bolsheviks Come to Power.* New York, 1976.

———. *Prelude to Revolution: The Petrograd Bolsheviks and the July 1917 Uprising.* Bloomington, Ind., 1968.

Radkey, Oliver. *Russia Goes to the Polls: The Election to the All-Russian Constituent Assembly, 1917.* Ithaca, N.Y., 1990; orig. pub. 1950.

Raleigh, Donald. *Revolution on the Volga: 1917 in Saratov.* Ithaca, N.Y., 1986.

Read, Christopher. *From Tsar to Soviets: The Russian People and Their Revolution, 1917–1921.* New York, 1996.

Rosenberg, William. *Liberals in the Russian Revolution.* Princeton, N.J., 1974.

Saul, Norman. *Sailors in Revolt: The Russian Baltic Fleet in 1917.* Lawrence, Kans., 1978.

Schapiro, Leonard. *The Russian Revolutions of 1917: The Origins of Modern Communism.* New York, 1984.

Service, Robert, ed. *Society and Politics in the Russian Revolution.* New York, 1992.

Shukman, Harold, ed. *The Blackwell Encyclopedia of the Russian Revolution.* Oxford, 1994.

Smirnov, N. N., B. I. Kolonitskii, and V. Iu. Cherniaev, eds. *Istorik i revoliutsiia.* St. Petersburg, 1999.

Smith, S. A. *Red Petrograd: Revolution in the Factories, 1917–1918.* Cambridge, England, 1983.

Steinberg, Mark, and Vladimir Khrustalev. *The Fall of the Romanovs.* New Haven, Conn., 1995.

Stites, Richard. *Revolutionary Dreams: Utopian Vision and Experimental Life in the Russian Revolution.* New York, 1989.

Sukhanov, N. N. *The Russian Revolution: A Personal Record.* Trans. and ed. Joel Carmichael. Oxford, 1955; orig. pub. in Russian, 1922.

Suny, Ronald, and Arthur Adams, eds. *The Russian Revolution and Bolshevik Victory.* Lexington, Mass., 1990.

Von Geldern, James. *Bolshevik Festivals, 1917–1920.* Berkeley, Calif., 1993.

Wade, Rex. *The Bolshevik Revolution and the Russian Civil War.* Westport, Conn., 2001.

————. *Red Guards and Workers' Militias in the Russian Revolution.* Stanford, Calif., 1984.

————. *The Russian Revolution, 1917.* Cambridge, England, 2000.

Wildman, Allan. *The End of the Russian Imperial Army.* 2 volumes. Princeton, N.J., 1980, 1987.

Document and Illustration Credits

ABBREVIATIONS USED

GAORSS LO. *See* TsGA SPb.

GARF: Gosudarstvennyi arkhiv Rossiiskoi Federatsii (State Archive of the Russian Federation). From 1961 to 1992 named TsGAOR (Tsentral'nyi gosudarstvennyi arkhiv Oktiabr'skoi revoliutsii—Central State Archive of the October Revolution).

RGASPI: Rossiiskii gosudarstvennyi arkhiv sotsial'no-politicheskoi istorii (Russian State Archive of Sociopolitical History). From 1991 to 1999 named RTsKhIDNI (Rossiiskii tsentr khraneniia i izucheniia dokumentov noveishei istorii—Russian Center for Preservation and Study of Records of Recent History). From 1956 to 1991 named TsPA IML (Tsentral'nyi partiinyi arkhiv Instituta marksizma-leninizma pri TsK KPSS—Central Party Archive of the Institute of Marxism-Leninism Under the Central Committee of the Communist Party of the Soviet Union).

RGVIA: Rossiiskii gosudarstvennyi voenno-istoricheskii arkhiv (Russian State Military History Archive). From 1941 to 1992 named TsGVIA (Tsentral'nyi gosudarstvennyi voenno-istoricheskii arkhiv SSSR—Central State Military History Archive).

RTsKhIDNI. *See* RGASPI.

TsGA SPb: Tsentral'nyi gosudarstvennyi arkhiv Sankt-Peterburga (Central State Archive of St. Petersburg). From 1941 to 1964 named GAORSS LO (Gosudarstvennyi arkhiv Oktiabr'skoi revolutsii i sotsialisticheskogo stroitel'stva Leningradskoi oblasti—State Archive of the October Revolution and Socialist Construction of Leningrad Oblast).

Also named LGAORSS (1964–1974) and TsGAOR Leningrada (1974–1991).

TsGAOR. *See* GARF.

TsGVIA. See RGVIA.

TsPA IML. See RGASPI.

DOCUMENT CREDITS

1. "Long Live Free Russia," by Mikhail Serafimovich, a private in the reserve cavalry, March 1917. GARF, f. 1244, op. 2, d. 31, l. 39. Manuscript. Ellipses in original.

2. "The Russian National Hymn," by the factory worker "Muzhik Mikula," Novgorod Province, March 1917. GARF, f. 1244, op. 2, d. 31, l. 14. Typed.

3. "On the Old Tsarist Regime," by Fyodor Korsun, a private in the infantry reserves, Orenburg Province, March 1917. GARF, f. 1244, op. 2, d. 31, ll. 15–150b. Manuscript. Ellipses in original.

4. "To the Fallen Freedom Fighters," by metalworker Demian Semyonov, Viazma railroad depot, Smolensk Province, 17 March 1917. GARF, f. 1244, op. 2, d. 31, ll. 38–380b. Manuscript. Ellipses in original.

5. "Dawn Has Broken," by the sailor Stepan Stepanov, Baltic Fleet, 28 March 1917. GARF, f. 1244, op. 2, d. 31, ll. 43, 440b. Manuscript.

6. Letter to Minister of Justice Aleksandr Kerensky, with a cover letter to Chairman of the Petrograd Soviet Nikolai Chkheidze, from worker and deserter A. Zemskov, Kuban region, 26 March 1917. GARF, f. 6978, op. 1, d. 296, ll. 39–450b. Manuscript. Ellipses in original.

7. Appeal to soldiers from the workers of the A. M. Ouf machine, metal, and engineering factories, Petrograd, 28–29 March 1917. *Rabochaia gazeta,* no. 24 (6 April 1917): 2.

8. Resolution of workers of the Putilov metal and machine factory, Petrograd, 31 March 1917. *Pravda,* no. 23 (1 April 1917): 3.

9. Resolution of workers of the Petrograd Pipe Factory, printed 4 April 1917. *Izvestiia,* no. 31 (4 April 1917): 6.

10. Resolution of the workers of the "Old Parviainen" metal and machine factory, Petrograd, 13 April 1917. *Izvestiia,* no. 41 (15 April 1917) 3; *Pravda,* no. 35 (1 May / 18 April [old style] 1917): 4.

11. "From the Council of Elders of the Tula Brass Cartridge Factories," printed 15 April 1917. *Izvestiia,* no. 41 (15 April 1917): 3.

12. Appeal to the Petrograd "People's Committee" from Matvei Frolov, day worker on the Perm Railroad, 25 April 1917. GARF, f. 6978, op. 1, d. 354, ll. 10b.–2. Manuscript.

13. "To All Russian Women and Mothers" from the Smolensk Initiative

Group of Women and Mothers, printed 5 May 1917. *Novaia zhizn'*, no. 15 (5/18 May 1917): 4.

14. A letter to *Rabotnitsa* from a restaurant worker in Petrograd, printed 20 May 1917. *Rabotnitsa*, no. 3 (20 May 1917): 7.

15. From the protocol of a general meeting of workers of the Okulovsky Paper Factory and local peasants of Krestetsk Uezd, Novgorod Province, 21 May 1917. GARF, f. 6978, op. 1, d. 354, l. 5a. Typed.

16. Appeal to workers from the Committee of Elders of the Atlas Metal and Machine Factory, Petrograd, printed 11 June 1917. *Rabochaia gazeta*, no. 78 (11 June 1917): 4.

17. Protocol of a general meeting of workers and employees of the Vysokovskaia Manufacturing Company Cotton Mill, Moscow Province, 14 June 1917. GARF, f. 1778, op. 1, d. 194, l. 67. Typed and signed.

18. Resolution of the workers of the "Old Parviainen" metal and machine factory, Petrograd, printed 18 June 1917. *Pravda*, no. 85 (1 July / 18 June 1917): 3.

19. Telegram to the Provisional Government and Congress of Soviets from a meeting of twelve thousand workers, soldiers, peasants, and Cossacks in the Kuban region, 18 June 1917. GARF, f. 1778, op. 1, d. 364, l. 165.

20. Letter to working women from Maria Kutsko, a worker at the Petrograd Munitions Works (*Orudiinyi zavod*), printed 25 June 1917. *Rabotnitsa*, no. 6 (25 June 1917): 14.

21. Telegram to the Executive Committee of Workers' and Soldiers' Deputies from soldiers of the administration of the 17th Mortar Artillery Division, 9 March 1917. *Izvestiia*, no. 19 (19 March 1917): 5.

22. "Letter from the active army," 10 March 1917. *Izvestiia*, no. 19 (19 March 1917): 6. Ellipses in original.

23. Appeal to soldiers, workers, and other citizens of Russia from the 8th Siberian Rifle Division, 16 March 1917. *Izvestiia*, no. 28 (30 March 1917): 4.

24. Letter to the Petrograd Soviet from soldiers of the 61st Siberian Rifle Regiment, 18 March 1917. *Revoliutsionnoe dvizhenie v Rossii posle sverzheniia samoderzhaviia* (Moscow, 1957), 636–637. Source: TsGVIA (now RGVIA), f. 2048, op. 1, d. 3, l. 13.

25. Appeal to Petrograd workers from the Tsarskoe Selo Garrison Soldiers' Committee, 24 March 1917. *Rabochaia gazeta*, no. 19 (29 March 1917): 2.

26. Letter to Chkheidze from "Sick and injured Russian warriors," 31 March 1917. GARF, f. 6978, op. 1, d. 297, ll. 45–46. Manuscript.

27. Letter to Chkheidze from soldiers of the 2nd Battery Assembly, Caucasus army, 3 April 1917. GARF, f. 6978, op. 1, d. 296, l. 89. Typed.

28. Letter to Chkheidze from soldier workers of Transport Repair Workshop No. 2, Uman, Kiev Province, 3 April 1917. GARF, f. 6978, op. 1, d. 296, ll. 90–90ob. Typed and signed.

29. Letter to the Soviet from Sergeant Ia. Z. Mazur on behalf of soldiers of the Mortar Artillery Division, 11 April 1917. GARF, f. 6978, op. 1, d. 296, l. 107. Manuscript.

30. Letter to Minister of War Aleksandr Guchkov from soldiers of the 64th Infantry Division of the active army, 13 April 1917. *Revoliutsionnoe dvizhenie v Rossii v aprele 1917 g.: Aprel'skii krizis* (Moscow, 1958): 497–498. Source: TsGVIA (now RGVIA), f. 2003/c, op. 2, d. 118, ll. 251–255ob.

31. Letter to the chairman of the Soviet of Workers' and Soldiers' Deputies from soldier Yegorov in the 753rd Reserve Regiment, no date (content suggests late April). GARF, f. 6978, op. 1, d. 296, ll. 1–2. Manuscript.

32. Appeal to all the soldiers of the 12th Army from the 186th Artillery Division, 4 May 1917. GARF, f. 6978, op. 1, d. 353, l. 17. Typed and signed.

33. "A Voice from the Trenches," 30 May 1917. GARF, f. 1244, op. 2, d. 10, ll. 177–178. Manuscript.

34. Appeal to reservists from a soldiers' committee at the northern front, June 1917. GARF, f. 1244, op. 2, d. 10, l. 387. Typed.

35. "Letter from the Front" to the Bolshevik newspaper *Pravda,* 7 June 1917. *Pravda,* no. 75 (20/7 June 1917): 3.

36. Resolution of the soldiers of the 1st Infantry Reserve Regiment, 18 June 1917. *Pravda,* no. 85 (1 July / 18 June 1917): 3.

37. Letter to "Comrade Patriots" from soldiers in the trenches, 27 June 1917. GARF, f. 1244, op. 2, d. 10, ll. 358–359. Manuscript.

38. Letter to *Izvestiia* from the peasant Nikolai Burakov, Perm Province, 30 March 1917. GARF, f. 1244, op. 2, d. 5, ll. 3–3ob. Manuscript.

39. Appeal to the Orel Uezd Land Commission, Orel Province, from peasant farmer Nikolai Savinykh, 6 April 1917. GARF, f. 1796, op. 1, d. 95, ll. 46–46ob. Typed copy.

40. Letter to the Petrograd Soviet from the peasants of Rakalovsk Volost, Viatka Province, 26 April 1917. *Revoliutsionnoe dvizhenie v Rossii v aprele 1917 g.:* 642–644. Source: GAORSS LO (now TsGA SPb), f. 7384, op. 9, d. 236, ll. 58–59.

41. Letter to the Petrograd Soviet from "a peasant," 27 April 1917. GARF, f. 6978, op. 1, d. 297, ll. 74–77ob. Manuscript.

42. Resolution of an assembly of heads of households from seventy-five villages, Istra Volost, Liutsinsk Uezd, Vitebsk Province, early May 1917 (received by Soviet Central Executive Committee, 6 May). GARF, f. 6978, op. 1, d. 247, l. 141. Typed.

43. Letter to *Izvestiia* from a peasant and former soldier, Andrei Sunin, Novgorod Province, early May 1917 (received 16 May). GARF, f. 1244, op. 2, d. 5, ll. 41–43ob. Manuscript.

44. Letter to *Izvestiia* from a peasant and former soldier, Nikifor Tatianenko, Poltava Province, 12 May 1917. GARF, f. 1244, op. 2, d. 5, ll. 29–30ob. Manuscript.

45. Appeal to the peasants from a Committee of Soldiers' Deputies, printed 12 May 1917. *Rabochaia gazeta,* no. 54 (12 May 1917): 2.

46. Resolution to the Soviet and the Provisional Government from peasant citizens in the villages of Osnichkovo and Andreevo, Petrograd Province, 11 May 1917. GARF, f. 6978, op. 1, d. 244, ll. 4–5ob. Manuscript.

47. Letter to *Izvestiia* from a village in Ukraine, 21 May 1917. GARF, f. 1244, op. 2, d. 5, ll. 55–55ob. Manuscript.

48. Protocol of a meeting of the Sadki village committee, 8 June 1917. GARF, f. 6978, op. 1, d. 244, ll. 50–50ob. Manuscript.

49. Resolution from "citizen-tillers of the soil," Kursk Province, 29 June 1917. GARF, f. 1244, op. 2, d. 10, l. 340. Manuscript.

50. Letter to the Soviet from peasants of Lodeina village, Vologda Province, 3 July 1917. GARF, f. 1244, op. 2, d. 5, ll. 65–66. Manuscript.

51. "A Flame of Gold Ablaze," by Pyotr Oreshin, worker, soldier, and "peasant poet," printed 14 May 1917. *Delo naroda,* no. 49 (14 May 1917): 2. Ellipses in original.

52. "In the Fields," by Pyotr Oreshin 28 May 1917. *Delo naroda,* no. 60 (28 May 1917): 2. Ellipses in original.

53. Resolution on the July Days by workers of the Shlisselburg Powder Works, Petrograd, 4 July 1917. *Perepiska sekretariata TsK RSDRP(b) s mestnymi partiinymi organizatsiiami: Sbornik dokumentov,* vol. 1: *Mart—oktiabr' 1917 g.* (Moscow, 1957), 139. Also published in *Revoliutsionnoe dvizhenie v Rossii v iiule 1917 g.* (Moscow, 1959), 20–21. Source: TsPA IML (now RGASPI), f. 17, op. 1, d. 154, l. 2. Typed and signed.

54. Resolution on the July Days by representatives of Petrograd printing workers, 8 July 1917. *Delo naroda,* no. 95 (8 July 1917), 4.

55. Resolutions on the July Days by workers and employees of the Petrograd Metal Works and by the Executive Committee of Bolsheviks at the factory, 11 July 1917. *Delo naroda,* no. 100 (14 July 1917): 4.

56. Resolution by the printing workers of the former Markus press, Petrograd, 13 July 1917. GARF, f. 1244, op. 2, d. 10, l. 239. Manuscript.

57. Letter to citizens from workers at the Putilov factory, Petrograd, 11 July 1917. *Novaia zhizn',* no. 75 (15/28 July 1917): 3.

58. Resolution of a meeting of workers in twenty-seven small enterprises from the Peterhof district of Petrograd, 27 July 1917. *Rabochii i soldat,* no. 11 (4 August 1917): 4. Reprinted with minor orthographic corrections in *Revoliutsionnoe dvizhenie v iiule 1917 g.,* 377–378.

59. Letter to Kerensky from Pyotr Arshinov, railroad workshop storeman, Orel Province, late July or early August 1917 (based on the dates of publication of the Bolshevik proclamation referred to). GARF, f. 1778, op. 1, d. 366, l. 138.

60. Anonymous note to the All-Russian Central Executive Committee of Soviets, late July 1917 (received 4 August). GARF, f. 6978, op. 1, d. 269, l. 1. Typed on a small piece of paper.

61. Letter to the editor of *Izvestiia* about a Literary-Musical Evening in Petrograd, 31 July 1917. GARF, f. 1244, op. 2, d. 35, ll. 72–72ob. Typed and signed.

62. Resolution by the cultural commission of the Berg factory, Tver, 17 August 1917. GARF, f. 1244, op. 2, d. 12, l. 258. Typed.

63. Resolution by the workers of the Erikson Telephone Factory, Petrograd, printed 18 August 1917. *Proletarii,* no. 5 (31/18 August 1917): 4.

64. Resolution of a general meeting of the union of forestry workers, Dubovki, Saratov Province, 27 August 1917. GARF, f. 1244, op. 1, d. 17, l. 426. Manuscript. Previously published with corrected punctuation and spelling in *Revoliutsionnoe dvizhenie v Rossii v avguste 1917 g.* (Moscow, 1959), 243–244.

65. Telegram to the Provisional Government from workers and employees at the Georgievsky Company Sugar Factory, Petrograd, 6 September 1917. GARF, f. 1778, op. 1, d. 234, ll. 142–143. Telegram.

66. Resolution of all the political factions of the Slutsk Soviet, Minsk Province, September 1917 (received 20 September). GARF, f. 6978, op. 1, d. 247, l. 60. Typed and signed.

67. Letter to the Soviet from the soldier Yurchenko, in the trenches at the front, 8 July 1917. GARF, f. 1235, op. 53, d. 9, ll. 48–51. Manuscript with signatures. Previously published with corrected punctuation and with the author's rank omitted in *Revoliutsionnoe dvizhenie v Rossii v iiule 1917 g.,* 407.

68. Letter to the Bolshevik party from two soldiers on the southwestern front, 8 July 1917. *Perepiska sekretariata TsK RSDRP(b) s mestnymi partiinymi organizatsiiami: sbornik dokumentov,* vol. 1: *Mart-oktiabr' 1917 g.* (Moscow, 1957), 436. Also published in *Revoliutsionnoe dvizhenie v Rossii v iiule 1917 g.,* 406. Source: TsPA IML (now RGASPI), f. 17, op. 1, d. 376, ll. 4–5.

69. Resolution on the July Days by the soldiers of the 22nd Railroad Battalion, 9 July 1917. GARF, f. 6978, op. 1, d. 254, ll. 4–40ob. Typed and signed.

70. Resolution from soldiers of the 2nd Caucasus Engineering Regiment, July 1917 (received 21 July). GARF, f. 1244, op. 2, d. 10, l. 247. Typed, with handwritten note added.

71. Resolution by a general meeting of soldiers and officers of the 3rd Company of the Ust-Dvinsk Fortress Artillery, Gulf of Riga, 27 July 1917. GARF, f. 1244, op. 2, d. 12, l. 223. Typed, with handwritten note added.

72. Letter to the minister-president of the Provisional Government from Staff Sergeant (Fel'dfebel') Safonov, July or August 1917. GARF, f. 1778, op. 1, d. 368, l. 93. Manuscript.

73. Letter to the Central Executive Committee of Soviets from the soldiers' committee of the 129th Bessarabian Infantry, received 5 August 1917. GARF, f. 6978, op. 1, d. 519, ll. 272–273ob. Manuscript. Previously published with corrected spelling, grammar, and punctuation and with one sentence removed (see notes to document) in *Revoliutsionnoe dvizhenie v Rossii v iiule 1917 g.*, 436.

74. Letter-essay to "Comrade Citizens" from soldier A. Kuchlavok, approved by the regiment, received by *Izvestiia* 7 August 1917. GARF, f. 1244, op. 2, d. 35, ll. 140–141ob. Typed. Some punctuation has been added for clarity. The original is written as a stream of clauses, divided mainly by commas and an occasional colon, ending in periods only very rarely.

75. Letter to the Central Executive Committee of Soviets on behalf of positional soldiers, 9 August 1917 . GARF, f. 6978, op. 1, d. 528, l. 181. Manuscript. Previously published with corrected spelling and punctuation in *Revoliutsionnoe dvizhenie v Rossii v avguste 1917 g.*, 259–260.

76. Letter to the Central Executive Committee of Soviets from a soldier at the front, 9 August 1917. GARF, f. 6978, op. 1, d. 531, ll. 4–5. Manuscript. Previously published with corrected spelling and grammar in *Revoliutsionnoe dvizhenie v Rossii v avguste 1917 g.*, 260–261. Ellipses in original.

77. Appeal to the soldiers of the telegraph company, 7th Engineering Regiment, from the soldiers' committee of the telegraph company, 13 August 1917. GARF, f. 1244, op. 2, d. 12, ll. 259–259ob. Manuscript. Ellipses in original.

78. Letter to Kerensky from soldiers at the front, 18 August 1917. *Revoliutsionnoe dvizhenie v Rossii v avguste 1917 g.*, 269–270. Source: TsGVIA (now RGVIA), f. 366/c, op. 1, d. 334, ll. 467–467ob. Copy.

79. Poem sent to *Izvestiia* by the soldier P. Anoshkin, in the active army, received 16 August 1917. GARF, f. 1244, op. 2, d. 31, ll. 3–3ob. Manuscript.

80. Letter to the Socialist Revolutionary newspaper *Delo naroda* from I. Morozov, artillery soldier at Vyborg Fortress, end of August 1917. *Delo naroda*, no. 147 (6 September 1917): 2.

81. Resolution of the soldiers' committee of the 92nd Transport Battalion, 1 September 1917. GARF, f. 1244, op. 2, d. 10, ll. 55–57. Typed and signed.

82. Letter to the Central Executive Committee of Soviets from soldiers at the Caucasus front, 16 September 1917. GARF, f. 6978, op. 1, d. 534, ll. 238–239. Manuscript. Previously published with corrected spelling and punctuation in *Revoliutsionnoe dvizhenie v Rossii v sentiabre 1917 g.* (Moscow, 1961), 431.

83. Poem sent to *Izvestiia* by a wounded soldier, Ilya Ladanov, received 22 September 1917. GARF, f. 1244, op. 2, d. 31, ll. 84–84ob. Manuscript.

84. Appeals to the country and the soldiers from the Soviet of Soldiers' Deputies of the 12th Army, printed 7 October 1917. *Izvestiia*, no. 191 (7 October 1917): 3.

85. Letter to *Izvestiia* from a soldier and member of the Petrograd soviet, received 4 October 1917. GARF, f. 1244, op. 2, d. 35, l. 215. Typed and signed.

86. Appeal to the Provisional Government from soldiers at the front, early October 1917 (dated by content and placement in archive file). GARF, f. 1778, op. 1, d. 369, ll. 402–402ob. Manuscript.

87. Instruction (*nakaz*) to the delegates to the Second All-Russian Congress of Soviets from the Congress of Soldiers' Representatives, 6th Army Corps, 18 October 1917. GARF, f. 1235, op. 1, d. 16, ll. 41–41ob. Manuscript.

88. Resolution of the soldiers' committee at the front, 2nd Company, 11th Siberian Rifle Regiment, received 23 October 1917. GARF, f. 1244, op. 2, d. 12, ll. 555–555ob. Manuscript.

89. Letter to *Izvestiia* from Mikhail Savin and the committee of wounded soldiers, mid-October 1917. *Izvestiia*, no. 210 (29 October 1917): 4.

90. Letter to the All-Russian Central Executive Committee of Soviets from the peasant Ivan Pastukhov, Vologda Province, received 7 July 1917. GARF, f. 6978, op. 1, d. 523, ll. 246–247ob. Manuscript. Previously published with corrected grammar and punctuation in *Revoliutsionnoe dvizhenie v Rossii v iiule 1917 g.*, 448.

91. Resolution of Gagarin Volost assembly of peasants, Kostroma Province, 9 July 1917. GARF, f. 1778, op. 1, d. 205, ll. 1–3. Manuscript.

92. Letter to Kerensky from Ivan Shabrov, Ryazan Province, 13 July 1917. GARF, f. 1778, op. 1, d. 366, ll. 72–73ob. Manuscript.

93. Letter to the Bolshevik newspaper *Rabochii i soldat* from Timofei

Gurov, an injured noncommissioned officer, 9 August 1917. *Rabochii i soldat*, no. 15 (9 August 1917): 4. Reprinted with orthographic corrections in *Revoliutsionnoe dvizhenie v avguste 1917 g.*, 308.

94. Report addressed to Kerensky from peasants in Valdaisk Uezd, Novgorod Province, 19 August 1917. GARF, f. 1778, op. 1, d. 363, ll. 244–244ob. Manuscript.

95. Declaration to the Provisional Government from a village assembly, Tambov Province, 21 August 1917. GARF, f. 1796, op. 1, d. 71, ll. 76–77. Manuscript.

96. Petition to the Ministry of Agriculture from Andrei Kulagin, peasant in Penza Province, received 21 August 1917. GARF, f. 1796, op. 1, d. 37, ll. 174–174ob. Manuscript.

97. "Man and the Land," letter-essay by Semyon Martynov, a peasant from Orel Province, August 1917 (dated by content and placement in archive files and in relation to a second essay by Martynov, located in GARF, f. 1778, op. 1, d. 234, l. 91, received by the government and numbered after this one; that essay refers to a press article of 19 August 1917). GARF, f. 1778, op. 1, d. 234, ll. 88–89ob. Manuscript. Emphasis in original.

98. Letter to Kerensky from G. Korotkov, a worker in the provincial town of Slaviansk, Kharkov Province, 26 August 1917. GARF, f. 1778, op. 1, d. 362, l. 1. Manuscript. Ellipses and emphasis in original.

99. Telegram to Kerensky from the "working peasantry" of Botsmanovo-Ivanovsk Volost, 2 September 1917 (dated by position in archive folder). GARF, f. 1778, op. 1, d. 364, l. 268.

100. Resolution by a general meeting of peasants, Petrograd Province, 17 October 1917. GARF, f. 1235, op. 1, d. 19, ll. 3–40b. Manuscript. Previously published with orthographic corrections in *Revoliutsionnoe dvizhenie v Rossii nakanune Oktiabr'skogo vooruzhennogo vosstaniia, 1–24 oktiabria 1917 g.* (Moscow, 1962), 453–454.

101. Plea to the soldiers from Iskeevsk Volost, October 1917. GARF, f. 6978, op. 1, d. 247, l. 142. Manuscript.

102. Pyotr Oreshin, a "Song of Freedom," printed 17 September 1917. *Delo naroda*, no. 157 (17 September 1917): 5. Ellipses in original.

103. Ivan Loginov, "To a Worker Friend," printed 25 September 1917. *Rabotnitsa*, no. 10 (25 September 1917): 14. Ellipsis in original.

104. Resolution of the workers of the Kushnerev Printing Works, Moscow, 1 November 1917 (dated by content). *Pechatnik: Organ Moskovskogo professional'nogo soiuza rabochikh pechatnogo dela*, no. 7–8 (28 November 1917): 7.

105. Resolution of the workers of the Baltic Shipbuilding Works, Petrograd, 2 November 1917. *Izvestiia*, no. 216 (4 November 1917): 7.

106. Letter to the Central Executive Committee of Soviets from a group of Putilov factory workers, Petrograd, received 5 December 1917. GARF, f. 6978, op. 1, d. 247, ll. 118–1180b. Manuscript.

107. Resolution of workers and employees of the Bogomdarovannyi mine, Yenisei Province, to the Commission on Elections to the Constituent Assembly, 10 December 1917. GARF, f. 1781, op. 1, d. 42, ll. 321–3210b. Typed and signed.

108. Letter to Lenin from "a former Bolshevik," Rostov-on-Don, 19 December 1917. GARF, f. 1235, op. 140, d. 8, ll. 41–410b. Manuscript.

109. Letter to *Pravda* from Frants Kontaka, a worker at the Obukhov Metal Works, Petrograd, printed 3 January 1918. *Pravda*, no. 1/228 (16/3 January 1918): 4.

110. Resolution of the workers of the Petrograd Military Horseshoe Factory, 4 January 1918. *Pravda*, no. 5/232, (20/7 January 1918): 4.

111. Resolutions by "The Working Masses on the Disbanding of the Constituent Assembly," 7 January 1918. *Pravda*, no. 6/233 (22/9 January 1918): 3.

112. Letter to Trotsky, shortly after 5 January 1918 (dated by content). Stamped received 10 January. GARF, f. 1235, op. 140, d. 8, ll. 83–84. Manuscript.

113. Letter to the Central Executive Committee of Soviets from F. Petrov, between 5 and 11 January 1918 (dated by content; received by the Executive Committee 11 January 1918). GARF, f. 1235, op. 40, d. 8, ll. 97–970b. Manuscript. Emphasis in the original.

114. Resolution of soldiers of the Preobrazhensky reserves, Petrograd, printed 2 November 1917. *Izvestiia*, no. 214 (2 November 1917): 6.

115. Resolution of the soldiers of the Reserve Electrotechnical Battalion, printed 2 November 1917. *Izvestiia*, no. 214 (2 November 1917): 7.

116. Resolution of the Regimental Committee of the 20th Siberian Rifles, 6 November 1917. GARF, f. 1235, op. 1, d. 19, l. 15. Typed.

117. Appeal from the Extraordinary Congress of soldiers' committees of the 12th Army, 17–21 November 1917. *Izvestiia*, no. 231 (21 November 1917): 8.

118. Appeal from the soldiers' committee of the 1st Cavalry Corps, printed 30 November 1917. *Izvestiia*, no. 240 (30 November 1917): 7. Emphasis in original.

119. Appeal to soldiers from the soldiers' committee of the Volynsky Reserve Guards Regiment, Petrograd, printed 3 December 1917. *Izvestiia*, no. 243 (3 December 1917): 3.

120. Instruction from the soldiers' committee of the 22nd Infantry Division at the front to the committee's delegate to the All-Russian Extraor-

dinary Congress of Peasants' Deputies, 2 January 1918. GARF, f. 1235, op. 2, d. 23, ll. 8–9. Typed copy.

121. Letter from a soldier in Petrograd to Lenin, 6 January 1918. GARF, f. 1235, op. 140, d. 8, ll. 156–1570b (original continues to l. 159). Manuscript.

122. Letter from the front to Lenin, received 15 January 1918. GARF, f. 1235, op. 140, d. 8, ll. 121–122. Manuscript.

123. Resolution to the Main Land Committee in Petrograd from a village gathering in Kherson Province, 9 November 1917. GARF, f. 1796, op. 1, d. 71, l. 156. Manuscript.

124. Resolution from an uezd "peasant congress," 22 November 1917. GARF, f. 9550, op. 14, d. 1, l. 1. Printed leaflet.

125. Instruction (*nakaz*) to the Constituent Assembly from representatives of peasant communities, Voronezh Province, 27 November 1917. GARF, f. 1781, op. 1, d. 1, ll. 34–35. Manuscript. Ibid., ll. 36–360b. Typed copy.

126. Instruction to the Constituent Assembly from citizens of Viazhishchensk Volost, Petrograd Province, 31 December 1917. GARF, f. 1781, op. 1, d. 42, ll. 309–3120b. Manuscript.

127. Letter to Lenin from five peasants, Moscow Province, received 7 January 1918. GARF, f. 1235, op. 140, d. 8, l. 35. Manuscript.

128. Letter to the Bolshevik leaders from a peasant, Orel Province, 10 January 1918. GARF, f. 1235, op. 140, d. 8, ll. 154–1550b. Manuscript (in red ink).

129. Resolution to the Constituent Assembly from peasants, Kursk Province, 13 January 1918. GARF, f. 1781, op. 1, d.42, l. 247. Manuscript.

130. Pyotr Oreshin, "What Chasms to Us Have Opened," 24 December 1917. *Delo naroda*, no. 241 (24 December 1917): 3. Ellipses in original.

131. Vladimir Kirillov, "To the Proletariat," January 1918. *Griadushchee*, no. 1 (January 1918): 3.

132. Aksen-Achkasov (Ilya Sadofiev), "We Go On," January 1918. *Griadushchee*, no. 1 (January 1918): 2. Ellipses in original.

ILLUSTRATION CREDITS

1. Soldiers posing by tank after joining the revolution, February 1917. Russian State Archive of Film and Photographic Documents.

2. Soldiers at the ceremonial funeral for the fallen in the revolution, Mars Field, Petrograd, 23 March 1917. Russian State Archive of Film and Photographic Documents.

3. Women demonstrating, Petrograd, March 1917. Russian State Archive of Film and Photographic Documents.

4. May Day demonstrators, Palace Square, Petrograd, 18 April 1917 (postcard). Russian State Archive of Film and Photographic Documents.

5. Demonstrating restaurant and café workers, Petrograd, spring 1917. Russian State Archive of Film and Photographic Documents.

6. Soldiers, possibly deserters, spring 1917. Russian State Archive of Film and Photographic Documents.

7. Soldiers participating in a political demonstration, Petrograd, 18 June 1917 (postcard). Russian State Archive of Film and Photographic Documents.

8. A worker, a soldier, and a peasant—studio photograph taken in the first days after the October overthrow of the Provisional Government. Russian State Archive of Film and Photographic Documents.

Index

alcoholism, 25, 100–101, 230, 288–289, 294

Alekseev, Mikhail, 343

All-Russian Extraordinary Commission for the Struggle Against Counterrevolution and Sabotage (Cheka), 266, 343

anarchism, 76–77, 90, 102, 126–127, 340

April Days, 74, 133–135, 340

April Theses, 75, 340

authority: of Bolshevik party, 258–260; Cheka, 266, 343; of factory workers, 64–66, 96, 105, 255–257, 342; after February revolution, 10–11, 85–87; military rank and, 67, 257, 343; after October revolution, 271–272; Okhrana (security police), 39, 51–52, 111, 114; soldier-officer relations, 21, 27, 67–69, 108–109, 178–180, 234, 257, 343; in villages, 64, 69–70, 128, 129, 237, 350, 351; workers' authority in factories, 64–66, 96, 105, 175–178, 190, 256–257, 342. *See also* dictatorship; freedom; power; soldiers

Avksentiev, Nikolai, 287, 291

Bebel, August, 91

Birzhevye vedomosti (newspaper), 93, 124, 145, 351–352

Black Hundreds, 39–40, 117, 142, 189, 201, 292

Bloody Sunday, 53, 187, 188, 271

Bolshevik party: Anarchist Bolsheviks, 126–127; Bolshevik Central Committee, 77, 170; Bolshevik Military Organiza-

tion, 150, 154; and coalition government, 74–75, 260; Committee for the Struggle Against Counterrevolution, 164–166, 198; and Constituent Assembly, 262–264, 280, 292, 342, 348–349; Council of People's Commissars, 251–252, 342, 348; and July Days, 153–155, 239; lower-class Russians and, 29–30, 75–76, 164, 171; Military Revolutionary Committee, 173–174, 342; newspapers, 75–76, 98–99, 155, 352; October revolution, 21, 252–253, 342; peasants and, 19, 236; Petrograd factory shutdown (8 June), 76–77, 340; popularity of, 76, 170–172, 258–259, 271–272, 286–287; *Pravda*, 75, 76, 93, 124, 155, 239, 352; press closures, 190, 205, 260–261, 292, 342; Provisional Government, 75, 102, 154; Red Guard, 95, 173–174, 346; soldiers and, 126, 172–173, 180, 200, 201, 213–214, 283–284; workers and, 101–102, 172–173, 185. *See also* Kadets; Kornilov mutiny; Lenin, Vladimir; Menshevik party; Russian Social Democratic Workers' Party; Socialist Revolutionary (S.R.) Party

bourgeoisie: April Theses, 75, 340; Bolshevik revolution against, 74–75; Constituent Assembly elections, 262; and counterrevolution, 19, 122, 166, 188, 195–198, 221–222, 245; democracy, 89, 221; government in aftermath of Kornilov mutiny, 167–168; intelligentsia, 88–89; and July Days, 159; proletariat